A GUEST

AT THE

SHOOTERS'

BANQUET

By the Same Author
The Wild Field (poems)

More Praise for *A Guest at the Shooters' Banquet*

"[A] powerful consideration of what happens when reality contradicts our belief 'that those we love or have loved are good.'" —*The New Yorker*

"Maturing from childhood to adulthood means accepting a place in family stories. Checking treasured myths against historical facts is like a second coming of age, and one rarely achieved. This true-life Bildungsroman sets an example, in its honesty, industry, and artfulness." —Timothy Snyder, author of *Bloodlands: Europe Between Hitler and Stalin*

"Intense, moving . . . A deeply personal and important addition to Holocaust literature." —*Booklist* (starred review)

"Heartfelt . . . Gabis paints an engrossing portrait of the snake-pit of ethnic animosities in wartime Lithuania and of the intimate horrors of the Holocaust." —*Publishers Weekly*

"A journey of discovery . . . Thoughtful." —*Library Journal*

"Intricate and intimate . . . Rita Gabis brings macrocosmic Holocaust horror into the microcosm of our dining rooms, kitchens, and bedrooms—a noble feat." —*New York Journal of Books*

"*A Guest at the Shooters' Banquet* is Gabis's gripping, psychologically acute account of her search for the truth about [her grandfather], a wrenching personal journey . . . Gabis's resolute hunt and expressive prose really illuminate these years of anguish." —*BookPage*

A GUEST
AT THE
SHOOTERS'
BANQUET

**MY GRANDFATHER'S SS PAST, MY JEWISH FAMILY,
A SEARCH FOR THE TRUTH**

RITA GABIS

BLOOMSBURY
NEW YORK · LONDON · OXFORD · NEW DELHI · SYDNEY

Bloomsbury USA
An imprint of Bloomsbury Publishing Plc

1385 Broadway   50 Bedford Square
New York   London
NY 10018   WC1B 3DP
USA   UK

www.bloomsbury.com

BLOOMSBURY and the Diana logo are trademarks of Bloomsbury Publishing Plc

First U.S. edition 2015
This paperback edition published 2016

© Rita Gabis, 2015

This is a work of nonfiction. However, the names and identifying characteristics of certain individuals have been changed to protect their privacy, and dialogue has been reconstructed to the best of the author's recollection.

ISBN: HB: 978-1-63286-261-7
ePub: 978-1-62040-129-3
PB: 978-1-63286-623-3

LIBRARY OF CONGRESS CATALOGING-IN-PUBLICATION DATA IS AVAILABLE.

2 4 6 8 10 9 7 5 3

Designed by Elizabeth Van Italie
Typeset by RefineCatch Ltd, Bungay, Suffolk
Printed and bound by CPI Group (UK) Ltd, Croydon, CR0 4YY

To find out more about our authors and books visit www.bloomsbury.com. Here you will find extracts, author interviews, details of forthcoming events, and the option to sign up for our newsletters.

Bloomsbury books may be purchased for business or promotional use. For information on bulk purchases please contact Macmillan Corporate and Premium Sales Department at specialmarkets@macmillan.com.

IN MEMORY OF MY FATHER

FOR ALL THE MIRELE REINS

We were riding through frozen fields in a wagon at dawn.
A red wing rose in the darkness . . .
O my love, where are they, where are they going

—CZESŁAW MIŁOSZ

———————————————————

Sventiány was remembered by the hussars only as the drunken camp . . .
Many complaints were made against the troops, who . . .
took also horses, carriages, and carpets.

—TOLSTOY

———————————————————

We were dreamers, now we have to be soldiers

— ABRAHAM (AVROM) SUTZKEVER

CONTENTS

A NOTE ABOUT THE TEXT

As I MENTION in the text, names of people and places in the borderland this book is concerned with vary widely in spelling and pronunciation. These variances depend to a large degree upon the source—Lithuanian, Polish, Russian, Hebrew, Yiddish, and German primarily—in which the name appeared or in the particular usage of an interviewee. Although the standard for publication is to "silently correct" these discrepancies, the more interviews and research I did, the more valuable, even given the inherent confusion, the variances of place names and surnames became. They represent part of the rich essence of a multicultural borderland where people lived as neighbors yet had different names for their streets and their towns, for the food they ate, and different spellings for the names of their children. I have tried, as faithfully as possible, and I hope without too much trouble for the reader, to render place names and the names of individuals as they appeared in source material and as they were spoken to me. The complexity of rapidly shifting borders and the unique heritage of different population groups seemed best represented by these choices. Below is a truncated list of place names with their variations for three towns that appear frequently throughout the book. For further clarification, JewishGen.org is a wonderful resource.

Švenčionys (Lithuanian)
Sventzion/Sventsian (Yiddish)
Święciany (Polish)

Švenčionėliai (Lithuanian)
Nei-Sventsian (Yiddish)
Nowo-Święciany (Polish)

Vilnius (Lithuanian)
Vilne (Yiddish)
Wilno (Polish)

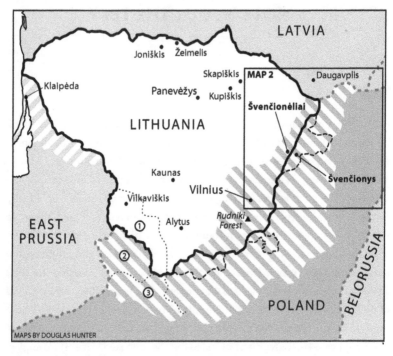

MAPS BY DOUGLAS HUNTER

Klaipėda region. Taken by Lithuania in the 1923 revolt. It was returned to Nazi Germany after an ultimatum on March 20, 1939.

Territories within the 1920 border of the Lithuanian Republic claimed by Poland.

① Lithuanian territory requested by Nazi Germany in German-Soviet Boundary and Friendship Treaty on September 28, 1939. It was occupied by the Soviet Union on June 15, 1940. Nazi Germany relinquished its claims on January 10, 1941.

② **"Suwałki Triangle."** Polish territory claimed by Lithuania. Occupied by Nazi Germany in September 1939.

③ **Southern Suvalkai Region.** Polish territory claimed by Lithuania. Occupied by the Soviet Union in September 1939.

— Territory of Lithuania under the Soviet-Lithuania Mutual Assistance Treaty on October 10, 1939, including the western Vilnius region, which had been claimed by Poland.

----- Section of the western Vilnius region transferred to Lithuanian Soviet Socialist Republic on November 6, 1940.

——— Territory of the Lithuanian Soviet Socialist Republic on November 6, 1940.

——— Territory of Lithuania under the administration of Nazi Germany after the June 1941 invasion.

▨ Region of the Belorussian Soviet Socialist Republic within Nazi Germany's occupied Lithuanian territory.

- - ▪- - Administrative region of Švenčionys under German occupation.

TWO DREAMS

Dream one: I'm being hunted down. Whoever is after me and the reasons for their pursuit aren't clear. I know they carry rifles. I know they have an instinct about small places; shelves with false backs that open into alcoves, shadows behind bulky furniture. They know where to look. They know how to listen for my frightened breathing. In the dream, my sense of the hunters is that they are methodical, zealous, unstoppable. They are after me; it's a fact. Usually it's night. I'm barefoot. Footsteps, heavy—slow at first and then louder, faster, clamor of voices, a sweep of light. I close my eyes, try to make myself invisible. My tongue sticks to the roof of my mouth, the spit sucked away by panic. The dream is one of the earliest I remember from childhood. I had it for years. Often, in those days, my hiding place in my dream was my own house, on Greenway Terrace in Kansas City: house of our cat Mitzi, house with the doorway from which my mother called me in at dusk in her broken English. What was Lithuania to me then? It was a rag wrapped around my mother's tongue, the dark bread of the embarrassing sandwiches she gave my sister and me to take to school. The crust hard as the curb of a road, the meat inside an uneven slab. I wanted a white lunch. I wanted to sleep without dreaming.

Dream two: I'm a murderer. It's not clear who my victim was. It's also not clear that there is just one. I've buried whoever I've killed. I had help. There was planning involved in the placement of the graves. Often my dead are buried near a construction site, a place where concrete will be poured, where floors will be laid, where the dogs (Lassie and Rin Tin Tin, because again, this dream began in childhood) will sniff and paw at the ground, at the just-laid turf, at the stone steps and the hedge of fresh ground around the foundation. The dogs alert only to the ordinary; leaves, bits of gravel, the clanging of a copper gutter, the evidence of a recent rain. In the dream I've forgotten the reason for the killing. I just know that I've done it—and the knowledge folds over and over inside me like one of those combines in the fields outside the city, in Kansas where my mother's brother and his wife had a farm, where my Lithuanian Catholic grandfather lived the last years of his life. The steel teeth rend me. Guilt, I'll call it later, when I dream the dream in my twenties and wake trembling because this time the dogs and the detectives are pulling down wallboard, bringing the heavy machinery in to break into the truth, dislodge it.

"You're very angry," a therapist I was seeing at the time said. Her name was Eva Brown.

Eva Brown. Eva Braun. Hitler's mistress is your shrink. Who said it? Maybe the lanky, drunk philosopher who bartended at the restaurant where I worked during college, maybe my Jewish father, who didn't believe in therapists. Though he wouldn't have used the word *shrink*. He would tell me the story again, of my paternal great-grandfather, Wolf Treegoob, an inventor and village elder who left Vyazovok in the Cherkasy Uezd (*uezd* means "county") of the Kiev Gubernia for Kalnybolota in the late 1800s, at a time when Ukraine and Lithuania—and indeed, the whole of Eastern Europe—were teeth in the mouth of the Russian Empire.

Wolf Treegoob's family name appears variously as Tregub, Trigub, or Tregubas, depending on where you look: a tax registry; a ship manifest; on JewishGen.org, the Vsia Rossiia business directory—a kind of yellow pages that listed businesses throughout Russia, updated several times during its existence in the late 1800s and early 1900s; Yad Vashem's Shoah Victims' database; a three-by-five card typed out during his processing at Ellis Island—the last time he would use the name Trigub. When he moved to Philadelphia in 1908, the name would be forever Treegoob, a name I would one day touch on a plaque in a forest in Plugot, near the town of Kiryat Gat in Israel on a stunningly hot day, driven there in a car courtesy of the Jewish National Fund. The fund's warm and informative representative Avinoam Binder arrived at my hotel in East Jerusalem and presented me with maps and a colorful version of *The Book of Blessings* for the Jewish holidays—a gift the serious young uniformed Ben Gurion Airport police in Tel Aviv would grill me about incessantly a week later (the luggage contents of noncitizens to and from Israel are routinely scrutinized).

"Anyone who had a problem would come to your great-grandfather for advice," my father intoned. "That's how it's done. You don't need someone to fix you. You don't take your problems to strangers, especially someone named after Hitler's girlfriend." I seethed. I held up my love for Eva Brown like a flag. I buried the little seed of doubt my father had planted. Was she German? Was she corrupt, untrustworthy? She passed along no information about her personal life. I studied her dress; formal, stylish in a sedate way, nothing to call attention. Nice shoes. Skirts, pants sometimes but only with a jacket to match, or a sweater with pearls. I told her my dream of murder. I told her that every time I left the house, I panicked, fearing it would burn down behind me.

If my father were alive, I'd tell him what I learned about Eva Brown years after I stopped seeing her. She's Jewish, like him. She's a child survivor of the Holocaust. In her later life, transgenerational silence became a clinical and personal passion. I draft an e-mail to her that I'm too shy to send in which I tell her what I've discovered about my recurring dreams, with their ubiquitous motifs and durability. Whatever permutations of meaning they have in the immediate geography of my life, it turns out they are mirrors of what my grandparents on both sides of my family—Lithuanian and Jewish—actually lived. I, without knowing, dreamed parts of a truth about Lithuania. One part is this: my grandfather on my mother's side was a murderer.

Or was he?

I

CHAPTER I

A SMALL THING

On a freezing Wednesday morning I stood in front of the Immigration and Customs Enforcement (ICE) division of Homeland Security, a few minutes early for my meeting with Michael MacQueen, a war crimes investigator. A storm was coming up the coast. My gloves hid in some crevasse of my bag. I clenched and opened my hands in the bitter air. The sky spread out in an even blue, and morning sun hit the glass doors in front of me. A hundred miles south, cars fishtailed on highways. Ice and snow crashed down branches and power lines. Here, just the barest scent of moisture in the harsh wind; the scent of rain, actually—unexpected in the deep heart of winter.

MacQueen was the first investigator sent by the Office of Special Investigations (OSI) at the Department of Justice to Eastern Europe in the 1990s. He was tasked with the painstaking work of sifting through archives for evidence against Nazi collaborators who had made false statements on their immigration and/or citizenship applications and were living quiet postwar lives in the United States. He went to Lithuania, where my Catholic maternal grandfather, grandmother, and their three children were born. He taught himself the language. He was, he would tell me, in the early days of his work there, always followed by two tails, one KGB, the other Saugumas, the Lithuanian security police.

Among the cases OSI made because of MacQueen's tenacity and thoroughness, one involved a Vincas Valkavickus, who was deported back to

Lithuania. There, during World War II, Valkavickus had been employed as a guard at a mass shooting of the Jewish population in the Švenčionys region, famous for lakes that make irregular circles on a satellite map, dark, as if they are solid matter interrupting the forests and meadows. In this same region my grandfather once lived and worked, before the war ended and he emigrated with a sister and my mother and her two siblings to the country where I was born. This country.

I pulled up the blue hood of my down jacket. The Holocaust Memorial Museum is six blocks from ICE. I'd been there many times, and was returning briefly after my meeting. Each time I traveled from New York to D.C., the contrast always struck me; D.C.'s buildings low squares, long rectangles of park, wide sidewalks soon, on this day, to be hidden by snow. I looked down Twelfth Street and gauged the quick, frigid walk to the museum; blocks of straight lines and hard turns. Still, I thought of a circle. I thought of my Lithuanian grandfather, all he might have hoped for as he wrote his name and the names of his children on the immigration form that sits on my desk. Did fear accompany his hopes? It was not an emotion I ever witnessed in him as a child, but then, I was a child.

MacQueen had explained in a quick phone call that when I got to ICE, I should go left to the Visitor's Center. I pulled my hood back, ran a few fingers through my hair, and, forgetting his instructions, went in the front, through the wrong doors. I was quickly ushered out again to the glass door on the left. The friendly security officers scanned my bags and jacket, gave me a temporary pass, and offered me a seat.

A few days earlier I'd reread a write-up about MacQueen done under the auspices of his alma mater, the University of Michigan. A black-and-white photograph led the piece. A man, thin, hands clasped behind him, walked away from the camera on a gravel path lined with stones embedded with small plaques. A memorial.

The thin legs and straight narrow back of the man caught by the camera set up an expectation: here was the man I'd been exchanging e-mails with for months. Even more than our time together, it was this assumption that would seem, when I stood later in Union Station with frantic travelers trying to stay ahead of the weather, part of the circular and often errant nature of my own efforts the last handful of years. I'd expected the man in the photograph, but the man who opened the door from an interior hallway, shook my hand, and said "Labas"—Lithuanian for "Hello"—was someone else. MacQueen, but not the man in the photograph.

Expectations endure. During our conversation, MacQueen inexplicably remained both to me: the helpful, shrewd, wry man behind the cluttered desk and the unknown other. Several weeks later I contacted the photojournalist who had gotten credit for the image. She had no memory of ever taking the picture. Perhaps the editor of the piece got the credit wrong. A small thing. A lapse. A missing detail. Not really important, but it needled me.

Back in Union Station that late afternoon, I shifted my weight in the long, snaking line. All around me people unwound scarves, dismantled some of their armor against the cold; down and wool coats slung over shoulders, tucked under an arm. We juggled coffees, cell phones, bags, briefcases and, here and there, children. I thought of the wrong door I'd entered at ICE, of all the wrong doors I'd walked through over many months, only to backtrack, go a different way. I thought of how, very early on, trains, travelers, crowds of people ushered together, began to create a small panic inside me that has remained for every trip I take, every ticket punched, every stamp on my passport.

What I'd started with at the beginning was an incongruity—like the scent of rain in winter—in the history of my family as I knew it, in what was, when I began, the present moment, and what continues to be the storm of the past.

My FATHER'S PARENTS came to the United States from Belarus and the Ukraine in the early 1900s. My mother and her family, Lithuanian Catholics, emigrated to the United States after World War II. The two sides of my family remained, through most of my life, separate—with the exception of a week or two during the summer when my mother's relatives would come east to visit. Growing up, I thought this separateness was a simple issue of geography; my Jewish relatives lived on the East Coast, my mother's Lithuanian family, after they moved early on from New Jersey, were Midwesterners. I never imagined that their histories, their lives, intersected beyond a gathering for a birthday, a cookout on the beach.

In memory, my Lithuanian grandfather is tall and wide. He's a wall. He's a tree with low, spreading branches. Even though I knew him both as a child and a young adult, the images of him that dominate come from childhood. His hands, for instance, his right hand around my hand, the large fleshy enclosure, the calluses, the safety of it. I called him Senelis—Lithuanian for "Grandfather." We're walking somewhere—to the bakery maybe—in Jamesburg, New Jersey, where he ended up with his sister and my mother and her siblings after four years in a displaced persons camp in Germany at the end of World War II. It's the early 1960s. I'm four or six or seven, on a street with only a few shops. It's that lazy Sunday after-church time, in the spring. My coat is unbuttoned. Senelis doesn't have a jacket on, just a plaid shirt, neatly tucked in. He's freshly shaved. Maybe a white bit of shaving cream somewhere. The scent of it mixes with the smell of leaves and marshes. He shares a house—it's more of a shack—outside town with his sister, my Krukchamama ("Godmother" in Lithuanian, which she was to my mother and became to the rest of us). It's a wild place where rain pools and cattails grow. When the sun goes down, crickets call up from the crawl space under your feet in the little hallway between the kitchen and Krukchamama's bedroom, with the crucifix above the bed and the lumpy mattress. Senelis's neck, a little grizzled, is the only thing about him that looks old. He fishes and hunts. He doesn't sit in a chair all day and read like my father. He's a man who can move.

The woman behind the counter knows him. Everywhere we go, he introduces me: "This is my granddaughter," he says, putting the accent on the middle syllable instead of the first. I choose the flaky sweet pastry called "butterfly," but before the woman behind the counter can reach into the glass case and retrieve it, Senelis says, "More, choose more." I ask him how much more. He sweeps his arm across the small room. "Anyting," he says.

It must have happened more than once, but I remember it as a singular event; the woman behind the counter picking up a big white box and proceeding to fill it at my command. Two more butterflies. An éclair. A sugar cookie. Amazing.

When the box is full and tied up with that string so deftly measured and cut, Senelis pulls a wad of bills out of his pocket and peels off the cost of "more." We wander out into the sunlight. I half expect him to stop before we cross the street and tell me it was a joke, that we have to give back all but my half-eaten butterfly, that he is testing me to see how greedy I really am.

Over and over my mother told me stories of privation in Lithuania during the war and in Germany after. People sucked on pebbles because there was no food to eat. She begged for bread with her small brother and younger sister. My grandfather never spoke about the war like that. "Anyting," he said to me.

Was it the next day, or the next? He was arguing with someone back at the shack near the marshes. Maybe his son, my uncle Roy, who later moved to the farm in Kansas but at that time lived down the road with his wife Agnes. Or maybe Krukchamama, or my mother. I was in another room. Or I was outside and heard the shouting through the window.

"What was it about?" I asked my mother after I'd gone in, or she'd come out to find me for dinner.

"Money," she said, and didn't elaborate because what did a child know about immigrant grandfathers who hunted and played cards and made cherry wine by the case that tasted of time itself, the sticky sediment trapped at the bottom of the dark glass bottle?

My stomach twisted with guilt—that white box of more. All the little artifacts of my desire I'd chosen and gobbled up. The dollar bills my grandfather delivered with ceremony into the hands of the woman behind the counter. Out of love for me, my grandfather had incurred wrath. The pastries, for all I knew, cost as much as the electricity that flickered into dimness when too many lights were on in his house. But along with the certainty that my greed was at the root of the bickering I'd overheard, another thought came to me: my grandfather, who counted out the bills without any hesitation in the sugary air, was not rich, was not what he pretended to be.

CHAPTER 2

FAYE DUNAWAY AS AN INVADED COUNTRY

Whenever I think of Lithuania, I remember a scene in *Chinatown*: Jack Nicholson is trying to extract the truth out of Faye Dunaway, who was raped by her father and then bore his child—a girl.

"Who is the girl?" Jack Nicholson asks.

"She's my sister," Faye Dunaway replies, sobbing.

Nicholson slaps her. Asks the question again.

"She's my daughter," Faye Dunaway says.

Another slap.

"She's my sister and my daughter," Faye Dunaway cries.

In August 1939 the Molotov-Ribbentrop Pact between Nazi Germany and the Soviet Union assigned Lithuania to the German "sphere of influence." Then, as a result of the German-Soviet Boundary and Friendship Treaty of September 28, 1939, Lithuania became a Soviet satellite state.

In June 1940 Lithuania lost all independence to the Soviets. In early June of 1941, Russian soldiers arrested and deported thousands of Lithuanians to Siberian Gulags; Senelis's wife, my grandmother, was among them. On June 22 of that same year, the Germans invaded the Soviet Union and quickly "liberated" Lithuania from Soviet control. In the beginning, the Reich's strategy was to allow an autonomous Lithuanian government to form within the occupied country. This nod toward autonomy was short-lived. In mid-July of 1941 the Reichskommissariat Ostland—the German Civil Administration—was established in Lithuania, as well as in Latvia, Estonia, and parts of Poland and Belarus.

One truth about Lithuania is that, as a country, it is indistinguishable from the invaders, collaborators, ghosts, heroines, thieves, defenders, and healers it contains. It's the raped woman and the father and the child. It's those who know nothing about what went on behind closed doors and those who stood by and watched, those who shrugged and walked away. Those who hid strangers, who carried messages, who didn't betray the hunted. It's the hunted themselves.

It's a prism. It belongs to anybody who wants it. It even belongs to people like me, who for many years hated to pronounce its name. Not because I had any special empirical knowledge of Lithuania. I had the lullabies my mother sang to me so I'd sleep and the stories she told that kept me from sleep—the ones about war, the ones about the potatoes that made her fat in the displaced persons camp. As a small child, I was well aware that my mother had lost her own mother to war. This deficit, this wound, was always present, even when it was not spoken about directly. "Vat do you vant from me?" she'd say. (I wanted her to talk like the other mothers I knew.) When she was angry, she became more explicit. "I had nu-ting!" she'd cry out. Meaning, of course, no mother, no grocery shelves stocked with twenty different kinds of cookies, no meat three times a week, no Disney, no childhood. I conflated my mother's anger and sadness, the disappearance of her own mother, the war itself with Lithuania.

Years later, in 1990, when Lithuania declared independence from the Soviets, stood fast in the face of deadly retaliation, and, remarkably, became its own nation, my mother traveled back to the country of her birth (she had also gone there during the Soviet occupation). She invited me to go with her. The ticket she wanted to buy me seemed an invitation to enter into the deepest sorrows of her life. Whatever Lithuania was, if I stepped off the plane onto the foreign tarmac, it would never let me go. I turned her offer down.

Memories from the months after 9/11 also made me think of Lithuania. A week or ten days after the towers fell, some of us who had jobs downtown were allowed to show ID at a police checkpoint set up along Canal Street and go to work—for me, an office at the Tribeca Film Center, a few blocks up and west from Chambers Street. The area was desolate, shops closed, faces grim. Sirens wailed back and forth from "the pit." For weeks the air stank—the smell can't be described, though many of us have tried to. Glass, fuel, death. After work, I walked home, back through the checkpoint, north by thirty blocks and east. I ate. I showered. No matter what shampoo I used, no matter how hot I let the water run, I couldn't get the burnt odor from my hair. It was in my clothes, the palms of my hands.

It's not memory of that odor, though, that brings to mind Žeimelis, a little Lithuanian town near the Latvian border where my mother and her family lived when she was a girl. Or Švenčionys, where the family later resettled minus my grandmother (my Babita, as I learned to call her, though the proper, if now somewhat archaic, version in Lithuanian is Bobute), who by then had been arrested by the Russians and was gone, the small library she administered boarded up. Every trace of her a rumor.

It was the palpable presence of absence.

"Do you feel it?" people in Tribeca asked one another about what was both amorphous and irrefutable.

"Is it their spirits?" someone would say. Someone you would never expect to utter such a thing; the angry Greek waitress at the corner diner, maybe, or the producer who flew in from L.A. when planes were airborne again and stood in the middle of the brick street looking up, as if at a hovercraft or as if he were trying to locate the source of a din in the air, in a pitch humans were never meant to be able to hear.

The dead exerted a pressure on the burning wind. They crowded into the mockery of the light that day after day dazzled us as we walked the unconsoled ashy streets. They grabbed at our warm hands. We held on to cell phones, coffee cups, children's hands, so as not to feel the emptiness.

This was how I learned that mass murder alters matter separate from the dead. The air changes. Gravity shifts. Time bends and breaks everywhere you look.

In both Žeimelis and Švenčionys, Jews were herded together and massacred. My mother was in her early adolescence then.

"Aside from my grandmother, what do you remember about the people who vanished from the towns you lived in?" I asked her during a visit she made to my home in New York City in 2010.

"Nothing," she said, immediately.

"You knew that Jews lived where you lived?" I asked.

She thought for a few seconds.

"Yes," she said.

"And then what?" I prodded.

"And then they were gone," she said.

In 2010 the Lithuanian Parliament declared that 2011 would be the "Year of Remembrance of Defense of Freedom and Great Losses" (during the Russian occupation) as well as the "Year of Remembrance of Lithuanian Citizens Who Were Holocaust Victims" (during the German occupation). How Lithuania storied its past was something I'd never considered. My conversation with my mother grew out of a desire to uncover—what, I didn't know. I couldn't name it yet or understand it, but I had begun the kind of amateur genealogical quests I'd always disdained, focused first on the Jewish side of my family, then quickly encompassing the Lithuanian side as well.

Like all overnight genealogists, I turned to ancestry.com, Internet archives, books, disparate questions thrown at surprised family members. I watched myself print out passenger lists, names of camps that Stalin's roundup squads populated with Lithuanians, saw myself become more and more like those people who zealously collect trinkets from the past; obsessive Saturday garage sale patrons who pick through the broken, the smelly, the stained, the puzzles missing three large pieces, the cardboard box of shells, the bikes with no brakes and busted chains. There are thousands of us on Internet search sites, millions of threads. *My grandfather Horus was the village baker in such and such a time in such and such a place, does anybody know anyone who bought bread from him? My mother Ruschka taught piano to three children in ⸻ before the war. Are you one of these children? You would remember my mother. She had beautiful hands. A laugh that often turned into hiccups.*

I searched to find out what I was searching for. The name of a town? The birthplace of a great-uncle? The date that a Russian noble, impressed by my great-grandfather Wolf Treegoob's engineering skills (he'd fixed his shtetl's decrepit grain mill), invited/commanded him to convert to Christianity and move to St. Petersburg? My great-grandfather refused, and shortly afterward, at the age of forty, fled with his family to London.

Every tidbit sent me searching for the next; a naturalization card, a long roll call of Lithuanians on ancestry.com with a version of the Treegoob name, the address of a hardware store in Philadelphia where my father had worked as a boy; he made the rounds each week to collect dime payments from the African Americans who had come up from the South with their hope, who paid on time for their refrigerators and stoves in tenements on pushcart streets.

I read books about Siberia and realized one day, with a small shock, that I couldn't in that particular moment remember Babita's first name. By the time my mother came for her visit in the fall of 2010 and we first spoke about Švenčionys, a longing I hadn't expected—a question that wasn't on the list in my notebook of, among other scribbles, Russian place names next to their Yiddish or Lithuanian or Belorussian or Polish counterparts—waited for her.

We sat at a side table against the wall in a large, airy café on the Upper West Side. Her gray hair was freshly cut in an attractive bob. Her eyes were clear. Her purple cashmere sweater showed off her trim waist. She loves cities. She's traveled the world, my mother, without my father, who never liked to go anywhere.

For many years I went nowhere to make sure I would never become like her. Now, her cosmopolitan bent is one of the things I love about her. The way she'll stop at a busy corner and take in the chatty Mandarin of the two elderly women with a grocery cart, the young man speaking a rapid Spanish into his cell phone, the little girl crossing the street with a pink backpack, holding tight to her frazzled mother's free hand. Really take them in, the way some people shut their eyes and then open them at a bakery counter, in Paris maybe, near the Luxembourg Gardens, in a small shop overheated from the oven in back, where a woman of indeterminate age in a smock slips a delicacy into a thin paper bag, pleased not so much to serve you as to bestow upon you a prize that can't be earned, only savored.

"China," my mother will say about the two women with the cart, "from the north." Then recall a homely detail about the Great Wall or the dense, earthy taste of the mushrooms at a hotel banquet in Shanghai. Which will lead to a memory of her father, my Senelis, who tramped around the parks off the tennis court in Oak Bluffs, on Martha's Vineyard, where we spent our summers when it was still possible for middle-class families to have a second home there. He wandered for hours with a paper bag, looking for mushrooms: strange, bulbous, the caps soft as a deer's pelt, the stems clotted with sandy dirt. His skill as a forager cultivated long before he briefly took to the forests and marshes of Lithuania and fought, along with his fellow partisans, the Russian invaders before the German invaders arrived.

At the little table amid the bustling clatter of cutlery and chatter and milk being steamed and plates set down, my mother sighed. She was happy. I didn't encourage her visits very often, but lately it had occurred to me that the energy required to keep her at arm's length, to refuse her love, was itself a form of furious attachment. I was happy to see her, to sit with her. This astonished me, in the moment, though later it occurs to me that it's predictable, what time allows. If you're lucky enough to have time.

The good coffee came. The sandwich with a bitter olive paste. Her hands were sun-marked. I used to examine them over and over when I was a small child, marveling at the infinite, tiny crosshatches and lines in the soft skin on top of her hands and at the joints of her fingers. Her palms always smelled vaguely of almonds.

I started to tell her about my haphazard family research. At a certain juncture I put my fork down, sat back. Said I had a question for her, which was not, after all these years, another accusation, that there were just certain things I was trying to understand.

"Where did the violence on your side of the family come from?" I asked.

She looked me straight on, took in the absence of vitriol in my voice, straightened up a bit, as if I were the teacher and she the good pupil. By "your side of the family," she knew I meant her and her sister and her sister's husband.

"Well, there was the war," my mother said.

"But lots of people lived through the war and didn't end up doing—" I didn't elaborate.

Our waiter interrupted with dessert specials, his face open, something sturdy about his hands—a carpenter's hands, or a painter's. From the table next to ours, a whiff of just-cut oranges.

"Do you remember your mother ever raising a hand to you?" I asked.

We locked eyes. My mother's face was thoughtful. "No," she said, "never," and then added what she had shared with me before: Babita didn't like her daughters very much, was practical, efficient, remote.

"And Senelis, what about him?"

My mother shook her head. She took a sip of coffee.

"Never. He was never that kind of father. My mother was the cold one. But he had a love of life, and he loved us, always."

I pushed my plate to the side. The morning rush was subsiding, and the café was quieter. At the end of our row of tables, our waiter wiped a cloth in a slow circle.

I asked my mother if she was sure.

She considered, leaned forward, looked up. We were both quiet, and then, almost as an afterthought, she remembered something. "He did beat my brother Roy in the DP camp."

(After the war, displaced persons camps were established and run under the aegis of allied militia in specified zones and the United Nations Relief and Rehabilitation Administration.)

My mother paused. She spoke again slowly, drifting back to an interstice in time that began to take on dimension, particularity. "They were terrible, those beatings."

I'd always been able to see the girl in my mother's face, even when she was in one of her rages. I saw it then; the oldest child, her cheeks fat from the starchy DP camp diet. Braids down her back.

"Why did Senelis do it?" I asked. It was hard to imagine Uncle Roy cowering before anyone. Him of the Brut cologne he must have showered in; when he visited, that pungent drugstore scent took over every room. A big man with a large tattoo on his huge right bicep, he had been a flight mechanic for the army on a base in Kansas, pigheaded as a teenager in Germany in the deportation camp, the war still breaking up inside him. But he was smart. Math and biology came easily to him.

"I don't know why. Arguments, Roy disobeyed him, I don't know," said my mother.

"Did he use his hands?"

"Sometimes. Mostly, I think—a belt."

My mother and I looked at each other.

"Tell me more," I said, "about my grandfather."

What exactly did it mean, I asked, to have fought in the resistance? Who was he resisting? My ignorance appalls me now.

"The Russians," my mother said.

And what did he do when the Germans came into power?

She paused.

"He was a police chief," she said.

"Under the SS?"

She paused again before saying, "Yes."

EVERY YEAR FOR MANY years when I was younger, my mother would send me a pretty journal. Often the cover was of flowers, butterflies. Sometimes the motif was Asian—a water bird standing on one leg by a still pond. Lotus blossoms opened against a gilt background. Always, in the card that accompanied the journal, she would scribble, "Write happy thoughts." This, of course, made me furious, made me immediately pick up a pen and write down one ugly thought after another. Many of them were about her. Raw and venomous. She wanted to suffocate me. I hated her. She, in her heart, hated me. Periodically I tore up the pages of most of my journals. The fantasy was, I think, that something would happen to me and my journals would become a marker of my life. Even if only one person read them—the language of what was to some degree pretty standard mother/daughter hostilities and to another degree the brokenness I carried out of the chaos of my early life—that reader might imagine this was the sum of me. Tearing up the pages felt like a self-betrayal and a rebellion—a way of enacting a freedom from the past that I didn't feel yet, but hoped to.

When I conjure up that young woman now, writing with intensity and suffering, perhaps in a room in Massachusetts on a side street three blocks north of Emily Dickinson's house, or at an alcove desk in a suburb where I was once an improbable boarder, or in the sand on the beach at Martha's Vineyard, jittery from the gallon of coffee I drank through my morning waitress shift in Edgartown, I seem astoundingly fortunate. I could write. I could rip pages up and start again. I had a room and a bed. I went to college. I worked and was paid. I lived in time with language. I was born.

I WAS RAISED in a secular household. We went to mass (without my father) on holidays with the Lithuanian Catholic side of my family and celebrated the Jewish holidays with my father's side of the family. Yet when asked what I was, I always responded, "Jewish." Technically I was not; my father had married a non-Jew. However, my Jewish grandmother, Rachel Treegoob Gabis, believed her will and wishes superseded rabbinical law and conveyed to me her notion of how I was to think of myself.

She made her pronouncement the summer I was twelve, on Martha's Vineyard, where she lived the last half of her life and where, along with my parents, various aunts and uncles spent parts of each summer.

It was a hot day, and I was hanging out by the side of the local movie theater on the corner of Circuit Avenue in Oak Bluffs. A new poster was up advertising a movie I wanted to see. What was it? *Jaws* comes to mind, but probably it was another movie. The sun was bright with that salty white glare that only happens near the ocean. I was wearing a tiny gold-plated cross around my neck that I'd bought at the town drugstore because my summer girlfriends in Oak Bluffs (mainly Polish Catholic daughters of plumbers and rooming-house owners) all wore them. Absorbed in the movie poster, at first I didn't see my grandmother drive up in her used gold Impala. Ignoring the traffic, she put her car in park, threw open her door, and made it to the curb where I stood before I could completely register the fact of her. She reached for me, tore the little necklace with the cross off my neck, and threw it on the sidewalk.

"I never want to see such a thing on your neck again," she said.

I looked down at my ruined necklace, and then back up at her red face. She was always fiery, loving, dominating, but I'd never seen her so angry before.

"You're Jewish," she spat, then turned, jumped back into the Impala, and sped away.

* * *

In the café with my mother, the ambient noise buzzed in my head. I felt hot, folded and unfolded my napkin as if it was one of the cards Senelis used to send me. He never learned to read English very well. "To My Dear Son-In-Law," the front of a birthday card might say. Inside it, a worn-out five-dollar bill, his uncertain handwriting. "Anyting," he'd said.

But he had said other things to me, too, when I was young. That I was not to be like my father, an admonition that caused me enormous distress until I could make out from my grandfather's stumbling grammar that he wanted me to be a Catholic. I was eight or nine at the time. It was summer again. Oak Bluffs again. My grandfather had been drinking. We were alone on the scruffy side porch of my family's rambling house built by a sea captain who designed the interior beams to be curved like those of a ship. Senelis's eyes were round and glassy. I'd begun to recognize the appearance of that sheen as well as a haranguing repetitiousness that came over him and connect them to his beer breath or a half-empty bottle of too-sweet wine. His English always got worse when he was drunk. "No be like your fader," Senelis said. Why? What was wrong with my father? "Jews no good," he explained. I remember being both confused and relieved. It wasn't my father completely, the whole man, who Senelis thought was bad, only one part of him. I had no idea why Senelis felt that way. I promised him I'd go to church, knowing that I wouldn't. I knew also that I would never tell my father what Senelis said.

The waiter brought our check, and without me asking, or her telling me, I knew my mother had had enough of the past that day.

We walked out to Broadway. A man with a wide face on a bike with a food delivery, going against traffic, careened past. My mother chattered. We walked slowly past the gym, the fruit stand, a bus stop where eight or nine preschoolers stood, roped together by their cheery, watchful minders. The children gawked at the mannequins decked out in spandex in the gym windows—ready to run, leap. Question after question tumbled through me—all really the same question. *Did Senelis hurt anybody?*

* * *

THE NEXT MORNING my mother and I sat in my study in our pajamas. The one large window framed her in light. In her white nightgown, she stretched like a sleepy cat. We sipped our coffee. She tucked her knees underneath her on the old, elephantine sofa. I had a felt-tip pen and a piece of paper. I asked her to write down the name of the town where my grandfather had worked for the Germans. *S-V-E-N-C-I-O-N-Y-S*. She became again the language teacher she had once been, laughing a little at my difficulty pronouncing the name. She said it again for me, slowly, and then again. And then—stopped. Something was there:

She spoke dreamily. "I remember the grown-ups talking,"

Was Senelis there? No, he wasn't.

"Something happened." She reached for it, the past. "Germans had been attacked in a car, and there was a translator with them who wasn't German. All the Germans were killed, but she lived. And I said to someone, maybe Kruckchamama and one of her friends, that was a good thing—she was alive! But they said no, better she had been killed given what would happen to her."

My mother was quiet for a minute.

And what was that? I pressed.

"The Gestapo, torture . . . some horrible death."

I waited a beat. "Who was she, the translator? Did you know her name?"

My mother just shook her head, as if shaking off the past, the emotional capital these moments of remembering cost her.

The translator. What happened? Was my grandfather there?

MY MOTHER RETURNED to Martha's Vineyard, where she and my father had moved from the Midwest after retirement and before my father's death from cancer. I missed my father terribly after she went. I wanted to talk to him about what my mother had said. I wanted to ask him what he thought of Senelis, if he knew anything about what Senelis did during the war. I wanted to tell him, belatedly, what Senelis had said to me on the side porch that summer.

Soon after my mother's visit, on an Upper West Side morning, light refracting off every hard surface, I stood with our two dogs on 104th Street. They yanked on their leashes in the direction of a cabbie's honking. A tall teenager (shouldn't she have been in school?) in leggings and frizzy red hair passed, holding a bag from the McDonald's on Broadway. The smell of salty grease made my mouth water. Half a block away, the corner market boasted white plastic buckets of flowers that looked like daisies dyed a garish blue, a fake purple. They probably *were* dyed. I thought about the amazing shimmer of a red maple I'd watched all fall in the park; the real and the not-real. I turned away— And there was my father walking up from Broadway toward me, a gray wool cap on his head. His stride was eager and determined. He'd never been a large man, but age made him more compact. The khaki pants. His air of distraction and curiosity, his sweetness. He got closer. Any second he'd look up. Oh, the happiness at seeing the missing one again! It surged up into my chest, my throat. Then my father turned a certain way, tilted his head to the sun—vanished into someone else, younger now, I could see, with a sharper chin, a different mouth. I stopped, let the man pass, vaguely embarrassed, vaguely demolished, but oddly joyful for the almost incarnation of physical shape, molecules, feet hitting the pavement, heart beating, lungs working. I see my father this way sometimes three times a week, sometimes once every few months. This would please him, I think, if he were living. "Really," he would say, "really, you thought it was me!" This is a fact I've learned from his death, from the deaths of my grandparents, the deaths of friends—that the experience of their absence is something you end up wanting to talk about with those who are gone. And the questions—the particulars only they can tell you, their secrets, a nuance of a story, shimmer like maple leaves with their palmate lobes, a fact of nature and time you'll never touch, hold in your hands, crush.

If my father were alive, I'd ask him about Senelis, ask him why, especially when my father got older and Judaism became central to him, he never spoke to any of his children about the way we were raised—with the trappings of two religions and the substance of neither.

If his mother, my grandmother Rachel, were alive, I'd ask her what being Jewish meant to her. If Babita were alive, I'd ask her what my mother was like as a child.

If Senelis were alive, I'd present him with my checklist:

Were you a member of the LAF—the Lithuanian Activist Front?

No answer.

Were you a member of a partisan unit in hiding during the Russian occupation of Lithuania?

Yes; check.

And when the Nazis violated the Molotov-Ribbentrop Pact and entered Lithuania in 1941, did you come out of hiding?

Yes; check.

Did you then become chief of police under the Gestapo in Švenčionys, Lithuania?

Yes; check.

He pushes his can of beer or glass of cherry wine to the edge of the waxy tablecloth. He whistles a little, as he did after scraping the scales off a fish he caught onto newspaper in the sun.

What did you do during that time? Who did you become?

He sighs. He rubs at a callus on the fat chuff of one of his hands, says my name, rolling the *r*, landing hard on the *t*, picks up the can of beer and in a glass meant for orange juice or whiskey shots, pours a little for me.

I E-MAIL THE Lithuanian Central State Archives in Vilnius, not sure what to ask for, not sure, at first, what I'm looking for. I ask for a copy of my grandfather's internal passport during 1941, the document that's supposed to show his comings and goings inside the country. I ask for the names of the Gulags where my grandmother served her time after she was arrested by the Soviet secret police or NKVD. I ask for any information relating to my grandfather's activities as police chief in Švenčionys in 1941 and his brief arrest three years later. I ask for a specific file—a pay voucher for local police in the Vilnius district in 1941, submitted to the German command. I give the file number, the page numbers. Two weeks later I get an e-mail back. I'm asked to wire the equivalent of thirty-five dollars into a Lithuanian bank account. I'm told that after I do, there are three documents they'll send me.

It's the end of my teaching semester. True winter has set in. Snow stops the city. Juvenile red-tailed hawks in the park go hungry. Buses skid sideways on every icy avenue. Cars hibernate in hard-pack drifts. I get sick. Too sick to go to the bank and wire the money. I'm ill for weeks, feverish, my throat swollen.

Every day I think about the wire transfer I need to send, the thirty-five dollars. I don't send it. I don't go out. The fever continues. Every day I think of the archivist in Lithuania with a stack of requests. If I ever get around to sending the money, she'll have put my questions into the bottom of the stack. It makes me crazy. But I don't go to the bank. *Stupid woman,* the archivist is probably thinking anyway. *Her grandfather's dead. Why put us to work for a date here, an accusation there? Doesn't she love him? Doesn't she have other things to do with her time?*

For weeks the snow continues. For weeks I read and sleep sitting up because of the coughing. And the stack gets taller and the answers to my questions get farther away. Finally, six weeks after the archive's request for money, I stop off at the bank after a trip to my doctor, who says, "Welcome to the age of the superbug." She's sick too, coughing in her little examining room, covering her mouth with her hands.

At the bank, the wire transfer takes all of ten minutes. That same day, I e-mail the archives again, inform them I've wired the money, give them the confirmation number. Weeks go by, I'm waiting. I want those documents. I hate those archivists in Lithuania. Hate the piles of requests with mine lost somewhere, shuffled into the did-not-follow-up stack or the took-too-long stack. I want my information, and I want it now. How American!

EVERYBODY HAS A secret. Everybody has a locked door, a dream with a message. In my family, I blurt the secrets. I jimmy the locks on the doors. All my life, I thought of myself this way. But somehow, during those homebound weeks, the weeks the money didn't get wired, the follow-up e-mail didn't get sent, I realized this was false. All my life I've said just enough to survive. I wrote just enough to step over the threshold of silence. Then I stopped.

I have no family members with whom I can talk about what went on in my life as a child, compare notes, affirm one another's microversions of the past.

What redeems the brutality of the larger past, in the macro history that contains us all? Every day I ask myself that question. The only answer that ever comes is this: To make the past manifest.

WHILE I WAS sick and the snow fell and I shuffled around the apartment and our two dogs lavished their cold-nosed love upon me and my husband brought me soup and my stepdaughter told me to spit after I sneezed and the days went by and the weeks fled, it seemed more and more possible to stop asking questions about my grandfather. But when my fever spiked, the dead in my life pulled at me as if they were still here, as if Senelis still drove the horse and cart between two front lines, his children on a bed of straw behind the buckboard. He lived in me. He was a wheel that turned endlessly in my family's path without any of us knowing, exhausting the road, running across the shadows of who we all were and who we would become.

I sent out another query to another archive in Lithuania and again, in a few weeks, got a reply:

"We . . . beg to inform you that in archival fund of department of Committee for State Security in Lithuanian SSR, in card index for operational registry files, there is a card which contains a record that Pranas Puronas had worked as a chief of Švenčionys police department during German occupation . . . If you wish to have us carry out a search for persons who testified on P. Puronas and for activities of Švenčionys police department as well as for related files . . . then we beg to inform you . . ."

"Yes, I wish you to search," I wrote back right away.

CHAPTER 3

WORD GETS AROUND

Everyone knew he was a Nazi," Aunt Shirley said, when I phoned her about Senelis.

The list of living family members I am in touch with is small. Aunt Shirley, my father's sister, is one of them.

"What do you mean by Nazi?" I asked, unhelpfully.

"Oh, you know, they all were, all the Lithuanians."

Did she mean my mother too? Did she mean my Lithuanian grandmother?

"What did my dad say about it? What did Nana say?"

"We never talked about it. We just knew," Shirley said.

"*How* did you know?"

"How do you think?" Her voice was louder by a few decibels. My obtuseness was starting to irritate her.

She lives thirty blocks or so away from me, also on the Upper West Side, in an apartment by Central Park that has grown cavernous since her third husband, the composer George Perle, died. Urbane, artistic, worldly—she used to frighten me a little when I was a child. I felt ignorant in her presence, Midwestern, simple. Her beauty has morphed into a diminutive elegance. She tends to laugh, a little caustically, at that which is dark. She gave a quick laugh now, a pause during which she considered how to tackle my ignorance.

"Everyone hated the Jews." The decibels climbed again.

She sounded just like her mother—my grandmother Rachel—giving my father what-for about his right-wing politics, or imploring one of her errant grandchildren to take her advice. I suddenly felt like I was talking to Aunt Shirley and my grandmother at the same time: Nana, who could cut you off for twenty years if you betrayed her—not a phone call, a letter, a nod at a party—or claim you, as she claimed a number of troubled, broke, and talented artist friends of her daughter's, lodge you permanently in her heart, as she did me.

Since my mother's visit, I missed her as much as I did my father. Beyond the world of books and his political leanings, my father could be impossible to talk to. His mother was different. She was, like everyone, full of contradictions: unaware and intimate, coarse and gentle, self-possessed and haunted.

When I hung up with Aunt Shirley, I went to the rickety wooden cabinet in my study and opened a file of old letters. My grandmother had lovely penmanship before cataracts clouded the page of stationery before her. She pressed hard on the nib of the fountain pen she used, which left little blots of ink here and there, like space dust in the galaxy of her thoughts. *Dearest*, she began before she told me what I should or should not do—*appreciate your father more, never forget how much your mother suffered, the family is your home. You belong here.*

Grandmother Rachel, born in 1899. A century and change earlier, her birthplace would have been part of the Grand Duchy of Lithuania instead of the ever-expanding Russian Empire.

She relentlessly stabbed at the eternal weeds in the sand and moss of her large yard in Chilmark on Martha's Vineyard. When she reached her hundredth year and couldn't stoop to the ground anymore, she dragged herself, seated with a collection of sharp instruments, from one defiled spot to the next. Before her lipstick kiss, she grabbed our cheeks hard enough to rearrange our faces. Pain and love were intermingled—her life, the lives of her children and grandchildren, depended on this knowledge. Otherwise, how could any of us prepare for whatever forces might be bearing down, preparing to extinguish us?

She hated Christianity. "Bullshit," she called it. One of my cousins thinks she conflated Christians with the Cossacks who terrorized the village where she lived as a small child. By the start of World War II, she'd divorced her husband (Harry Gabis, slim, dapper, seller of fine men's suits), stopped keeping kosher, stopped the ritual dunk in the mikvah ("tub of stinking water") and was raising her children alone, cutting hair, which she hated. As it had been for a time in Lithuania among a cross section of Jews and non-Jews, communism, with its egalitarian promise, enthralled her.

"I never signed anything," she said once, referring to some document that would have signified actual party membership.

She sat across from me at her supper table. Out the two windows on our left, late spring and the hour did something to the pink-red of her azaleas; the iridescent color seemed to hover over the blossoms. Stains marked her table-cloth. She couldn't see them anymore. We had wandered into an area of her past she didn't want to speak of.

(It occurred to me at that instant that *We Never Talked About It* could be the generic title for all family reminiscences written until the current age of memoir when *I Talked Too Much About It* seems a better fit.)

Politics and her own personal liberation created a rift in the family; once she stopped keeping kosher, her father, Wolf, and her mother, Ḳlarah, never set foot in her house again. But as it did for many, my grandmother's brief entrancement with communism ended in anger. She had been duped; she hated the brutal machinations of the Soviet regime. The generals of Stalin's army—some Jewish, some not—who pressed on to Berlin at the bombed-out end of the war, their exhausted troops freezing to death during brief night encampments in the first push through East Prussia, walked away from the war weighted down with medals. Shortly after, many were executed or sent to the Gulag for one treasonous act or another. In 1939, the famed Yiddish poet Peretz Markish was awarded the Order of Lenin. In 1949, the ubiquitous knock on the door summoned him to his death. "You'll pay with your head for the love you bear the world," he wrote. When my mother came into her life, my grand-mother was horrified by the imprisonment of Babita, lost, probably dead in some unmarked frozen grave in the Gulag.

But for a time, while she cut hair and raised children and had romances, my Jewish grandmother must have felt modern, part of something grand, beyond the shtetl, beyond the long, dark, narrow apartment where she was raised after emigration. If only the children would behave.

Time after time she exhorted Leonard Bernstein, a chum of Aunt Shirley's, to stop banging so loud on the piano in her Philadelphia apartment or they'd all be on the street. The landlord had already complained. Bernstein didn't stop. My grandmother and her three children were evicted for their noisy love of music.

She often spoke of Israel to me, but rarely of the Holocaust. Certain subjects evoked so much passion that words left her. She'd moan. She'd throw up her hands, *Oy*. The subject wasn't forbidden, but language couldn't grasp it.

There she is; the not-quite-typical Jewish grandmother with her early divorce and secular ways and *Oy vey is mir* and chicken soup. "He was a Nazi," Shirley said. And we all know what Nazis are, don't we? Psychotics in knee-high boots. Killers. And in fact, I have a photograph of Senelis in those tall, dark boots.

But Senelis, I'd been told, hated the Gestapo.

A FEW DAYS after my talk with Aunt Shirley, my mother-in-law came over for lox and bagels. I told her about Senelis. "Oy vey," she said, and put her head in her hands. Always ready to talk about the persecution of the Jews, she didn't want to talk about this. It occurred to me that she was afraid it might compromise her love for me, even if she didn't want it to. Instead we talked how she, like my grandmother Rachel, grew up in a Yiddish-speaking household.

"It's a beautiful language," my mother-in-law said.

I'd never thought of Yiddish as beautiful before. The Yiddishisms of my grandmother were delivered with the force and bluntness of jackhammers.

"Take *a shayna maiydelah*, for example," my mother-in-law said. "The English—'a pretty girl'—doesn't have any of the heart of the Yiddish. The Yiddish has such tenderness to it, and it can't be translated."

And because she's told me, I hear it suddenly, in that particular phrase. *A shayna maiydelah. A pretty girl. Brief, that beauty. Of the daughter, the niece, the granddaughter, the childhood friend.*

CHAPTER 4

BAD STUDENT

Finally, another letter from the archives; a thin, this time larger envelope, a small sturdy thread secured around a circle below the flap to seal it closed. Even in my dread, I loved the antiquity of it. Inside was a pay roster with names I would parse through dozens of times in the months to come. On two other pages, in Lithuanian, was a list of file numbers. A brief summary of their contents led me immediately to Google Translate. There, of course, I ended up with a strange mishmash—a telephone operator who heard on this day and has since was . . . 1941 saugumas . . . not mentioned . . . something about my grandfather . . . shooting . . . 7,000, 200 . . . testified . . . when . . . gone . . .

My immediate reaction was not to swiftly find a professional translator but to decide on the spot to learn Lithuanian—a task that would take time, and so was partially a stalling tactic, a division inside me; to want to know, to look away.

When I was very young, when Senelis and my aunts and my mother chattered in the warm holiday home in Hammond, Indiana, and I colored or watched cartoons, their words seemed almost like English to me, ordinary, knowable, at least to a certain degree. Then came a day, another holiday, when I was older, seven perhaps—oh, so grown up. My mother and her sister were in the kitchen. Perhaps my aunt snapped a dish towel, the drying done. Perhaps my mother lit one of her Kent cigarettes. Those details elude me, but what I do remember is that their mother tongue was now utterly incomprehensible to me. I was locked out of it. Whatever capacity I'd had for recall and comprehension vanished. I marked it, for it was one of those moments when a child feels the weight and separateness of a self. My hands, my hair, my thoughts, my wishes, my worries, my—life.

AND SO I FOUND Aldona, an old friend of an old friend, a second-generation Lithuanian. Her real profession was massage therapy, but she had two daughters who had both learned Lithuanian at her kitchen table. When the girls were small, she demanded that only Lithuanian, no matter how clumsily, be spoken at dinner. In six months, both were fluent. Because I had told her that when I was very young, I could understand much of the Lithuanian spoken around me, she had expectations.

Our few meetings took place in a small spare room, several floors up a cranky elevator, the same room where she worked on her clients. Stocky, with unruly short hair, she was warm and smart. In her presence, I felt the weight of her life, as if I were lying on her massage table and she was leaning into me, a forearm pressed hard on my shoulder blade, her knuckles kneading hard on my thigh. On her large desk, she flattened out the pages from the Lithuanian archives. She tried to get me to work at the words. She scolded; she insisted. I fumbled. I immediately wanted to sleep. Black out.

She went through the Lithuanian vowels and asked me to mimic them. I tried, immediately forgot. "Again," she demanded. I couldn't. I wanted her to do the work. I'd steered clear of the Lithuanian side of my family for so long that the intimacy of learning the language, of incorporating its sounds (right out of my childhood, right out of my grandfather's mouth), was more than I could manage.

"Just read it to me," I asked/begged/demanded.

"It's your nickel," she said, sighing, but resigned for the moment.

A fair number of the files from the Lithuanian archives mentioned my grandfather. They confirmed that he was chief of Saugumas in Švenčionys from 1941 to 1943. In the small room over Union Square, my tutor, who was not Jewish, who had Lithuanian family members turned in, so she said, to the Soviets by Jews and killed, read brief notes about a series of shootings aloud—no context given, just a trace, a notation, and then she stopped. Horror played long and deep across her face, and she looked at me finally and shook her head.

"What is history?" I asked her.

"History is who you've lost," she said.

A SCHEDULING GLITCH forced me to cancel our next lesson. I didn't go back. Aldona's kindness and depth, the strictness of her instruction, were too loaded for me, though I'll brag to my aunts from my mother's side of the family (whom I'll soon see for the first time in decades) and to my mother that "I'm learning Lithuanian"—which meant by then that I'd purchased the Pimsleur Lithuanian language tapes, downloaded them onto my phone, listened to Lesson 1 for a minute—"Ar kalbate lietuvių?" (Do you speak Lithuanian?), and then pressed stop.

In February, a call came from my mother. In the clipped, awkward manner she adopts when she mentions her sister to me, she told me that my beautiful Aunt Karina with my shy and direct Aunt Agnes, a onetime amateur bowling champion in Kansas, were both traveling to Martha's Vineyard for a visit. I immediately asked to come and interview them about Senelis. Permission was granted. And so on a cold Friday, my husband boarded the train with me at Penn Station, and we headed north.

The train rattled up the coast of New York and Connecticut on our way to a bus in Boston, then the ferry to the Vineyard.

Across the aisle, a girl my stepdaughter's age chattered into her cell phone. The car smelled vaguely of cigarettes, even though they had long been banned in transit. The conductor, his waist too big for his blue suit, swayed up front as we rounded each curve. We reached a familiar shimmer of water on the right— Connecticut, home of my first marriage.

My then-husband and I were welcomed to the area with a small dinner party given by one of his colleagues at the maritime museum where my husband built boats. Seven or eight of us sat sated after a rich meal of cassoulet—the room still redolent of the dense mix of beans, sausage, and meats. The boat talk put my husband at ease. I was silent, a good listener, my strategy when I felt shy.

Bottles of wine caught the light. The other guests, strangers to me but for the few hours of this dinner together, were telling jokes. Someone was interspersing the joking with a discussion of Mike Plant, a world-class sailor from Jamestown, Rhode Island. He and his boat *Coyote* hadn't been heard from for two weeks. Overwhelmed by working his boat into seaworthy shape and finding sponsors for a race, Plant hadn't registered his EPIRB (emergency position-indicating radio beacon). A distress signal from his boat could be picked up, but the signal wouldn't reveal the vessel it came from or its sailing path. Was it a fatal error? No one knew yet.

The man at our table talking about him, handsome, his face colored by a late-fall tan, was also an experienced sailor and calculated Plant's odds like a surgeon talking about possible outcomes of a risky case. He spoke quietly, intelligently, and something about his considered speech made the sailor's fate more real to me. Most of the dinner guests sailed. Their faces were pondering, grim. We sat with candlelight and dessert; somewhere in the ocean, Mike Plant foundered amid salt, cold, storms. Then jokes began again, maybe to dispel the sense of the ominous.

Another dinner guest, gray-haired, a bit corpulent, apropos of nothing it seemed, wisecracked, "How many Jews does it take to screw in a lightbulb?" I'm sure there was a precursor to the joke, but I've forgotten it. I don't remember the punch line.

Did I interrupt the laughter at the end of the joke? I don't think so. I draw a blank when I try to recall the rest of the dinner party. I'm like my mother in this way; memories of my own cowardice or moral failure can immediately become vague. What I do remember is that eventually I signaled to my husband that it was time to go. I was disgusted. The person who'd made the joke was intelligent, educated.

I was stupid and naive, caught out. On the way home my husband, Seattle born, from a family of Baptists and Protestants, joined me in condemning the crudity. In the dark of his truck that always smelled vaguely of the cigarettes I railed at him for smoking (nicotine yellowed the windshield), reminiscent of all the cigarettes I sucked on before I quit, I leaned against the passenger door. I thought of Mike Plant holding on to a bit of planking, or the grip handles of an inflatable raft, told myself I was lucky to be settled in a marriage, a life ahead of us in a beautiful place, even if a few people said ugly things there.

ON THE TRAIN, I pressed my forehead against the window as if I might see, in passing on the station platform, one of the kind, elderly members of a historical society ("We're the hysterical society," the woman had joked with me early on) whose property my husband and I lived on and cared for. All the society members were deeply committed to the preservation of local history; many had family ties to the region that went back centuries.

My father was still alive when I lived there. The year of that dinner party and the lightbulb joke, my Jewish grandmother was 103 years old and still kept her own house in Chilmark. I could call her on the phone, hear her voice, the little cough at the beginning of the call, the clipped bit of British still there—*Darling.*

The local Mashantucket Pequots hadn't broken ground yet on the casino that would change the night sky into a permanent fluorescence. I loved the old stolen farms on land that had once been the domain of the tribe. North of Mystic, where the historical society was, sugar maples flared orange in the fall. A huge mulberry sailed green into summer. A cold millstream ran under our house. Each night dusk quieted the world.

Once a week I ran a dustrag through the small genealogical library on the first floor of the old house we cared for. Before the house was given over to the town, the last family inhabitant had lived there alone, wan, bespectacled, a local cultivator of the arts. The cavernous attic had numerous middling paintings he had done, but among them, stashed away in rolls in the eaves, were quick and lovely sketches of naked young men. I periodically laid them out flat and wondered. They made me melancholy, made me think of hidden life, hidden desire.

The hopeful faces of far-flung library visitors with Maryland and Florida even California license plates who tapped on the door, welcomed by the docent librarian, mystified me. To drive all this way to put your finger on a line in a ledger—such-and-such relative died of pig fever, great-grandfather so-and-so sold a barn. Why? I picked up broken robin's eggs, pale blue in the grass. I made the rash mistake of pulling, from gaps in the front stone wall, some kind of precious historical, almost extinct, vegetation I'd taken for weeds encouraging cracks in the granite. I was forgiven.

As THE TRAIN moved beyond my old life, I thought of my current husband's first mother-in-law, Grace, who loved travel of any kind and was a committed genealogist. We had met at her eighty-eighth birthday party in a Turkish restaurant, belly dancers and all, six years after her own daughter's death from colon cancer. A Lithuanian Jew, she put a remarkably unlined hand against my cheek.

"You have a hamish face, dear. Do you know what that means?"

The Yiddish escaped me.

"It means familiar," she said.

Two years later, Grace would phone my mother to ask for permission to be my "other mother." My mother agreed.

Yet even when Grace, whom I loved, tried to interest me in all the Litvak history and genealogy she'd immersed herself in over decades, I could only pretend to care. Her stack of photographs, shtetl histories, mini-biographies of relatives from Vilna—the Jerusalem of Lithuania—laid out carefully for me in her small, nearby studio apartment, pained me. "I'm a speed reader," I told her, as I pretended to zip through what it had taken her decades to assemble.

Her Lithuania had nothing to do with me then. I was like my Jewish grandmother: repudiating, turning away from. Looking forward instead of back.

MY HUSBAND SHIFTED in his seat, tall, his legs stretched out awkwardly, half in the aisle. I watched him doze. He's an investigative journalist. I thought about questions he has and hasn't asked me, and I him. What we keep from each other. What we reveal.

Mike Plant's boat was found finally. Capsized. The hull was painted black, making it hard to pick out from the dark swells. My Jewish grandmother lived on until my second year in Connecticut. At four o'clock one morning the call came; she had had a stroke the week before and for the first time in her life (excluding childbirth) been admitted to the hospital.

My first husband and I tried every fertility treatment available to conceive a child together, but could not. My second husband, asleep beside me on the train heading to Boston, adopted, with his first wife Lisa, a girl from China, my beautiful stepdaughter; my *shayna maiydela*.

CHAPTER 5

IT'S OPRAH'S FAULT

You may encounter reluctant witnesses. Attempt to gain their
cooperation by appealing to their sense of civic responsibility . . .
At this stage of the investigation, you cannot be certain of anyone's
degree of involvement or knowledge of the crime.

—*HOMICIDE INVESTIGATION STANDARD OPERATING PROCEDURES*

On the hulking ferry from Woods Hole to Vineyard Haven, my husband went out onto the upper deck while I stayed below, away from the wind and cold, though the stink of fuel wafted through the grimy seating area. Car alarms kept going off, loud, annoying. A few islanders sat behind me and tried to guess the make of the car from the sound of the alarm.

"Mercedes," one said.

"Black BMW," said the other.

A baby wailed, the sound traveling from the indoor deck upstairs.

The familiar rumble of the engine, the slight pitch of the hull against the swells, always reminded me of the family summer crossing, of being young. Was Aunt Karina nervous about seeing me? Did Aunt Agnes remember what I looked like?

I'd thought I would never see my mother's sister Karina again. Every once in a while, I fantasized about a final meeting with her at my mother's funeral. I'd heard she'd put on weight. I imagined we would nod to one another, separate in our grief. She would be large and still lovely, wearing a big woolen coat. She would be alone because I wouldn't have allowed her to bring Uncle Alan. We would say nothing to each other.

Out the window, the churn and spread of the sea, dark blue with winter, was comforting. What would Aunt Karina really look like? She had been a surrogate mother to me during my eleventh year, when our family left Columbia, Missouri, and moved in with her and my uncle Alan, who was a successful contractor in Hammond, Indiana—a relatively short train ride from Chicago. My father's sabbatical necessitated research at his alma mater, the University of Chicago. He was writing a book on secrecy in politics that he wouldn't finish. He got his book contract shortly before Watergate and perhaps would have made a name for himself in academia, worthy of his beloved mentor Leo Strauss, but he was not a man given to completion.

He loved to study and hypothesize. He was a dreamer, my father. He should have been walking with Emerson or Wordsworth while Dorothy Wordsworth was at home making soap and stew and darning socks and transcribing poems and giving William bits of her diary he could make poems out of. He liked ambulating with silent, thinking men. He liked being alone in the spare bedroom, turned into a makeshift study for him in Aunt Karina and Uncle Alan's apartment, a room littered with pipe ash and spent matches and stacks of books and legal pads covered with his small, inscrutable handwriting. He liked pondering the idea of secrecy in, well, secret.

He was not able to grasp that stocky, gregarious Uncle Alan's attentions toward me were a signal of something other than familial affection. The long photography sessions during which I arranged myself on the couch in clothes that Uncle Alan picked out, usually dark—black turtlenecks, tights—while he fussed with lenses and lighting; the weekly all-day Saturday outings. My increasing attachment to his compliments and our physical closeness and jokes were noted by everyone as a sign of a mutual devotion that was perhaps a bit excessive but also enviable—a club no one else belonged to.

While my father was busy with Machiavelli, Uncle Alan and I roamed the city and ate salty french fries and the best hot dogs in the small city. Not that year, but earlier, when I was perhaps eight or nine, one outing had ended with Uncle Alan requesting I straddle him in the car and "hug him very tight." After the protracted hugging session he asked me to make it our secret, and I remember being surprised by his request; he was my uncle. I loved him; he loved me—this was common knowledge, wasn't it? I complied, of course, because even before the sabbatical year, I adored him.

When my father's sabbatical was ending, I let it be known that I didn't want to go back to Missouri. I don't remember if Uncle Alan and Aunt Karina first suggested that I stay on with them, or if I started to campaign to stay. They both doted on me. My school year with them had been the happiest of my life. I started writing, and received accolades from my trim, energetic fourth-grade teacher, Mrs. Laws. I had many friends. I loved Hammond.

Aunt Karina was as steady as my mother was volatile. She read out loud beautifully, without the heavy Lithuanian accent my mother would never lose—*The Hobbit*, *The Wind in the Willows*, *Jane Eyre*. I loved the luxury of nights spent listening—a gift that has endured my whole life—in the small back room off their kitchen, in the trundle bed, with my sister beside me, the vague odors of the night's meal still in the air, rain beading on the sill that was always a little gritty from the Midwestern wind. A few blocks away, the red neon light of a hotel shone. Perhaps it flashed off and on, I don't remember—just that it was part of the theater of the stories my aunt read with such engagement and authority.

"You love Uncle Alan more than you love me," my father said, emerging from his temporary study one afternoon after school, during the time when I was to make my decision about where I wanted to live. It was a pronouncement, not a question. His glasses were pushed up. His hair, bristly and thick, stuck out. His shirt pocket was stained with ink. He looked at me with both sadness and absentmindedness—as if he couldn't quite place who I was but knew that I was on the verge of abandoning ship. "No, I don't," I told him, not knowing how I really felt.

I ended up going back to Missouri. My father, perhaps in an effort to reclaim my deepest affections, began to talk with me on a regular basis about Aristotle and Plato, and then quiz me on our discussions, in the dialectic mode of one of the other eras he should have been born into.

And then, of course, it vanishes: those fictions of childhood in which heroes and enemies are clearly identified and love is inviolable. Several months later,

during a much-anticipated holiday visit back to Hammond, Uncle Alan moles-
ted me on a night when we were alone in the house—though one could argue
that the hugging event in the car a few years before fell into the same category.

When he slipped his large hand under my turtleneck and started circling
my still-flat left breast, asking, over and over, "Will you be my baby?" I remember, aside from the overwhelming panic, wanting to shake him, to wake him.
His actions in the hours as they unfolded felt practiced, rote—acts committed
by someone to whom I was suddenly a stranger. Not even an anonymous child.
Not even, somehow, there.

I told my parents everything several weeks later when we were home
again, burst out with it as I was coming down the stairs from my bedroom
because, hand on the wooden banister, I'd heard them in the living room below,
planning the next visit to Chicago. I wept, even shouted as I spoke, but all the
time I felt as if it was someone else, not me, talking, weeping, explaining when
my father called me to him and insisted, detail by detail, I tell him all of it.

My mother was outraged. I was a liar. No, my father reasoned, a child
wouldn't lie about such a thing.

I would ruin Aunt Karina's life if I said anything! my mother declared.

They had already lost so much in the war!

My father listened and then said, "I want you to understand that some men
have a kind of sickness. They can't help it."

The next visit to Indiana, when I refused to leave the house with Uncle
Alan for our ritual day in the city, my mother hissed in my ear, "Go." She didn't
want Aunt Karina to think anything was amiss. It was my father who very
quietly entered the kitchen where we were having our showdown and said,
softly, firmly, slowly, after taking his pipe from his mouth, "She doesn't have
to go if she doesn't want to."

I loved Aunt Karina, but understood that my rejection of Uncle Alan, my
unwillingness to ever be alone in a room with him, broadcast something not to
be delved into. I held knowledge that could destroy her, and because wherever
she was, Uncle Alan was too, we were through.

At fifteen, in part but not exclusively because of this turn of events, I
decided to leave home. Shortly after my mind was made up, I found a boarding
school in Massachusetts that gave me a scholarship. (As it happened, the

school's founders and a certain portion of the faculty were Jews who had fled different parts of Europe, Germany in particular, when the war broke out. The family histories of some of my teachers would become increasingly meaningful to me the more I learned about Senelis.)

YEARS AFTER BOARDING school, when I was grown, during a visit with my mother on the Vineyard, Aunt Karina called the house and began to sob, begging my mother to tell her why I would not come to the phone, why, for all these years, I had refused her affections when we had been so close, in the old trundle-bed days. My mother put the phone down. She came upstairs to my father's study, where I was looking through his books. He was at the beach, walking the tide line with one of his philosopher friends, Stanley Burnshaw, a poet and one of the early editors of the the *New Masses*, a Marxist magazine that attracted, in the 1920s and '30s, writers like Langston Hughes and Dorothy Parker. He was sharp and bent like a gnome and loved my father for one of the reasons intimacy was difficult for him: his preference of books over people.

My mother asked if I would give her permission to tell my aunt why I had pulled away from her all these years. My mother was now willing, perhaps because of her sister's distress, to let the secret out. I agreed and immediately wished I hadn't, though part of me went on bird-dog alert. Would my aunt be mine again? Would she hold her husband accountable? In graduate school I had written him a letter threatening to kill him if he hurt another child. Of course there was no way I could know if he had done to others as he did to me.

I was too anxious to go downstairs and listen to my mother's side of the conversation, but later, with a paucity of detail, in her own words, she related my aunt's understandable shock and then her attempt to seal her husband off from my wild claims.

"It's Oprah's fault," my aunt had cried. "All that recovered-memory stuff Oprah started, all those crazy people coming on her show saying this happened and that happened, things they pretended to forget and then imagined they remembered. They just made it up because they're sick and confused and Oprah took advantage—look what she's caused." And my mother, though the elder sister, couldn't muster a rebuttal. So afraid of losing her Karina, she couldn't insist on the truth—that I had revealed what occurred with my uncle several weeks after the event, not years later. When I told my father and mother about Uncle Alan, Oprah was still a girl living in Kosciusko, Mississippi.

THE LOUDSPEAKER BLARED; drivers should return to their vehicles. We were getting ready to dock. The announcement was flat, crackly like the static on one of my father's old radios. I zipped up my coat and went in search of my husband, climbed the stairs against the stream of passengers, climbed with a little shrine to Aunt Karina inside me. I was eleven, in the steamy kitchen, and she was making me a grilled cheese sandwich. Christmas Eve, before midnight mass, she was showing me the right way to put on my special white gloves. Her stockings made a sound when she was dressed up. Her fur hat, in the fierce Midwestern winters, felt alive and soft. At church; the processional, white smoke, wool coats, candles, singing echoing up to the vaulted ceiling—the gathering only mattered to me because it mattered to my aunt, whose face was radiant. She squeezed my hand to keep me from falling asleep.

My husband and I walk through the slightly rickety side door of my mother's house, bringing the cold into the warm kitchen with us. Aunt Agnes and I embrace, her face just as I remember it, only ringed by gray. Aunt Karina prefers to greet us from a distance. She has a cold, she says, and doesn't want us to catch it. I thank her for being willing to talk about my grandfather, and after she hunches over briefly with a deep, rumbling cough, she straightens up, with the impeccable posture I recall so vividly from childhood.

"Of course," she says. "I remember everything."

CHAPTER 6

INTRODUCTIONS

Do you keep a kosher house?" Aunt Karina asks.

My secular husband looks down and smiles.

Nervous, I strain not to laugh at the formal politeness of the question. Welcome the stranger from the strange land, the half-Jew with the Jewish husband. Is there something beyond politeness in Aunt Karina's deference? I feel it; it's an echo, hardly there, nothing Aunt Karina is conscious of. The villager taking note of the oddly dressed neighbor who speaks in a soft, volatile gibberish and doesn't go to church, and if a child happens to go missing from some ruined farm or a town an hour down the road, well, maybe we better take a closer look. What do they do on Friday nights? What's beneath the long shawls, the stinky broad-brimmed hats?

I chide myself for my paranoia. Aunt Karina is just being gracious and I'm just used to New York City, where I'm rarely asked this question.

Aunt Karina coughs again. The dark, soft wools she wears shift, settle; an autumn forest I want to lose myself in, back in the shadows of childhood. An elegant strictness rules over her old beauty; the full mouth, lavish deep green eyes. As she stands, she crosses her arms over her broad chest as if I might rush for her, disassemble what the years demanded she guard herself with; sheets of tin, boards nailed one over another, prayers, the on-goingness of life itself.

Her husband—ask anyone—he's devoted to her, and that other thing, that thing that this meeting threatens to provoke, is something she's never seen or perhaps witnessed only in the rarest of moments. And this woman before her who had been a girl once, why did she suddenly refuse to even look at a man she'd adored, clambered on as if he were a jungle gym, secluded herself with for hours on end in the small city full of grit and paper flowers and ruin and good well-meaning people like themselves?

The air in the kitchen is thick, stultifying. We all stand slightly frozen, wait, as if for an explosion. The old farmhouse odors assail: lemon oil, a smear of it still bright on the kitchen table. The pungency of an oversize rosemary plant drifts in from the other room. Four feet from me, my mother's huge dog half barks, growls.

I'd rescued him from a kill shelter in New York and brought him to the Island after my mother's old black Lab died. He'd been dumped at the shelter on Thanksgiving, full of ticks, his thick russet fur matted, fear rife in his dark liquid eyes. My mother named him Homer.

"It's me," I whisper to him, then bend down, wanting to be known. He's been out. His soft ruff is rank, cold. He sniffs my hands for a treat, licks at my palms with his large, mottled tongue, then grandly lumbers back to a spot between the small sink and the refrigerator. A photograph stuck on the white refrigerator door catches my eye. Uncle Roy—my mother and Aunt Karina's brother. A summer barbecue. He's scowling with tongs in his hand. He's the spitting image of his father; wide face, a bit of hair over his upper lip.

The photograph socks a knot in my stomach, a small shock, as if any second Senelis could tramp in, blustering, shaking off winter, loud like his son. I look out the kitchen door we just shut behind us. The door hangs a little sloppily on its hinges, grimy, paint-peeled, the works of the lock liable to be undone by a strong wind. All those comings and goings! I resist the urge to slip on my coat, grab my husband's elbow, beat it out of there, out of the past, out of the village huddle, away from the elderly gray women.

Aunt Agnes starts to cry. I move to embrace her.

"I never did think I would see you after all these years," she says, flat gray curls like a little cap around her face.

She's almost trembling. She has a certain way of speaking that I love, diction like a thumbprint. I've missed it. I've missed her. I hug her, shut my eyes, open them, responsible, suddenly, for her happiness.

My mother quickly points out a winter bouquet—a centerpiece on the large kitchen table—evergreens, bittersweet, something else—pink or white.

Clematis maybe. Or maybe a bowl of oranges stuck with cloves; the punctured skin of the citrus and spice, the ache of an old perfume.

The central purpose of my visit begins to get fuzzy. No one else in the room, except my husband, wants to find out what I want to find out about Senelis. (And what is that exactly? What am I doing, striding in from the dark as if I have rights to other peoples stories?) *Just be quiet*—the refrain of my early life.

But there were at least two slaughters in the town where my grandfather had supposedly, presumably, most assuredly been chief of security police; eight thousand dead in the first, four hundred dead months later. I don't have any particulars yet, only an intense need to know. During the killings, where was he? Who was he? Every time I ponder it, the same fantasy comes to me—right out of *Casablanca*. Oh, he was playing cards, in some curtained-off room, or the empty office at the end of a gray hall. He and his cronies smoking—one with a bit of tobacco stuck to his upper lip. The slap of two jacks on the table. As if no other sound existed in the world. No stink of cordite. No little jingle of shell casings. No cry.

"Gosh, it's already such-and-such o'clock," I announce, gesturing toward the scrim of dusk at the windows, the slight warp in the old glass panes somehow appropriate to the moment. The room unfreezes. Quickly Aunt Karina takes the lead. There is a plate of sausage and crackers. Cheese. Water put on for coffee. A bottle of wine my husband brought. We make a little parade into the living room.

The wide, pitted floorboards haven't been cleaned lately. This means my mother's eyes have gotten worse. All weekend I'll see cobwebs, little clouds of dust, small dead flies on a sill in the downstairs bathroom where once, in the last months of his life, my very ill father fell into the bathtub at night and, too weak to call or get up, lay there until morning.

"You might want to try it, sometime," he had quipped to me over the phone the next day. "Quite comfortable." His particular brand of stoicism.

"Darling, move over so your husband can sit by you," Aunt Karina commands, and then seems to catch herself.

The old familiarity.

We sit.

I ask Aunt Agnes, on my right, who touches a sore on her leg that won't heal, if she still bowls.

"I don't bowl no more, not since Roy died."

I look at the empty rocker where my Jewish grandmother used to hold forth in her old London silks and deep red lipstick. Gin and tonic in hand, she lambasted my father for voting for Bush, an ornate necklace heavy with semi-precious stones around her neck, that bit of a British accent in every word she spoke, even her Yiddish.

I pat Aunt Agnes's knee, and she jumps a little, as if she isn't used to being touched anymore. If Uncle Roy were alive and present, he would have nothing of this digging around the past. "Pop was Pop," he would say or fill the room with a version of Senelis's nationalism: the old, lost, pure Lithuania, the Communist devils, the partisan warriors who drove them out.

My husband sits on my left, Aunt Karina on a settee catty-corner from us. The sausage on the table has a little sheen, a little nitrate sweat. Aunt Karina reaches for a cracker. Her fingers—they're like Senelis's now. Working hands. The nail beds a little stumpy. The hands slightly ruined by sun and time and effort. Everyone sits poised. My aunt's willingness, her particular bravery to deliver over her memories, has stunned me into a kind of idiocy. She's gone quiet along with everyone else. My mother maneuvers into the old caned rocker, hands in her aproned lap. What is Aunt Karina waiting for? A log falls in the woodstove, softly, a ghost shape in the fire.

Oh. She's waiting for me.

CHAPTER 7

FATHERS AND SONS

This is a map of Poland and Prussia published in 1811, after the 1795 dissolution of the Grand Duchy of Lithuania, after which Lithuania became part of the Russian Empire. It was still part of the Russian Empire the year Kazimieras Puronas was born.

My grandfather's father, Kazimieras Puronas, was born in 1850 in Gindviliai, a tiny farming village in northeastern Lithuania where each year Marytė, a cousin of my mother and her sister, visits the graves of my great-grandmother Barbara (Senelis's mother) and Barbara's sister. My mother and my aunt will tell me Gindviliai doesn't really exist anymore, which only means that immigrant knowledge is different from the knowledge of those who stay behind.

A knowledgeable map collector cautioned me about the lack of accuracy in maps of Eastern Europe made before midcentury, but I fell in love with this one by the British cartographer William Darton. Darton learned printing from his father, and in 1804, opened his own shop in London, Repertory of Genius. I wonder what kind of nod that was to his father. Was it "I'm the best, Dad, thanks to you" or "You thought you were smart, Dad, but I'm a genius!"? Darton Jr. died seven years after my great-grandfather Kazimieras was born.

I'm not sure why I care about this, but I do. Maybe it's because I love the name of Darton's shop. (No self-esteem issues there.) Maybe it's because of the beauty of the map and its particularity. Or because a map implies, once the drawing and engraving and printing are complete, established knowledge, continuity, reliability.

Much of the story of my family and the story of Lithuania is a live grenade, a gun going off by accident in an attic, life up for grabs, countries changing hands so fast the local sign makers couldn't keep up—what was in Polish had to be in Russian, what was in Russian had to be in German, then Russian again, then miraculously, Lithuanian. And as for Yiddish, that wild mix of German and Hebrew and Aramaic, that language I always thought of as the "village talk" of my Jewish grandmother, there is silence, the barking of a dog, a diesel-fueled used VW van backfiring in a gravel lot, a man in an undershirt pulling a rusted screen down over the window of a house whose owner won't ever come around to make a claim.

The year 1811, Darton traces the Bug River, a watery dividing line at the start of World War II between German-occupied Poland and the Russian-occupied Baltics. But that war isn't history yet. Napoleon still has to invade Russia. Europe is going to enter the age of empires. America will turn on the British. Darton works on a drafting table in London near a window for the light. Perhaps he imagines his childhood river, thin bodies of fish, cold against his palm, stones and currents, but not those who will try to cross the Bug in flight from the Germans, nor the completed territory of his own life, the final boundary.

My Jewish great-grandparents—Wolf and Ҟlarah Treegoob, Israel and Esther Gabis—had by 1850 been forced from interior Russia to the Pale of Settlement. The Pale, or Черта́ осе́длости, was a series of borders that determined where Jews could and could not live. Established in 1791 in imperial Russia by Catherine the Great, the Pale was in part an attempt to prevent Jews from commercial enterprise in highly populated areas where they were or could become a competitive threat to non-Jewish trade and business. The creation of the Pale prohibited Jews, as well as Poles, from buying and working land beyond a small allotment. They had to lease instead of own, and Jews paid multiple taxes far beyond what was levied upon the non-Jews in their midst. It was these hardships, coupled with strategically implemented pogroms in the late 1800s, that compelled my Jewish great-grandparents to leave for England and then the United States.

The map is a chimera. A ghost. Once the Grand Duchy of Lithuania was a vast multiethnic geographic entity that spread out in all directions for more than three hundred thousand square miles. Within that reach, all my forebears lived.

The map reflects, among other things, Russia's partition. What the map doesn't show is one of partition's dictums: the outlawing of Latin and the Lithuanian and Polish languages. Space and speech. When both are claimed by someone else, what do you do? As a child, my own tendency was to become immovable and silent. But Kazimieras, like many other Lithuanians, sent his son, my Senelis, into local homes, where at considerable risk, teachers secretly taught children to speak and write the illegal language.

He wanted Senelis to become educated. He wanted him to have more than the two-room dirt-floored house with the few outbuildings for subsistence farming of wheat and potatoes and flax. Unlike his wife Barbara, Kazimieras was not completely illiterate, but he saw in his sons a vision of a life that outstripped his own in every way. They would have fluency. They would have more land. They might not even work the land.

My great-grandmother Barbara, from whom I inherited my middle name, bore twelve children with Kazimieras. Four died as infants, leaving two girls and six boys. But because there are several four- and five-year gaps between births, I suspect my great-grandmother was pregnant more than twelve times. My grandfather, my Senelis, Pranas Puronas, was her fourth child, born on the cusp in 1899, five years after his brother Jonas. After my grandfather was born, there would be another child who did not survive. The family's firstborn, Ona, my Krukchamama, would live with my grandfather for much of his adult life.

When Senelis was seventeen his father got sick. It was "gumbas," Aunt Karina told me. The literal meaning in Lithuanian is "nodule," but Aunt Karina said the word covered "a multitude of sins." Some kind of cancer brought him down, in from the glistening field, the precious cows, the herbs his wife dried in huge bunches upside down and tied to the rafters in what passed for a barn.

A pragmatist, as Senelis turned out to be, Kazimieras had a coffin made, as was the custom of his time, and kept it propped up against the wall in the room he slept in. It gave him comfort, I was told, to know that his wife wouldn't have to be bothered. So he lay there with the raw sweet/bitter scent of the new planks, and perhaps a swirl, as he got sicker, of the old images: the pagan horse slaughtered when the master dies, two moons in one sky, the faces of his parents, his children—Krukchamama, Senelis, the others I never knew.

Barbara was an herbalist and a midwife. She must have treated his pain, so add the stink of valerian to Scotch pine and the hard-packed dirt floor and, in the other room, the fire. A few centuries earlier, they would have had a grass snake in a clay bowl in a corner inside for luck.

Kazimieras died in 1916. In 1918, after the war, came independence from the Russians. Lithuanian farmers were allotted plots of private land. My great-grandmother, with the help of her sons, dismantled her house and moved it, as did all the inhabitants of the small village, to the new site of her allotment. The town's name never changed, but the sun threw a different angle of shadow on every threshold, and every child learned a different way home.

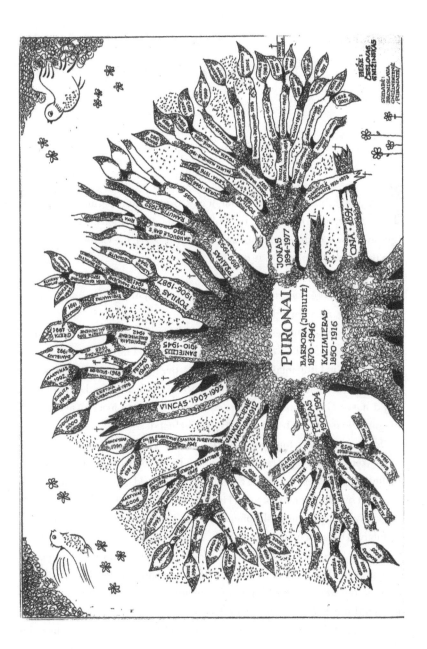

CHAPTER 8

AN EDUCATION

In regular school, Senelis was taught in Russian," Aunt Karina says.

My mother interrupts, her voice soft, a bit querulous. Didn't Senelis fight in the war of independence against the Russians, the German Balts, and then the Germans proper in 1918, 1919?

"No, no," Aunt Karina dismisses her.

A puzzled look comes over my mother's face, but Aunt Karina, who is right in everything, must be right in this, too.

Aunt Karina continues. "They were all so poor the boys had to stay home and work on the farm. In 1918, when the Germans [in Lithuania] went against the Russians [in Lithuania], the Germans took our grandparents' last horse and Senelis went begging to have the horse back to plow their fields. Otherwise, they'd starve. Grandmother Barbara's youngest child was just two at the time. Imagine. No food. The horse gone. His father just dead."

She's asked me to imagine, so I do.

A young man runs. The mud of the road leaks between his toes. Already the little blue flowers are in the first ridges of the fields. *Lina*. Linseed. Linen. The cloth his mother makes. Rain. His is a rainy country. He runs like an ape, legs awkward, sometimes slipping in the mud and then wiping his hands on his thighs. He can see them now.

Up ahead, a little convoy in the drizzle. The smell of petrol makes the sky seem grayer. The family horse, old, is a light bay with thin legs, a Þemaitukai, a classic Lithuanian breed known for dexterity in battle, durability on the farm, and the ability to survive on feed from starvation harvests. He looks weak, is anything but. He's already outlived his master, with whom he headed out to the fields as if the plow was a swallow on his back. Now useless, tied to the back of a stupid German truck with iron wheels that tear up the road. The poverty of that army. No rubber. A truck with a steering wheel you turn as if you are opening a manhole, bent close to it, hands almost bloody from it. The driver sucks on a Reemstma cigarette. Only a year older than my grandfather, but his face is screwed into itself like a worn-out clock.

"Prasome atiduoti arklys," the boy my grandfather was says. *Please, give back the horse.* "Bitte giv die Pferde. Bitte. Bitte."

What does my grandfather look like at that moment in the rain? Poor. Begging. He gets the horse back, but it's not really clear how. Does he steal it? Does he somehow appeal to something in the soldier riding the back wheel casing? A soldier who maybe has a younger brother back home, or is sick of war, ready to defy the orders: *We're short on horses (and everything else), resupply any way you can.* About to leave the fucking country anyway, so who cares?

My grandfather is like the light bay, untied now. A little whinny or snort. They head home where the barn is, where food is, fat a gold skim on a broth of last fall's potatoes, new dill like hope in the thawing ground. Senelis looks like a beggar, but he doesn't have a beggar's heart. He'll just do whatever has to be done, in the moment. He'll snivel. He'll offer the soldiers women, liquor, cigarettes. He'll get them a hundred packs. Just give the horse back.

I always knew this about him. He could take off his pride and put it back on again. My hero.

THERE'S A GREAT shortage of officers in the Lithuanian army. A call goes out for new recruits. Three hundred and thirty-six young Lithuanian men apply. Strapping farmers. Lithuanian exiles from Vilnius, now overrun by Poles, who have the audacity to call it Wilno. Lads who can't read. Boys whose fathers were killed by someone—a Russian, a Pole, a German, the crazy son of a neighbor who had fits and should have been drowned in the river at birth. Those who are accepted to the Military academy are all born between 1887 and 1899. Their studies last three months. Senelis is among them. Lucky boy. He's the first in his family to go to secondary school. How proud his father would have been.

Senelis in 1920, upon acceptance into the Military Academy.

The new military academy is in Kaunas, sixty miles, give or take, from Vilnius/Wilno or Vilne, as it is known by the roughly sixty-five thousand Jews who live there. In the unforeseeable future, when the Poles are gone, the Jews are gone, and Vilnius is corpselike, all bone, no life, the academy will relocate there and be called the General Jonas Žemaitis Military Academy of Lithuania.

Almost every public building or institution in Lithuania carries a complicated archaeology of the past, ancient alliances and enduring enmities. In the days of the Grand Duchy, Lithuania's military school was bankrolled by the king of Poland himself.

But the Grand Duchy is gone. It's 1919, and then 1920. A Soviet-Lithuanian peace pact has been signed: the Moscow Treaty gives the Lithuanians autonomy as long as the Russians can use Lithuanian territory (both undisputed and not) to act against the Poles. The embryonic Polish Legions run riot in Wilno; their light cavalry parade in front of the cathedral, their horses shit on the brick streets. They conduct *pogroms*, a word that can't fully evoke the slightly open mouth of a dead man in a photograph taken as trophy or evidence after one of the killing sprees of those days: his impossibly thick hair (how his mother must have loved it) up past his high forehead, lean body slack in the cloth stretcher set down on the cobblestone street that trips you up if your ankles are bad and your heels are high.

At night in Wilno, Polish young men my grandfather's age drink *siwucha*—vodka flavored with flowers—like water. Sing "Strzelecka gromada" (*Shooters' squad*), a line from the new song "My, Pierwsza Brygada," which proclaimed the start of the Polish Legions and sounds like war itself, year after year after year.

In Kaunas, when my grandfather enters the academy, two-thirds of the Jewish population of Lithuania lives and works and prays there. They call the city Kovno. The academy exists because the Moscow Treaty exists. Lithuanian Jews from Kovno and the far shtetls answered the call to arms and joined long before Senelis's first day at the academy. As volunteers or conscripts, they fought on behalf of the Russian Empire during the late 1800s and now into the new century. In the Sixth Infantry Regiment the Jew Nisonas Mackebuckis falls in battle. In the Fifth Infantry Regiment Jokubas Chaitas falls in battle. Lieutenant Colonel Moshe Dembovskis is a military doctor; he treats gangrene, syphilis, cupronickel-lead core bullets invading the mess of a leg, an arm, the soft sausage nest of a man's intestines. He uses chloroform, mercury. Dembovskis survives, for the time being, when peace briefly descends. Having served in the Russian army when Lithuania is still part of the Russian Empire, he returns home to an autonomous Lithuania for more war. Let's follow him back to the village of his birth, Vilkaviškis. The huge synagogue made of wood planking. To walk inside it must have been like walking into a forest.

I don't really understand any of it: Poles in Wilno, Germans in Memel. The Russians everywhere; I look at Darton's map again and again, at many maps, each from a different time, the borders so slippery, they seem meaningless. But they're not, especially to the people who live within one, outside of another. People like my Jewish great-grandparents, in London by now, fleeing like thousands of others—including non-Jewish Lithuanians—because of poverty or because someone is always coming to slaughter them within those borders.

By the time Senelis goes into the academy, he speaks Lithuanian, Russian, a bit of German, and Polish. Maybe even a little Yiddish. If you gave him a drink or two, my mother says, he'd swear he knew French.

For now, the little aside, the mini-biography of Lieutenant Mausa Dembovskis, seems simpler, easier to understand.

But I must close this small page of his life. I'm like Aunt Karina, who marks the spot in the book and pulls my covers up to my chin. (I'll push them down again.) "Laboniktas," she says with a kiss. *Good night.*

AT THE END of the three months, my grandfather has gone from beggar to officer. Because the military school is still so new, many of what will become long-standing protocols and rituals aren't in place. Unlike later graduates, Senelis is not called upon to kneel before the president of Lithuania and affirm, as the president touches a sword to each young man's shoulder, "You shall not draw the sword without a cause nor sheath it without honor."

My grandfather is seated in the middle. The photograph is undated.

IT'S ALMOST DINNERTIME. In the kitchen, skin crisps around the roasting chicken, the pot of drained potatoes steams—a dot of butter, a white spoon of sour cream whipped into the starchy cloud.

Aunt Karina is flagging but stalwart. She's a piling on the dock jutting into the sea of time. She asks for a bit of wine and coughs. The living room has gone cold. Time to throw another log into the stove. Did I do it? I don't remember. Who fetched the wine? My husband? I don't remember. No, it must have been my mother—my aunt's supplicant.

"Should we stop for now?" I say. She's sick, and I'm making her talk, talk and remember, talk unto death.

She presses her lips together and shakes her head. "No, let's go on," she says grimly.

This is costing her in ways I can't know.

Almost dinner, and Aunt Karina is plodding through the years long before the war I need to find out about. I sink into the couch. I'm afraid I'll cry. A small panic flutters in my throat. We'll never get there. She'll talk and talk, but my questions will never be answered. I try to rally.

Aunt Karina takes a small sip of wine, the glass too delicate for her hand. The shadows under her eyes are darker. Homer is beside me again. My aunt brushes a stray white wire of hair from her face. She's old. I won't speak with her again in this lifetime.

I bow my head so she won't see that my heart is broken. I listen.

"Your great-grandmother Barbara was younger than her husband," Aunt Karina says.

Oh god, she's gone all the way back to my namesake and to Senelis's father, Kazimieras.

"Long before they were married, when the horses were being hitched up for her baptism, a young man [Kazimieras] saw her up in the wagon and said, 'There goes my bride,' and sure enough, they were married. She was an illiterate midwife."

But you've told me this already, haven't you?

"She knew a great deal because women would come for help to her. She would wash, put on clean clothes, go and stay through the birth and after. She learned by watching a doctor who one day told her she knew enough to do it all on her own. She was also very knowledgeable of herbs."

Here, I stop listening. I'm thinking of my mother, who tends the long herb sheds and herb garden of a large nursery and landscaping business up the road. It's summer. She still has most of her sight. (Macular degeneration will slowly rob her of it.) The show garden she's made is round, like a planet. I'm impatient. Awed. She points at the waist-high chamomile, the purple sage, the flowering mint, the soft, invincible thyme, the high lavender, not stunted and lost in dry grass as mine is. It's her gift. She's in the middle of it all. A world that, for a moment, is only about life.

But life is full of reversals.

Suddenly, Aunt Karina is talking about Senelis.

"He met your Babita in Kaunas—his cousin introduced them. Some time later he was on leave from military duty, in Kaunas again, and decided to stop and visit her. She said, 'Let's get married.' Just like that. She was very unhappy. Actually, she was engaged to someone else who was a policeman away at some convention for work he wouldn't take her to. She wanted to get back at him. She and your grandfather even had to get a special license to get married so fast. She never loved him. When she saw him through the window or walking down the road she used to say, 'Here comes my ass.' "

My Babita: her name was Ona—Anna in the Anglicized version—Puroniene. (In Lithuania, women's last names have a feminine ending, *iene*; the phonetic pronunciation is ēně.) Ona, not exactly the dutiful wife/grandmother who sucks on caramels and clucks her tongue at curse words and massages the cold flat feet of her husband with goose fat, who crouches before him, the bursitis in her knees like little ponds that spread under the weight of her thighs and wide hips and heavy breasts. My grandmother, my Babita, was thin as a match.

"She'd even been engaged before, to a doctor, older, very smitten with her. But one day she looked at him and said, 'What am I doing with this old man?' and that was the end of it."

"Tell me about her family," I say.

Her story, in brief, is the story of the Grand Duchy of Lithuania, of Polish and Lithuanian nobles, all who speak Polish across the elaborate tables as the candles throw their tapered shadows and teeth grind and shred the meat of fallen animals, the Christmas goose, the "smoked meats all cured with juniper smoke," in the words of the poet Adam Mickiewicz in his famous elegy to Lithuania, *Pan Tadeusz; or, The Last Foray into Lithuania*, written in the early 1830s. A poet who—like the city Wilno/Vilnius—both Poles and Lithuanians claim as their own. Nevermind that much of the Lithuania he describes in his poetry is now Belarus.

"Babita's father was the caretaker of a huge estate, responsible for all the forests. When her father married, the [Polish] nobles he worked for gave him a whole big farm, so they were very prosperous." Aunt Karina takes another sip of wine. "Babita said they had six teams of plow horses plus carriage and riding horses and someone who lived on the premises just to take care of the poultry! Her father had a large library with books in many different languages. Farming equipment from England. Parquet floors!"

Aunt Karina looks at me for a long beat to make sure I have taken in this very important detail about the floors. In my prewar apartment in New York, strips of thick oak lie atop the subfloor of the living room. Parquet. I'm too spoiled to really grasp the splendor of it.

Parquet, from the French, not the dirt floors of the shack Senelis grew up in. Parquet—of Versailles, the winter palace of St. Petersburg. My grandmother learned to read: Polish, Russian, Lithuanian. She walked on bare feet on those bright floors. She followed the poultry manager on his feathery clucking rounds. The hen smell and feed dust conjoining in the light of a changing century.

"After Lithuanian independence"—in 1920—"the large estates were all to be divided," said Aunt Karina.

No more large landowners lording over peasants. For a country to last, all its people had to have a share in something.

"Your grandmother's father was so damn mad, he said, 'Take it all.' He sold all of his land and built a house in town."

Gone the McCormick land tractor, the pulsation milking machine, the sheen of inlaid wood the length of the library. Who were these people? Selling, marrying—in an instant. Petty. Desperate. Well-off. Poor. I love you. I hate you. You want my land, take it. You want my hand, it's yours.

Aunt Karina lets out a long sigh, so loud that Homer looks over, his huge lion's face impassive but inquiring just the same.

"We need to stop," I say.

"Yes." She's too tired to look at me.

Aunt Agnes, in her acrylic sweater and Kansas polyester pants, announces at the doorway to the kitchen, "We eat now."

We stand. My husband moves toward the food, but Aunt Karina catches me by the elbow. "I want you to know something," she whispers, raspy.

Again, the bird dog alert.

"Your Aunt Agnes doesn't know anything. Don't listen to anything she tells you about the past."

"Okay," I whisper back, feeling instant loyalty to Aunt Agnes.

Aunt Karina looks satisfied. Apart for thirty years, and now we're suddenly conspirators. We share a secret about Aunt Agnes that lies on top of an even bigger secret, one neither of us will name. I nod to her solemnly to seal my oath of understanding, my allegiance to Aunt Karina's superior knowledge, and because she is the elder and I am the younger, she goes before me to the table.

THERE'S NO MORE talk of family history at dinner. We all eat quickly. Sucking the meat from the bones. Taking seconds. Eating the spears of broccoli whole, like forcing little swords into our mouths. Salt. Something sweet—a pear crisp. The scoop of ice cream on top demolished instantly by the sugary heat.

I thought this would all happen so quickly, thought my husband and I would be at the house for one afternoon, and if there was anything to be learned about my grandfather's collaboration we'd learn it lickety-split—or I'd know right away that this was a futile journey. "Of course," my husband and I say, we'll be back in the morning for Aunt Karina's pancakes and more talk. The aunts retire to the living room. We tackle the dishes. Aunt Agnes returns stealthily, stands very close to me, like a horse sometimes does when you've got a bucket of feed or a carrot in a pocket.

She whispers, "Don't listen to your Aunt Karina. She don't know nothin'. It's all made up stuff."

"Really?" I try to look shocked and disapproving of Aunt Karina.

"She tells a big bunch of lies, but she was so young she don't remember," says Aunt Agnes.

"Thank you so much for telling me this." I kiss Aunt Agnes on the cheek. Among my mother and Aunt Karina, she's the underdog. I love her.

"You remember what I tell you," she says.

I promise I will, even though I believe that Aunt Karina, up to this point anyway and insofar as she is able, is conveying to me the bits and pieces of family lore that were given to her firsthand by her own grandmother and mother and father. Up to this point. Insofar as she is able.

ON THE DARK road back to the hotel in Vineyard Haven my husband and I both start talking at once about Aunt Karina. Not the particulars of the stories. Not the brooch on her sweater or the cough that fills her chest, but her. There's a pressure zone around her. It's the zone of a woman who is fighting to hold on to her own story. The one she's lived by in which a man loves her and praises her work in the church and talks about every little thing with her through all the days of their years together, and is innocent of any wild, indecent claim. She's holding a pack of ten wild dogs on ten thin leashes. She's looking into my face and forcing herself not to consider my clarity, my steadiness, my lack of a wigged-out Oprah affect, which, if I had it, would cause accusations to fly from my mouth the way they do sometimes from the mouths of the hurt and homeless in the city. On the subway once, a woman (impossible to tell her age) bundled in stinking dirty rags stood up and screeched at me, "You whore, you dirty whore." I instantly believe I'm guilty of anything. I looked down at the scuffed subway floor, got out as soon as we reached the next stop.

The hotel room is small and the heater noisy: floor-to-ceiling windows look out onto the very still Main Street. We come in from the cold and fall into bed, rummaging for extra covers in the closet first. Not even bothering to wash or brush our teeth. Soon my husband sleeps. The bed has one of those mattress pads that seem to be made of plastic. Every time I shift and turn, it crimps and crackles. I give up. Stand. Open the double doors to winter.

I've known the street before me all my life. I had my first waitressing job at thirteen at a café in an earlier incarnation of this same hotel. At the end of the summer I called the Labor Department on the management because they were shorting us ten cents for every dollar we made. And I was an under-age worker to boot. The grizzled, sweaty Portuguese fry cook who'd been my friend cursed me for ratting out the bosses. I took it on the chin, as they say, even though I was surprised he didn't believe in justice and ten cents for all.

My arms are freezing. That hotel burned down, this one built right in its place, a replica, a fake. But the little street is as it has always been, and suddenly—I smell it before I see it—snow. Sparse, the flakes individuated. I try to follow different ones: dizzying. A cold bit of memory. Hammond: I'm still a child. It's Christmas, and we're staying with Aunt Karina and Uncle Alan. But he and I are alone on the street outside their apartment building, looking up at a thicker, faster snowfall quickly covering the base of the lampposts, sidewalks, the slick roofs of large gas guzzling cars, our hats, the long bridge of my uncle's nose. Maybe a cab goes by. Maybe Susie the cat sits fat and regal high in the yellow-lit window above us. Of those things I can't be sure.

The memory is this; he catches a flake and shows it to me on a dark sleeve or in a gloved hand and says, "Look, each one is different." Because I am small, he seems as tall as a lamppost. I suck in the cold air at the wonder of it, the tops of our shoes already white. The intricate design. The infinite daunting splendor.

CHAPTER 9

AUNT KARINA'S PANCAKES

Brilliant sun. Now the kitchen seems open, the wood floors gleam. The cloister of shadows is gone. I hang our coats on the hooks in the pantry—there's my father's jacket my mother sometimes wears when she brings wood in. I press my face to the waterproof fabric. For a second, I have him—then he's gone.

There's a trick to the batter only Aunt Karina knows; something to do with egg whites and cottage cheese and lots and lots of butter. We hardly eat butter at home. I'm drunk with it now. This morning Aunt Karina seems revived and Aunt Agnes tired. The wound on her leg. A child she gave away in Germany at the end of the war—a brief encounter with an American GI—she can't find a trace of her boy. He's a man now, in the States, but where? After breakfast I find her crying on the couch in the living room. Even in her the war continues.

My husband and I eat and eat. The warm syrup pours like water. The coffee gives a jolt. I never want to talk about Senelis again, but can't stop myself. After the sticky plates are cleared, the little digital tape recorder is brought out again. I'm terrified I'll erase what I recorded the afternoon before, confuse which little arrow means things disappear and which button will hold hostage the details of these women's lives.

Aunt Karina begins again:

"Your grandfather was still in the army, so they lived where he was stationed. All three kids born in different places—Kaunas, Trakai, Žeimelis. For a while we lived on an island outside Vilnius, and had a horse, a high-strung, skittish Arabian. Once your Babita was driving the cart across the narrow strip of land to the island and someone had dropped a bag in the road and that darn horse stopped and wouldn't go and backed up right into the lake."

Aunt Karina tries to remember the horse's name—Amazon. She'll remember the name differently later, but I'll forget her correction and the recorder won't be on. So it's Amazon, defiled by my forgetting, Arabian, white, long-necked, the withers a defined ridge—one of the few creatures on earth to best my Babita, my thin one, my shrew.

Aunt Karina goes on, but it's my Jewish grandmother the horse makes me think of. London, 1910. Her family has fled there from Ukraine. My Rachel, my Nana, nine, ten years old, loves to watch the farriers at work. She sidles in, with her own stubborn beauty, among tall men and stalls and manure rakes and listens to the hammering. The gorgeous, frightening creatures whose bodies give off steam, whose lips, huge, take in and gum the straw; the chewing, the filing, the shoes strung on the rack—how she loved it all, she told me. She stood there for hours, men pausing to take her in, as here they look out from their work, out of their time, at me.

Blacksmiths and Farriers, London, 1910

"It's late," my mother says, high-pitched, a cup rattling a little in the saucer she holds in her hand. Aunt Karina has just started talking, but breakfast took over the morning.

I attend the moment. My husband and I agree to take a different boat, a later train home. The recorder is recording. It even records my secret memory of my grandmother Rachel.

SENELIS'S FAMILY SETTLES finally in Žeimelis, a town on the Latvian border. Senelis is chief of border police. He rides a high horse in his polished boots. He patrols.

My mother (the oldest) and Karina (the youngest) and their brother Ramutas (Roy) are kids and do what kids do. They play "Indian," smoke peace pipes with tobacco made from weeds, only Karina isn't allowed; she's too young. The older kids won't let her do so many things. Roy catches fish, my mother cooks them outside on a Primus stove, and they run away from Karina with the fish and gobble them down in the outhouse while Karina cries and cries. They're scientists—try to kill burdock by pouring vinegar on it. They bury apples in the fall to see if they'll last through the winter. They dig them up when they are eight months older—the children and apples—the fruit not quite rotten, but soft, riddled with the slow burrowing of new worms.

Babita complains unendingly about Senelis. Where are her parquet floors now? Their house is small, owned by a Jewish family that lives across the street in a two-story building, a small notions store below. They are older people, the woman a seamstress. In Babita's house, there is a backyard with chickens, and in the kitchen a huge brick stove. One night Senelis comes home drunk and threatens to shoot himself because she's unfaithful.

(My mother related this incident to me during her earlier visit to New York City. When I bring it up again now, I watch my mother's face when Aunt Karina says she doesn't remember their drunk father, the gun, the threat. I watch my mother waver, silently will her not to surrender her memory to her younger sister's. She doesn't.)

Babita isn't unfaithful, but she still corresponds with the aged doctor who would take her and the children in a heartbeat, take her away from Žeimelis, away from the blustering man with a gun who falls in bed beside her like a sack of feed and doesn't remember what he said the next morning. She can't do it. One sister is divorced. Another went into the convent, and then left it. Too much shame for the family to bear.

At least Senelis's work keeps him away. She's grateful for that. When he comes back, it's with armloads of stupid things. Blue velvety slippers for Karina. A sleigh. Sausage made from venison or boar. It drives Babita crazy. To appease her, Senelis crosses the border and buys potatoes from a Latvian farmer, bushels of potatoes, all the potatoes in the world. And it's not enough.

Babita takes a librarian course in Kaunas and then in Žeimelis works in the town library. She's crazy for order. She doesn't like girls very much, even her own. But her house is neat and her food is good. Whatever goes on between her and Senelis, they make four children together.

Four?

I stop the recorder.

All my life, my mother has told me the war story of her life, her face growing red and swollen, the tears plopping down while I ate my graham crackers and drank my milk or came home late and stoned, my eyes bloodshot as if I too had been crying. She told me when I was ten and nineteen and thirty, told me as I walked out the door, told me even when I was gone.

But not once did she mention the lost one.

The proper village burial.

Senelis comes home, takes leave from his job as chief of the border patrol between Lithuania and Latvia.

SENELIS, IN UNIFORM, holds Aunt Karina. My mother and Uncle Roy are in front of him. Babita is in the larger dark hat, Krukchamama to her right in the smaller dark hat. The photograph is undated, but my mother looks like she is six years old, or a small seven, which would make the funeral year 1936 or 1937.

It's Aunt Karina who has brought the photograph. The little death that calls, like all deaths, for silence.

CHAPTER 10

WAR

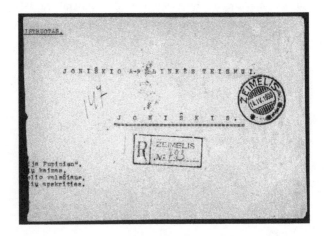

On the eve, what was Žeimelis like?

There was a market square the shape of an envelope, with a lemonade factory, a library (where Babita scowled at those who entered with torn pages, overdue books, lame excuses), an agricultural school, ten Jewish shops, a Jewish bank, a separate Jewish library, and a synagogue. Žeimelis: the root *Zeim*, from *ziema*, "winter," where a Livonian knight Otto Grothus lived in the fairy tale of long ago. In 1937 there were nine Jewish tailors, three Jewish butchers, two bakers, one tinsmith.

"There was a Jewish boy," my mother begins, as she leaves the dishes stacked in the small kitchen sink to return to the table. She sits, speaks slowly, as if sleep is overcoming her. "I played with him. I even went to his house." She stops, corrects herself. "No, I never went to his house."

Aunt Karina garners my attention. The look on her face is the look she wore when she told me about the parquet floors.

"Once," she begins, "when I was very small, your grandfather and I were walking through town and a rabbi passed us. I was so frightened of him—his long beard. His hat, his flowing black robes. Your grandfather said, 'Don't be frightened. This is a very important man. He's like our priest.'" She pauses, studies my face, gauges the impact.

I don't know what she wants me to take from this.

The rabbi—was he the famous Rabbi Kook? Rabbi Yakov Dov? No, they were all gone by then, to Palestine, away from the northern village, the cold coming, the Russian Cossacks with their whips.

One day in 1939 Aunt Karina was at the library with Babita. How high the library windows seemed back then! You could see the whole square. And there, suddenly, men were racing and ransacking the marketplace. Aunt Karina wanted to go out and buy Babita cigarettes and with the change purchase a huge ginger muffin. But the whips and the men. God, they were riding cows (she'd never seen pinto horses before)! Swords and smashing and crashing. The Russians had come snorting and stamping and smelling like wolves. No more trips to the market. My grandfather was a member of the Šauliai, the Lithuanian Rifleman's Union, to which Babita also belonged. Ultranationalistic, charged with defending a pure Lithuania, the Šauliai were a threat to the Russians. Senelis was, in fact, a Šaulių leader of a platoon of anti-Russian partisans, and was gone, hiding in the woods, a wanted man. (*Šaulių* refers to the Lithuanian Rifleman's Union, *šaulys* to an individual member.)

But just before all this happened, one of the last beauties of childhood: a trip to Gindviliai to visit Grandmother Barbara, who was what Babita should have been: warm, always a bit of something sweet in her pocket—dried blue-berries, the like. Senelis is home from the border! Babita stays behind. She has her job at the library. She has the chickens to feed. So Senelis drives the cart full of his children, stops at a certain place—green inner world of a forest, the clayish soil, pine litter. Out of the cart they go to hunt mushrooms, and it's Karina who discovers the largest, the most stupendous mushroom of all. Senelis throws up his hands. *Ah—it's the best!* Praise she'll remember her whole life. She adores him for it. The youngest. The left-out one.

In Gindviliai their Grandmother Barbara sings to them and cooks for them and brings them to her small garden and pets them and prays over them and when it is time to leave says, "Tell your mother I still have one tooth left in my mouth." Then they are gone.

TIME HAS CAUGHT up with us. There is a boat to catch. A train. Quickly, my mother and Aunt Karina describe the Russians crashing in first, nationalizing all the little businesses, killing, making promises, promoting this one and that one to fake party jobs, then the Germans chasing out the Russians, bombing and burning. Aunt Karina recalls a little ditty in Lithuanian from wartime whose lyrics roughly translate into "Red shirt/brown shirt," the first as evil as the next. I decide to press her.

"What exactly did Senelis do for the Germans?" I ask, as if I don't expect any particular answer. As if I'm not waiting like Homer for a dry bit of bread that will satisfy, even in the most minute way, my terrible need to know.

Aunt Karina is offhand. "Oh, something. I don't know exactly. Something with administration and so on, army security."

Then she changes the subject.

Our coats are on. The little tape recorder tucked away. Kisses all around. Chicken sandwiches offered and refused. (The train is hot; mayonnaise spoils.) We're stuffed anyway. The pancakes! I'll remember them, like Aunt Karina's mushrooms, for the rest of my life.

My mother is pleased we've come. "I'm proud of you," she whispers to me.

Aunt Agnes is radiant. Her gray halo shines.

Aunt Karina, before she holds me to her and tells me she loves me, her voice breaking a little, stands in the doorway between the kitchen and the heat of the great ceramic stove in the other room.

"So, the Jews," she says.

I stop. Put down my bag. Can't breathe.

"It's true your grandfather didn't like them."

I say, in as noncommittal a tone as I'm able, as if I'm not a hungry dog, as if I don't really care, "Did he think of them all as Communists?" (As so many Lithuanians did during the prewar Russian occupation, and after.)

Aunt Karina shakes her head.

"No, he just didn't like them. But he had Jewish friends, so go figure." She shrugs a little, pauses to consider, then continues, matter-of-fact. "Everyone needs a scapegoat. The Jews were his."

CHAPTER II

THIS KIND OF WORLD

J ust off the train, I drop my bag at my hotel and walk in the naked morning light the twenty minutes or so to the library and archives of the U.S. Holocaust Memorial Museum in Washington. These days every library, even this one, makes me think of Babita in her library in Žeimelis. Cigarette between her thumb and index finger, her mouth a straight line, she calculates the odds of getting the children out, away. In Lithuania now there are the Soviets; in Poland, the Germans, after a swift, devastating assault—the main arteries outside of Warsaw glutted with the wounded, the overnight refugees, cows, broken soldiers, a dowry chest in a ditch, a feather bed on the side of the road.

Over and over I've magnified and scrutinized this photograph taken when Łódź, Poland, was overcome in the fall of '39. The three different faces of a particular kind of shock; a hand to the forehead, the almost sheepish smile of the man on the right—perhaps reflexive, even in the moment; a picture is being taken, after all, but what face to show to the enemy? The woman on the left, a quick glance front and behind. Make a decision. Go to the store and buy . . . a phone call before the lines are cut. Shrewd, maybe hopeful. *We'll survive, we'll suffer but survive*—Jewish, a third of the population of the central manufacturing hub of Poland.

I am projecting, of course; three faces, the obliterating advance of three German flanks, among them one soldier and his scrapbook of the adventure of war from which this photograph comes. Łódź, where the pianist Arthur Rubinstein was born in the late 1800s. In the disarray of his study, my father and I used to listen to the Chopin Nocturnes. No. 2 in E-flat Major, the needle in the groove of the old prized recording; note by note, a world of such precision and delicacy and restrained power you know it has to end when Rubinstein's hands come to rest at his sides. And it does end in Łódź. If you were a Jew in 1939, Lithuania, compared to Poland, was briefly a haven—if you could get across the border.

I stop for a minute across the street from the Willard Hotel, just to orient myself. A breeze takes up the hotel's flags and awning, blows them back. I fish in my bag for the glossy map from my own hotel—I've been here more than once, but my sense of direction is terrible—find instead of the map a ticket stub, an envelope, those illegible taxi receipts, like chewing gum wrappers. I think suddenly of the feel of the envelopes in a large packet in my study, the old hard creases in those tragic packets of letters in Yiddish from my mother-in-law's relatives in Nowogrod, Poland, written around the time the German soldier snapped his picture in Łódź.

In one of the letters: "Life like a dream—bad or good. I'm sure you know what's going on here . . . does it pay to live in this kind of world?"

In other letters, gratitude for packages sent, for money, but what's desperately needed is a way to escape. Who do you pay off now that visas are no longer being issued? Who might hide you or your children?

What last-ditch presence of mind would guide you, as it did one of my Jewish boarding school teachers, who as a boy on the run when the Germans completed their takeover of Czechoslovakia in 1939 found the right train track, the freight car under the belly of which he'd ride, his torn hands holding tight to the iron underpinning, gravel pelleting his back. Those fists never unclenched, even when he came to America. Even when he led a group of young people through the Berkshire woods and pointed out the white on the wings of a mockingbird that makes up its song from the songs of other birds, from barking dogs, even from your own whistle in the clear air, a stream nearby.

My paternal Jewish great-grandparents, Israel and Esther Gabis, lived in what is now Belarus, just across the border from Švenčionys. They've gone to America by 1904. Wolf Treegoob, after taking his family to London, became a master horologist—a fixer of watches and clocks on Third Street in Philadelphia, "a genius" with anything mechanical. There he is, behind a cubby with a window, among small glass disks, hour wheels, and minute wheels. He fixes time with his dexterous hands, fastidious, the hairspring, the balance arbor perfect when he returns the piece to its owner.

I give up on the map, look at my watch, a gift from my husband. I blot Senelis out of my head.

Compared to New York, central D.C. always feels compact to me, organized, though in truth it's a city that sprawls without an even grid to follow. At this early hour, even as I pass the gargantuan Willard Hotel, pedestrians are scarce. I think about the standing order the D.C. metro cops must have: keep the riffraff away from the tourists. The poor congregate in the little triangles of parks and benches between angled streets.

On Fourteenth Street, the wide sidewalk is immaculate. I've missed the cherry blossoms, but the air still smells of them—only fainter, like the scent of roses in a room when the vase has just been whisked away. The warm spring sky has a slightly opal cast. The grass spreading out from the Washington Monument is a green fluorescent mirror back to the sun. I feel dizzy. Tired. More and more often, I'm tired. I don't know what I'll find at the Holocaust Museum, why I'm going there. Every time I try to articulate a formed intention about what I'm doing, it slips away. I'm left with just questions:

Did he hurt anybody?

The translator . . . Her name?

Did he carry a weapon?

Chief of what?

Saugumas?

Of course I've looked things up, am reading too many books at once. "Sowgoomas," Michael MacQueen will pronounce it when I meet with him at ICE. To really know the word you have to know the country, and I don't.

On the wall just inside the museum, there's a large photo commemorating an African American security guard gunned down by a neo-Nazi. Stephen Tyrone Jones smiling in his uniform. Forty years old. A son, two stepsons. Von Brunn, his killer, in the notebook he kept, wrote, "Obama does what his Jew owners tell him to do."

Two years earlier, I had visited the museum for the first time. Like everyone, I was given an ID card of a Holocaust victim; mine was a young Jewish girl from Lithuania with serious eyes. I look at the face of Stephen Jones and think of her. Turn away.

I'm not a researcher. I'm not a historian. My grandfather did something—I don't know what. Upstairs, the entrance to the archives and library has those sensors that go off if someone tries to head out with archival material. I expect it to sound an alarm as I pass through.

When I pick up my first of two-hundred-something microfiche reels at the reference desk and settle in at my cubby with the viewer and computer to scan what I might find, the first thing I do is take the reel out of the small white box and drop it, reflexively, into my bag. As if I'm a thief, a criminal. As a child I flagrantly disobeyed library rules. All my books were late, months late, years late. I had been told that my lost Babita had been a librarian and was locked up or dead. I doubt this influenced me, but you never know how deep the family story turns inside you. Sometimes I stowed books under my jacket, avoiding the checkout process altogether. I was an outlaw reader. And in the end, my parents would have to pay up.

I immediately pluck the white box back out, look around. The slightly harried reference librarian with her loose dress and quick smile is as congenial in person as she was via e-mail and has no interest in my sudden reflexive transgression. She doesn't care that my grandfather worked for the SS. I'm searching. She's helping me.

It's only later that someone will politely suggest that I shouldn't bring my bag into the microfiche area but leave it in a locker in the hallway. Meanwhile I've done all the wrong things. I have a chocolate chip cookie with me. My cell phone. Both not allowed.

I break the rules, as if I were a girl again. Then I begin.

I start out with the records of the Gebietskommissar Wilna-land, accession number 1999.A.0107, five microfiche rolls from the captured German administration records from the time of their occupation in the Vilnius district of Lithuania. Only five rolls to start with because I've limited my search geographically. Senelis worked in Wilna-land, north of Vilnius itself. My mother speaks German, used to teach it. (Of course, she would never utter a word of it in the presence of my nana, my Jewish grandmother.) I don't really know it, but it's a knowable language. If you look at it long enough. If you stare at document after document, if you grew up in several households and heard Lithuanian, German, Yiddish, a bit of Russian, Polish down the block in Oak Bluffs in the summer. And then there are those loan words from the French and the Latin that make German familiar. Take *terror*, for example: *terror* in Latin ("great fear"), *der Terror* in German, *terror* in English.

Juedische. A name: Jakob Zimon. "Bei 50." Age fifty. My plan was to look for letterheads that mentioned Švenčionys, where my grandfather worked. My plan was to focus only on correspondence, edicts, orders that concerned Švenčionys and Wilna-land dated from 1941 to 1943. I don't.

Jakob Zimon. "Juedische Kommunistas in Litauen." This is a list. They're after him. "Erotisch abnorm"—the description continues . . . an insinuation perhaps that he's not only a Communist but homosexual as well. The Communists/Jews were the first victims of the roving baltaraiščiai—the Lithuanian "partisans" who wore a white (*balta*) strap or band tied around one forearm. The smallest gesture toward a uniform, that white marker—in the open, a young man among other baltaraiščiai brethren must have felt as if he'd kicked open a door of his life.

In a few weeks' time, the Germans trample in and make a false offer of autonomy to the Lithuanian government, then quickly install their own superstructure over a command chain primarily of Lithuanians, including the white bands whose violent zeal makes them difficult to control, makes them useful.

Zimon is in Kaunas/Kovno, where Elena Buividaite-Kutorgene, a Lithuanian physician who refuses to follow the edict that forbids doctors from treating Jewish patients, is keeping her diary. "Perhaps world society does not know what is happening here," she writes. Jews forced to gather excrement with their hands. Everywhere the snatchers, the catchers, the kidnappers. (Someone is coming. Get off the street. Leave your house. Forget the dinner on your table, the cat, the baby's toys.) Lithuanians with guns. Looting. Raping. Going after some of their own as well as the Jewish population. Wild murder before the killing becomes more organized. Kutorgene will bribe a policeman and throw food over the ghetto walls. Read Tolstoy at night, an Asian travelogue, Turgenev, for escape, for "oblivion."

Jakob lives at Maironio str. 18. I want to tell him to get out of there. Run. Flee on your own or with the departing Soviets who according to this list you so loyally served with distinction. In other words, promoted, uppity, parading around, upsetting the old order of things. Maybe he was a true believer. Maybe everything written about him is a lie.

And then there is another: Leib Schaus, twenty-six years old, blond, tall, wrote newspaper articles that agitated against Germany. Good information has it that he took off from Lithuania several days before the Germans trooped in. Wife in Minsk. I stare at the words on the list, on the pages of the five rolls of microfiche. For hours I'll stare.

I turn the dial. Glass and light. All the records stored during World War II and immediately after on microfiche are perishable because of the film's acetate base. Of course, by now, thanks to places like the Holocaust Museum and other archive treasuries, many of these records have been transferred to film without this flaw, or digitized. But not as many as you'd think, living here in the United States, sitting, for the moment, at three in the afternoon, in a chair with arms that make it impossible to get close enough to the bright screen, so I scowl and lean in, cookie crumbs falling from my shirt, second after second disintegrating before me.

On the screen appears the first major order in German and Lithuanian signed off on by Gebietskommissar de Wilna-Land Hingst. I can't work the scanner right: big dark letters, tacked up everywhere in the cities and then the towns. I end up copying only a slice of the Lithuanian text that sits next to

the German, a list of orders on official paper that began to appear on public noticeboards, on telephone poles, in mail slots, on the outer doors of the libraries or police stations, at street entrances on August 2, 1941.

Looking at my scan later, I'll think of the paradox of nationalism—how it slices away, eviscerates the richness of identity, of place, including Švenčionys, where my grandfather would soon be working. I'll think of the yellow star (the size and placement would change and change again), the rule about walking in the gutter instead of on the sidewalk, the rule that forbade all Jews to enter parks and squares. There would be no strolls along the gravel walkways between beds of summer flowers outside the large stone imperium, once the mansion of a duke but now housing the offices of the SS, with the delicate crocus just outside, while across the street spread purple rock cress with leaves like velvet sandpaper, yellow-gold rue—the herb of repentance, the Lithuanian national flower. The movement of time in the passage of the noon sun expanding there like a door pushed open after the short days and still, cold nights of a late spring.

"Yes, I do remember the yellow stars and that they had to walk in the street," my mother had said at the February gathering with my aunts on the island. Fragments of her past had started to come loose, a glacier breaking up, but just a little, and never for very long. She spoke soberly but without emotion, as if carefully recalling a detail about a medical procedure that happened to someone else or remembering a long-ago visitor, whose face, the purpose of the visit, was lost to her. Because at the time we spoke, the only country I'd visited outside of the States was France, I imagined people walking off the sidewalks in a place like a medieval village in the Languedoc. The little streets all steep and mazelike. Summer disappearing into stone. Wisteria dripping down, that seasonal oblivious beauty.

Aunt Agnes had barged into the conversation, uncharacteristically specific, intense. She's German, was a child there during the war.

"I remember I was in dis store and an old man was in line in front of me to pay and someone—I don't know who, maybe it was an officer or just someone ordinary—said to me, 'You get in front of the line, all Jews at the end of the line.' And I felt so darn bad. I was so embarrassed. I'd always been taught to respect my elders and dat stuff. I always remember dat."

I FOCUS AGAIN on the hypnotic typeface, out of horror and habit. My father collected old manual typewriters. I turn my chair away from the screen because it's easier, just now, to think of him, remember our visits to the "genius" type-writer man on Circuit Avenue in Oak Bluffs, up a flight of stairs to a room full of little jars and cubbies with typewriter parts. Oil. Grimy rags. I remember the typewriter man as slight, tired, with gray stubble on his face. My father wanted to know everything; platens and key strikes. How did you learn your trade? Where were you born? Was there ever one you couldn't fix? What did your father do? The man flattered at first, then *God, get this customer out of here.*

Periodically, my father would hand off an old typewriter to me. Underwoods were his favorite. We would talk about the action of the keys (the way his sister would talk about a piano) and about typefaces, so it's something I notice. Even now, before a whole vocabulary of erasure.

The type before me looks like Fraktur, rejected by the Reich as "Jew letters." *All type would be Latin!* Martin Borman, one of Hitler's devoted, decreed in January 1941. Latin from now on, in every typewriter key over all the many German-ruled lands. But how impossible to accomplish this—there were war shortages, after all. Slave labor was needed for munitions production, not type-writer keys. The German officers in Litauen (Lithuania) already had their type-writers, thank you very much. Wanderer-Werke Continental Silentas, possibly, or Gromas, thought to be Hitler's favorite. A Groma from his bunker said to be his is on display, in of all places, Bessemer's Hall of History Museum in Alabama.

In a civil rights unit I taught years ago, we read, in letter form, the reminis-cences of a former slaveowner, Mr. O. J. McCann. They unfolded in a wobbly, tentative script. When I looked at the cursive trying so hard to stay in the margins, the misspellings (*skilet/skillet*), I felt an odd unwarranted tenderness that had nothing to do with the text but with the effort—"it was very seldom the [slave] huts had a window in them"—an effort Senelis made, in the holiday cards and the birthday cards, chosen for their sparkle and prettiness, the few words he wrote in a script so awkward and careful it made English seem like a kind of calligraphic penance, attempted only because he loved me.

The heavy black letters of the German documents make it hard to breathe. I think of my father's maternal grandfather and grandmother again.

Wolf Treegoob, Ḳlarah Treegoob

Though my father was the first academic in the family—a Ph.D., imagine!—I never heard him speak about Plato or Aristotle with the same reverence with which he extolled the gifts of the typewriter man or the college kid at the bike repair shop or the mechanic who repaired the engine of his ancient, rusted-out blue Volvo. All versions, I think, of his "genius" grandfather.

You can hold a Tiffany, a Hamilton, a Gruen, in your hand. You can observe, as my great-grandfather did, the end of the era of timepieces: the pocket watch gifted, inscribed. Weigh out, in your palm, the three ounces, close your hand around it. Something real, something the sheen of your sweat, if your palm is warm, will mist a little, until you take a cloth and shine the evidence of yourself away from the crystal and gold. But nothing on the pages before me can be fixed, or made whole. I've made myself a few promises; one is never to use the words *unbelievable, unimaginable,* as I read. Not to think them or say them. They're a write-off, a way of disposing of. I'm already too good at splitting off, abstracting.

I click and scan a letter that has only one link to Senelis—geography. I know that after his three years as chief of security police in Švenčionys, he was sent to work for the SS in Panevėžys (Ponewesch in German). This letter, from 1943, is a complaint written from one Röhler, the commander of the security police in the Ponewesch field office, to the Kauen/Kaunas/Kovno commander of the security police (his name is not visible on the document, only his title) about the Jewish labor battalion under Röhler's watch. Röhler wants him to know that Jews have escaped from a work detail, and they haven't been supervised properly either. I go over it and over it: the Lithuanian versions of each Jewish name. The space between the letters of their surnames, like a chasm, an abyss, an accumulation of obliteration.

I use my own fumbling linguistic skills to unpack the last three paragraphs (later I'll hire a translator to go over the material and be surprised how close my own patchwork of words and sentences is to his formal translation).

> *Levinas . . . number 15, has been treated in a special way, shot during his escape and seriously wounded. One could expect him to die anyway.*
>
> *I ask for a decision and a message what is supposed to happen with the Jews. If there is no special treatment planned, I suggest to relocate them from here and to accommodate them somewhere else, because the prison is overcrowded.*
>
> *I ask to consider a special treatment for the Jewish policeman, Bakas, because he failed to report about the incidents, even though he knew about them. Besides, B. had been strictly warned once before . . .*

Some of the escapees are still missing. But there is an informant who has even drawn a crude map of the street, showing the house where the men are hiding.

Special way, special treatment. Shoot to death, beat with the back of a shovel, pull the skin off first to use as grafts for wounded soldiers, say "You're spared" to a trembling man, a physician in his former life, then—a Mauser to the forehead. A crumpled body.

If Senelis killed anyone, I have to know who it was. Otherwise, there is only that blankness, the spaces between the type, the perversion of language. The letter is dated November 4, 1943. "I ask, I ask, let me explain about the special treatment," writes Röhler. Perhaps the writer has to take care to justify the execution of a Jewish worker because by that time, in Lithuania, there are hardly any Jews left for the labor that war requires.

I stop, click, scan a page, scan another. But I don't actually want any of the pages accumulating on the flash drive I've brought from home. I don't want to be here. I'm still not sure why an old man being shoved to the end of the line, a story that hurts my Aunt Agnes, should be repeated, brought into view like a scar. Everything I read, scan, concerns private lives. Private deaths. Turn, click. "Aktion"—a word that infers damage, a roundup, an implementation of a particular policy on a particular day in large, dangerous letters stamped sideways across certain pages, not to be confused with the more innocuous "Akten," which simply means files. After a time, in my cubby at the museum, I start to conflate the two words; typewriter keys clacking throughout the occupied territories, carriage returns thrown back, fingers smudged from ribbon changes, the old ribbons burned because of the imprinted keystrokes on the long spools, letters that spelled the ends of lives, the latest order.

I have a small timeline in my head:

The Germans take Kaunas on June 23, 1941, Vilnius on June 24—the whole country by June 27. The days are long; it is only June, but it is hot. Dust on the roads; rubble clouds in the blown-up towns. In the German newsreels you see soldiers in tanks, on bicycles, horses. So odd, that—invade Ostland on a bicycle, as if you're on your way to a picnic or delivering a telegram. Shirtless boys in the heat, tramping up and down, mug their righteous vigor for the camera, but also, now and then, there is a flicker of discovery, a shade of disorientation, wonder on a quickly vanishing face. Weirdly lazy summer clouds drift overhead as you push on, the convulsive forward rampage of war in a country you didn't grow up in, go to school in, fall in love in, learn to drive in, yoke an ox to a plow in, get drunk in as you might have back home, maybe in one of the famous Munich beer halls that became rallying sites, knocking back dark wheat beer after beer while speeches were made, curses spat, slap after slap on the back—all the younger boys your brothers, all the older men your father. There's a purity law even for beer in the homeland. Six glasses, and the 5 percent—give or take—alcohol content knocks you on your ass, brings you to your knees in an alley, your friends laughing while you retch. It's a joy. It's an antidote to all the loneliness of the world.

The Red Army tries to fight back, according to a German newsreel about the taking of Jonava and Šiauliai. Burning the towns as they retreated, leaving only the synagogue standing—for the Communist "Jewish scum of the earth." But neither my mother nor her sister recalls this. The towns they saw were intact. The farms working. The roads passable.

The panzers come in ahead of the infantry. Their tanks are too light for the Soviets, but in Lithuania the Red Army is so undersupplied, it doesn't matter. Locals give the Germans flowers, dark bread, and salt—the traditional welcome. But not every local. Not Elena Buividaite-Kutorgene. Not my great-grandmother Barbara, who my mother remembers saying, "It's terrible—what they're doing to the Jews." Though my mother is not sure when or where these words were said.

Back in Germany (it's not like the last war when Senelis went running after the family horse), the light tanks would be retooled and upgraded, the task made so much more efficient by slave labor for Henschel, Alkett, Daimler-Benz—later bought out by Chrysler.

Click, scan. My Jewish grandmother's friends who had numbers on their arms, my fascination with that blue-black ink. I wanted to touch it, try to rub it out. To speak of it was forbidden. To be caught staring meant being pulled aside, something clawlike about my grandmother's arthritic hands when she was upset. *Scram. Gei shoyn.*

My back hurts. *Ten more minutes,* I tell myself. The man with small eyes and large glasses long gone from the cubby in back of mine. The helpful reference librarian yawns, catches herself, puts her palm to her mouth. I go to the bathroom. Come back. Sit, force myself to look at a few more pages. Press the button that makes the pages fly past too fast to scrutinize. *No cheating,* I tell myself. *Why?* I ask myself. Then.

My grandfather's name, in his handwriting. His signature on the document is at eye level. An affront. A dare. As if it wanted to be found. All the writing in the body of the document his, in Lithuanian. One document with his signature at the top. And then another and another and another and another.

CHAPTER 12

A GOOD GET

The handwriting. My grandfather is front and center. He's with me, his clean folded handkerchiefs—thin cotton with the smell of the press of the iron, his small green (or was it black) tackle box with line, sinkers, single and double hooks. His face is red. He's roaring a laugh. He's dead.

The handwriting is the handwriting of a younger man. Do I know him, inside the older man I did know?

I leave the archives at closing time. Walk in long shadows. The hotel is quiet, the lobby smells nice, the light just so, a vase of something tall and springlike—forsythia? The first thing I do in my compact room is close the thick curtains of the two windows that look out on a row of windows of other rooms. I turn on every light, strip, get in the shower. Make the water hot, then hotter. My hands shake under the bright stream.

I order so much food from room service that the man who takes my order repeats it all back to me slowly, twice. The food arrives under shiny domes and thick creamy napkins. I've only eaten the one cookie all day. I pick up a roll, put it down. The food sits until it congeals. A waste.

I got a cheap price for a great hotel. It's a thing I do, the way my Jewish grandmother used to: get the bargain, but not just for any random purchase. I stare at the food and think of her, of what she would say about my day at the Holocaust Museum archives. Would I even tell her? She of the yards of Liberty silk bought during a trip to London to visit her sister Sally, or a kilim rug, a beautiful drop-leaf oak table. And then, chocolate. "Wait here," she'd command, after she veered her car into the long driveway of the Chilmark chocolate store. She'd slam the car door behind her and then begin to hobble as part of her faux decrepitude—ninety, she was still climbing ladders and

From right to left: my grandmother Rachel; her mother, Klara; my grandmother's sister, Bertha, 1925

pruning her trees, obsessively lugging all the border stone around her entire property an inch this way, then an inch back. Not small, skip-in-the-flat-salty-bay stones but boulders, stones as big as a small dog.

In the store, she'd buy a small bar of the darkest chocolate, her arthritic hands shaking. Propped against the counter, she would take a few minutes to catch her breath. Often, as part of the endless thrift that was the flip side of her love of fine things, she made shirts out of torn beach towels. I see her, in orange terry. Safely out of view of the store window, she strides quickly to the car. To me she gives the small chocolate bar. For herself, she has a pound of chocolate, the broken pieces presented to her in a white bag—a gift for an old woman on the brink.

"You privilege yourself," a friend accused me once during an argument, scathing. Something about sheets and thread count. Good coffee as opposed to well, not-good coffee.

My grandmother would have found such an accusation incomprehensible. An Eastern European Jew, a woman, she shoved and bargained and worked her way out of a very particular impoverishment. Despite her father's consid-erable business success, her parents had remained fixed in their cloistered old-world life. She broke into the larger world. She read voraciously—Dickens was a favorite—took the children to concerts and museums. She used part of her limited income to buy the work of young artists brought to her door by her pianist daughter, my aunt Shirley. She was both repressed and rapacious. *You're alive. So live! But watch out every second because life is a disaster.*

I look at the rolling cart of food. She would have made me pack it all up and take it with me when I left D.C.

Wrapped in towels and a terry robe, I phone my husband and tell him about the documents my grandfather wrote: *protokolas*, "reports," with place names I can pick out, the names of people. That's it. My Lithuanian tutor Aldona was right. I should have tried harder because now, not being able to decipher the pages on my flash drive is unbearable.

"That's a good get," my husband says about what I found. Newspaper parlance.

For a second, I hate him for it.

Whatever is on those handwritten pages isn't good.

After we hang up, I think of calling my mother. Reading the words on the pages to her as best as I can. See if she can tell me what they mean. The thought lasts a second. She's recently told me she doesn't understand Lithuanian anymore, though we both know that I know that each week she has long conversations with Aunt Karina in Lithuanian. And anyway, I've made another promise to myself and to her. I will not tell her anything I find out about her father unless she asks a specific question, unless she wants to know.

I wheel the food cart out to the hallway.

I turn the lights out.

The bedsheets are heavy and soft. Even so, they bother a blister on my left foot. I wasn't wearing socks with my sneakers on the walk to and from the museum. I keep seeing my grandfather, then not seeing him. I walk backward in my life, this way and that, in my head.

In 2006 I was in a book group on the Upper West Side that lasted for one book: *The Odyssey*. The eloquent man who led our discussions is the only person I've ever met who lives up to the cliché of being someone who could entrance just by reading a phone book aloud. Our discussions went on through long dinners and even back out into the old elegance of West End Avenue on late spring and summer nights. Our leader was writing a book about his Jewish family and relatives who had perished in the Holocaust. One night, at the dinner table—a few oily, desolate leaves left in the huge salad bowl, a hunk or two of bread, an empty bottle of wine—talk turned to his work, to World War II.

"The Lithuanians were the worst," he said, punctuating "the worst." Many nods around the table.

I looked away, to my side, to floor-to-ceiling bookcases crammed with books our host, also a writer I greatly admire, had inherited from his father. My father was four months dead, his overloaded bookcases not yet taken apart. Our host's beautiful wife had died suddenly a few weeks after my father. The two deaths are incomparable. My father was in his eighties. Still, my father. And since his death, I heard things differently.

In the Boston train station on my way back from the horrible faux living room of the Vineyard funeral home—with its stuffed striped sofas, gilt frames around neutral paint-by-number paintings, the bizarre catalog of urns—I thought I heard someone announce on the station's PA system, "Will all passengers whose fathers have died come to the ticket counter?"

The Lithuanians were the worst.

The words cut through me, stuck. In the moment—an image of my grandfather, the freedom fighter, running across a field, in a country I'd never seen. Running into my life.

I got up, clattered a few dishes together. Ashamed. Embarrassed. Something. But not enough of something to ask any questions of any family members. Start reading. Wondering.

Until now. Eight years later.

Exhaustion hits. I float a little, close to sleep.

Before the unremembered dreams, a little half-dream—mountains, denuded, strange. Not a real place. It's the past—somehow I understand. But how to get there? How to come back?

CHAPTER 13

OUR ANNE FRANK

The next morning I'm at the archives again. One day I'll be able to read, with a fair amount of exactness, what my grandfather was writing about in Lithuanian in the captured German records. But now, at the Holocaust Museum, I can't.

A little bomb is busy constructing itself in my chest. A dry cough rests in the back of my throat—no lozenge or syrup or hot tea chases it away. My hands are sweaty, and my eyes in the mirror of the quiet bathroom down the carpeted archive hall seem too shiny, a gaze without clarity or depth.

My mother had a private liturgy I inherited: disappearances are utterly possible—people, houses, goats, carefully stitched slippers (a bit too tight but beloved), her mother with her familiar officiousness, her subtly acrid sweat, the nails of her thin fingers clipped and clean. They're here. They're gone. Better stay put. Better hold on tight. Better doubt than believe. I download all the records from Lithuania again. Next, on a different flash drive, red like a stoplight, I download only the files in my grandfather's hand, in case the first flash drive vanishes between D.C. and New York.

All I want to know is what my grandfather's reports say, but I make myself continue with other files I've ordered.

FOR MY MOTHER, Babita was the victim of a terrible magic trick. No one mentioned her after she was taken; no one explained. So my mother waited. Spring rains churned an unfamiliar road into muck, washed out paths to door-ways of strangers and relatives who hid my mother for a while, and then passed her on, sometimes with her brother and sister, sometimes alone. Once in a while, when circumstances demanded it, someone led them all into fields, burrowed them at night in a trough of ground that smelled of the molting of animals and tall broken grass.

My mother, the oldest, had a duty to her brother and sister to discern, predict; what had happened to the imperfect order of chickens, the apples she and her brother buried, the vinegar they poured on burdock? Was their mother's disappearance an irrevocable event? The old life was close enough still—when would it enclose them all again like a coat my mother could hand down to her younger sister, like the heat from the great brick stove?

In the white boxes tagged at the long, low archivists' desk, my next batch of microfiche reels waits. Every reel they contain is in Russian. I can't read the Cyrillic typeface or handwriting. I've been tricked by my own half-conscious expectation—everything important in this world is in English, or at least Latinate.

The Cyrillic alphabet creates a whiteout in my brain. And because it was the Soviets and their local collaborators who, in the early summer of 1941, surrounded my Babita's house in their long coats, I think of her again. Of the wire sent for Krukchamama, Senelis's sister, to come collect the children. Then Babita fled to a hiding place in her church rectory closet until the fourteenth of June.

I knew some of her story from my interview with my mother and my aunts on Martha's Vineyard, and from Babita's arrest files sent from the Lithuanian archives. Months later, I would get them fully translated, but they were instantly evocative with their official headings and a blurry photograph of Babita's membership card for the Lithuanian Rifleman's Union (Šaulių Sąjunga).

On the morning of June 14, 1941, Babita left her hiding place in the rectory and took a quick detour back home. It was dangerous, foolish, but she couldn't help herself (we have all done some small version of this: in the middle of a personal hurricane, watered a plant, straightened a portrait on the wall of a house that won't exist in an hour's time). She went to feed the chickens one last time. She worried for them. The domestic routine that was hers, her hours, as she lived them; she had to let them go but couldn't, not quite yet, not her yard, her birds, their eggs, rabble and scratch marks in the dirt, her fate.

Afterward she'd simply walk away, take to the road, quickly but casually, a scarf around her head, as if heading out to mushroom, pay a call, take eggs to someone old and homebound a half mile away. She stood surrounded by chickens, her hands empty with the last of the feed, by the sand pile her children dug through to foreign lands. Then the Soviet secret police (the NKVD) were everywhere—backyard, front door, side alley, at the window with the broken pane.

The ubiquitous gas seal revolvers, an old Russian make good for seven rounds, weighed down their side pockets. They had their lists, their processes of inventory and arrest, had gone to the home of the janitress at the rectory as well. She was missing, but her child was there. They took the child.

The page of Babita's KGB (what the NKVD morphed into) file that lists the minimal contents of the family home speaks of a Comrade Jakuchonas who is part of the two-person processing team—a man or woman, one can't know.

The inventory paints the scene: a thin woman cursing herself for stopping home one more time, watching two "comrades" rifle through coats, rip through the feathered interiors of pillows she stuffed and sewed, put their hands, their scent, on all she has to leave behind. The stubs of her cigarettes, perhaps, to check the brand, a bit of blanket her boy used to suck on when he was teething. Babita watches; even in her panic the details won't evade her. One agent's eyes linger a bit longer on the Philips radio, the other strokes the velvet fabric of the couch.

"It was her Jewish neighbors who turned her in," Aunt Karina had said on the Vineyard, somber, matter-of-fact. Turned her in because she was married to the chief of the border police, a Lithuanian military man, was educated, was, as her Rifleman's Union card indicated, a nationalist, not a good Communist, turned her in because my grandfather was fighting the Russians, because Stalin in June 1941 had ordered a purge; anyone who might be a threat to his regime was to be arrested, collected, vanished. The order brought forth informants quick to make their own allegiances clear, or perhaps settle a score, or both.

Prior to the actual roundups and deportations, the Soviet secret police gathered denunciations. Their "interviews" had a single set of answers and a

I, the authorized operative officer Patsenin of the Mnel'sky Inter-Regional
Office at the NKGB BSSR, in the presence of the Head of the Regional
Executive Committee "a", Comr. Gitzer and the member of the All-Union
Communist Party of Bolsheviks, Comr. Jakuchonas, have made the property
inventory of Puroniene Ona, d. of Rulenas [sic], residing at As Daruyeriu St.,
township of Zeimeris, Shavol'sky County, Zeimerskaya Volost, LSSR, as follows:

1.	Table 1 (one)
2.	Chairs 4 (four)
3.	Sofa, velvety one
4.	Beds 2 (two), iron.
5.	Radio-set one, Philips brand.
6.	Watch made of yellow metal one.
7.	Jacket, diagonal one.
8.	[Army] overcoat " ——— " one.
9.	Fur-coat covered with woolen cloth one.
10.	Pillows 3 (three).
11.	Electric iron one.

The inventory was made following the protocol and without [unintelligible].
Authorized operative officer Patsenin 6/14/41.

The property has been transferred for keeping
to the Regional Executive Committee.

Property delivered by auth. oper. officer	[Signed: Patsenin]
Property accepted by head of REC "a"	[Signed-1]
ACP/b member	[Signed-2]

single purpose—to justify arrest, jail, torture, and/or deportation of the "criminal." The following "Record of interrogation" was badly handwritten, but the
gist is clear.

[?] *Salote _neidiene, daughter of Jakubas, [born] 1895 in Koenigsberg [?],
Germany. Illiterate, no party affiliation [residing at] Žeimelis.*

*Question: When did you become acquainted with reserve lieutenant Pranas
Puronas?*

*Answer: I've known Pranas Puronas for about 6 years. He [was] the border
commander and an active rifleman organizer. He was a very ambitious man
and paid no heed to anyone, especially proletarians [or "working
people."]. He covered [provided protection for] various fascist
demonstrations. Now he seems to have gone somewhere else. His wife lives
in Žeimelis, has 3 children, an 8-year-old son, a 7-year-old daughter and a*

small 4-year-old son Darius [the list of children is all mixed up] . . . *She has worked since 1937 at the library, now the state* [library]. *Over all, the reserve lieutenant and former regional border commander is and was an active worker for the capitalist system. I have nothing further to testify. This testimony has been read to me and is written correctly.*

[signed] *S.* [?]

[signed] *senior district authorized executive Stokauskas* [?]
May 31, 1941
Žeimelis

[signed:] [illegible]
chairman, Žeimelis rural district executive committee

[stamped] *Žeimelis Rural District Exec. Committee*

The name of Comrade Jakuchonas on the inventory form is a Lithuanianized version of Jakushok, a Jewish name. In Žeimelis and nearby Panevėžys, the Jewish family name Jakushok appears on countless tax lists, necrologies. Names were routinely altered; depending on the native tongue of the person who asked the voter, the arrestee, and the taxpayer, and then licked the pencil lead, writing it down. So one must look at a name and imagine a Russified version, a Yiddish version, the Lithuanian one with the different endings for masculine, feminine, married, unmarried. I wonder if "Jakubas" on the interrogation record is my translator's mistake in light of the difficult script—it's just close enough to Jakushok. One of the neighbors who is saying what she knows she must say, or maybe she never liked my grandfather. Maybe he was too loud, drunk and carousing. Perhaps he included her in his hatred of the Russians and of the Communist Jews.

Babita was taken on June 14, 1941. But war is a quick-change artist, a con done so swiftly—the shuffling cards and the money you put in the game fly off the table long before you understand you're the mark. In a few weeks' time those who gave the order to shove Babita first into a truck, then the truck to a train, must themselves take to the road or they're dead. Dead if they can't outrun the baltaraiščiai—Lithuanian partisans wearing white armbands, intent on exacting revenge from anyone who supported the Russians—and the advancing German army. On August 8, baltaraiščiai and Germans gun down a mother and daughter who bear the Jakushok name, along with the rest of the Jewish population of Žeimelis; roughly 160 people. Families with children. Widows. Wayward sons.

Jakushok/Jackuchonas. On June 12, 1941, the paperwork on Babita and Senelis and their children was stamped and sealed. When the time comes for payback against those who helped implement the purge, the baltaraiščiai, young, barely literate, good Catholics or drunken thugs or midlife lawyers, doctors, business owners (before the Soviets nationalized their livelihood), leave their houses in Žeimelis or jostle in a truck from Panevėžys, with rage, a long list of old humiliations that can be rectified now that the Russians are out and the Germans are on their way in. The baltaraiščiai won't worry about derivations of a name before they shoot, won't pull on the threads that bind rumor and fact. The fact, for instance, that as late as 1938, there were 1,004 members of the Communist Party in Lithuania—among them 303 Lithuanian Jews (Litvaks) and 598 Lithuanians. Though they kill Lithuanian Communists as well, in the end it will be the Jews of Lithuania who are seen as Bolsheviks—all of them, devils of Stalin.

My mother had told me that she thought that after the war, relatives of either Babita or Senelis were able to retrieve some of the family property in Žeimelis. This amazed me, that one could go back, claim the coat with a fur collar, the electric iron. I imagined a huge warehouse. A thousand radios, bedsteads piled haphazardly, stacks of chairs, as in the basement of a thrift shop. She later surmised that it probably didn't happen; she had remembered wrong, or perhaps gotten errant information in a letter from a Lithuanian relative.

Stowed in my bag, on this return visit to the Holocaust Museum, in a narrow locker out in the hall, is a thick book: *The Last Days of the Jerusalem of Lithuania: Chronicles from the Vilna Ghetto and the Camps, 1939–1944*. Meticulously edited by Benjamin Harshav and translated by Barbara Harshav, it is a large compendium of diary entries made by one Herman Kruk, who created the library in the Vilna ghetto, and was also conscripted into the German work detail, Einsatzstab Reichsleiter Rosenberg. Kruk's diary is, among many other things, a record not only of the people of the ghetto but of property lost, destroyed, stolen, hidden.

Alfred Rosenberg, chosen by Hitler to lead the Reich Ministry of the Eastern Occupied Territories, was also the head of the Einsatzstab Reichsleiter Rosenberg. He conscripted ghetto prisoners to sort, destroy, or box for shipment to Germany looted art and books, including centuries-old Judaica—all for a macabre, grand showcase, reaped from destroyed public institutions and the private collections of Jews and other Untermenschen (subhumans) who, by the time Rosenberg's museum was a reality, would all have been obliterated from the earth. Rosenberg was a dandy, obsessive about his clothes, a needy sycophant. Like Kruk, he too kept a diary, but of a different sort—a scribble here about a night when Hitler invited him to pull his chair closer to the fire, another scribble about a dinner when, like a bad father, Hitler cast him out of the magic circle with a glance, a whisper in another direction. Though he was instrumental in constructing the murderous analytics that justified a doctrine of racial purity, he never achieved the full approbation from either Hitler or his peers that he so keenly sought.

Partial interior of the Vilna ghetto library, 2014

Kruk and others (including the Lithuanian Ona Šimaitė, a librarian at Vilnius University), at great personal risk, took advantage of this work detail to aid in the smuggling out and hiding of precious manuscripts and books to stock the Vilna ghetto library on what was then Strashun Street. The ghetto prison sat just across a small courtyard visible from the library windows. The library was a sanctuary. Resistance fighters held target practice in the cellar.

As I sit in front of the microfiche machine, I think of Babita's name: Ona, like Ona Šimaitė. How differently their lives splintered forward. Šimaitė received her library training in Moscow, Babita in Kaunas. Šimaitė wasn't deported during Stalin's early purges. In 1944, as Julija Šukys, her biographer, notes, the Gestapo arrested Šimaitė and "burned the soles of her feet with hot irons."

ANOTHER SECONDHAND STORY, from the past. I'm a child; either my mother or my aunt tells me that after Babita's arrest, after the crowded, stinking cattle car and the brutal interrogations, the inscrutable system whereby she was shuttled from one prison camp to another without warning, a particular Gulag guard took a liking to her and out of kindness and pity (certainly it wasn't passion for a woman so stern and ossified—was it?) gave her a little milk, a little extra bread, and so saved her life.

But during the February meeting on the Vineyard, neither my mother nor aunt remembers this small story. The details brought me comfort as a child, and so I carried them into adulthood. They had made me happy for a grandmother I'd never met. In the great frozen expanse, Babita had a tin cup of milk! On the Mongolian border (wherever that was), a bit of bread was stashed in her hand, food the most essential possession.

Men starved first, then children. Women survived the low caloric intake the best, though thousands died anyway. If not from hunger, from typhus; if not from typhus, of infection from a wound incurred in the forests, a beating doled out by a fellow inmate or a guard, anemia (even though menstruation stopped), suicide. Late in Babita's sentence, conditions began to improve. One day a cat was spotted wandering delicately between barracks, a cat no one had killed and skinned for a scrawny bit of meat.

The truth, it would turn out, was that for the luxury of cigarettes—Babita was a chain smoker—and perhaps, now and then, milk or bread, she bartered, made a trade. She stripped the threads from bandages and, a beautiful needle-worker, stitched delicate "gifts" for the wives of the guards. Nothing was free. Not in the desolate Siberian camps, not in Švenčionys.

I COPY RUSSIAN files from one reel, then another. In the postwar interrogations conducted and compiled by Soviet commissars and their secretaries who fanned out across the Baltics, some schooled in forensics, some barely literate, intentions were multifaceted. Enough testimony about the crimes of the "fascist invaders" might (though this was unlikely, given the Allies' efforts to rebuild and stabilize Germany) entitle the Soviet Union to reparations. Collaborators like my grandfather had to be hunted down. Their punishment sent a message to the occupied population—rebellion, even small acts of defiance, would be met with swift repercussions.

Investigations that produced information troublesome to the regime were quashed. The religious and cultural identity of the victims was ultimately forsaken—for the murdered, an after-death death. If there had been a Holocaust, it had been a Holocaust of brave Soviet citizens (excluding criminal Soviet citizens like Babita who, before the war, were justly sent away to the Gulag). Otherwise how to account for the numbers of brave Soviet citizens walking around in the shoes of the Jewish dead, making soup in their houses, riding their bicycles? Focus must never be on *Jewish* victims, survivors, or partisans. The few Jews of Lithuania and other Baltic countries all now part of the Soviet Socialist Republic, as well as the Jews in Russia proper who survived World War II, would be targeted again when the wheel turned in the grinding Soviet machine.

In his *Prison Diaries*, Edward Kuznetsov used the same word Aunt Karina had when she referred to my grandfather's anti-Semitism, though Kuznetsov, a Soviet-Jewish dissident, was referring to the plight of Jews in Russia in the 1970s: "The most accessible scapegoat? Indeed!" (He also wrote passionately about the Soviet persecution of Catholic Lithuanians: "He who does not bow the knee must rot his time away in prison.")

I press on with my attempt to reach back in time, scan the unreadable like a blind woman, even the pages of microfilm that bled from front to back, one side a mixed-up mirror for the other.

Finally I stop. Once my mother knew Russian, but as with her knowledge of Lithuanian, when I ask her about it, ask if she can help me, she'll demur: "No, I never really could read it, a few words maybe but that's all." And my memory of her in our house in Kansas City with a loud-voiced émigré, a Russian she met during her graduate work in languages at the University of Kansas, booming out phrases that she responds to in kind—teeters, becomes a half dream. (I always thought of him as rotund, large; but my mother has corrected me—he was a slight man, a poet whose voice traveled ahead of him, took up all the space in the room.)

I GO BACK to the hotel to shower and change, take a taxi to an event at the hard-to-find Lithuanian Embassy on Sixteenth Street. The talkative cabbie pulls first into the drive of an apartment building, calls dispatch for directions, backtracks, and finally spots the small, elegant building opposite the park side of Euclid.

The lush Meridian Hill Park exists because Mary Henderson, wife of the Missouri senator who introduced the constitutional amendment to abolish slavery, made it her mission. When I was a schoolgirl in Missouri, Henderson's name (the he, not the she) was drilled into us. Back then, white boys still went "coon hunting" into the African American neighborhoods, the engines of their cars ramped up, their beer bottles smashing against the curbs outside low stretches of apartments that contained lives the boys in the cars could not conceive of.

Our cleaning lady lived in one of those apartments. She stood barefoot in our kitchen and ironed my father's shirts and did not genuflect or pretend to enjoy vacuuming and dusting. My mother taught German at the local high school, and that was the only reason we had "help." Our cleaning lady's broad-shouldered son was the president of my seventh-grade class. My mother, out of her teaching salary, made some modest contribution to the cost of his mother's eye surgery. We stood with flowers in her crowded living room after she was home from the hospital: a television on somewhere, awkward thanks, my mother's accent made more pronounced by the cramped, low-ceilinged acoustics. It would take me a long time to understand how many strange doors my mother opened in her life, out of kindness, desperation, bravery, ignorance.

The spring evening was just beginning. Here a Norway maple, there a red oak. Soft wind jettisoned the new leaves. I have a little fantasy—I'll ask someone in attendance at the embassy to translate my grandfather's pages on the spot. It's more than a fantasy, actually. It has the energy of compulsion, so perhaps it's the effort of restraint that will make me feel, the whole time I'm inside, as if any second I'll knock something over, blurt out of turn, my voice querulous and then increasingly loud. Copies of Senelis's reports are stashed in a notebook in my bag. I stand to the side of the walkway. Shadows cross the wind, beautiful. Better to stay out in the dusk.

Of course I go in. It's a book party for a wonderful young-adult writer whose first effort is about a girl deported to Siberia during the purge that swept up my grandmother; a book I wish had been in print when I was growing up in Missouri. It would have explained so much about my mother's chronic sadness, would have given me words to use when my Missouri friends asked me about my grandparents instead of "One grandma is missing."

The incomprehension of my small classmates matched my own.

"Where did she go?"

"She might be in a prison somewhere."

This always aroused curiosity: images of an old woman with blue beauty-parlor hair robbing a bank or holding up a cashier at Kroger's with a Civil War–era rifle.

"What did she do?"

"Nothing."

The answer was unsatisfactory. Neither titillating nor familiar, just—other. Inexplicable.

("Meeting with the KGB is extremely hard on anyone," Kuznetsov wrote, "let alone a woman.")

A young, formal embassy guard greets me at the entrance. He speaks with a Lithuanian accent, and this surprises me because it's familiar. I don't routinely visit embassies so the fact that each job represents a foreign posting is new to me. Wouldn't it be cheaper, I think in the moment, to hire someone local? As if Lithuanian pride and identity had no meaning. In the months to come, when I don't want to think about anything else, I'll remember the embassy employee, thin and proper and correct. Young—does he miss home? Is he rotated out? His voice is the first Lithuanian voice I've heard other than my mother's for many years, with the exception of the recent visit with my aunts on Martha's Vineyard. But my Aunt Agnes is German, and Aunt Karina's Lithuanian accent is almost undetectable. When I left the Midwest in my teens, I left with a flat twang and an annoying penchant for calling people I didn't know "hon" and "sweetie," a habit picked up from the seasoned waitresses at Stuckey's Pecan Shop off the interstate, where I worked the Friday-night fish fry and Sunday's biscuits-and-gravy extravaganza. Missouri, the state I grew up in, Lithuania, the country I've never seen—two places on the meridian of my life.

In my high-heeled sandals my feet hurt. I clatter into the room where the reading is, the seats already almost full. The author, Ruta Sepetys, has a wide, friendly face and a shock of blond hair. Her editor, who looks much younger than me, sits to my left. Two gray-haired women on my right strike up a conversation with me before the program begins. Both are Gulag survivors. It will turn out that many in attendance survived the Gulag. One of the things that will stun me when the room is finally full, the reading over, the Q and A in full swing, is how young some of the Gulag survivors look, early sixties perhaps, or even late fifties. In my mind, that part of history started and stopped with my own grandmother. But of course the purges and arrests and deportations went on and on and on.

Mikhail Suslov, a name heading many of the KGB interrogations I'm destined to read, distinguished himself for his brutal service in Lithuania during the early years after Yalta. (The infamous Yalta pact made by Churchill, Stalin, and Roosevelt in 1945 ceded, among other nations, the Baltics and eastern Poland to Stalin. In exchange, Stalin agreed to go to war with Japan as an ally of the West and help to demarcate and maintain the war-torn zones of Europe after the demise of the Reich.) The Yalta pact was Suslov's "pass go" card. As is explained in his obituary in the *New York Times*: "As a member of a Central Committee task force, at the end of World War II, it was Mr. Suslov's job to supervise the political integration of Lithuania with the Soviet Union, including the deportation to Siberia of thousands of people whose loyalty was suspect." Looking around me as the seats filled, I wagered that at least some of the faces I saw had once looked into the face of Suslov, who had already decided their fate.

He died in 1982, a year before the poet Czesław Miłosz—born in the Kėdainiai district of Vilnius County—published *The Witness of Poetry*.

Miłosz spoke, when the book came out, in a large hall at the University of Massachusetts to a standing-room-only crowd that came expecting to hear poems from this man whose impossibly bushy eyebrows lived their own life; bristly flags raised, a furrowed line closed in a forbidding ridge. "I would like to talk about the existence of evil," he began, in his drawn-out, heavily accented introduction. Faces looked down, hidden smiles. *How, well, Catholic—how old world*, the hip, politically savvy students and faculty from five colleges planted in the dreamy beauty of a green valley might have thought.

My Lithuanian relatives who did not emigrate would have accepted his opener as a given. For decades after World War II they never, at the local postal exchange, accepted a letter or package from the United States. Tear open an envelope from America, and you could be hauled in, accused of a foreign plot. Frustrated in their efforts to arrest my grandfather, the postwar Soviet secret police (formerly the NKVD, now called the NKGB until the intelligence service arm that contained the police was renamed the Ministry for State Security or MGB in 1946) came nightly, with tragic consequences, to the house of Senelis's brother Paul. For years they came: pounding on doors, screaming, dragging the whole family outside in their nightclothes. Chests of drawers were pulled out, the contents dumped, pictures ripped from walls. Dogs howled as the police tormented Paul, his wife, and their children in the rain and the snow and the late northern light of summer evenings. One such night, Senelis's pregnant sister-in-law could not, as the police ordered her to, move quickly enough down an attic ladder. She fell beyond the arms of her husband. The child born after that fall, still childlike though she is grown, is cared for today by her older sister, Marytė, and is held close by her entire family. When I met her she half smiled, her face shining, though she did not, in my presence, speak.

MEMBERS OF THE Lithuanian parliament sit in the first several rows. A few look at notes, others chat, a bit stiff, decorous.

Before the reading, Ruta Sepetys gives a brief introduction, complete with slide show, about the horrors of Stalin. There he is, the monster with the mustache. She's singing to the choir, so to speak. People nod as she speaks. There are tears on some faces, tears of memory, I imagine—not of him, but of the ruin his dictates brought down on them. I don't remember the slides that follow. Perhaps there are cattle cars. Perhaps there are faces of purge victims, returnees from Siberia, a pair of shoes made of a bit of timber, a diary scratched onto bark. At a certain point Ruta Sepetys's large, lovely eyes brim over. How is it possible a system of criminality could inflict such pain upon a population? Babies thrown from trains. Families separated. She seems innocent to me, open. All this evil—and growing up, no one spoke to her about it!

But I know, I want to say. It's the only story of my mother's family, told again and again.

The protagonist of Sepetys's novel is named Lina.

"She is our Anne Frank!" someone declares during the Q and A.

Anne Frank was real, I almost snap back. Though of course I understand that the fictional Lina represents all the real children, children who were, as my mother would have been if she were not in hiding, taken away with their Babitas and Senelises, their mothers and fathers, the men quickly separated from the women.

Still, I'm so disturbed by this comment, so disturbed by the papers in my bag, that faces blur. And it has nothing to do with Ruta Sepetys, whose book *Between Shades of Gray* is a marvel and who once posted a bit on her author's site about her writing process. Her account of her endless redrafting, her refusal to lighten up what was inherently tragic so it would be more palatable to potential publishers, instantly won me over.

In Sepetys's book, the grown-up Lina returns to the repressive Soviet-occupied Lithuania and buries her drawings and diary notes from her time in the Gulag in a large glass jar, because people are forbidden to discuss this saga of personal reality, record it, publicize it. Then in Kaunas, in 1995, shortly after Lithuanian independence, two construction workers unearth Lina's hidden testimony.

"She is our Anne Frank!" When I read about the glass jar in Sepetys's book, I thought immediately of the diary kept by one Kazimierz Sakowicz, a Pole born in Vilna and trained in the law, though he ultimately became a journalist. Poverty drove him from the city, with his wife, to a rural outpost called Ponary, less expensive in the deteriorating economy of wartime. Sakowicz, for reasons we won't ever know, took cryptic and sometimes not so cryptic notes on the human slaughterhouse, conceived by the Germans and manned almost exclusively by Lithuanians, that Ponary became during the war. There, before fleeing the country, the Russians had dug out huge pits meant for the storage of gasoline. Approximately eighty thousand people, the majority of them Jews, were shot at the edge of one of twelve pits. Most of the Lithuanians who signed up as shooters were members, like Senelis, of the Lithuanian Rifleman's Union, Šaulių Sąjunga.

Sakowicz buried many of his observations of their savagery in lemonade bottles that were subsequently unearthed. Like Lina's glass jar.

Only—not like Lina's glass jar.

I WAIT, AFTER the context given for Stalin's purges, through Ruta Sepetys's brief but moving reading from her book, wait as the different members of the Lithuanian parliament stand and make speeches. Their central point, apart from praising Sepetys's book, seems to be "Finally, somebody in the West is writing about what happened to *us* and people are reading it." I wait for some mention of the nonfictional lemonade bottles and the people who were once lined up at Ponary, their naked backs targets for the Lithuanian shooters. Wait for mention of the odd neutral weather reports that often precede Sakowicz's notes on the continual carnage at the pits. "A nice day." "Clouds, a bit warm." (Senelis's handwritten reports from the microfiche file at the Holocaust Museum, printed out from one of my flash drives in the hotel business center, seem to grow heavier, larger in my handbag.)

After Ruta Sepetys signs my book for my mother, after I congratulate her on a job well done, she says something to me about her book being for all of "us." But I don't feel like I'm part of the "us," or that the "us" includes my Jewish grandmother and grandfather and their parents and grandparents. The two elderly women who sat next to me during the reading write their addresses on a piece of paper and tell me to let them know if I ever publish anything about the Gulag. I, who save everything, immediately lose that piece of paper. I've looked for it, through stacks of files, in pages of books, the corners and shelves in my study many times since, but it's gone.

The parliament member I end up speaking with is Adomenas Mantas: Oxford-educated, part of the Lithuanian right, though I don't know that then. I ask him why he went into politics. He shrugs. It's what his family does, he quips, but when our talk turns to the issue of wartime collaboration he speaks about the Truth and Reconciliation Commission in Rwanda and about how attitudes can't change unless a structure for change is put into place. I have a cracker in one hand, a cup of seltzer in the other. He's short, elegant, though his clothes seem somehow to be choking him a bit, sleeves pulling, collar maybe leaving a red mark at the back of his neck. He tells me a joke. The gist of it, as I remember, is something like this:

A group of people just come home from the Gulag are swapping stories.

What did you do to get twenty-five years? Answer: I killed someone.

What did you do to get fifteen years? Answer: I robbed someone.

What did you do to get ten years? Answer: Nothing.

BABITA WAS SENTENCED to fifteen years' hard labor in the Gulag. She was a librarian. So the joke fits her and doesn't fit her, and I don't fit in with the grateful audience at the embassy.

In our family narrative, Babita was tortured for a year in Lubyanka. This will turn out to be not entirely true—it was several weeks, not a year. But maybe time in the death cell does that to you—alters hours into weeks. The scars on her forearms where the skin was pulled out with pliers—

"Where is your husband?"

"Who were his accomplices?"

"Where are your children?"

"Admit to your crimes!"

All night, all day. For many days. Time crushed like stones.

THERE ARE NO cabs outside. I walk and walk until the blisters on my heels force immediate action, slip out of my sandals, the pavement cool under my bare feet in the dark. After the green of Meridian Park is long behind me, a cab finally rushes up. We travel (slower than cabs in New York), back to the center of the city. Out my window, the moon is so huge it seems to need a crane to keep from falling.

The Lina/Anne Frank comparison confounds me; the packed room of people confounds me, people who unlike Anne Frank had their books signed, tried out the Brie and delicately sliced meats, left half-empty wineglasses on a mantel and windowsills, withstood the flashes of the cameras—a picture for an old acquaintance or a friend the busyness of life has kept them from until this evening, pictures to show grown children or grandchildren or even great-grandchildren.

I've known a few people more dead than alive, who've gone into some broken or corrupt hovel of the self no appeal or offer of assistance can reach. The finality of their ruin is hard to grasp at first. And when you do, ultimately, you force yourself to back away, to understand you're powerless over a despair that no entreaty or born-again motif countermands. But as far as I could tell, I had been among the living all evening—people who had stabbed at ice to build a road under the snow, people freed by an official document made of paper thin as onionskin, come home to a Lithuania under siege, come here. I had documents stamped by an archive, a long recording of a hesitant conversation with my mother, her sister, and their brother's widow. I had those pages of my grandfather's handwriting, but not his streets, not the particulars of his innocence or his crimes. I had a book I wish I'd read as a child, but not the country where the story began, the scent of juniper, the feel of the land. I had nothing to do then, but go.

CHAPTER 14

THE HUMAN HEART

JUNE 2011

My plane ticket to Lithuania was in the travel-agency envelope on my desk. In Vilnius, a young woman named Viktorija whom I'd found through the chair of the English language department at Vilnius University was busy ordering files for me from the Lithuanian archives. A "fixer" named Rose waited for me, a woman originally from Belarus, who had lived in Lithuania for many years and was recommended to me by a colleague of my husband's at the *New York Times*. I was reading about war. It was making me very tired, and I didn't want to read with numbness and stupidity about the slaughter of Carthage by Appian of Alexandria, "torn asunder in all shapes of horror, crushed and mangled," or the battle scenes in *War and Peace*, turning the pages mindlessly, as if I was looking through an Ikea catalog. But I couldn't shake my fatigue.

Instead of excitement and/or trepidation about my fast-approaching trip, all I could think of was a chair: a big chair with torn upholstery like the ones upstairs in our apartment. When I thought of the chair, I imagined myself sitting in it for a long time, not reading, not watching television, not listening to music or talking. Just sitting, very quietly, until my weariness lifted like the mist of morning from the field of battle. My days, as they say, were numbered, only I didn't know it. I only knew that when I ran through the green profusion of Riverside Park, past the roses, the buds still sealed and secret, out of the shade of the chestnut trees, I was cold, even as the sweat ran down my face and I took the concrete stairs back up to the street two at a time.

Three months earlier I'd shared a plate of beets with a friend in a restaurant;

wood, dim lighting, a step down in the foyer that could trip you up if you weren't looking. The next morning my urine was pink-red. I didn't know that could happen with beets. As a child they made me gag, though I loved the look of the borscht my Jewish grandmother made with the swirl of sour cream and so clamored for it right up until the moment the spoon was at my mouth. My mother's Lithuanian version was different, sweeter somehow, equally loathsome. Every year I picked the red beet slivers out of her winter salad. Then suddenly—like my stepdaughter, who overnight lost her hatred of onions—I wanted them all the time; roasted, steamed, turning my hands the color of roses.

And eventually the right beets at the right time saved my life. The pink-red urine set off an alarm; I was sure it was blood. My internist ordered an abdominal CAT scan. The results were insignificant but for "an isolated 0.4 cm pulmonary nodule." We had an aha moment in her office when I talked to her about the beets, the timing of the tinged urine. But now there was the nodule; it was most likely nothing, but protocol required a chest CT in three months. It had been three months. If I left for Lithuania without doing the test, the "probably nothing" would needle me the whole time. In Lithuania I'd dream of tumors and labored coughs. Anxiety is its own brand of self-absorption. *Get rid of it,* I thought, and scheduled the test.

My internist (her grandparents, as it would turn out, were from Rokishok, or Rokiškis as their Gentile Lithuanian neighbors knew it) is usually prompt and scrupulous. This time, however, she was late with my test results, even though she knew my plane tickets were squared up next to my laptop. There, one early-summer morning, while I squinted at the too-bright sun through the one long window in my study, my CT results from New York-Presbyterian hospital appeared in my e-mail.

I logged in and began to read, from the top of the report to the bottom, then from bottom to the top. Over and over, like the Pimsleur language drills I was doing twice a week now during the New York City reality show known as alternate-side-of-the-street parking, which from time to time results in usually docile people screaming at one another from car windows, ramming fenders, swearing at the neighborhood traffic cop who has heard it all before. *Ar Lietuvos? No, I am American.* There was more than one small node. There were several. But the nodes weren't the headline.

I had a bicuspid aortic valve: two leaflets letting blood flow in and out of my aorta, instead of three. I had a 4.9 cm thoracic aortic aneurysm. (Actually, 5.0 cm, my trim, remarkably dedicated cardiologist would tell me after my echocardiogram.) It was ready to blow apart like an overinflated balloon. Kill me. "You have a time bomb inside you," someone helpfully advised me a few days later.

At my desk, I called to my husband. He came to my side, tall, stooping in the light to read what I was pointing at on the laptop screen.

"The trip is off," I said.

"No," he said.

"Yes."

Then I called my internist's emergency number so I could yell at her for not returning my calls, and she, beloved and practical but never stern, raised her voice so I would shut up and listen. She'd seen the report. She'd put a call in to her go-to cardiac person so she could refer me to the right thoracic surgeon or cardiologist or both, instead of simply calling and saying, "You have a time bomb inside you."

The day before I read the report, I'd dead-lifted a hundred and fifty pounds in the small, ratty gym ten blocks down Broadway with my high-octane Italian trainer, who believed all women should attempt forty-pound lat pulls and fifty-pound chest presses and dead lifts—just the kind of physical activity that places inordinate stress on the heart and the aorta. I was lucky a hundred times over. *I'm breathing,* I started saying to myself. *I'm walking. I'm reading. I'm turning on a light. I'm brushing my teeth.* A mantra of my luck that continues to this day. *I'm writing this. I'm remembering: Carthage. Lietuvos. The low bench in the gym, my trainer spotting me while I lay on my back and heaved the barbell up, straightened my elbows, my face turning—yes, beet red.*

A little more than two weeks later a very talented surgeon used a special saw to cut open my chest. His father had been a mechanic, I'd learned from a newspaper piece about him. In our first brief meeting he leaned close to me and listened with his stethoscope to the little *whoosh* of a heart murmur I'd had all my life, then lightly touched his index finger to my skin at a place below my clavicle and told me where the scar would begin and how long it would be.

CHAPTER 15

WATER

Ten weeks later, at nine in the evening, I opened a spiral notebook. "I think I can start again," I wrote, then closed the notebook, turned out the light, and fell into one of those deep, cushiony sleeps still new to me postsurgery.

I heard my husband's voice. Yelling. In a dream that wasn't a dream.

He was in the living room, the room with the large chairs where I had, indeed, sat for many hours, quietly, not speaking or reading or even looking out the window, just—being.

In the not-dream I woke up and padded into the living room. The sound of a river was coming from somewhere. I looked at the television, thinking my husband had wanted me to see something, but he was pointing to his feet. Water was up to his ankles. I'd once lived near the Bay of Fundy, where the tide comes in with one long, loud rush, and that was the sound I heard. It displaced me. But the Bay of Fundy is numbingly cold, and the water rising quickly over my ankles was warm, almost hot.

My husband's face was frantic. He and I stupidly looked around. Up at the ceiling. Out the window. My stepdaughter appeared on the stairs, and in the teen voice she used with us then—a voice of condescension and affection, and in a crisis, utter calm, said: "I think you two should know that water is pouring out of the light fixture in the kitchen." She paused a half second for effect. "And the light is on." Then she looked down at her feet; the rushing river. Water splashed down the stairs to the first floor of our duplex. It wasn't coming from the most obvious place, the upstairs bathroom. The hallway to that bathroom was, in fact, the only dry place upstairs.

In two or three minutes our super, who was in his car ten miles away, began racing back to the building. Robin, who was running the elevator that night, got Zaico, the super from across the street, to come over. Our neighbors, some we knew well and loved, some we'd hardly met, immediately started a bucket brigade—not small buckets, but large utility trash cans. People began giving directions. My husband quietly unfroze and went to the fuse box. Someone brought flashlights; a young woman appeared with mountains of towels. Sanjay, father to a new infant daughter, said, "It's going to be a long night," and rolled up his shirtsleeves.

In my study, I picked up my laptop—an idiotic choice, as it was on my desk, high above the watermark. All my books about Lithuania and the war, all my research notes and papers in Lithuanian and Russian, were stacked on the floor. Along with them, the red flash drive I'd used on my first visit to the archives of the Holocaust Museum. That night, someone would inadvertently step on and crush the flash drive, proving true at least part of my mother's liturgy about the propensity of the people and objects of this world to vanish.

The neckline of my nightgown revealed the ragged train track of my sternum scar.

"It will be all right," our super kept telling me when he finally arrived.

Later, he confessed he was afraid I would have a heart attack.

Everyone on our floor worked while the water poured. It took a long time to pinpoint the origin of the flood. Water rose into electrical outlets. Our neighbor's son, terrified of dogs, bravely took our dogs away into someone else's apartment. His mother, a friend and journalist, had the good sense I didn't. She grabbed my papers from my study floor. One was my grandfather's file from the Office of Immigration and Naturalization. Soaked.

"It's ruined," I told her. Even in the chaos, I was aware that I half wanted it to be ruined. All of it. Thrown away. "You'll have a new apartment," our super kept saying to me, directing me to a chair each time I got up and joined the brigade. His words made no sense. Mopping, I thought, a few days of fresh air from open windows—the rugs hauled off and cleaned . . . but he knew the subfloor would rot, mold would take over the walls, doors and cabinets warp, come off their hinges.

Long after midnight, the right riser found, the water shut off, the initial mop-up over, I heard a crash downstairs, put my boots back on, grabbed a flashlight and made my way to the kitchen. There, a large, open set of shelves had buckled. It hung precariously half off the wall. The long, partially collapsed shelves were laden with books and irreplaceable pottery collected by my husband's father, but one small copper jar, handmade in Russia in the days of the czar, given to my Jewish grandmother by her parents, bore all their weight. The bit of copper was wedged somehow in exactly the right spot, so that although a few books and bowls had slid off, one end of each shelf rested on the tarnished jar that was as small as the palm of my hand. I stood on a stool and item by item, took everything off the waterlogged shelves and then finally held my grandmother's jar in my hand, marveling.

The day after the flood, our apartment already stank. Only our bedrooms were untouched. Downstairs, on our long dining room table, neat rows of the pages of my grandfather's A-file from the immigration archives in Kansas City were the only sign of order in the room. In the rank air, they were already almost dry—yellowed, but my neighbor Susan had salvaged them. They included at least three or four copies of the two photographs that came with the A-file. I'd scanned the photographs as soon as I received them, then made copies, because, well, you never know what might happen . . . I looked at one yellowed set of photographs in particular. Senelis looked back at me. A man already in his fifties. Ravaged. *You think you know me; you don't know me.*

The source of the flood turned out to be in a wall of my study. A hot-water pipe there had been closed off when the upstairs and downstairs apartments were joined and my study was turned from a kitchen into my stepdaughter's bedroom and then, when she outgrew it, my workroom. The pipe had blown out. There was a hole in my study wall the size of a small suitcase. When I picked up the books piled on my floor, they were sodden sponges. The carpet squished. If I'd been superstitious, I'd have thought it was a sign. *Whatever you're doing in here, stop.*

The crime scene encompasses all areas over which the actors—victim, criminal, and eyewitnesses—move.

—James W. Osterburg and Richard H. Ward, *Criminal Investigation*

Of all the places I lived, emotionally I am attached to Święciany, which I carry in my memories and heart (and often miss).
That is where I was born, my parents were born, my extended family lived. On my father's side the family name was Rudnitzky and on my mother's side Chermetz. There, in my hometown, while walking the streets between the small one story wooden houses, where here and there a brick one- or two-level house sticks out, I felt "heimish" (there is no exact Hebrew word for this Yiddish word, but the word heim means "home" or "homely," "homeland").

—Yitzhak Arad

Erev Sukes (Sukkot) 1941 returning from work at four o'clock I met the Jew Yudl Khartaz running. I asked him where he's running and he answered, "It's not a happy time." Other Jews were running also. Shloime Shmirt with an axe, Yisroel with other Jewish boys on the street. There was a lot of noise. A Christian, familiar to me, called out, "Khone, leave me as a memento your shoes because tomorrow will be your end." Coming into the house my mother asked me, "What are we going to do?" I looked through the window and saw many families . . . One woman was carrying her paralyzed husband on her back. The Lithuanians just stared and didn't do a thing. People ran without a plan through fields and forests.

—Khone Zak

CHAPTER 16

YITZHAK ARAD

He is eighty-six. The wood, the tools, the worktable—all younger than he is. A man of contradictions: his compact build is slight now but sturdy. He is sweet but fierce. Focused, but easily pulled this way or that by a quick greeting and a bit of gossip from a friend, a phone call, perhaps from his children or one of his grandchildren.

He lives next door to a cemetery. The sun throws white heat across the graves; it's summer in Ramat Hasharon outside Tel Aviv. It is cool and spacious inside the elegant residence where he lives, an assisted living complex full of his contemporaries—some old dear friends, one his beloved wife for more than sixty-five years, Michal. You can get a coffee and a savory and sit in a comfortable chair. You can walk out on the patio and drink the mineral-rich water to balance out the sun's work on your shoulders.

In the craft room at the complex other people create animals, wonderful landscapes, perhaps toys for their grandchildren. He admires their work, but it doesn't interest him. His own efforts are slow. He is creating those who vanished, using photographs and memory. His efforts are painstaking and utterly absorbing. He has waited many years to do this, years in which he lived as a fighter and a scholar.

Over time, the extraordinary happens with each figure whose image he works into the wood. The past spills into the present: a callus on the thumb of his grandfather's hand, faces in summer by a lake, soft skin at his mother's neck when she bent to whisper over him before sleep, nuanced timbre of voices, a song his mother sang, the sound the scissors made during his father's first career as a barber (later a cantor), his schoolboy dreams, even snow, falling lightly again. In the wood, those he loved returning.

A BOY AND his sister in the snow. Rachel and Itzhak Rudnitzky. She's fifteen; he's thirteen. It's December 1939. The snow has a blue cast under the moon. Sometimes it has a glassy crust they have to break through with their heels. The winters of 1939 and '40 are notoriously brutal. Where there is no icy sheen, they sink in the cold white powder up to their knees. There are wolves. They each carry bundles of clothing and food and a bit of money, maybe a trinket that could be traded for something, small gifts for their grandparents in Święciany.

Their parents are smart. They have prepared their children for the trek as best they can. They are headed from Warsaw to Święciany, Poland, the family's hometown, the town where Itzhak was born. Their father, Israel-Moshe, cantor at the Moriah Synagogue at 7 Dzielna Street where the family lives, and their mother, Haya, have promised to follow in short order. They hope to be repatriated back to Święciany, now in the Soviet sphere of control.

7 Dzielna Street, Warsaw, 2013

The Germans and the Soviets are not quite at war yet. Warsaw is under siege. Correction: Warsaw is taken. During the taking the bombs create so much smoke that the Luftwaffe bomb their own troops on the ground. The bombs are deadly versions of nested Russian dolls: bombs within bombs that cover a vast area and ignite, bombs with relay boosters, magnesium, gunpowder, and shrapnel. On the streets there are fires, dead horses, bodies of those who didn't run for cover quickly enough or whose cover was blasted into flame.

Poland falls without aid from Britain or the United States. Suddenly you can be killed for owning a radio, or just killed. A wave has begun that will spill into Lithuania. The Germans want the money of the Jews, the goods of the Jews, the houses of the Jews, the free labor of the Jews, but more than anything they want the Jews removed, along with other segments of the population deemed *Untermensch*, "subhuman" — Poles, Russians, Byelorussians, and Communists among them. The Germans need room for Germans. At the same time, they allow a small number of Poles to be "Germanized" — many of them children and infants who have Aryan features and are taken from their parents to be raised by real Germans.

In 2013 in Warsaw, I spoke to several people unsure of their ethnic identities — Polish, German, Jewish? Family histories contained vagaries they were afraid to try to clarify. Some of the fear had to do with a possible discovery of Jewish heritage. This fear was not strictly anti-Semitic; things had been very bad for the Jews once, and they could become so again.

But it's still 1939, and perhaps Rachel and Itzhak's parents will be allowed to leave. For now they pay a Polish smuggler — who suddenly has a new source of employment — to transport their children (an older couple they don't know is also on this trek) to the border of Soviet-controlled territory, from which the two will make their way to Święciany. The smuggler charges 250 zlotys — roughly five hundred dollars in U.S. currency at the time. The Germans have frozen the bank accounts of the Jews in Poland, first requiring all Jews to deposit most of their money in these same accounts. The 250 zlotys is part of the 2,000 zlotys allotted to each family to subsist on. That leaves the Rudnitzky family, after paying the smuggler, 1,750 zlotys, unless they have hidden money away — a crime for which they could be killed. Some of the allotment has surely gone into the snow with the two young people, or has already been spent on food, or given to those with nothing, or parceled out in a crucial bribe.

Rachel, the older of the two children, has already, in late fall, gone on a reconnaissance trip to Święciany to see if the town, under Soviet influence, is safer than Warsaw. It is, she reported back when she returned. The Soviets have even given some of the local Jews positions in government, a fact of prewar Sovietized Lithuania that the Germans will skillfully exploit with the help, early on, of the Lithuanian Activist Front (Lietuvos Aktyvistų Frontas, or LAF).

Though ensconced before the war in Berlin, the LAF actively disseminated radically anti-Semitic, anti-Bolshevik, and anti-Polish propaganda inside Lithuania—often mentioning the ruinous Jews and Bolsheviks together—calling upon Lithuanians to "do their duty" when the time came. But the time hasn't yet come, and the extended family have instructed Rachel to tell her parents that they should all leave ravaged Warsaw as quickly as possible and come to them in Święciany.

I think about that reconnaissance trip, made when Rachel and her younger brother and her mother and father were required to wear the Jewish star, when the borders were still porous but full of danger. She was fifteen.

Warsaw to Święciany—south to north—is about three hundred and thirty-seven miles; now, she has her younger brother in tow. At the train station at the start of the journey there is one last glimpse of home, their father's face as he waves them aboard; then the train's huffing and all the other faces, those in flight, or with military orders, or in disguise (Itzhak and his sister have slipped off their starred armbands on the train).

There is snow, a river to cross. There are wolves. Their belongings are stolen.

In Israel, Itzhak, now Yitzhak Arad, will report this detail to me with the briefest smile—a bit of irony in the smile, perhaps, about a world that quickly became rife with thieves of all kinds. Or perhaps I read the smile wrong. Perhaps it was a remembrance of and fondness for the innocence they quickly lost. It is their Polish guide who steals their belongings on a trek that includes an encounter with a German cavalry patrol, Itzhak and his sister running at times to keep warm, alongside a sled meant to carry them.

The smoke of their breath, declension of horse hooves in the moon-crossed roads and fields. How quickly the snow fills up the trace of the animal's progress.

The smuggler looks at the running children, notes perhaps the boy's height, measures it against the height of his own child. Or perhaps he has no children, but he has cunning. Perhaps he has always been someone who knows how to find an opportunity when it appears, or perhaps this is a recently discovered talent.

"Oh, I wrote it all already in my book," Yitzhak Arad says to me, shaking his head. He's a bit mystified to see me; anything of any import about his experience in Święciany he wrote in a book I carry. On the worn red paperback cover: *The Partisan — From the Valley of Death to Mount Zion.*

The name of the high school library that ultimately deaccessioned it is magic-markered out with a thick, uneven black line, like the dark water under the ice of the Bug River.

Which is, of course, the river Yitzhak Arad and his sister Rachel had to cross; the ice they tested with each step ever so carefully, the pine scent sharp in the back of the throat, and the brazen clarity of winter stars.

They make it to Święciany. They are there on June 14, 1941, when the Soviet purge that consigned my Lithuanian grandmother to torture and imprisonment sweeps through. In *The Partisan* Yitzhak Arad noted that among those arrested throughout Lithuania at the time were Polish officials, political activists, and people with influence and wealth; five to six thousand Jews among them. "The social elite of the Jewish community," Arad wrote — but that fact would evaporate even before the first Soviet freight car of those purges vanished with its stunned cargo of human lives.

CHAPTER 17

ANIMALS

A green park studded with little white flowers. A breeze like a soft scarf one wears in late spring. The fabric caresses, almost weightless, smelling of the night's perfume. The fields outside of town have been plowed up for planting. Another weightless gift—that scent of day and new heat in the turned earth and beyond—forest, lakes. The Vilnius highway, the one main road from Vilnius to Švenčionys, is a straight shot. Hawks circle in the light. A single cloud moves a silver shadow here, then there.

A young woman with a leg that doesn't work right maneuvers down the sidewalk across from the pharmacy; she hitches up one hip to drag the useless limb forward. At day's end my fixer, Rose, and I will enter the small pharmacy at almost the same time as the young woman, and the effort she has to expend to cross the threshold will seem heroic, her face determined, tight and fatigued, as if she were thirty or forty instead of nineteen or twenty. She'll look at me, bored, dismissive, imperious, then move with great complication out the door.

Švenčionys is roughly fifty-three miles from Vilnius; I'd expected to get out of the van and see—what? At the end of a street that is not as wide or grand as it is in the old photos before the war, my grandfather walking toward me, his vigor restored. He's eager. Happy. It's his town; a town that feels strangely in suspension. All of Lithuania that I discover on this trip will feel the same way. Waiting. Everywhere. A black dog on a chain hyperalert in a dusty pen. When the knock on the door comes, will it be a lover? A brother? The one you cross a river to wait for? The one you drowned as casually as the unwanted litter of puppies a friend of mine's neighbor down South bagged up and threw, with a stone, into a pond?

But I'm no longer waiting to learn about the contents of the first of my grandfather's reports I discovered at the Holocaust Museum. It's about gold—the missing gold of missing Jews. It's an interview in 1942 with Kazys Šuminas from nearby Ignalina who is informing on Juozas Miciūnas, who apparently has been seen with a golden bracelet and a gold watch.

These interviews are part of the German Civil Administration's attempt to halt the dispersion of Jewish wealth into the hands of police chiefs, German officers and administrators, and locals via thievery or bribes. All over Lithuania, men like my grandfather are conducting these interviews. All over Lithuania they make it clear to the peasants they bring in to "testify" that there is to be no mention of Jewish goods, especially gold, in the hands of Lithuanian police chiefs, their cohorts, and their favored underlings.

A German document puts the house where Senelis lived on "Commissar Street"—but no such street exists. Rose, my fixer, is convinced this was just another name for the Vilnius highway. "He was an important man," she says. "He would have lived out front, on this road." She speaks with certainty. I'm not so sure. Though perhaps she's right; perhaps Commissar Street is a name the Russians gave Vilnius highway—which is a real highway, though without western modernity (no six whiplash-fast lanes, no tall buildings bumping the sky, no exits leading to sprawling suburban outcrops).

It is a highway I'll be on weeks later, my heart rhythm slightly awry, my blood pressure spiking, when a thought like a whisper will come to me—*You won't live very much longer*. An intuition that feels more local than personal, less nightmare than fact—but not a fact from my own life. It might have been a disconnected fear, a result of having had my chest cut open, my heart stopped and fixed and started again. Or something else, inexplicable, subtler, as if a door to the past of this place was left ajar—a few words, a private prayer. The door slams shut, and I'm back in the van, video cam and papers and water in my blue canvas bag, the tic tic tic of the turn signal as Petras, the driver who often works with Rose, pulls into the usual gas station for a pit stop.

FOOD POISONING BROUGHT me to my knees a few nights before the moment of terror on the highway. I felt it coming on at the hotel while I watched, on the big flat-screen television, a Lithuanian-dubbed version of Edward Zwick's *Defiance*—the saga of the Bielski partisans (born in what was part of Poland before the war) and their forest camp. The movie was filmed in Lithuania in 2008, though the events of camp life it depicts took place across the border in Belarus.

I'd eaten pork that night. I hadn't had it since childhood, hated it. Fear, hatred, self-hatred; whatever it was that made me order it, I watched the waiter arrive with the large, white, elegantly plated hunk of meat and forked it into my mouth, even though it made me gag.

My stomach cramped while Daniel Craig, stocky, wary, rallied his camp members in an English/Belorussian accent while on the half beat after each word, the Lithuanian voice-over chimed in. Confusing, it matched my own confusion; Jewish, not Jewish, Lithuanian-American, American. The cramping worsened. I felt sicker and sicker. A neighbor of mine in New York had gone to school with a boy whose father, a truck driver, was one of the Bielski brothers. (The Bielskis' famous forest camp gave shelter to over a thousand Jews hiding from ghetto incarceration and death. It offered one of the few options to families on the run, men and boys whose prewar lives had never taught them to fire a weapon or survive in the open.) The father of my neighbor's classmate never talked about his time in the forest. There were no class visits on what-do-your-parents-do days. No sign on his truck: YOU'RE SAFE WITH US. YOU CAN TRUST A BIELSKI.

That night, soon to end in a narrow hospital bed in a clinic off the Vilnius highway, I remembered a passage from Yitzhak Arad's *The Partisan*: "On the way to a small island in the marshy swamps north of the Kozyany Forest, I watched the faces of the people as they passed, dragging along with their last ounce of strength . . . the only survivors of tens of small Jewish communities wiped out . . . struggling to save themselves and their children. I stood there

. . . powerless." No camp for them, with love affairs and brotherly feuds and green-black potatoes to share. No time or means to help them, no shelter to offer.

"This is the one place in all of Belorussia where a Jew can be free," Daniel Craig proclaims in the Belorussian/Lithuanian woods—"Tai viena vieta visi Baltarusiją, kur Judėjas gali būti nemokamai!" I thought of a Jewish woman living in Moscow I'd interviewed recently by phone; she remembered the sting of peroxide on her forehead, poured on her dark hair to make it blond by the wife of the Polish couple from Švenčionys who had taken her in as a child.

In Švenčionys (then Polish Święciany) in the interwar years, a Lithuanian *gymnazija* (school) had, before first the Poles and then the Russians shut it down, also served as a meeting hall. There the Lithuanian minority could gather, celebrate national holidays, and vent its anger at being locked out of the best jobs, just one more proof of what was viewed by some as the treachery of the Poles.

Švenčionys gymnazija *that became, in 1941, a Kasino and banquet hall.*

For proof, go back to 1920 when the (Lithuanian-born) Polish general Żeligowski mutinied against the soon-to-be leader of the Second Polish Republic, Józef Piłsudski (born in the Święciany region), by marching on Vilnius, thereafter to be known as Wilno. It is the stuff of international intrigue;

Piłsudski was actually behind the "mutiny," the stealing away of Vilnius, all the while pretending to negotiate a mutually acceptable border with the Lithuanians while his general "betrayed him."

This is, of course, a gross simplification of an event preceded by border battles, interventions by the League of Nations, the Polish-Soviet War, and the Lithuanian struggle for autonomy. The theft of Vilnius, their glorious capital—where Polish and Yiddish were the dominant languages—was an assault on a complicated Lithuanian dream. For some, like Senelis, the dream was the return of a Lithuania with borders as vast as the old, vanished grand duchy, a Vilnius that could not be taken from them, and a population that might be polyglot, but was purely Lithuanian. It was partly a fiction and partly a refusal to be broken by a series of invasions, demands, and gifts with hidden price tags. On October 10, 1939, the Soviets offered to return Vilnius to the Lithuanians if they allowed Soviet military installations within their borders. The Lithuanians got Vilnius back, but with the Soviet military in place, their country was soon overrun and in 1940 the Soviet occupation and purges began.

In Švenčionys, Jews and Poles and Lithuanians and Russians knew their own history; they had their own divergent and sometimes overlapping narratives, interpretations, travesties experienced by one but not another, wars fought together or against one another. In 1941, during the German occupation, the Švenčionys *gimnazija* was no longer a place for the Lithuanian minority to commiserate. It became a watering hole for the local German command, the Saugumas—the Lithuanian security police headed up by Senelis—and other branches of the Lithuanian police. The *gimnazija* turned *Kasino* was full of black-market and ration-card food, cards, and liquor, with Gestapo from Kaunas or Vilnius on the scene when events required their presence. (By this time the local Jews were incarcerated in the small ghetto, soon to be hit by a typhus epidemic.)

In the hotel room, I was sick for hours. A cab stinking of diesel fuel sped me off to a clinic. The cabbie and my husband banged on the front door until a nurse came from some interior room and let me in. Three IV bags later, the lovely high-heeled doctor said in slow, heavily accented English, "I think you will be very fine." I'd asked for apple juice long ago, and it hadn't come. Even with my husband in a chair by the bed, I was lonely and scared and furious, the fury from dehydration and disorientation, but even more so from the past I was chasing down, so hard to find in the Lithuania present, yet at the same time everywhere. That week I'd gone to the death pits at Ponary and again thought of Kazimierz Sakowicz's notes buried in lemonade bottles, of the demonic inventiveness of the Germans who stumbled upon the huge, deep wells in the earth that the Russians had dug out for petrol storage, just close enough to Vilnius to make them convenient, just far enough away in a wooded area to make a perfect, secret (at least for a time) killing ground.

After the doctor (beautiful as so many Lithuanian women are) click-clicked elegantly from the room, a nurse in a smock entered, holding carefully on a tray a glass full of foamy liquid. They'd had to go to a store—waiting first for dawn and places to open—for apples to press into the fresh, incredibly delicious juice. I marveled. The juice instantly made me think of my grandmother Rachel, who always had Mott's apple juice and apple sauce on hand—she would have made *matzah brei* for me, a special treat even though it wasn't Passover. "For your strength," she'd say. "Eat!"

"I want to go home," I said to my husband.

"You have to stay," he said, softly, but with great seriousness, stroking my hand. "You have more work to do."

WE DRIVE SLOWLY, Rose, Petras at the wheel, and I, looking for my grandfather's long house, really two houses with two front doors, two glass porches, one on either end, like an antiquated duplex. For a time, Aunt Karina had recalled, a Polish family lived in the adjoining house. A gate of wrought iron—or was it wood? (here my mother wavered when she tried to remember for me during a phone call before my flight out of JFK)—then a paved walkway that led to the front door, but first, in the yard, a profusion of flowers. Cosmos, she recalled hesitantly, then with more conviction. Tall, fuchsia and white, brilliant at the end of summer. Did the German officers notice them on the walkway to my grandfather's door? *Kosmosblume*; they shine even when the sun goes down, as if each flower contained a battery.

My mother remembered the officers in stages. *No Germans ever entered our house.* Then, *Yes, it was a soldier or two, they never stayed long, I never saw them.* Finally, *Officers from Vilnius.* Uniforms a young girl's eyes were drawn to, low and then loud voices. Clatter of forks and knives on dishes during the welcome dinner the children didn't take part in, shuffle of good-byes at the door, the end of a drunken joke.

My grandfather's unmarried sister Ona/Anna (she had the same name as his vanished wife), helped from time to time by my namesake, my great-grandmother Barbara, cooked for the German visitors. My grandfather was a hunter, so deer probably. Or rabbit, still studded with a bit of shot. Maybe wild boar. *No*, my mother says, *not boar*—then, *Yes, perhaps*.

My mother remembers that after my grandfather's three-year tenure in Švenčionys was over, after he had moved on and was working for the Germans in Panevėžys and the children were with Krukchamama in Gindviliai, he came to visit once with *a whole ham*! Where did the ham come from? A black-market coup? Payment for a job well done? A bribe? A small, dumb question—it haunts me.

Petras parks opposite the imposing Catholic church my mother went to as a child, her ankle socks clean, mud brushed hard from her shoes.

Švenčionys Catholic church

She had one friend. The friend lived far from Švenčionys, so my mother barely saw her; in fact they only played together a few times, and then the girl, who spoke Lithuanian instead of the locals' impenetrable Polish, was inexplicably gone. But when one friend is all you've got, you claim her as such, even if you only nod to each other in the street, or meet briefly every few months, or have a picnic and then part forever.

"Are you a big shot?" my mother asked Senelis when they moved into Švenčionys.

"Yes," he said. This makes her proud, but her mother's absence is a splinter in her heel; every step hurts.

A BROAD-SHOULDERED BELARUSIAN, Petras, our driver, wears dark glasses; he looks tough, lounging by his dependable secondhand van as if it were a prized horse that must be guarded from market thieves. And in fact the first place he parks, opposite the church, is on the edge of what was once the crowded market square.

It smelled of fish, someone I'll interview remembers; many horses, feed buckets, warm flanks, and in winter the white clouds of horsey breath, smoke above the trampled snow. Animal life and the crush of buyers and sellers were overwhelming for a small child: the jammed stores and crowded stalls, the tannery, the apothecary, the expert tailor's shop, two book binderies, one in the basement of a large stone house where among the supplies was gold leaf for the rare order that spared no expense—a book like a jewel, like an inheritance.

Petras speaks almost no English and offers little candies in the van when the miles drag out between Vilnius and Švenčionys. The van is solid as a tank. Gas is astronomical here, cheaper in Belarus. And because he has a Belarusian passport, Petras is permitted to wait hours at one of two border crossings to visit his mother and fill up the tank; if it's a lucky day, two hours; an unlucky day, seven or eight hours or more.

Rose, my fixer, has a great, albeit condemnatory, fondness for the home country she shares with Petras, even though it's more or less a police state. "Things work there," she says. Farmers plant and sell. In Lithuania everything is imported now. After communism, the small farmers who used to belong to collectives couldn't afford all the big equipment agriculture requires. They couldn't beat the import prices. Hundreds of acres are idle. She can't abide that—the waste of it, the poverty it signifies.

Before Petras turns off the van's engine, we drive slowly up and down the Vilnius highway into the town center, then back out again. We look on both sides of the road for the front-yard flowers, the two glass porches. It feels futile.

I wish I could ask my uncle Roy questions about his visit back to Švenčionys, but then I remember what Aunt Aggie told me: "He wouldn't talk about any of it," she said, not once, but several times, when I pressed her, during phone calls before my trip, to make sure. "It" was the war, Švenčionys, the DP camps, the loss of his mother. Uncle Roy never wavered in his view of Jews and their corrupt dominance over world affairs, particularly economic affairs.

I'd thought, before I came to Švenčionys, that I'd find the house he'd lived in with his father and my mother and my aunt and that the house would be an orientation point: I'd know the sidewalks my mother walked on, the distance between Senelis's house and the jail, the ghetto, the roads to different borders, different towns. I stare out the window of the van and make a different kind of map in my head. The Belarusian border is a half hour's drive away. An old

Russian Orthodox church, blue and wooden and beautiful, sits just beyond the town center on the Vilnius highway—continuity in the midst of so much change.

In the pool at my hotel in Vilnius, Rose swims in a striped bathing suit that looks as if it was made in Russia in 1920 and so is instantly hip, contemporary. (In Soviet times she worked as an engineer in the telegraph office, transformed now into the very hotel where we wade into the pool.) She does the breast stroke carefully with her head out of the water at all times, like a woman from Missouri in 1962 who gets her hair done twice a week and doesn't want the orange-juice-can curls to flatten out. But Rose doesn't have this kind of vanity. In the van with Petras she pulls obsessively at her lovely tight curls. If I had to go to war, I would want her by my side. She is strident and delicate. She teases me like a sister, eats like a forager, nothing thrown away. Handfuls of berries. Hard ends of cheese. Bread. Presses it on me. As if I were withering away. As if my life in New York guaranteed a vitamin deficiency she is required to correct. Over the months we work together, I come to love her. This first trip though, I'm appalled by her blunt approach to potential interviewees. People run from her. An old woman shakes her head furiously, *No no, I don't want to talk about the war*, and totters away as quickly as she is able, Rose shouting after her.

We make a good team: She's bold. I'm overly decorous. Soon we'll be joined by a third, Viktorija, fresh out of graduate school at Vilnius University; her braids and braces and glasses make her look sixteen. Her intensely blue eyes are lively, lovely. For a long time during our work together, the only history she'll care about is Putin, the madman, the gangster—and it's not really history, not Putin of the past, but Putin of the future. He's gunning for Lithuania. She knows it. Dreams of it sometimes, wakes, frightened. Holds her landlady's cat that came with her apartment. Her landlady is Jewish. Her friends make comments. *The old Jew landlady who counts and recounts the rent payment, in case there's a lita missing.* She tells me this without a filter, worries that I'll find it offensive, but because I've asked about her generation and its attitudes toward history and ethnicity, she remains stubbornly truthful. Her transparency makes her invaluable.

* * *

NEXT TO THE Catholic church, in a small row of buildings, is the Nalšios Muziejus, the Švenčionys Museum. Nalšia is an old tribal name, a throwback to the pagan. Which was what the country was through the 1100s: a people who worshiped trees, goddesses and gods, cohered into tribes by geography. Dalia, the weaver of fate. Dievas Senelis, the wise god in beggar's clothes who could warn you when you were about to lose your soul by doing harm to another—a shuffling old man like a moral stop sign: retreat, put the club down, go back. The "old believers" still existed, here, over the border in Belarus, in my Lithuanian family tree.

The glass doors of the museum open into a small, cool, rather sleek lobby. No one is at the front desk. We climb one set of stairs. On the walls, tastefully matted photographs turn back time; Švenčionys when it was Polish, Russian, finally Lithuanian. Schoolchildren. A field of flax. A day at a shimmering lake. The photographs make you want to unpack your suitcase. Find a canoe. Bring along some dense, dark bread and lie back in the narrow hull, let the slow current of the nearest river carry you until sundown.

In 1941, the year my grandfather came to Švenčionys, roughly 30 percent of the regional population was Jewish, though this is not evidenced by the photographs, and only barely noted in the even chillier exhibition room off the first-floor lobby, its formidable door unlocked by a rather formal and very sweet museum employee. She wears a suit jacket and a wide smile that is at once proud and serious and nervous and enquiring.

The exhibition room opens into darkness and smells like a church before mass—polished wood, fingerprints buffed from glass with a mix of vinegar and water. Our guide switches on a light, and as objects in the room take shape, Rose heads for a locked case. There a prayer book in Hebrew, a siddur, one of the few artifacts of Jewish life here, is propped upside down on a carefully arranged shelf.

"This should be fixed," Rose says abruptly, pointing and striding as if the museum is her castle and she is the grand mistress. "This—upside down, you see," and the museum employee looks dubiously at the upside-down Hebrew writing, murmurs an acknowledgment. A year later, when we return, the book will still be upside down. And again, the next year. The museum has a limited staff. They are working hard to expand and contemporize and in fact have just digitized an extraordinary array of photographs; so of course there are oversights, forgotten tasks—an upside-down book among them. I write this without irony, but the oversight gnaws at me like the unknown provenance of the ham my grandfather shows up with. What did he trade for the momentary appeasement of his children's hunger, for the special treat in the upside-down world?

WE TROMP UPSTAIRS into a large, light-filled room. Our host at the museum is Naderda Spiridonoviene. With her is Giedrė Genušienė; she is blond, with a thin musical voice that quivers a bit and is somehow at odds with her sturdiness. I find out later she's a woman who walks a lot. She notices the seasonal alteration of pines—their litter of brown needles, silver underside of green—and, seeing the mark of tractor tires on a dirt road, can calculate, like a detective, how long ago the tractor broke up the ground. Employed by the municipality in the cultural department, she used to work for the museum, fund-raising and promoting cultural exchange. One of the heritage projects the municipality contracted her for was the small book *Švenčionių Krašto Žydų, 1941–1944* (*The Tragedy of the Jews in the Švenčionys Region, 1941–1944*).

Naderda fetches a thin file of museum material Giedrė used for her book. Aside from the file, Giedrė did interviews and archival work. Perhaps most significantly, she met and became close to Blumke Katz. Jewish, a formidable Yiddish scholar, Katz left Lithuania for Russia in 1935 after the Polish occupiers of Vilnius made Yiddish study impossible. In Russia, in a purge that predated the sweep in Lithuania that swallowed up my grandmother, Katz's husband was murdered and Katz herself sentenced to twelve years in a labor camp. She returned to Lithuania after her sentence with vital memories of prewar Jewish life and an encyclopedic knowledge of Švenčionys as it had once been. She taught and befriended many. She died in 2006. Giedrė's voice grows softer when she speaks of her. She misses her. (I think of my mother with her one friend.) "Spirituality is not really valued these days," Giedrė says when I ask her what the young people in town think of their local history.

Giedrė used to walk with Blumke Katz, long beautiful walks and walks of vigilance that were part of a territorial claim Katz kept over a place known as the Poligon or Poligony or Poligon or Polygon—a vigil that Giedrė keeps now. We agree that we will walk together, in a few days time, the route Giedrė took with Blumke Katz to Poligon.

Giedrė checks her watch. This is her lunch break—she needs to get back to her office. We agree on the date and time of our walk, weather permitting—it's the spring rainy season.

"Lithuanians care about what happened here," she says. And yet, the sparseness of the museum's file is stupefying.

POLIGON MEANS "RANGE" in Polish—it connotes a military camp for Polish soldiers. Just outside of Nowo-Święciany (the Polish name; Švenčionėliai in Lithuanian)—a town a little under seven miles west of Švenčionys—Polish soldiers once kept horses and practiced their shooting.

Poligon is not a particular place name; it is as generic as "railroad" or "museum." But history has made it code for something else in Švenčionys and nearby Švenčionėliai (Nei-Sventzion in Yiddish—to add another version, another population to the town) and the other nearby villages: Ignalina, Daugeliškis, Lentupis, Khone Zak's Podbrodz, Adutiškis, Stajatzishkis, Tzeikiniai, and Tveretzius. Perhaps in Švenčionys a woman, one day when it was still spring in 1941, saw a girl walking on the Nowo-Święciany road—a girl who grazed cows at Poligon, someone the woman's family knew, because the girl's cousin, local to Švenčionys, did washing for them from time to time. And the girl's face brought to mind a milk cow, a green stretch of land beyond a barren plateau trampled down by the past presence of horses, and then a river—a quick collage of images the woman's mind didn't work at or hold, a *poligon* that did not signify. Distance; the girl grows small, becomes part of the road and the spring land that borders it. New barley, field pansies—white petals at the top, bright yellow below—and though the future for both woman and girl gets a little bit closer, it is not within reach.

AFTER OUR APARTMENT flood, in the long, perpetually dark rented apartment ("Wonderful light!" the agent had said) where we lived while the walls and floors of our apartment were gutted and rebuilt, I did a phone interview with Jonathan Boyarin. At the time, a scholar in the Religious Studies Department at the University of North Carolina at Chapel Hill, Boyarin translated Lithuanian survivors' testimonies from Yiddish to English during his days as a somewhat impoverished grad student at the New School.

The collection of testimonies was painstakingly gathered and assembled by Leib Koniuchowsky, a survivor of the Kovno ghetto. After the war Koniuchowsky, fulfilling a promise he had made to himself and to those who begged him to record their fate (he was trained as an engineer, which is perhaps why his interviews are methodical and comprehensive), sought out and interviewed Jewish survivors from his home country who were living in the DP camps in Germany, where Senelis, his sister Ona, and my mother and her sister and brother had also been sheltered.

On the phone Boyarin and I talked about small things—how much Koniuchowsky paid him to do the work, how long it took, what it was like for Boyarin to do the translations, and finally, why Koniuchowsky had such trouble finding an American publisher who would print the testimonies in their entirety. Then we veered off.

"History is by its nature retrospective," Boyarin said at one point.

So obvious, but I'd never thought of it before. His words utterly changed the way I considered the past.

"We give order to it, as if it was orderly. But the people who lived it or died during it—there was nothing retrospective about their experiences, about what they thought would come next, how they interpreted, for instance, a day of brutality. How could they know, the way we know, what would follow?"

ROSE AND I are on our way out of the museum, but Naderda wants to show us more exhibitions. In one expansive, bright room, ancient farm and fishing equipment hangs or is propped against the walls. A large, frightening scythe with its quarter-moon blade stands at the ready.

Fifteen minutes later, at the entrance to the Jewish cemetery, a man holding a twin of that scythe will appear and start working it methodically across the high grass, a little apologetic; with the heavy rains, it's been hard to bring down the thick green, to thin out what looks like a mix of honeysuckle, wild rose, and Queen Anne's lace to the right of the main path.

I'll have the sense of history stalled, a town where time doesn't accrue but circles back, forward, then back again.

But before the Jewish cemetery, as we walk from one room to another with Naderda, she points out a huge old loom used at the museum to demonstrate the art of weaving, the art of the goddess of fate. I think of my great-grandmother Barbara, an old believer, it turns out. A spell caster. The loom is extraordinary, but whose fates are remembered by its presence?

Naderda unlocks another door. For a moment, I don't know what I'm looking at. It's a taxidermy show. Extinct wildlife? Naderda corrects me. Most of the stuffed birds and mammals here can still be found in the countryside, on farmland and the acres of parkland that surround many of the local lakes. In my small blue notebook Rose scrawls a few of the Lithuanian names: *kranklys*—raven, several of them, the huge black wingspans stiff and stuck; *tigero*—tiger; *vovere*—a frozen squirrel stranded on the white floor of one display. The whole room is dead.

In our interview, Boyarin said that what haunted him most after he was done with his translations were the accounts of humiliation that so often accompanied or preceded the slaughters. The hacking off of beards while German soldiers jeered, snapped trophy photos. Elders commanded to strip and then dance, perhaps on a Torah or clumsily on the corpse of someone they went to shul with, broke bread with.

Often murder is written about as animalistic, beastly. People who torture and kill are swept up in a deep reversion. They are actually pre-people, unleashed. I scan the group of trapped and shot and stunned creatures, the glass eyes, iridescent feathers, the long brindled animal claws. *Beasts* and *animals*—there must be other words to describe those who took part in what happened outside the door of the museum, in the priest's field near the Catholic church, through the entrance of the Jewish cemetery and to the left, in a well down a side street, at police headquarters, at the Poligon outside Švenčionėliai, in my grandfather's house, and elsewhere.

Those who let it happen.

CHAPTER 18

MIRELE REIN/
HIGH HOLIDAYS

FALL 2011

I heard all things in the heaven and in the earth. I heard many
things in hell. How, then, am I mad? Hearken! and observe how
healthily—how calmly I can tell you the whole story.

—EDGAR ALLAN POE, "THE TELL-TALE HEART"

That fall, rain every day, then every other day. Our postflood rental was on Edgar Allan Poe Street, a designate given to West Eighty-Fourth in honor of the poet and mystery writer who lived there before the city sprawled north. Almost every day I saw his name on a nearby street sign, and thought of Dupin, Poe's amateur sleuth who seeks out the savage murderer of a mother and daughter on the rue Morgue. A plague of mosquitoes descended upon Poe's street (and only his street) the months we were there. Somehow this seemed fitting. It was written up in the papers; something about mosquito traps in clogged sewers. Our neighbors slept under netting. The invisible buzz and bites kept us up at night right until the first snow.

In a small back room of our rental I put my computer on my transported desk and unloaded a box of books that had been out of reach of the deluge. From Lithuania, Viktorija, at the time still working on her graduate degree in translation, sent me several hundred pages, in hard copy and disc, of KGB interrogation files from the Lithuanian Special Archives. In many Senelis was mentioned, but I had also requested any files related to Poligon, as well as Babita's arrest file. I found a Russian translator who conveniently lived on the Upper West Side, downloaded the material (most of it interrogation files) and sent it to her.

It was, of course, raining, the night I walked a few blocks uptown to pick up the first set of translations. We hadn't spoken by phone. I imagined a deep, heavily accented voice. I imagined someone like Krukchamama, only younger—thick-soled shoes, kerchief around her head.

Anastasia was thin, a lovely sparrow. Trained as a lawyer in Moscow, she was studying for the bar exam in the United States and earning her keep as a translator. Her fair, almost translucent skin instantly made me worry; did she have anemia, mono? I would see that same pale skin on the lovely cheekbones of Lithuanian women in the streets of Vilnius in less than a year, and she would prove herself to be rugged and sharp. She'd put on lipstick for our meeting. She slid the packet of typed pages across the table at Starbucks.

"The language is very formal, very dry," she said. "But somehow I could picture it; a man in a room somewhere. A desk. A light. The interrogator. It was"—she paused—"moving."

I didn't ask her what the pages contained. She shook my hand in a gentle, slightly decorous way and went off into the night until our next meeting.

Back at the apartment I shut myself in the small room. The ceiling light was dim—the apartment seemed to resist illumination the whole time we were there. I'd found two desk lamps and put both on the floor near the only outlet. So there it was: the chair, the desk, the lights—two white ovals overhead.

Of course I looked first for my grandfather's name. I found it in an interrogation on June 19, 1952, conducted by Senior Lieutenant Suslov. On June 12 the subject of the interrogation, Stasis Gineitis, had been sentenced to twenty-five years in a Gulag camp. For a short while longer he would be in custody in the dank KGB prison in Vilnius. He was thirty-three years old. Since he had already been sentenced, the number of interrogations he'd undergone was not listed in this particular file. Does a man who already knows he's heading off on a train for twenty-five years bother to hold back, obfuscate? Even though he was sentenced, he could still be tortured. I thought of his family; if they were in the country they were vulnerable. Suslov knew this. Gineitis knew this.

He knew my grandfather, Pranas Puronas, but first was asked about Iozas (Joseph) Breeris, the warden of the Švenčionys prison—a man my grandfather had frequent dealings with, a man Gineitis worked for as member of the prison police in a jail built from the ground up for the occasion of war. Most of the records created there were destroyed near war's end or sent down straightaway to the Gestapo in Vilnius. My grandfather's office and the office of Jonas Maciulevičius, his direct superior, were above the cells, the barred windows. Across a utilitarian hallway, one secretary ran between them, placed their phone calls.

> Suslov: Who and under what circumstances took a group of arrestees from the prison in spring of 1942?
>
> Gineitis: Spring 1942, after the German commandant of the town of Švenčionys Beck had been murdered by Soviet guerrillas, one afternoon I stopped by the prison (I was on authorized leave at the time), and there in the yard I saw a group of prisoners, two or three German officers, the head of Saugumas Puronas [in other documents my grandfather is referred to as the "chief" of the region's Saugumas, or security police], and the prison governor Breeris. Puronas was instructing the prison governor as to which prisoners had to be brought from their cells . . . Puronas asked everyone's last name and suggested that some of them be taken aside . . . Where to the arrested Soviet citizens had been taken away from the prison was unknown to me . . . I learned that they had been gunned down . . . outside the town.

For two years, every time I read this section of testimony, I'll read it wrong. "Puronas suggests that some of them be taken aside"—this means, I think, that these prisoners head back to their cells, that the names he calls are not the group gunned down. I see my grandfather's face cloud over. One of the German officers has a Walther pistol with a wooden grip shoved into Senelis's back, growls in German: "Read the list . . . That little daughter you love, the money we pay you—do as we say, or . . ." My grandfather can't do much, but he can do this; choose a handful to be spared. Even with the Walther digging into his right kidney.

I misread, but at the same time some part of my brain gets it right.

I wonder about the translator my mother mentioned—the woman who was in the vehicle with the ambushed Germans and survived. Is she among those driven off and shot? Her face battered. Her feet swollen from a truncheon smacked against her insteps until they disappear. Is she in one of the two isolation cells? Two boards across a floor. No light. Rats.

I hate the fact that I'm still healing from surgery and my family and our home are in limbo and shambles and I can't get on a plane and go to the faraway place where there might be answers. "Saugumas Puronas." I'm glad my chest hurts and our apartment is ruined and I have to stay.

According to Gineitis, the doomed are driven away. Another description of this event comes from Yitzhak Arad, who witnessed a march on that day from the prison yard to the Jewish cemetery: "I encountered the prisoners being led away from town in threes, under escort of several Lithuanian policeman and two Germans. Most of the men were familiar to me. This was the elite of local Polish society, a few priests among them. They walked quietly and soon disappeared around a curve in the road . . . they were all shot at the edge of a pit that had been dug that night. Two Jews from the ghetto, for some unknown reason, were included and murdered with the hundred Swienciany Poles."

A hundred victims, not ten. Over time, these two versions of one event will multiply into six versions, a dozen, more—combined they form a kind of hologram of the past.

Gineitis is on leave, but he happens to "stop by the prison." Which of course sounds like a man trying to inoculate himself—he's describing part of a crime scene. He's either there because it's an event worth coming to for the show or because his "leave" was suspended for this special occasion. I don't know yet how deep the local antipathy between the Poles and Lithuanians runs. I don't know yet that the translator my mother mentioned has been taken by the Gestapo down to Lukiškės prison in Vilna with her mother and her sister. Tortured again. I don't know that she's a Pole from Wilno/Vilna who arrived at the age of twenty in Švenčionys in 1939, speaking perfect German. I don't know that she's beautiful.

I put Gineitis's file down. In the moment, I have little context for any of this; only Arad's version and the interrogation record. I'm sickened, but also feel a small relief; the German officers were there, so my grandfather with a list was following the orders of war, their orders. "We did it!" the German historian Joachim Tauber will tell me one day in an outdoor café in Berlin. His face vital, elastic somehow, opening to the import, the drama of the moment, the declaration. "No way around it. Guilty." The context at that juncture of our conversation was admission—how "guilty" only arrives after any kind of plausible denial is turned on its head. Done. Bombed away. Had it been possible for the Germans to create a fiction about the atrocities ostensibly committed in the service of Lebensraum, "living space," they would have.

I pick up another file. My chair is stiff-backed and overstuffed. I move to the floor by one of the lamps.

This one starts midinterrogation and concerns an earlier time, 1941. Bronius Gruzdys, a police chief in Novye Sventsyany (Russian for Švenčionėliai):

> Along with the other Volost police chiefs, I was secretly
> instructed . . . to place all citizens of Jewish nationality, men,
> women, and children, into the barracks located on the artillery
> practice ground . . . and to confiscate their property.

This is Poligon.

> I ordered all my police officers . . . to go along with my Acting
> Chief to the Jewish quarter and without delay huddle all the
> residents into the above mentioned barracks . . . Once the Jewish
> population from all Volosts of Sventsyany County had been
> huddled . . . there were over 7,000 . . . In early October 1941, the
> Chief of the County Police Januskevicius arrived . . . with two
> Gestapo representatives . . . He informed me that by order of the
> German authorities all the Jewish population of Sventsyany
> County had to be executed by firing squad.

The grave has to be dug. Three hundred workers with shovels are enlisted from their minuscule farms and railroad jobs and torpor and poverty and fear. Each signs a paper. Fail to show up, someone will come looking.

On the following day, October 5, 1941, when the ditch was
ready . . . a punitive squad of up to thirty people arrived at the
township of Novye Sventsyany from the city of Vilno. The squad
consisted of Germans and Lithuanians under the command of
Lieutenant Siblauskas.

In addition . . . about eighty police officers had been sent to
assist . . . In the morning . . . Siblauskas' punitive squad and the
assisting [officers] under his orders began taking the people
doomed to execution by firing squad out of the barracks in
groups of forty. Taking them up to the ditch, they shot them dead
with rifles and pistols . . . The execution . . . lasted exactly two
days . . . I ordered the workers to backfill the ditch . . . Despite
that, however, the blood . . . was still showing through.

I turn off the light nearest to me. A little *click*. Anastasia is an expert translator. The word *huddle* is as close to the English (from the Russian) as one can
get. That one word robs me of protection against what I've just read. A human
word, used here in a way it would never be used in English.

Those people, those families, those children. The different occasions in
life when you draw close—dancing at the Purim ball; linking arms before
the soccer goalie gets in position and the kick off sends time spinning in
the spring grass; the violin players in the orchestra, first chair, second
chair, three others tuning together, leaning in to hear over the shuffle of the
audience; the games of hide-and-seek—the grown-ups play too. Twilight in the
field. A boy whose mother you know, nine or ten or eleven, shares your spot
behind a fallen tree. He smells of boy sweat. The acrid scent of manhood not
his yet. He whispers in your ear about where the others might be, and you
realize he's in the last few weeks of childhood. Hear, somewhere, where night
begins, the Ural owl, with a syrinx instead of vocal cords, a call that's made
from membranes and pressure and air and vibration that carries so far it seems
the round face should be before you, then the boy is gone, the fallen tree
is gone, the owl is a hunter, the huddled have broken hands and cratered
empty eyes.

In one file my grandfather holds a list. In this file he's invisible.

*   *   *

AN INVISIBLE MOSQUITO wakes me mid-dream that night; it's a dream about Krukchamama. My mother has opened a long, low cupboard in her kitchen on the Vineyard. Krukchamama is wrapped in linen, the fabric just tight enough not to drape away from her corpse. She's been dead for a long time, but no odor comes from her body. No decomposition has begun. Autolysis halted. The skin cells still alive. Her chest cavity neither bloated nor collapsed.

"In the spring," my mother says, "when the ground softens, we'll bury her."

I slap at a buzzing in the air. Hear shovels lifting dirt. Loamy. The *ping* when metal meets rock, finds it, works around it. The diggers were afraid they were digging their own grave, but they were reassured. *It's for the Jews, not for you.* How long does grief last? I'll see it all differently when I take my walk with Giedrė, surrounded by new-growth timber, trees that were not there when first the men, then the women and their children, were marched from barracks to ditch. Not even leaves for them, shriven by fall, or glistered into a transfusion of color: red, gold, crimson.

Something's been hidden away, the dream says to me. "Exactly two days," Gruzdys reported, the time it took for the shooting. There was an aftermath, there were aftershocks; they've never ended.

IN 1925 A center for Jewish history and culture, rooted in the study of Yiddish, was founded on Wiwulski Street in Vilna. YIVO, originally the Yidisher Visnshaftlekher Institut, became a home to the poet Avrom (Abraham) Sutzkever, among many other writers, educators, and progressive intellectuals. Max Weinreich, an early force in the creation of the institute, would be instrumental, when war became a reality, in developing the New York–based branch of YIVO as the new anchor for the institution that was being destroyed an ocean away.

On yet another rainy day, I take the train downtown to Fourteenth Street, walk east and up two blocks, check my coat, and take the elevator to the YIVO archives.

The back room is windowless, so the rainy day disappears. The carpeted floor makes the room even quieter, though there is much chatter at the reference desk. There are books from floor to mezzanine and from mezzanine to ceiling. I think of my father. Insofar as I know, he never came here when he traveled to New York to visit his sister and, a few times, me. He would have loved it. He would have driven the reference librarians nuts. He would have stood for a long time just looking at the sliding ladder and the old bindings and the students bent over a ponderous text or working the keyboard of a laptop, faster than the fastest typist could fly over the keys on a manual.

I stand still for a minute, as he might have; my thoughts jump. His mother, my grandmother Rachel, once saw Queen Victoria go by in her carriage in a procession in London. Grace (my husband's first mother-in-law, my "second mother") wrote that her great-grandfather Archie "watched the troops of the French Emperor Napoleon . . . along the roads and through the fields toward . . . Vilna . . . Weak soldiers who could barely walk, were pulling carts of wounded men. Thousands of horses, along with their riders, had been killed." I think of time all the time now—just as I think of Senelis, make and remake my questions about his wartime life.

The librarian brings a large cardboard sleeve from the massive collection of testimonies gathered by Leib Koniuchowsky after the war. The 297 pages I'll end up copying concern all the towns that make up the Shventzionys region— Shventzionys, Shventzioneliai, Ignolina, Daugeliškis, Padbrade, Adutishkis, Stajatzishkis, Lentupis, Tzeikinia, and Tveretzius. They are a fraction of the work he did. The attestations, signatures, witnesses to the signatures at the end of each narrative speak to Koniuchowsky's meticulousness and also, I think, to some prescient awareness that as time passed the reliability of the testimonies he collected—traumatized individuals recalling the collapse of a world a second after it happened—would be questioned. He was right. But of course his work and that of his initial translator, Jonathan Boyarin, followed by the remarkable collection assembled by the late David Bankier at Yad Vashem (not yet in print when I went first went looking for Koniuchowsky's material) stand.

Sometimes repetitious, when Koniuchowsky summarizes to offer the reader the sweep, the scope, each time I open the white binder of hole-punched pages, more of life appears. Loan societies spring up, teenagers back-float in

Lake Kochanowka, an old smithy brackets a leg back to a chair. Shokar had an iron business. Yankl Svirsky, a woolen boot factory—his four or five employees worked the good wool and the not-so-good wool, the gloppy oil, pressing and sizing. Whatever yarn goods came his way, Svirsky saved the best for his granddaughter's dresses. ("I was a spoiled girl," she'll tell me, shrugging one shoulder, leaning slightly to that same side, as if listening to those who loved her, just out of sight in the other room.)

I read the pages at YIVO quickly at first; skimming, skipping, stopping and going back again, looking for Senelis's name. Not there. Not there or there. The horror of Poligon is mapped out; the roundup day, September 27, 1941; the Sabbath of Repentance. The Haftorah reading is Hosea 14:2–10.

> *Take words with you/and return to the Lord . . . Forgive all guilt/And accept what is good . . . I will heal their faithlessness; I will love them freely, for my anger has turned from them.*

Just as at the Holocaust Museum in the spring, I'm about to turn away. I've gone through two-thirds of the material. The Germans Metz and Beck and Wulff are mentioned. Skarbutenis. The Lithuanian Antanas Kenstavitzius. My copy to take home will be ready in a week. I can retrieve it, read in privacy, read alone. I think of the dark apartment, keep going. *Take words with you, take with you words*—suddenly, there is a girl. Suddenly, there is my grandfather.

The girl is the cousin of Fayve Khayet, one of those whose testimonies Koniuchowsky recorded on April 30, 1948, at the Feldafing DP camp in Bavaria—the same region of Germany where, in a remote hilltop village, my grandfather and his children, having left Lithuania with the retreating Germans, waited for the war to end, watched the Allied bombers head for Munich, using the church steeple as a coordinate.

The girl's name is Mirele Rein. She's "very pretty . . . didn't look Jewish and she spoke Lithuanian perfectly." She is rounded up and taken the roughly thirteen miles from Tzeikiniai to Poligon with her family, with everyone she knows. On Wednesday, October 8, when the shooting begins, a Lithuanian policeman she can plead to with his own language, a man who remembers her lovely features—he's seen her, maybe even knows her name—covers her with branches in a gulley, a pit in the earth different from the mass pit prepared with the work of the three hundred shovelers. "All day Mirele watched as groups of men, and then groups of women and children, were taken out of the compound to be shot."

With the help of the policeman she makes her way to the Vidzy ghetto, a far fifty miles from Poligon, in what is now Belarus. When the Vidzy ghetto is liquidated and the Jews fit for work transferred into the crowded Švenčionys ghetto, Mirele Rein "stayed at Fayve Khayet's house . . . for exactly two weeks." There she describes Poligon, the sound, when the children were killed, the "terrible weeping and screaming . . . like a slaughterhouse."

She's fifteen or sixteen, relentlessly determined to live. She leaves the relative safety of the Švenčionys ghetto and goes "to see the wife of a Lithuanian police-man who had promised to obtain papers for her. Instead the woman reported the matter to the Lithuanian Puronas, the head of the security police . . . [Mirele Rein] had been a member of the Communist youth in Tzeikiniai under the Soviets." My grandfather "summoned" the head of the ghetto, Moshe Gordon, along with Dr. Taraseysky, a member of the Jewish Council. He demands the girl be brought to him. The beautiful girl who speaks perfect Lithuanian. I can see him, slamming his fist on the table. What was started at Poligon can't be undone. She won't come to his office and get a reprieve. She won't be put in a cell and sent out on a daily work detail. She'll be shot, as she should have been on October 8, 1941, the third day of Sukkot—a time of joy and deliverance, when one dwells in a homemade hut under a roof of leaves. I see them in front of the synagogues all over New York City in the dark chill. They remind me of Missouri fields. Of cropland starting the winter rest, of the moon and childhood. "Bring her to me," my grandfather demands. She finds out she's been betrayed, takes off for Pastoviai, is killed when the ghetto there is liquidated.

I write her name in a small notebook, close the large file, and leave it behind me on the reading table. I don't stop to thank the archivist. I don't ask about the pickup time for my copies the following week. It's already dark when I leave. I think I'm weeping, but I can't tell. I can't feel anything. Only late fall and, when I look up—rain.

CHAPTER 19

CHAYA PALEVSKY NÉE PORUS

FEBRUARY 15, 2012

The entryway of the Bronx apartment opened into a narrow room cluttered with life; newspapers, books, art on the walls. It was raw outside, so the heat was like pulling on a sweater. A radio tuned to a continual news cycle in the kitchen scanned the five boroughs in loud, clipped voices so it seemed, at first, as if more than just the two of us were there. Something both formal and familiar in her welcome: "Yes, well, very good to meet you." And also a bit of wariness. How much to tell? Who was I, with Senelis in the background of my life, and my Jewish husband in the present tense of my life? "And your husband is Jewish"; she nodded, a bit pleased, I think, after she asked the question, though in the end, for her, it was the transmission of history that mattered most.

Chaya Palevsky had given me very thorough instructions on the phone— *You must write them down*, in the manner of my Jewish grandmother—for the least expensive car service to take, a phone number that she repeated slowly twice.

"THIS WORLD TODAY—unbelievable," Chaya Palevsky will say to me; astonished that after the carnage of war people would create more carnage, more war. After we meet, I will think of her often, think of a cup of water filled with small worms a Lithuanian guard offered her father, of the unexpected, the deadly, think of the resolute intelligence I could see she'd had since she was young. She had been a little breathless on the phone, a year away from ninety and fighting a cold; courteous, precise, thoughtful, her Yiddish accent more pronounced than my Jewish grandmother's, and instead of the bit of British, a small undertone of Polish. One of her sons had vetted me for this meeting, then e-mailed to say his mother was ready for my call.

And so I called, which means I entered the past of a stranger my grandfather might have seen in passing in 1941, when she was just out of her girlhood and ran in utter horror with her family down a road in late fall, all of them refusing the wagon that waited to take them (for a price) away from the barracks at Poligony, as she called it, taking the paths and the roads without stopping until Sventsian (her spelling) came into view. Which was home. The steeple of the Catholic church, the Orthodox priest's field, the late grasses there tamped down into mud, a shoe, a few rags, a piece of soap, a bit of bread, some cutlery perhaps, maybe a handful of photographs strewn as well in the field that cold had frozen brittle the night before. A field in which everyone they knew had been gathered several days earlier and at dusk into night marched west, those who could not march beaten or shot or borne in wagons the locals offered or were ordered to present themselves with at a certain appointed hour.

They ran more than six miles. Her father. Her mother—were there heels on her shoes? Her younger brother. The hair of her sisters, perhaps flowing long and disheveled. Why were they taking the road in a panic, almost flying, almost mad? Did my grandfather know what they were running from? Where was he, as they passed the field? The question of proximity will never leave me. Of distance, of closeness. How long does it take a family to run seven miles? How long did it take my grandfather, in his motorcycle with the sidecar (perhaps abandoned by a fleeing member of the Red Army, or war booty, the soldier dead) to drive, if indeed he did, from the gray, serviceable office not quite in the town's center, not quite within sight of the Sventsian ghetto, to Poligony? Maybe he rode a German BMW, the ubiquitous retooled R75, a light version, but still able to cover upward of fifty miles in an hour. So if he drove the Nei-Sventsian road in the opposite direction of the Palevsky family, he would have reached the witness house in less than fifteen minutes, a wooden, now tumbledown affair, with opaque windows and overgrowth close to the road at the fork where the right meant death and the left meant other houses on a sandy lane, where even at night the inhabitants on September 27, 1941, must have heard the farm horse clatter, the frightened jostle of men marched ahead of the women and the children and the elderly, wagon after wagon stubbornly clearing ruts left by rain, hardened now, like sinews in rigor. A curtain drawn. A lamp put out. The report of a revolver, then a kind of after-stillness amid the noise of the exhausted and confused.

On the wall near the table where Chaya had prepared an elaborate meal for me—fruit cup, a frittata, bagels with guacamole (a combination I've never had before), store cake, cup after cup of instant coffee, bitter and hot—there was a painting of a violin, in vivid reds and browns: a violin just like her father's. She saw the painting in a shop window years ago when she was a new immigrant in New York, the city strange and expensive but livable. The painting stunned her, as if her father might come out the shop door, a little tin of resin for the bow in his hand. She had to have it. It was much too costly, so she made an arrangement. It is easy to imagine how she drew herself up outside the shop, perhaps arranged her scarf in the partial mirror of the window. A perfunctory cough before the storekeeper, who would never know the mix of shock and desire the painting of the violin called up inside her. Only a few other customers, and even then she was a commanding presence. She would pay perhaps a dollar a week, as long as it took until the painting was wrapped in brown paper and she squared the frame under her arm and took it home.

A violin. So her house in Sventsian, as it partially appears in the left-hand corner of the postcard above, next to the old synagogue (the new one is out of view, across the street), was a house of music. A house with wood siding and a stone foundation with a window that could be opened from the outside by sticking something in the hook of the lock and lifting it free.

Inside the huge finished half-basement, there were two bedrooms, a kitchen and two large rooms with two typesetting machines, the leather bindings and threads for the books (Chaya shows me, holds up a book and makes a stitching motion). There her father, Eliyahu—*Elias* in Polish and *Elyohu* in Yiddish—often helped by Chaya and one of her sisters, sewed the typeset pages and perhaps, after work was done, took his violin from the case upstairs and played.

We ate and stopped eating and ate some more. Chaya talked, sometimes stopped to grab the right word from the air so that the radio—*Dobbs Ferry, Long Island, terrorists*—intruded; the present veered into the past and then faded out.

They have a little dog, Funya. When Funya is fourteen and blind, she is given to a farmer many kilometers away. But one day, after several days, they watch, amazed, as blind Funya makes her slow way down Schul Street to their doorstep. Inside, safe across the threshold, Funya lets go and dies with the final accomplishment of return. There are cats too; kittens, so the children saw birth happen, the mother cat mewing or silent as the bluish clear sac fell on the paper or the rag, then another and another and as she licked and tore with her sharp cat's teeth, the blind new lives began moving against and atop one another toward the swollen belly to feed. As Chaya spoke, I remembered it from my own childhood, the scent of a little birth, the small scissors my mother used to spare our cat Mitzi the job of chewing through the little ribbon of umbilicus.

Jews had been in Sventsian since 1450, Chaya told me. Four hundred in the fifteenth century; after World War I, three thousand in a population of nine thousand—a town that had been famous for all the small and two quite large factories that produced the felt boots sold all over Poland (much like the felt boots used until recently by Russian soldiers). Sventsian was part of Poland, then incorporated into Byelorussia, and a few months later given to Lithuania along with Vilna. Chaya finished her high school years in the same school, only because of the Russian occupation, the Polish school became Russian (both her parents were fluent in the language). The Russian curriculum compared poorly to the Polish, but there she would learn about Darwinism for the first time and after school take a Red Cross course that, several years later, in the forests of the country she was born in, would be useful in ways she never imagined as she, all purpose, no nonsense, learned at sixteen or seventeen to tie a tourniquet. Focused, attentive, like her mother, as she was in our time together while she drew me a map of Sventsian from memory, peering down hard at the paper with her glasses on, apologizing for the partiality of it. This talk with me, one more mission out of the many missions of her life.

"I'm sorry to say it," she prefaced any ugly detail about the Lithuanians during the war—a gesture toward my own history, my Senelis. *Don't be sorry*, I wanted to tell her. *I'm sorry*. I would say those words to some of the other people I interviewed, but somehow her kindness and intensity and shrewdness silenced my apology. Coming too late.

So much running in a war; running to or away, running to the wild shouts of drunks who have sung and raped and shot off rounds near huge blistering bonfires the night through. Running in slow motion through the marshes. You can taste the carbon dioxide in your mouth, the oxygen in the air seems thin, your chest feels as though it might crack, pus pushes out of the blister in your ankle, your hairpins fall, as the stitching of your life is undone, and page after page falls away, as if it never existed.

CHAPTER 20

MESSENGER

All the Reins were beautiful," Zinaida Aronowa said, eyes wide, even as she grimaced. All painful; memory. Her husband, rugged and gleaming in the photographs, died in 1985. (Of the Reins she knew, none spoke of a girl named Mirele, a name that, given the complications of testimony and translation, could also be Mirl, Mirela, or even misspelled as Mary—all a derivation of Miriam in Yiddish.) Zinaida is Russian, born in 1920 in Vidzy, Belarus—where Mirele Rein apparently fled after Poligon. Zinaida married after the war; every member of her Jewish husband's family had been killed at the Poligon.

Next to Zinaida, on the couch in the boxy apartment in Švenčionys, her friend Teresa, her face as tanned and vital as Zinaida's is pale, held Zinaida close. I watched the two women, watched how Teresa marked Zinaida's grief, rocked her, but continued to punctuate any gap in our talk with loud commentary, smiling, serious, bright—pushing forward, as she did for thirty-five years on her bicycle, delivering telegrams to every home in town. Stocky, stalwart, she's a Polish version of my Jewish grandmother—doing the yard work of two men, her voice rising over other voices.

Rose and I had come upon her before our meeting at the Nalšia Museum, when we walked the small side roads and shaded yards beyond the town green and the Catholic church. We followed the lines of the town map Chaya Palevsky had sketched so carefully for me in the Bronx. (She had apologized for its roughness; I don't think she understood how grateful I was for her memory; the pen, the quick indications of a world.)

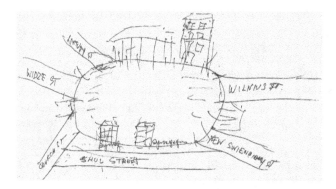

Chaya Palevsky's map

"BOB MARLEY" GRACED the side of an outbuilding. For a second I heard that rusted, sweet voice sing "many rivers to cross" and thought of home. Once a gutter carried waste water from the pump in the market square through the synagogue courtyard to the Kuna River. We turned away from the river and came up to a chain link fence around a huge garden.

Teresa hitched herself straight from a long raised bed (I thought I saw leeks and lettuces), shielded her eyes from the bright sun, and shouted, in answer to Rose's quick questions, "They were all here, all the Jews lived here, my mother did washing for them." We told her we had to go to the museum, would be back in an hour. She smiled and crouched down again. I wondered if she'd really be waiting for us. I hadn't moved into village time; in New York everyone, including myself, has to run out, take a call, is sorry—*forgot an appointment, stuck in a train*.

She was there. In her living room, her quiet, lovely daughter had laid a small table with sweets and coffee; a large ceramic fireplace took up a third of a wall. The tiles were bright and new. We talked of the past. Teresa was only seven when Chaya Palevsky was a teenager in the large house on Schul Street. I ask her if the name Porus (Chaya's maiden name) meant anything to her. No. She talked sometimes in a streak, mixing things up—said that Beck was killed in winter. Her best friend's Polish mother threw herself down a well to get away from the killers coming for revenge. The men were cloaked in white, their faces hidden (I think of the Klan), and pulled her out of the well's darkness. It doesn't make sense—not the winter, nor the white clothing (except that the anti-German partisans and the Soviet winter army wore white in the snow, loose coveralls that looked like they were made from old parachutes). But it makes a child's sense—seasons blurred, every murderer dressed the same.

A smile took over Teresa's face, exuberant by nature, when she showed us the certificate her aunt Anna and uncle Piotr Miksto received from Yad Vashem. They are counted as Righteous Among the Nations for taking in the Jewish girl with the peroxide-blond hair who grew up to be the woman I interviewed from Moscow, Karina Margolis. Only now Karina carries the last name Kavina, after the uncle who adopted her away from Teresa's relatives in a bitter court battle when the war ended. Kavina also because it echoes the last name of her biological mother, who, along with her husband, was most likely killed at the Poligon.

The Shpitz family, whose shirts and skirts and socks and pants Teresa's mother Salomeja scrubbed and rinsed (Teresa laughed a little, made sure we knew there were no washing machines back then), hid in an attic during the roundup for Poligon. Salomeja brought them food, but they were betrayed. At some point Teresa said "Lithuanians"—she'd said it outside too. "The Jews all lived here, the Lithuanians killed them." Her voice carried. I cringed, thinking of her Lithuanian neighbors, their ire. I realize now, in hindsight, I was thinking of my own Lithuanian-American family.

TERESA DID HER knees in biking through snow, though she was always warm enough, she said, in her messenger's uniform. For those who couldn't read, or couldn't read the language their telegram was written in, she translated. And for those who had to send news of a birth or a death, she often composed the short missive—the details in Polish or Russian or Lithuanian or Belorussian. In this way, she was the first to learn about all the large events of her town. Knows them still, sings at every funeral. ("I'll be home," she said when we arranged to meet her again, "unless someone dies.")

Some of Teresa's memories are clearer; along with the Shpitz family, her mother, Salomeja, washed for the Roiphes, another Jewish family, and was friendly with many of the people who would one day cry out to her from the ghetto, a fifteen-minute slow walk from my grandfather's house. "Help us, help," Teresa remembered the pleading after the ghetto was formally sealed off. But she was too young in the fall of '41 to know any details of Poligon. Undaunted, she went for her phone book to find someone who might know more, called her friend Zinaida, older by ten years, and off we went.

Petras drove us away from the large backyard garden that made me want my old garden back, want to have dirt under my fingernails again like Teresa. We parked behind a low apartment building across town. There were versions of them everywhere; the same small stoop, the hall light you clicked on that lasted until you reached the right door. We climbed a flight or two of stairs.

In fifteen minutes Zinaida was overcome with weeping. She had spent the entire war in a concentration camp in Alytus, Lithuania—south, near swamps, crammed in with Russian prisoners of war, liters of blood drained out of her for wounded German soldiers. In 1944, the ragged end of the war still happening, she was liberated and met her husband, Solom Aron, in Švenčionys. He'd been in the Soviet Army on the Japanese front, had come home looking for his family.

I asked a question about life in Švenčionys in 1944, and Teresa chattered matter-of-factly about how nice the German soldiers were on their way out, the Soviets on their way in. They gave her chocolate, praised her grandmother for taking the children to church. She wasn't championing them, and she certainly wasn't devoid of empathy for her friend; she just said what she remembered, unfiltered, and when she talked about the chocolate Zinaida began to cry.

But before Zinaida's face went white and she put her palms to her cheeks and shuddered, she showed us a photograph of her husband and a group of other men—friends, one with the last name Rein—reburying remains from the mass grave at the Poligon. There, for years after the massacre, storms washed away layers of the pit and tides of rain carried bones off for miles into yards and farmers' fields.

The photo was dated on the back, "1950–1960"—vague, someone's guess, perhaps Zinaida's—but somehow I sensed it was taken earlier, soon after war's end. The men seemed so young, so determined to bring some dignity to a desecration. Zinaida could not, at our meeting, remember the names of the last four men.

From left to right: Rein, Aron (Zinaida's husband), Ushpilas

Zinaida told us something else: Moishe Shapiro from Pobradze, whose father (the barber Shapiro) survived Poligon, had donated the photograph I'd just been given a copy of at the museum. Neither Giedrė nor Naderda had known where the photograph came from.

"Blood, maybe?" Naderda had said, when she placed the photograph on the wooden table where we sat. She put her small hand near the rust marks on the image, as if she might touch to know, to learn.

I shook my head. Perhaps someone put a rusted open can on the photo, or a cup of strong tea that slopped a little, the tannins leaking onto the fraction of documented physical evidence that remains of the massacre. When I gain access to the forensic file of the Soviet Union's Extraordinary Commission in Moscow, specifically to see the Poligon photographs—which exist as only shadows or dark, blurred lines in the frames of the Holocaust Museum's microfilmed copy of the same file—they will be missing. So it's Zinaida's photo of her husband and the four other young men carrying a wooden crate, and the photo saved by the barber's son for documentation. And then, of course, the long mound of earth at the site itself where Rose does not go without a yahrzeit candle, without scouring the memorial to free it of dead pine boughs, spent matches, trash.

CHAPTER 21

LILI HOLZMAN

ISRAEL, 2012

On either side of the entrance to Jaffa Gate, two enterprising Arab men make a small market on top of two overturned trash barrels. A pyramid of huge oranges rises next to their juice machine. Atop the other barrel, gorgeous breads cover a board, every shape in the world, glazed or speckled with poppy seeds or long and braided, like thin challah. A lookout shouts— *Police!* —and in an instant the men (they look thirtyish to me) hurriedly stow the fruit and bread, tossing their wares in large plastic carryalls with such acumen that I suspect this scene is repeated several times each day.

One of the men curses as he shovels his bread away. Nadav, tall, more teacher to me than guide, his South African accent always a slight surprise, is proprietary in the Old City in the way my fixer, Rose, can often be in Lithuania. He interrupts the cursing man with the bag of bread, a man who has now worked up a sweat in the morning heat for nothing.

"Hey, it's the law," Nadav says, shrugging, arms out, palms up.

"Fuck the law. It's not my law," the vendor yells and goes running off, looking over his shoulder but defiant just the same.

In the Church of the Holy Sepulcher, amid the smoke and candles and singing and praying, two Armenian clerics in long black robes are having an argument with two Greek Orthodox clerics. "You pushed me," one says. "You pushed me first," says the other. Two Israeli police with guns slung over their shoulders are trying to mediate. In the middle of their argument, a solemn processional with prayers and candles surges through. Nadav takes me into the side room where supposedly Jesus was buried—a small cave with what looks like two catacombs, a candle burning on an iron grate on the floor. Just outside the cave, graffiti marks the walls, and on the ceiling the reddish trace of Roman frescoes appears only after Nadav points it out. Two other tourists wander in, graying, thin, friendly. They listen to Nadav tell the story of the rock in the cave mouth and the resurrection. The woman says, "But I thought the tomb was in there," pointing behind us to where the clerics are arguing and candles are sputtering all around a gilded structure. "That's just for show," Nadav says. He puts a hand on my shoulder. "My friend here is Catholic."

He knows I'm half Jewish—whatever that means. He's calling me Catholic just to explain to the tourists something about why we are there, about the Christian need to see *where things really happened*. But when he calls me a Catholic, I wince a little and think immediately of going to mass on Christmas Eve in Hammond with my mother and her family. How—apart from my deep love of Aunt Karina, my wish to emulate her—it always seemed like a very smoky, loud, highly organized party to celebrate a guest I'd never met before.

It's a momentary relief to be in the Arab quarter, on a dark, narrow street that smells of spice and dust and leather—a million little stands set back, almost like small caves in the walls, and the proprietors, all male, mostly older, paunchy, insistent, coming out to beckon you to buy, some with coins in their hands from their last sale, or clinking in a closed palm as a convincer. I recognize part of the scorn some of the sellers wear on their faces—it's awful to be dependent on the capriciousness of the tourist trade. But there's more to it; the darkness gets claustrophobic quickly.

In the stalls: sandals, old coins, more beautiful breads, other juice machines and piles of oranges, scarves and stacks of cheap-looking underwear. A group appears around a bend, heading in the opposite direction—men in their best suits, lovely dark-haired women carrying flowers. It's a wedding procession. A small black Mercedes slowly honks its way through. Beside the driver, in the front seat, the bride sits, her face covered with vibrant veils.

Because it's Shavuot—the Festival of Weeks that signifies the handing over of the Torah to the Israelites as well as the first harvest of the year—once we leave the crowds of Christian pilgrims following the Stations of the Cross, the Jewish quarter is quiet but for children playing. Jacaranda trees shed purple blossoms; the sound of Hebrew prayers from shadowed limestone houses spills out into the light.

I'M IN ISRAEL only briefly, to talk to two Holocaust survivors from Švenčionys: Yitzhak Arad and Lili Holzman (née Swirsky). Neither will remember my grandfather. I actually had not expected them to remember him, but maybe the name Mirele Rein (no; the last name maybe is familiar, but not the first). What I had hoped was that the details they remembered, or the archives at Yad Vashem, would help me develop more definitive information about my grandfather. I'd grown to hate the word *collaborator*—for myself I'd defined the term as someone who had intent, who stood to gain by participating in what the local authorities or German authorities requested of them. But the word doesn't say enough, do enough—it's an umbrella term, a word that quickly abstracts the moment of *yes*, the circumstances of *no*.

Yes, there was the testimony about Mirele Rein, but a historian whose work I had great respect for explained to me that had Senelis helped her and been found out, the German command would have considered his action a major crime, though perhaps not one worthy of a death sentence. He might have been sent off to a labor camp, certainly jailed—no one left to care for his children— and perhaps his children sent away with him.

But I wasn't sure of this explanation; I didn't know enough yet. Mirele Rein had been a Jewish member of the Communist youth. My grandfather hated the Communists/Jews. My grandfather was cunning when he had to be, an operator, a survivor. Wasn't he? The possibility of choice dogged me—did he weigh the risk to his own life and the lives of his children if he offered help? Did he judge Mirele Rein as one who belonged in the pit at Poligon? I didn't know.

IN THE PREFACE to his classic text on the investigation of unsolved homicides, Richard Walton, speaking of victims and witnesses, observes, "I didn't need clinical research and 'data' to tell me that the pain and the hurt are just below the surface. It always has been and always will be." He talks about the need to be able to *feel* something of the long-ago, the dimension, the threads, the gradations, the house in a space of green or snow where no house stands. The investigation of the past, the accumulation of some slight understanding of the intersection of trauma and memory, was not some intellectual pursuit for me. As time went on and my grandfather became more knowable—the man he was before I was, before immigration—the nature of individual testimonies, the verifiability of sources, became more complicated and more crucial.

What had happened at the Poligon was not a mystery, but what my grandfather had or hadn't done during the planning, the implementation, and the aftermath of that massacre was. If I didn't unravel it, it would unravel me. That's the thing about looking back, opening the door, asking the question: the past asks its own questions of you, asks and doesn't stop. The door—well, there isn't one anymore. It's off the hinges. Wherever you are in space and time, you've crossed a threshold, and unless you will your ignorance to overtake you again, you go where the questions take you.

"I WANT YOU to read this book," my father said to me a little over a year before he died. He stood in the Vineyard living room, thin but not yet too thin, his complexion chalky with what after his diagnosis I came to think of as the color of cancer, and held a paperback out to me: *The History of the Jews* by the Gentile British writer Paul Johnson. "Marvelous, the way he writes about the tenacity and brilliance of the Jews—"

My father must have seen something in my face.

"They're your people, you know," he said.

I raised my eyebrows, tipped my head toward the kitchen, where my mother was at the table reading, or by the stove cutting up potatoes for chowder.

"Half your people," he amended, smiling just a little.

"I don't have time," I said.

"Well, think about it anyway," he said, quietly.

If he was finally going to pass on something of Judaism to me, I wanted it to be by a Jew: an English translation of the Steinsaltz Talmud with a Vilna page; Tanakh, the Jewish Bible; *My Mother's Sabbath Days*, by Chaim Grade. The real thing. (There is no snob as great as an ignorant snob.) I said I might read the offered book down the road, and that seemed to satisfy him, for the moment. He shook out the folds of his newspaper, and I, in my busyness, took off—a very important walk on the beach with the dogs, or to the ferry, then the bus and the train back to New York, where, along with multiple student loans, a fund established by my father's Uncle Bernie, son of Wolf Treegoob, had helped pay for my graduate education. In what he titled a "Biographical Sketch," my great-uncle Bernie explained why he had made such provisions for his grandnieces and nephews: "Father, to me, has always been the greatest living personality of his day and it is to perpetuate the memory of this great man." Wolf Treegoob, who brought his watch parts to the dinner table and worked while he ate, would have been "the greatest engineer" of his day if he had gone to college. His son Bernie, who made big money selling Jeeps, wrote that with an education, he himself would have "gone through life with a clearer vision."

Bernard (Bernie) Treegoob, my father's uncle

And my own father, with his Ph.D., did what the next generation is supposed to do: went farther, accomplished, at least in terms of education, more. I'm not so sure, though, about clarity of vision. During the same war my mother survived, my color-blind father landed a desk job in Italy at a U.S. base that housed and trained army dogs to rout out bomb caches, alert sleeping soldiers, parachute under fire with their human partners. His service never brought him near the German front. Like his mother, he rarely spoke directly about the Holocaust. *If he'd asked more questions . . .* I thought at my hotel in East Jerusalem, wrapping a scarf over my scar by the side of the pool because strong sun would darken the still-jagged line, keep it from fading.

At a certain point my mother will tell me she's glad her younger brother is dead, because of what I'm dredging up. But she won't mention my father. *If he'd asked more questions* . . . I couldn't even really imagine him asking. My mother's early losses took precedence over any other legacy from the past of our immediate family—until the end of my father's life, until the offering of the thick paperback.

In israel, that visit, I was "too busy" to go to the forest named for my great-uncle Bernie's brother Joseph Treegoob. My one day in the old city with Nadav was all I saw of the country other than the roads to Tel Aviv and its suburbs. I worked in the archives at Yad Vashem and then, with Irit Pazner Garshowitz, who fit me in around her schedule with the *New York Times* bureau in Jerusalem, drove out to Ramat Gan and sat down for hours with Lili Holzman, her story as long as the war she survived, so long that I heard only half of it on that day, the rest on a return trip.

Lili began by elaborating the way she was "spoiled" as a girl. Listed in the Polish business directory circa 1929 that includes Święciany, written in Polish and French, is Lili Holzman's maternal grandfather's felt-and-fabric business: "J. Swirski (wojloki/feutre vegetal)" on Lyntupska Street. The business was in the basement of the large stone house where the best fabric was saved for the beloved granddaughter, Léye (Leah) Swirski, as Lili was known then. Lili and her mother, Rakhel, would take the best fabrics to the best dressmaker, Leah Murashky, on Szkolna Street, "tailleurs p. dames," where in the front room mother and daughter could look through magazines with the latest fashions, choose what was coveted, beautiful. Lili, with the steel eyes and small, warm smile and then a purposeful embrace, hello or good-bye: what it means to leave and what it means to come back never trivial for her.

From left to right: Lili's mother Rakhel; younger sister, Khanale; their father, Khaim; and Lili, in one of Murashky's dresses

So, THE SPOILED girl, and her grandfather's large stone house on the corner of the market square in Święciany, her father Khaim from Świr, in Belorussia, twenty-four miles from Święciany, her mother from Russia. Her mother studied dentistry in Warsaw. When she married, her husband gave up his big beer and alcohol business (a business often taken on by Jewish entrepreneurs, who were blamed, at various periods in history, for encouraging drunkenness among the non-Jewish population) and went to Berlin to learn dental prosthetics.

Lili grew up in the long family home at 11 Piłsudski Street. A house with two clinics, one for her father and one for her mother's work, two waiting rooms, and a lab her father built from scratch. He wasn't educated, as Lili's mother was, but he was smart, like Wolf Treegoob. He could make things, take them apart.

Young people would come to the dental clinic waiting rooms just to sit, because of the lovely mahogany furniture—a place to gather after school, a place to come in from the heat or the rain. Lili's mother took care of everyone's teeth; farmers, Jews, Gentiles, those who could pay and those who could only pay a little. (In Święciany, Teresa—gardener extraordinaire and retired messenger for the postal service—will remember going to a woman dentist, how the daughter sometimes was there, mentions it in a stream of talk in the van with Petras, and for a moment the present rolls back. Was it Lili's mother? Was it Lili? As it happens, two female dentists worked in Švenčionys before the German occupation, so no way to tell—still, like a pop-up card children love, the flat, lost past gains dimension for a second, then vanishes.)

THERE WAS A younger sister, Khanale, born seven years after Lili. There was help for the working mother and father. Anja, a woman from one of the farms outside of town, walked barefoot from their house to the Catholic church each Sunday, carrying her shoes in her hand to spare them from the dust, from wear. Lili had some colored paper, and before the walk to church, Anja would wet it and rub it on her cheeks to give herself some color. She was paid roughly twenty zlotys a month. Nothing now, but a good wage then, for a woman from a farm without schooling who helped run the busy home along with a gardener.

They shared a courtyard with another well-off Jewish family, all of whom were arrested and sent to Siberia during the first Soviet purge in Lithuania in 1940.

"A terrible tragedy," Lili says. "But they survived it."

She tells this small side story of the neighbors with something that stops just short of irony. They were dragged off without knowing that their Soviet captors were, in effect, saving their lives. Something else was coming to that part of the world, something after the Soviets, after more snow, after the hidden expanse of leaves and green sorrel picked young for the spring soup, something of a scope neither the neighbors whom the Soviets rounded up, nor Lili's family, could yet contemplate.

Light makes a thick, solid line across the round table where we sit. The mic of the video recorder picks up separate warbles from outside, small birds in the shade beside her walkway outdoors.

"Once I had season tickets to the Philharmonic in Tel Aviv. At intermission I stood up and looked around. I knew the auditorium held three thousand people, and it was full that night, completely. Three thousand—and I thought to myself, this is exactly the number of Jews from Svintsyan who were killed. Half the town."

But not the neighbors who shared the courtyard.

Her father Khaim, suffering from a stomach ailment, couldn't get through the sealed borders during the Soviet occupation to reach a bigger, better hospital. During surgery in Svintsyan, he died. By the time of the German occupation, her grandfather had died as well.

So on the twenty-seventh of September, it is Lili's mother and grandmother (also named Leah/Lili), and Khanale, who see, from the windows of the smaller house they have rented (the large house with the two clinics requisitioned for someone in the German command or some high-ranking Lithuanian working for the Germans), carts that pull up beside every house where a Jew is living.

"This proves it was the Lithuanians. The Germans were new. They wouldn't have known where the Jewish people lived," Lili said.

"Was there a list?" I ask, because in that moment I don't know what to say.

"There didn't need to be a list. Maybe there was, maybe there wasn't." Lili is politely exasperated with my question; it's of so little consequence.

She is not talking about names on paper but about the farm horses and the pregnant women and the bundles she and her sister and her mother and her grandmother prepared; food, clothing (all those dresses, the luxury of choosing from the magazines, the red paper, her father's laboratory that was part of him, proof of him in the other, impossibly huge bundle of the irretrievable, the stolen life). The wagon pulls up to their door. Lili is fourteen and a half. Her grandmother and seven-year-old Khanale go into the wagon bed. Lili and her mother walk. First they go to the field right outside town. It's still early in the day, and it takes a long time for the carts and the wagons to go back and forth, for families and men on their own and widowed women with in-laws and the sick and the community leaders and the very old to all reach the same place. Nothing to drink. A little food from the bundle. Infants wailing. Speculation. *They're taking us to work somewhere. They're taking us away so they can rob our houses, and then they'll bring us back.*

The Lithuanians wore some kind of uniform, Lili remembers. She thinks it was green. The Poles who came out to the street to watch, well, some were smiling, some not smiling, just looking. Of course I think of Teresa and her mother, Salomeja, who did washing for Jewish families, when Lili says this. Of my great-grandmother Barbara, of my mother that day—where were they? Of Senelis. I imagine him in a uniform indistinguishable from the other Lithuanians in uniform. He's not on the list of those "employed" for duty at Poligon (I had received a copy of a pay roster for Poligon in the old-fashioned envelope from the Lithuanian Special Archives, months earlier). The police station is perhaps a kilometer away from the field. It's hard work to move half a town in a day. If he's not playing cards, not at the station, not at home, where is he? This is why a list of the Jews to be taken is important to me. If there is a list, someone had to make it, consult it.

At dusk the panicked, thirsty group is commanded to move. Those who can't walk the distance are put back in the wagons.

"Mergaitė," one of the Lithuanians moving the group forward yells at Lili. He says it again. She imitates him for Irit and me, makes her voice gruff.

On the crowded road, she's wearing a woolen muff with a fur lining. It matches her coat, a muff with a zipper in it and a pocket that can hold a key or a bit of change.

"Girl, throw it to me, you won't use it again in your life."

She refuses, but in the shuffle of the crowd, the progress of night—just after the Lithuanian yells at her—comes a turning point, her consciousness shifts and suddenly, without any doubt, she understands that the rumors flowing among those trudging ahead and those walking behind are all false. They aren't being marched away to work. They won't return from wherever they're going.

When the crowd of thousands finally nears the turnoff to Nei-Svintsyan (Švenčionėliai) proper, where the train station is (perhaps they're going to be loaded on to trains), the police and Lithuanians in uniforms steer the long, weary group off the road instead, into the forest.

Almost immediately, in the distance, huge bonfires appear, and then a sound, like animals—not singing. "Shouting. Horrible. They were drunk, they had liquor there. My little sister was smart, she said to us, 'You and Mamen will just be killed, you'll be shot, but me—I'll be thrown into the fire.' "

CHAPTER 22

POLIGON

June 14: the air is warm, thick, perfect mosquito weather. Rain clouds billow up behind us as we drive toward Švenčionéliai. Giedrė is quiet. Shy, I think at first; then, not shy—something else. She brought her blue umbrella, just in case. In some weird disconnect, I flash on Mary Poppins flying down with her big open umbrella, about to set the Banks family straight. The Poligon signage to the right of the dirt road said, "I masinių žudynių vieta"—"To the place of mass murder." Ahead of us thin, scrawny pines cluster; farther in, alders rise, sweet briar already in bloom. I had come here a week earlier with my fixer Rose, but we did not walk beyond the memorial for those who lost their lives at Poligon.

There are so many places of mass murder in Lithuania—perhaps too many to allow for specificity on a wooden sign. In Stalag 343, the Soviet POW camp in Alytus where Zinaida was interned during the war, mass death from starvation and exposure was a purposeful tactic; no one wanted the captive Russians or Red Army soldiers, not even their own leaders strategizing far behind the front lines, not the Germans. Most soldiers were too weak for transport to work camps closer to the front; none were worth food. The stalags were scattered throughout Lithuania, some close to the ghettos, some farther away (but not too much farther, in a country the size of New Jersey).

But of course the vagueness of the sign is also another desecration, like the pile of human excrement in a coil at the back of the overgrown Jewish cemetery in Švenčionys. Did I mention this to Giedrė? I don't remember. I was still sick from the bout of food poisoning. I almost called her to cancel. Instead I clutch my bottle of a Lithuanian version of Gatorade. When the lush green of late spring starts to swim in front of me, I take a big swig, and the path and tree line come back into focus.

The left-hand turn we'd made off the paved road was not the ingress where Lili Holzman's family and Chaya Porus's family and Mirele Rein had been taken. Petras drives Giedrė and me, following forks in the bumpy dirt road on the way to the Poligon memorial identified by white markers paid for by someone from Britain, knocked down from time to time—kids, maybe. These are woods after all, almost a park, the long way to the Zeimena River. Not much to do in this part of the country. Not much left to knock down, tear apart, shit on.

Petras stops the van by the memorial in front of the long hillock in the earth in the shape of an L, partially obscured by spring brush. Would a large group destined for execution have been brought this way, the unwieldy path, the risk of mass panic at the site of stakes marking off the length to be dug out? Better to go another way, gather the eight thousand or so in sheds, in an expanse where mines were set around the perimeters. It's not the biggest killing site in Lithuania, nor the smallest. It's a void. A black hole. Incomparable. It is, itself.

Giedrė is hardier than I am at the moment. Petras stays back with his van. I want to stay back there too. Later, I would take pictures of the pit from every angle. Later still, I would light another yahrzeit candle at the memorial.

"You can feel the souls," Giedrė says.

No, you can't feel the souls, I think but don't say, only spiritless heavy air.

We've just climbed a little bit of hill. The sparse forest starts to close in. A sweet smell clings to the air—like the pepper bush from my childhood, but not that. Honeysuckle.

A gnat flies into my eye; just hatched, delirious with new life. My heart bangs against my chest. I swallow the lime-colored drink the texture of corn syrup, ask Giedrė to slow down.

The path turns into a wider road, the dirt loamy. Huge tire tracks have chewed up a parallel wedge of ground.

"They aren't supposed to do this." Giedrė stops. "These are new," she says of the wide welts in the dirt. Her voice is high and soft, a bit tremulous. This wouldn't be happening, this trespass, if Blumke Katz were still alive.

At the museum the week before, when she spoke of their walks, she mentioned that she and Blumke had found a few remnants of the barracks—the stables and long sheds where the thousands were shoved, where no private human endeavor was possible, where the kidnapped prayed and clasped hands and waited. Where some went mad and others prevailed and a woman leaked her afterbirth into the shadow beneath her. Through an opening in one of the barracks, during one of the days of their imprisonment, a Lithuanian guard, for fun, threw a grenade.

The walk is roughly a mile. We are trying to find a trace of the lost archaeology of the barracks, blown up to destroy evidence. I don't think of the man who pulled the pin from the grenade and lobbed it inside at the packed, despairing target. I think of myself, think I might vomit again. The sun drifts in and out. It's hot. If not for Giedrė's long stride, always a bit ahead of mine, I'd stop. Pride keeps me from turning around. Not reverence for the dead. In ten minutes, I'll run out of the corn-syrup drink, and then the dizziness will return, and I'll fall down. It occurs to me that I'm in exactly the right shape to take this road. That anyone who walks it should feel like vomiting. Anyone who passes the long, thin shadows of trees, the sky announcing the entrance of summer, should feel the earth spin and not be able to stop it.

Then—woods break into a clearing. Giedrė points to a packed-down road on the right—wide, usable.

"I think they were brought in that way," she says.

The road is sandy, stretches farther than I can see. One road? For eight thousand people? There must have been more than one. To my left, more woods, but it's new growth, the birch and willow of today that wouldn't have been an obstacle then. So maybe in that direction a second route was improvised—for captives who lived farther northwest. Perhaps a few charges were set off to break up the ground; perhaps brush was burned away.

It is all so speculative, like looking earlier, near the memorial and the long tomb that breaches it, in a wide angle across the visible land, and trying to imagine where Mirele Rein hid during the shooting.

I cross over the road to brush: sedge, willow saplings, a few large rocks. Suddenly my left foot sinks into a hole. I call out to Giedrė, and together we push away brambles and make out, underneath, a small corner of the foundation of a building, a structure. I want there to be a fence around it. I want it to be marked.

Giedrė points ahead. I'm hot and cold, looking down.

"See," she prods.

Beyond the declension in the earth—water suddenly, the Zeimena River, where salmon spawn and sand from the basin washes up on the road. To our left, at a clearing where someone had flattened the beer cans they flicked open, the remnant of a small fire blackens the ground. Only sedge stands between us and the lake the river makes here. We could roll up our pants legs and wade in. In the distance ducks troll their placid progress across the mirror; a breeze ripples every now and then when the sun shifts to clouds.

I'm thirsty. I look back at the brush, where the remains of a building are hidden. "The water was so close, but we couldn't get to it." Had Lili Holzman said it? Chaya? I'd imagined the river farther away, but six or seven long strides and I touch it, could splash water on my face, fill the empty bottle of Gatorade. Proximity. It drops me through time. I forget the honeysuckle, the matches, and yahrzeit candle back in the van where Petras waits.

CHAYA. I'M AT her table again with petits fours and rugelach and the awareness that even though the radio is on, I don't hear it anymore. Her father was sick, thirsty. Everyone was thirsty. Lili Holzman. Chaya's youngest brother. The teenagers and the grandmothers. Mirele Rein's family who are named without enumeration, just "the Reins" in the shtetl Ceikiniai's necrology (list of the dead), the shtetl spelled *Tzeikinia* in Boyarin's translation of Koniuchowsky's interviews. The family of Solom Aron was thirsty, Aron who will come a long way back from the Japanese front and use a wooden crate to carry the remains of everyone he loved who exist somewhere in a pile of femurs, articular bones, and mandibles of all sizes.

GIEDRĖ LOOKS DISCONSOLATELY at the beer cans, then at the water. I hadn't known it was possible to look at a river and at the same time be in the Bronx, be sitting at the long table cluttered, aside from our dishes, with the business of Chaya's life, the papers she'd brought out for me, the Švenčionys Yitzkor book that I had, for so long, avoided looking at online.

* * *

"POLIGONY?" CHAYA TURNED her face into a question. "Nobody knows what does it mean. Polish army kept their horses there. A camp? Barracks?" She remembered for me; across her face, incredulity first, then a freeze frame of panic, confusion. Followed very quickly by steadiness, resolve.

"My mother never lost herself. She was oriented. She packed for every child—a towel, soap, candle, food."

She pronounced *oriented* with the accent on the third syllable: ori*en*ted. A small bit of music that will stay with me always, will, whenever her version of the word comes to me, make me think of her mother folding the towels, calculating quickly, pushing away fear, answering the questions of her youngest children. Modeling, for all of them, a resolute sturdiness.

Chaya told me her mother was her best friend, that so many of the girls Chaya knew would come around to talk with her, be in her company. Ori*en*ted.

I asked her if she remembers Germans.

"For every one German, ten Lithuanians," she answered.

I know that part of her memory is more of a scrim, knew that the ratio of Lithuanians to Germans was actually much wider, maybe a hundred Lithuanians to four Germans. My *maybe* is not exact, so not reliable either. I made a note to myself to find a more reliable number and to look within it, around it, through it—and try to find my grandfather.

We both had stopped eating the sweets on the table. A sip of coffee. Chaya paused, went on.

"You cannot imagine. First of all, they were drunk. Didn't care. If someone couldn't go so fast, they were shot on the way."

Shot on the road I'd just swept past; Petras pointing out a thicket on top of a post—the good-luck stork nest. Giedrė quiet. Not really comfortable, but not unkind. Called to duty. Called to honor the memory of her friend Blumke.

Chaya was seventeen. Her sister Rochl (Rachel) was a nurse, trained in gynecology. Their father, well, he understood violins and thread and pages and gold lettering. (Before the Germans came in, the Russian in charge of deportations had put the whole Porus family on the list for the Gulag. And so Chaya's father made a stunning album—the Russian officer's name in gold—and with that gift, during that terror, a reprieve.)

"We saw a big fire—pieces of wood being thrown, but it looked like they were throwing live people then—children. When you came nearer—a bunch of"—she struggled to find a word that was strong enough—"hooligans."

A word for a woman with a keen sense of propriety, a word to lay shame on the men around the fire. Of course I knew what it meant, but it's a word from the days of my father's childhood and my grandmother's life. It has less damning connotation in my here and now: the boys who toilet-paper trees on Halloween, who break into the girls' locker room and spray shaving cream on benches and mirrors, who wouldn't know what a take-down lever on a Walther pistol is. I looked up Chaya's word when I got home from our meeting in *Merriam-Webster's*—"Shouldn't you hooligans be in school instead of threatening old ladies?"

Chaya had said it with force, but I thought *motherfuckers*. I thought of the smoke and the drink, the sparks in the dark and the dangerous escalating fraternity of men inventing strange screeching songs. If there were those they meant to avenge, lovers, family members—entombed or pistol-whipped or violated by the Red Army—they've forgotten them, forgotten what their pay will be, drunk enough to work without pay. One of the hooligans tries to light a dead cigarette in the massive fire and burns his hand. Another man feels like king of the land, notices a younger punk watching him, maybe imitating his pratfall or swagger. Or maybe the punk thinks of what a pig the man as old as his father is, how, once the action starts—a stray shot—it could be possible, or not.

What was my grandfather thinking?

("Yes," my mother told me, in a random moment of recollection. "I remember he said that about the Jews. That they were Communists.")

On one of the early nights in the packed barracks, a guard yells into the crowd for a nurse. Chaya's sister Rochl steps forward. She's anxious to help a woman somewhere out there who is biting on a stick to keep from screaming or curled in a heavy ball on cold ground. So she follows the voice of the guard, and they lose her to the night. A few moments later a shot rings out.

At that instant, the dark hair of Chaya's father turns gray. Strand by strand, in the choke, the press, as the whole family strains to instantly recall the sound of the gunshot: Was it close, was it far, how close, how far? Did anyone hear a cry afterward? Was it *her* cry—the young woman who is part of them?

In the morning Rochl comes back. In the morning Mr. Porus's hair is silver, all the fine dark gone. His daughter has delivered a baby. Hope shivers among them: if the guards allow a baby to be born, maybe we are meant to live, to work somewhere.

When the call comes for the barracks to empty, Chaya's mother takes the pot she packed in her bundle, and outside they collect small rocks for a meager fire. A little water is given; maybe there are buckets the guards have put down among the mass of dazed children and grown-ups trying to locate their family recognizing neighbors, sisters. Water is warmed for the babies. Potatoes are baked in the coals, split into pieces handed around as Chaya's mother's pot is passed from person to family to another group, and suddenly becomes an anchor, a part of the life they just left, a vital possession, a gift.

Wertvolle Juden ("useful Jews," a term invented long before the Reich claimed it) who avoided transport to Poligon bargain and bribe the authorities, and a few days later bring a cart of bread and more potatoes from the ghetto in Švenčionys to Poligon. A slice of bread. More chunk of potato. More water warmed in the pot. More hope. But it's a wild hope. It's a hope that smells of finality. A hope that has to hold up in the land-mined perimeter, in the splattered brains of the old woman who just had to get to the water, the cries of the girls who are pulled out and raped in the night.

Before me, Chaya mimes a spit on her floor to the side of the table.

"Dogs," her sister Rochl called their captors.

Seven miles give or take south, back in Švenčionys, back among kitchen tables and phone books and the water pump in the square and the faucet in my grandfather's house, the man who runs the largest felt boot concession in town, a man who is enamored of one of Chaya's sisters, has gone to the authorities (my grandfather, a German?) and declared that the Porus family, who have never worked in a felt factory in all of their combined lives, are his most valuable workers. To prove his point, he has had to regrettably stop production. He has no choice; it's a pity, every day the factory is still, the goods aren't shipped, the money doesn't come in—money that has to feed the machine of war now as well as the factory manager.

So the Porus family is to be released from Poligony. But first, they are searched. A call had gone out for a "contribution"—the gold of the Jews, the money of the Jews, the jewels—all of it had to be thrown into buckets. The Poruses are to be let go, but they must go without their wealth, their wedding rings, the rubles packed inside a double layer of Mr. Porus's shirting.

"Inside the barrack you could see coins and rings glittering in the dirt, thrown there by the people who would rather lose what they had that way than give it away."

Guards command the women and girls to strip. In the open air, Rochl, Chaya's older sister, and Chaya and her mother are naked. Their clothing is shaken out. Every bit of cloth that was on their bodies is touched. Their bodies are handled and searched.

"Even our vaginas," Chaya punctuated with a look that could wither an army.

Her naked sister spat, said, "I feel no shame, not in front of them—they're not even human."

And so the women of the family remain intact. The women turn shame back on the men who touched them, watched them, laughed at them, men amazed at the turn of events that make it possible to order a woman to strip and bend over. The clothes go back on. Chaya's father is perhaps suddenly stronger, a neurological switch thrown inside him—fear and escape.

I TURN AWAY from the water. At the same moment, Giedrė and I start walking back the way we came. We are quiet. The walk back seems so much faster. Where the hulk of earth begins, there is a large old-growth tree. A maple, I think, because of the grooved bark, except for a square indentation cut and made smooth, the bark peeled away to the living tissue of the tree. There, a kind of bull's-eye, a hard, fast surface just right for killing infants and small children by swinging them by their ankles or hips, saving bullet after bullet, as the soft fontanels and craniums shattered against the weapon the tree became.

"Now we have taken the last path of the victims, the last they saw in their lives," Giedrė says.

Cloud cover steals the light. In the van she quietly asks us to drop her outside of town. "No, no—don't take me to my house, I prefer to walk."

Only when she looks back as I call good-bye again through the open window of the van I see that she's crying. Almost immediately, a hard rain begins. Color catches my eye; stuffed in the corner on the other side of the seat is Giedrė's blue umbrella. But she's turned down a street. She's gone.

DURING OUR MEETING, Chaya had raised herself taller in her chair, leaned slightly forward, as if she might quickly stand, as if she was on the road heading away from Poligony again. "We ran like a storm," she said.

A side view of Poligon pit mound (left), and the Killing Tree (right)

CHAPTER 23

DAY OF MOURNING AND HOPE

JUNE 14, 2012

We outdrive the rain on our way back to Vilnius. I want to go back to the hotel and sleep. Vilnius is sunny—it's only late morning when we pull up to a corner where Viktorija is waiting—but it feels like a day has passed, a week. Viktorija's energy highlights my fatigue. She's translating for me; today Rose is off somewhere. Viktorija with her bright blue sweater and glasses and braces; she asks me how the walk with Giedrė went.

"Fine," I say, the word flat and blank.

Petras stops by a café so I can pick up a coffee. My husband is at the hotel, sick now also. Tomorrow we fly to Frankfurt, then home. I ask Petras to call Rose about Giedrė's blue umbrella. We have to get it back to her. It's a trick I've learned on this first trip; worry about something small and material. Wrap your sadness around it, your confusion, your rage. Focus on the coffee cup that's too hot. The impeccable makeup job on the face of a woman with long ash-blond hair and very white skin, clicking her heels past you in front of the coffee place.

Rose has arranged for me to get access to Lukiškės prison, where my grandfather spent ten days in October 1943. According to my mother and her sister, he was arrested for releasing prisoners. Many. Eighty perhaps. A hundred. He'd "had enough of it." Of what? As it happened, in fall of '43, when he was arrested, the Germans, increasingly short on labor, decided to conscript Lithuanians into labor camps and factories. I suspect, if the family story has merit, that it was a group of Lithuanians, rounded up in a sweep that filled the prison yard in Švenčionys, that Senelis "let go." But his reinstatement to the security police after his brief prison term, and the absence of any mention of his derring-do in Švenčionys in the considerable amount of German correspondence that mentions him after his time in Lukiškės, calls that part of my family narrative into question.

He told my mother, her sister, and I suppose his son that while he was incarcerated, a vision of the Virgin Mary came to him and let him know he would be freed. (Bribery for minor offenses was particularly effective, though I have no information from any quarter indicating the brevity of Senelis's prison time was a favor given for a favor received.)

Before prison, back in Švenčionys, he walked the children out of town to a friend's house, then left for Kaunas. It's quite possible that a connection with other Saugumas officials in Kaunas helped, for a short time, to keep the Gestapo off his back. He contrived to be arrested in a Kaunas newspaper office. He left his pistol in his jacket pocket and draped the jacket casually on the back of a chair when he arrived at the office, and made sure he wasn't in that room when the German police came and got him. How smart to be arrested at a newspaper office. Even with all the silence and propaganda and censorship that dogged each press outlet in the country (and there weren't many during the war), he was in a public place, around people who would take note of what was happening to him. According to my mother, he was afraid to be arrested in Švenčionys, where the Gestapo could just "shoot you." That kill first/ask later license is something I suppose he would know more than a little about, after almost three years as chief of security police there.

Even with his savvy, swiftly made plan, when he was put in the back of a car and driven on the street that led to the Ninth Fort, he thought he was done for. By the time the war is over, more than forty thousand people—infants and octogenarians; Soviet POWs, German Jews, Lithuanian Bundists, Zionists, and secular Jews; thieves and scholars; Poles and Lithuanian Communists; rabbis and kindergarten teachers—will have been shot at the Ninth Fort or one of the other forts that flank Kaunas.

I've wondered how my grandfather heard of the first mass shootings in Kaunas throughout October 1941. Over a dinner with Gestapo up from Vilnius?

Or perhaps from a friend, also police, but working somewhere else, visiting? From Jonas Maciulevičius, his boss, who perhaps crosses the hallway to sit on the edge of my grandfather's desk and have a chat?

Litvaks (Lithuanian Jews) killed in October 1941. On October 29, almost 4,500 of them were children. German Jews sent by train to Kaunas to their death at the Ninth Fort in November. SS-Rottenführer (section head) Helmut Rauca, a name my grandfather would have known, decided during the selection on October 29, 1941, who would live and who would die, his mouth full of a sandwich, his fingers wedged tightly into his gloves. He pointed one way, then the other. (Some months down the road, I'll find a long complaint against Senelis in the Lithuanian Central State Archives which will contain—among the scribbled names of several SS acknowledging they've received and read it—Rauca's sign-off, the dark *R* heavy on the ink from a pen held in the hand of the man who reigned death upon the Kovno ghetto.)

But the car my grandfather was in, a black Opel, glided past Žemaičių Street, took another road; even then the Virgin Mary must have been beside Senelis. Who knew what awaited him at Lukiškės, but at least he'd left that zone of horror, where prisoners scratched last messages into the cement walls—*On this day so many were shot*, a name, an outline of a face. It was 1943. Unlike the region around Poligon, where no large group was left to mow down, there were still many who would lose their lives in Kaunas at the fort, but not Senelis, not on that day. He was taken to Vilnius and remanded into Lukiškės on October 11 with 152 other people.

THE DAY HAS opened up: blue sky, a small cool wind in the shade of the trees outside the entrance to the KGB Museum. We park there because some event is going on along the green outside. Folding chairs are set up. We're early for it. A group of junior-high-schoolers and a woman in a white suit jacket clucking over them mill about as the same piece of music, valiant, melancholy, plays and stops and plays again. Petras sits in the van with the door open, but curiosity gets the better of Viktorija and me. We head over to the folding chairs and sit as a small crowd gathers. The schoolkids are like all schoolkids; they half ignore the woman who directs them this way and that across the grass, but when she claps her hands, they shake off their disregard; the thin boy with the striped shirt, the girl in black flats with a little purse slung over her shoulder, a few boys a head taller than the others.

It feels good to sit in the shade. White clouds bluster overhead. Press people are setting up behind us; a staging area for a television feed, cameras pulled out and lenses adjusted. Near the van where Petras waits, a station wagon pulls up. A woman with white hair carefully gets out of the back seat in a long skirt and little apron—traditional dress. Another woman, wide-hipped and also elderly, cradles a large bouquet of flowers as she heads for the green. The music starts again, and this time the marching children clutch suitcases of different sizes: old leather valises, cheap cardboard boxes; PETRAS, one reads. I take a photo of it for our Petras. The music gives way to the *chug, chug* and whistle of a train; the kids pick up their suitcases and march in a diagonal across the green, wave when the melancholy music again drowns out the train.

Then it hits me— June 14. Babita, the day of one of the huge Soviet deportations before the Germans came in, memorialized as "The Day of Mourning and Hope." The slightly embarrassed adolescents, a little bored with all the walking back and forth, smiling or practicing despair or talking among themselves as they march to the train whistle, are all so unlike my Babita as she's been described to me on that day in 1941, that the reenactment seems utterly dissociated. I wonder what the kids thought as they held their empty suitcases, moved through the grass with their crushes and mothers and fathers and summer jobs and homework over (thank god!) and the awareness of cameras that will shortly focus on their brief journey.

An honor guard of young Lithuanian soldiers strutted into view: white gloves, caps, too young—like soldiers everywhere—to be in the military. June 14. The schoolkids walk away and stand in the sun and turn and wave, and then they come back. A trim woman with gray hair moves next to me. I offer her my chair, but she won't take it. A man and a woman with a video camera sit behind us and eat ice cream that melts down their hands. It isn't a large crowd, but still too much noise for me. The train whistle keeps blasting. The waving. The music. Poligon, the Ninth Fort, my stern Babita combing the hair of her beautiful daughters, Ramutes, the youngest, on her lap. All too much.

It's time to go to prison. I take video of one more tramp across the lawn, and then we get in the van with Petras and go.

CHAPTER 24

ARTŪRAS KARALIS

I check in on my husband by phone. He feels better, wants us to stop by the hotel and pick him up. I shift my worry from the blue umbrella to him; he'd had his own surgery before our trip. While he woke up from the thick dream of anesthesia, one of his doctors took me aside in the hallway and listed the symptoms that would make it crucial he go immediately on antibiotics. He had the symptoms. The night before, in the Ramada Vilnius, we fought about it. I have amoxicillin in my suitcase; since my heart surgery, I always carry it when I travel.

While the endless loop of music by Sting played in the small courtyard out our window, I yelled at him to take the antibiotic, wore him down until he swallowed it with so little water I couldn't believe he hadn't choked on the capsule. I was thinking of Chaya's mother's pot when I yelled, of the candle stub, the scratches in a cement wall at the Ninth Fort, of Yitzhak Arad, who had left Švenčionys before the Poligon roundup, without his sister. How they had found each other in Głębokie in Belorussia. I was thinking of how stupid it is to refuse the luxury of help when it's right there, at hand. I kept at him even after he took the amoxicillin. But later, when we get out of the van in front of Lukiškės Prison and he asks me about the walk with Giedrė, I lean into his left shoulder and close my eyes. He puts his hand on the back of my head, and for a second, I rest.

At an earlier time in my life, I taught at a maximum security prison for women. Now I buzz the metal door to the ubiquitous double-glass checkpoint inside, oddly modern for a huge yellowish brick fortress with a Russian Orthodox church rising beyond the walls and coils of barbed wire—stained, leaded-glass windows and five domes. In a cramped entryway of buzzers and a guard booth that smells like a prison—strong floor cleaner, a way station, a holding pen—Viktorijia translates for me: the appointment time, the prison tour. The correction officer on duty checks a sheet of paper. I expect him to say there's no appointment, but he confirms it.

He tips his head in the direction of the door we just entered. "Wait outside, please, someone will be with you shortly."

Already there's a traffic jam. Two guards are coming on duty, one jocular and beefy, the other a bit sallow—both young, both preparing their faces for inside.

Outside, the sun cranks up. The morning's rain and flutter of humid wind from the river are a memory. Without shade, my husband starts to wilt, retreats back to the van and folds his long frame into the back seat. Viktorijia and I stand where women stood when their Jewish sons and husbands were being picked up in droves at the start of the German occupation and taken first to Lukiškės and then on to Ponary (Ponary of the buried lemonade bottles, the round tombs in the earth). Here the women cried out for them, tried to throw their voices over the walls, bundles of food, their love. When the German and Lithuanian collaborators who administered the prison vanished, the Soviets returned with new local lackeys and thousands of scores to settle.

The large electronic metal gateway, a kind of iron curtain that opens for vehicles and certain workers, gives way every ten minutes or so after the blast of a loud alarm. A fleet of prison buses go in, windowless in back so there's no way to see if they are empty or ferrying in arrests from outlying jails. A man passes through the open gate with a shirt and a paper bag; he's young. He doesn't look like an employee. He stops for a minute, looks at the lineup of parked cars across the street, as if hoping for a ride, someone he knows. There's no one. He lights a cigarette, studies Viktorija and me without much interest; we're just two women waiting at the place women wait. He lingers a little longer then lopes slowly down the sidewalk, looking back over his shoulder.

In the drill of the late afternoon sun, Viktorija and I are both sweating. She's taken off her blue sweater. "Two o'clock," Rose had said. "Don't be late." At two thirty we go in the small entryway again. The guard on watch is annoyed. He's held up; a meeting, we're told. I don't know who *he* is, suspect he's a corrections officer who doubles as a liaison with the outside, or someone from the public relations office, if they have one. In the prison where I taught, the COs were the ones who really ran prison life—doled out brutality, sucked up bribes, fought the good fight with press conferences when the suicide rate spiked. The warden, a woman whose portrait graced the lobby where the bondsman's desk waited, kept the same lax oversight after the multiple suicides, the same soul-killing processes and procedures.

I never met her, never even glimpsed her outside of the picture frame in which her hair was a frozen golden helmet around her face, so after an hour of waiting, I'm surprised when the director of Lukiškės emerges from the doorway and apologizes—*the meeting*—brisk but not unfriendly.

He studies us for a second: Viktorija with her braces, the green tint to my skin, the sweat matted into my hair, which I've pulled up and away from my face—thick hair, like my grandmother Rachel's, like a wool cap in summer.

"Artūras Karalis," he introduces himself. (In English, King Arthur.)

He's in his forties, sturdy, graying. There's a vague resemblance to my grandfather in a certain photo, when he was about the same age. Handsome, his face not undone yet.

Through Viktorija I explain that my grandfather was incarcerated here during the war. I'm writing a book about his life during wartime and want to see what the inside of the prison might have looked like to him in October 1943, behind the high barricade of brick. (Even as I say it, I feel slightly ridiculous; what I really want is source material that can confirm the reason for my grandfather's arrest.)

Karalis speaks rapidly, looking directly at me. He doesn't want to be rude, doesn't want to discourage me, but even though the exterior of the prison hasn't changed, the interior has been completely altered. There's nothing left of the old cells, the lonely passageways, the crowded loading dock where trucks would pick up the next group of men and later women and children for the convoy to Ponary—flaps pulled down over the sides so those being carried away couldn't track their destination, though over time one man, then a group of men, then the sick and elderly who had to be helped up into the truck (its shocks worn out so every incline, every rut, every stone buried in mud shook the travelers, jostled them further into shock, into a fevered escape plan, into an understanding no one wants to ever come to) knew, but perhaps hoped it was not so.

Karalis tells us that yes, there's another prison where you can pay a bit of money and spend the night in an old cell, a tourist thing—the look on his face displays what he thinks of that kind of adventure—but that's in Riga in Latvia, not here. There's a pause. I somehow can't quite believe there isn't one old cell left inside Lukiškės.

"The church is administrative offices now, since the Germans," Karalis says, in case the aged structure misleads us. Then again; "Inside nothing is the same."

For a second I consider thanking him and going on our way, but he waits and I wait and then ask if he'll talk about himself, about his experience as director.

He agrees, but continues to stress how much has changed inside since wartime. He doesn't want to discourage us, he's prepared to take us in if we're bent on it. But he wouldn't advise it. He circles back this way several times. A kind of official hospitality and also a respectful discouragement, for reasons that become clearer over time—reasons that have nothing to do with the modernity of the cell blocks, the dining area, the cage where a certain group of prisoners is allowed outside, inside the brick walls.

"I trained at a police academy and then got my master's. It was something I wanted to do, so I pursued it." Some pride there, at what he's achieved.

I tell him I used to teach at a women's maximum security facility. He raises his eyebrows just a bit and shakes his head. "Men are different," he says. "In here, all kinds." He shifts his weight, perhaps has something to say but doesn't say it.

I ask him a question, something about the most challenging aspect of his job, something a student would ask for a school paper about the work men and women do in their lives, a student like the kids with the suitcases in front of the KGB Museum.

Artūras Karalis takes the question seriously. "I have to wear many faces in here. I have to be many different people because there are many different types inside; petty criminals like thieves, and then the worst—murderers, mafia. I have to know how to relate to them all, so I can control them and then leave, at the end of the day, with my own face, my own soul."

His openness surprises us. I ask him if he thinks about the history of the prison much.

"All the time," he answers. He looks at the metal gateway, the barbed wire, explains that the prison was built on top of a Muslim graveyard, Muslim Tatar, I'll learn—a people who trace their ancestry all the way back to Genghis Khan.

The graveyard was moved when the land was purchased for the prison, but during construction, the workers kept finding bones as they dug.

Soon after I'd arrived in Vilnius, I met with Rachel Kostanian, an erudite woman both weary and indefatigable, whose efforts were evident everywhere at the Green House, a branch of the Vilna Gaon State Jewish Museum dedicated to the Holocaust. At the start of a long discussion she said wryly, "Well, of course the country is one big cemetery."

In the early 1900s, Vilnius was much smaller. The big new prison was at the edge of the city, surrounded by fields, isolated. "The spirit of the old times is here. I feel it every day," Karalis says, then insists again he's not trying to dissuade me. But over the course of several more minutes of talk it becomes clear that he's warning me. He's thought my request over, considered what he presumes I haven't.

"This place is a bad place. You walk in here, and it's like walking in mud. You're stained, and what stains you can't ever be washed off. You carry it home with you. That's why when I leave here, I won't ever come back. Five directors were here before me, and when they retired, they never came back to visit."

Viktorija and I look at each other. The sun has shifted. Half the block is in shadow. The one CO I liked at the prison where I worked was getting a degree in religion; he wanted to write a book about all the religions of the world. Reggie, his hair dark, not as close-cropped as his colleagues'. But even he, when the chips were down and it was time for a cell toss, or a midnight walk at rifle point in the yard in a storm for some group infraction, would toe the line. The next time I saw him, the animation would be gone from his eyes, his voice a monotone.

I say something about wanting to understand Senelis, and Artūras Karalis shakes his head, adamant. "Normal people walk away from the bad things in the past. People shouldn't keep pictures of funerals. Your Senelis wouldn't want you to come back here."

"But isn't remembering important?" I ask.

"Why?" He returns to the subject of my prison tour. "There are bad people in there, bad things happen. You go in and you'll be changed, but if you insist, I will take you through."

He waits. And perhaps because I've kept him talking this long, he expects a certain response.

"Well?" He's busy. He's been generous with his time.

I look at him; the square shoulders, a bit of steel in the nakedness of his eyes; a decent man, an articulate man. When he was young, did my grandfather envision a future version of himself—a position of authority like the one Artūras Karalis holds—envision how he would navigate through life with decency? Did he, at one time, want to be someone other than who he became? Or did he believe he was his best self, as his daughters knew him, remembered him?

I don't know who he was anymore.

Artūras Karalis looks quickly at his watch, asks again. I shake my head.

A bit of surprise flickers across his face.

I reach out my hand to clasp his, tell him I'll send him my book about my grandfather when it's done, see immediately that he would never read it, even if it was translated into Lithuanian—he has no time for a book about the past, about memory. But he wishes me well, then turns rather abruptly, and Viktorija and I watch him vanish. The metal door closes behind him and the muffled sound of a buzzer announces his reentry.

I step back and look at the security cameras, picture the new inside the old, the institutional paint of the cell blocks, the modern currency of prison favors, hope Karalis retires soon, but somehow can't imagine him with idle time. Though I have no doubt that when he's buzzed out of Lukiškės for the last time, he won't even glance at the rearview mirror as he pulls away from the parking space marked "Director" and drives, at the slow speed required for this particular roadway, into another life.

"I was surprised you didn't want to go," Victorija says as we walk to the van, now thankfully covered by shade.

I look at her lovely face. She's quickly become dear to me, and I'll miss her. We immediately go over what Karalis had to say, both struck by his depth—what he was willing to reveal to us. I film the two of us as we recall everything we can about what was said. Viktorija is happy because she's intrigued; we're getting somewhere, she and I. But privately I'm saying goodbye to her. I won't see her again, won't come back to Lithuania again. I've had enough. As we walk toward the van, I harden myself after the rollout of this last, long day, touch Viktorija on the shoulder.

"Time to go home," I say, as if that explains my refusal, my turning away.

III

The Shvenchionys area is famous not for its developed industry, but for its unique and beautiful nature: blue-eyed lakes, lush green forests, the sky blue Zheimena River and old mounds including burial mounds.

—ŠVENČIONYS MUNICIPAL DISTRICT TOURISM WEBSITE

CHAPTER 25

LOST

I think about the barracks at night. Not my New York City night, but the cold autumn evenings before Lili Holzman and Chaya Palevsky and their family members and the others they claimed as family in order to get them out escaped. I remember the road that leads back to Švenčionys, the quiet street where my mother slept, her hair still in braids, in the same bed as her great-aunt, the body heat of Krukchamama comforting in the chill. Frost has collapsed the flowers in front of the house, yellowed the grasses. In the other half of the house, the Polish family sleeps or looks through the window or speaks softly about the events of the last days. A family. It's all I know about them.

A woman had her ears torn off on the way to Poligon.

I think of her as Heida Lapido, as she is referred to in the testimony of Michael and Hirsh Rayak. I think of the variations I've found of her last name: Lapido appears in the necrology for Švenčionéliai as Lapidus—the unnamed wife of Henoch. In the Hoduciszki necrology, there is a Hava Lapide—also possibly Heida Lapido, because the Jewish residents of Hoduciszki were also taken to Poligon. Who tore the earrings from the ripped cartilage? Who undid the clasps and pocketed the shine? Who washed the blood from the gold or plated wire?

I've always hated questions without answers.

Was Senelis home the first night the bleeding woman spent in a barrack—his boots off, exhausted, asleep like a sack in his own room? Or was he in the outer glow of one of the bonfires? Was he at the *Kasino*—a late-night card game before the long duty ahead? Did he miss his wife? Did his mind wander from the thousands of prisoners a handful of kilometers up the road to a lover he'd taken, a promise he'd made, a grudge he was nursing? And then there were the babies; impossible not to see them unless he turned away or absented himself, the certain gesture with which a woman in a wagon cupped the back of her infant's head; her full breast and the baby's sucking covered with a shawl. The shawl falls, and someone—maybe a grandmother next to her—pulls it up again in the din of movement. Despite orders to be silent, it's just impossible for thousands of people to travel a road without a sound.

If Senelis is not there, he's near. How did he get there or near?

In 1920 my grandfather joined the Lithuanian Rifleman's Union, the Šauliai.

As a Šauliai platoon leader in the early 1920s he took part in the revolt of Klaipėda. Klaipėda was a sizable and important port city that since the Treaty of Versailles had been an international no-man's-land. The revolt was successful, and Klaipėda, where the Lithuanian population was already the majority, was won for the Lithuanians.

To be a part of the Šauliai meant, at least theoretically, that you were trained and prepared to pick up your arms and defend your nation. When in 1940 the Russians set up military installations in Lithuania and then absorbed the country into the Soviet Union, it was the Šauliai, like my grandfather, who took to the woods as anti-Russian partisans, nationalists committed to an independent Lithuania. This is just one reason why Senelis's family was marked for deportation during Stalin's purges. He had also been trained in the Lithuanian Military Academy; he was border police; Babita was a librarian. In the end, almost any reason was enough.

When the Germans occupied Lithuania in 1941 and promised an autonomous Lithuanian government, it was also the Šauliai who, joined by other local Lithuanians, came out of hiding and collaborated. The promise of Lithuanian autonomy was of course betrayed, but many men, like my grandfather, took positions that aided the German plans for Litauen (Lithuania) and Ostland (the East).

My grandfather wanted, above all, an independent Lithuania. But he also wanted a military career. In 1927 though, he was pulled from active duty, relegated to the reserves and a job as a police chief along the Latvian border, and continually posted farther away from his family in Žeimelis. He vigorously campaigned for his reinstatement to active military duty through a series of letters and several supporting notes of confidence he must have sought as, one by one, his appeals for reinstatement were denied. After the war, during a KGB interview, the same Bronius Gruzdys whose Poligon testimony I had read in the postflood rental, a man who was also a Shaulist, told Captain Buglan, chief investigation officer of the Fourth Division of the Soviet counterintelligence agency Smersh, which would morph back into the KGB, that my grandfather was discharged from the military into the reserves "allegedly for excessive drinking."

My grandfather stated the situation differently:

31st of January 1928
To His Excellency the Minister of National Defense

Request
　　Last year, on May 1st, I was dismissed from the military service. My commanders suggested that since I was associating with people from leftist parties, I should send a request for a transfer to the reserve. That unexpected claim, however, was pronounced without any reason. Throughout my entire life I have never been close to any political party. I went to military school straight from high school, and when I became an officer, I placed my service above everything and worked with as much dedication as possible.

> *I was delighted to know on the 17th of December in 1926 that
> our country would be ruled by really national minded people who,
> among other things, would restore the honor of the military officers,
> since in the times of the "real democracy" the status of the military
> officer was widely degraded . . .*

(My grandfather was referring to a coup that ultimately brought the
Lithuanian dictator Antanas Smetona, and with him the National Rifleman's
Union, into power.)

He writes again to the minister:

> *In 1927, after the uprising [in Klaipėda] . . . I was dismissed from
> the army and exiled from Kaunas. Later, I was offered a placement
> in the border police office, but all this time I was persecuted and
> tossed around from place to place.*

And then another letter, undated, to the president of Lithuania, Antanas
Smetona, himself—a letter in which my grandfather leaves out what was, in
effect, his discharge from the military:

> *It is an honor for me to ask Your Excellency to accept me back into
> military service.*
>
> *I graduated from the Lithuanian Military Academy on the 18th
> of December, 1921, and all this time, up until my transfer into the
> reserve, I was serving as an infantryman in the Fifth Regiment of
> the Grand Duke Kęstutis of Lithuania. I was transferred into the
> reserve on the 1st of May, 1927 on my own request.*
>
> *. . . Military service is my true vocation.*

(Antanas Smetona, with his white gloves and cravat, called unsuccessfully
for an armed revolt against the Soviet occupiers in 1940 and 1941, but ultimately fled the country and ended up in Cleveland, Ohio, of all places—just
one of thousands of strange trajectories the war created.)

Another letter to the minister of national defense in 1928:

> *Currently I am serving in the 7th category and with that salary it is*
> *difficult to support my family.*
>
> *I swear on my honor and my father's grave that I was*
> *unlawfully dismissed from military service. Since my early*
> *childhood I was very interested in my country's matters and*
> *stayed in the army; I did not belong to the party but always felt akin*
> *to it and now feel even more akin to the Lithuanian Nationalist*
> *Union.*

A Captain Stakonis vouches for him. A Colonel Birontas, who years later will appear on a list compiled in Israel of World War II Lithuanian killers and collaborators, wants it known that my grandfather would be reinstated, but for a dearth of positions. Senelis, Birontas assures, is deserving, and if circumstances were different . . .

My grandfather gets high marks in pistol shooting during his training in the reserves. But according to one ranking officer he pleads his case to, he has been in the reserves too long and so has lost the edge of a military man.

He has a wife who scorns him and children he rarely sees since his posting up the border. Then his wife is taken by the Russians and their helpers (perhaps Jewish, perhaps not).

The Germans occupy the country. Almost immediately they break all their promises, but they bring with them a gift for my grandfather. A job.

On June 28, 1941, the Lithuanian Colonel Jurgis Bobelis, who also supervised the creation of the Kaunas ghetto, called upon men like my grandfather—men stuck in the army reserves—militiamen who had just deserted the fleeing Red Army to come to Kaunas and sign up for active duty. I don't know if my grandfather signed up at that specific moment or not, but his letters seem to indicate that if the opportunity arose for duty, he'd grab it.

Chief of the Gestapo in Švenčionys, the aforementioned interrogation subject Bronius (also spelled in various documents Bronislaz) Gruzdys called him. But this is inaccurate. In late summer of 1941, my grandfather became chief of security police under the German SD, a substrate of the SS devoted to intelligence work. In Lithuania, during the German occupation, this meant many different things. In Švenčionys and the surrounding areas, officially, my grandfather was to rout out Communist Jews, Communists who were not Jews, Jews who were not Communists, locals who were hiding Jews, anti-German partisan bandits, and any last remnant of the Red Army that, on its way out of the country, had made a special point to savagely torture and kill those incarcerated in local country jails and the larger city prisons, easy targets whose deaths the Germans could use to incite and sustain an already activated and lethal nationalist fervor.

AT OUR FIRST meeting, Arunas Bubnys, the thoughtful, soft-spoken director of research at the Genocide and Resistance Research Center in Vilnius, took a key and opened a cabinet near the table where we sat in his office, in the building that houses the KGB Museum and was once headquarters for both the German and Soviet occupation administrative bodies. He pulled out a thin Wehrmacht directory prepared for internal use by the German administration.

The paper had the texture of soft sand: timeworn, friable. We found my grandfather's name and his phone number. I felt as though I should be able to dial it, the past that close. Bubnys, who has painstakingly created an archival record of Lithuanian collaboration under the Germans, was one of my teachers from afar. I'd read everything he'd written that had been translated and struggled with work not yet translated. Collaboration pained him; researching it pained him. He spoke with a slight grimace, but from time to time smiled at some small irony. I appreciated the unlocking of the cabinet, the slim phone book of proof of Senelis during wartime.

IN THE FIRST week of July 1941 a German advance team, heading for the Russian front, arrived in Švenčionys with a group of Lithuanian baltaraiščiai (white bands). Among them, Ona Cibulskiene, thirty-four years old, an elementary-school teacher from the outskirts of Švenčionėliai who walked with a limp and was an amateur actress. I tried to imagine what it was like to be her; to go from teaching the alphabet to farm children to walking through town with a gun (the fleeing Red Army left weapon caches everywhere—you could find a gun in a field, behind a barn, on the side of a road by a bloated body, or go ask Mykolas Kukutis, the Lithuanian white band leader for the region, what he could give you from a stockpile).

*   *   *

THE DAY BEFORE I left Vilnius, the careful translator of my grandfather's letters and also of dozens (still a fraction of the total) of reports Senelis filed from Švenčionys, particularly in relation to two events of railway sabotage, appeared at my hotel. He'd walked across town in the late afternoon. A bit pale, serious, impassioned, he handed me a plastic folder with the copied Lithuanian originals. The packet of papers reeked of cigarette smoke. I quickly saw him—working late, chain-smoking, with a black ashtray and cold black coffee—an instant fiction. He asked me quiet, thoughtful questions about my research. Though nothing he revealed about his own life flagged it, I felt I was in the presence of a person of courage. The years have confirmed this, in ways I would be at a loss to explain, even to him.

He hadn't realized, until halfway through the translating he'd done prior to my arrival in Lithuania, that Pranas Puronas was my grandfather. So he had sent a few comments about my grandfather via e-mail—just a notion or two about the man who was tasked, in the instance of these reports, with tracking down partisans and their helpers. What startled me was not his few innocuous comments—his goodwill had been evident since he'd begun translating for me—but my instant (private) defensiveness. How dare anyone refer to Senelis as if he was just, well—someone—a man dictating the same boring statement to an equally bored secretary, a man without a wife, a daughter, a granddaughter?

I can't remember the exact time frame—whether the information was in the plastic folder, or was something he'd sent later, when I was home in New York—but on his own, he'd also found something he thought would interest me. In a section of a list of Lithuanians who had murdered Lithuanian Jews, compiled by the Association of Lithuanian Jews in Israel, he'd found the name Puronas listed as a killer in the town Skapiškis, a town not far from Gindviliai where Senelis's parents had lived.

He'd also come across a section of testimony by Emilija Greibene-Laucinaviciene, born in 1912 in the Skapiškis area. On June 29, 1941, she and her husband were arrested by the white bands, "the punitive unit which ran rabid . . . at the time." They were taken to the commandant's office, where one of their captors said "to commandant Puronas; here we've caught a good

Communist." Her husband was forcibly separated from her and taken into a dark room. In mid-July, he was shot.

If this was my grandfather, it places him in Skapiškis at the end of June in 1941. But my mother and her sister never mentioned Skapiškis. Nothing in the Lithuanian archives, thus far, had located my grandfather there. No other documentation referenced Senelis as "Commandant."

My translator wouldn't take payment for what he'd passed on to me, had said, "Compensate me for two minutes' work on the weekend? That's really OK. Let me get the other stories to you tonight. All it says is something about a police commandant, nothing really. Could be anyone."

He mentioned that Skapiškis had caught his eye because it was near another town that had come up in the translations he'd done for me. He was trained as a journalist, so I took his "could be anyone" to heart—when I got home, the section of the list and the testimony went in a file marked "Questions." And then the file itself was quickly covered up with printouts of other testimonies, stacks of books, pieces of paper with inscrutable notes I'd written to myself—things not to forget, translations I needed, the many variations of a name in a town on a certain day in June of 1941. Heida, Hava. Lapido. Lapidus.

Before the violence befell her—before Poligon.

BEFORE: I'VE NEVER been able to absorb any information in a linear fashion. On a corkboard and sheet of poster paper, I make myself write out, again, a timeline of major events in prewar and wartime Lithuania. But for the timeline to have meaning, it has to contain the power shifts and vulnerabilities of Germany and the Soviet Union as well as Lithuania. It has to contain the gap between the Reich's ideal of a massive land grab and the experience of the foot soldiers and field marshals on a vast, muddy, freezing arena of battle that even the brilliant tactician Field Marshal Erich von Manstein with the Fourth Panzer Army could not hold, and so was forced to retreat from Stalingrad. And it has to contain the experience of the young: a boy, for example, no longer sleeping on his uncle's stove in Święciany because the weather has changed, winter to spring of 1941. The boy is Yitzhak Arad. Back in New York City, I watch the video of my time with him in Israel from the past summer, while outside my study window the cold days shorten.

"Now I'm going to speak as a historian," Arad says.

Stalin reportedly gives a speech to the Politburo in August 1939. War is certain and is certain to last a long time, leach out a country's resources. Let Hitler fight Italy or France or both. When the collapse comes, the Soviets will bring communism to a broken Germany, and/or to the already large Communist Party in a fallen France. I watch Yitzhak Arad's face, notice how his hands move as if he is touching borders, winters, time.

In 1940 Soviet-occupied Święciany (no longer in Poland, but deemed briefly to be part of Byelorussia) Arad learns Russian and sings songs in praise of Stalin at school during the day, steals Hebrew books from the shelves of the off-limits, boarded-up library at night. Each house has a kind of loudspeaker from which two Soviet "channels" broadcast approved news and music.

Over coffee, in the large common room in Ramat Hasharon in Israel, we spoke of the interstice of time in Święciany when the Soviets were fleeing and the Lithuanian police and white bands were roaming the wide main street, the square where the private shops and lively trade on market day were already a thing of the past, living only in local memory.

His uncle has no children, and his house is small, with a privy out back, another reason to be glad for the end of winter. He and his sister have been getting letters from their parents in Poland. One particular letter comes, urging them to return to Warsaw. Their parents have heard a rumor. Arad stops.

"So many rumors . . . in the ghetto, rumors all the time. Without rumors people couldn't survive. They needed hope."

The Germans had something called the Madagascar Plan—if the British navy came under their control, they could ship all the Polish Jews to the isolated island of orchids and coffee plantations and poverty. The plan was abandoned, but it fueled a rumor among Polish Jews that they would be ·allowed to leave for Palestine.

"Come home," the letter from his parents urges. Arad is fourteen now. He's quick by nature—the complicated events unfolding around him grow him up. No, he won't go home. Whatever will happen in Warsaw (perhaps he can't allow himself to think that *whatever* through) he should stay clear of it, even though his father and mother and their sisters and brothers and grandparents—every part of his clan not in Święciany—are there.

In late June, when perhaps someone named Puronas is behind a desk in Skapiškis, passing judgment on the captured Communists brought before him, Lithuanian policemen round up two hundred (the number Yitzhak Arad recalls) Jewish men in Święciany, fourteen-year-old Itzhak Rudnitzky (Yitzhak Arad) among them. To be taken for work? To be moved out of town to a ghetto? (There is no ghetto yet in Święciany.)

At the last minute a Lithuanian policeman looks into a crowded car and plucks out Arad, the youngest, and another, much older man to clean his house. Mud on the front stoop, road dust on the floor and carpet and windows, unwashed so long the nicotine of the policeman's cigarettes has yellowed the glass. The place stinks. And that's the great luck of the fourteen-year-old boy and his fellow worker, who rub corners with rags and push brooms and beat rugs and pull out wind-seeded wormwood and broad-leafed weeds waist-high on either side of the front door. They throw out buckets of dirty water and scrape the scum from the stove burners while, a few kilometers outside the city, the others who were rounded up are shot. Among them are three of Yitzhak Arad's uncles, including one who was an ardent Zionist. With him, bent over a forbidden radio, Arad would listen for news of Palestine.

Afterward the Lithuanian—a Lithuanian like my grandfather, in the power structure, with a "new" house that until recently belonged to someone else— administers a vigorous beating to his two house cleaners. The occasion of war or perhaps the arrival of the man's family required that the place be spruced up, and so Arad and his work companion survived the day.

IN THE SAME interstice of time, twenty-four-year-old Ḳlarah Gelman, a member of the Shomer HaTzaier, a secular Zionist youth group active in Lithuania among many of the young people until war came, is suddenly on the run. Before the war, she was happy, married to an engineer with a home in Kovno; life was good. The chaos of the Russian retreat and the German advance separated them at a critical time. In Pobradze (Paberžė, in Lithuanian) a local

Jew told her, "Don't go where there is no place for you. No one can let you into their homes right now. Continue walking."

So she walks the eighteen miles to Švenčionys, walks into the middle of a kidnapping. A woman and her son are captured by a "Lithuanian on a horse. He killed anyone he could get his hands on. He killed the boy. He took the husband's clothes, left him only with his white underwear. He also killed a woman, an old lady. He had this big sword and he stabbed her. I saw it all. He then took a pillow filled with goose down and threw feathers on us. One woman helped me. She took my feather-filled coat and bag and took me to her home and hid me . . . behind her stove."

When I reread Arad's account in *The Partisan* of the events he describes in our interview, time has either altered or sharpened his memory. In his book, the taking of his uncles and the cleaning of the house happen some days apart. Ķlarah Gelman's testimony, translated from the Hebrew from the USC Shoah archive, seemed at first slightly fantastical; the sword sounded more like a Cossack story my grandmother Rachel could never forget—something Gelman had been told about maybe by one of her parents or grandparents. I watched her tell her story in the online video archive. I saw, online, the photograph of her as a young woman—striking, unshrinking, a shock of dark eyebrows over large, intent eyes. It suddenly, belatedly occurrs to me that the horse and the sword suggested a military man—a clue to his identity. Later, his sadism will provide another.

CHAPTER 26

PLANNERS, DIGGERS, GUARDS, SHOOTERS

Horst Wulff's identity card

When the German field command arrived in town, they immediately ordered residents to put out buckets of water for the thirsty troops on the move to the front.

In *The Partisan*, Yitzhak Arad writes,

> In the beginning of August [1941], German civilian authorities replaced the military government in Lithuania. The country became a Generalbezirk [general district] . . . Swienciany was included in the Vilnaland Gebietskommissiariat headed by H. Wulff . . . The SD, the Security Service, was established, with the liquidation of the Jews as one of its prime tasks.

Joseph Beck in Švenčionys

Without giving a precise date, the Koniuchowsky overview of Švenčionys describes the arrival that summer of "ten men working for the security police . . . and two county agricultural directors, both S.S. men . . . Postal services [including censorship] came under the control of six Germans headed by the S.S. man Metz . . . simultaneously the military commandant of Švenčionys." It seems likely that my grandfather and his assistant, Feliksas Garla (mentioned in several sources I'd found, including several of the KGB interrogations) were among the ten men working for the German security police mentioned here, though the exact process of Senelis's hiring isn't clear.

Prison construction was well on its way. Iozas Breeris, director of Švenčionys prison, was hiring thirty employees, sending the applications down to Kaunas for final approval.

My mother recalled, "The Jews were made to wear ribbons at first." I'd never heard of the ribbons before, and for months dismissed this as a girl's imaginings. But in fact a survivor interview done in Israel mentioned the brief period of ribbons with the word *Jew* marked on them.

In light of the danger for men, as evidenced by the fate of Arad's uncles, one David Katz raced back to Vilnius from his grandmother's house in Švenčionys by the Kuna River. As he got nearer to the larger towns, he saw "different billboards and propaganda materials . . . a picture of Stalin holding a knife in his hand dripping blood . . . Another poster declared that the Jews started this war. I already felt as if I was guilty of something. I felt as if I was dreaming all of this . . ."

In her passport photo taken before emigration, my aunt Karina looks as though she's caught inside a dream that wasn't a dream. Five years old in that first year in Švenčionys, still—the air of violence was so pervasive, even a walk to church on Sunday would catch a child up; a truck with locals in the back, a few with sawed-off rifles, three or four members of the town's Jewish population patching holes in the road or painting a wrought-iron fence, men and boys watchful without watching, attentive, grim. Then there was the sound of rounds against concrete—too far away to place exactly, too close not to know the shooters were near.

Unless she and my mother were kept in the house all the time, kept behind the wrought-iron fence that marked the yard; she who longed to follow her brother and sister must have followed them sometimes, followed the official cars from Vilnius, followed the women in the late light, going to the stores during the shopping hours allotted to them, the hours when nothing is left but offal, the empty shelves that still smell of bread. (Though if you had a bit of a garden, or knew people who had bread, chicken, last year's potatoes, if you were rich and could buy from the black market, you could avoid the empty stores.)

When I pulled the passport photo of my aunt out of the small padded mailer she'd kept it in for me, her face struck me as familiar, beyond the grown Aunt Karina I'd recently spent time with again. In the rickety wooden cabinet in my study, I took out an old photograph from my own childhood, one that for many years I couldn't look at. Now the girl I was looks back at the girl Aunt Karina was: the shock in her young face, the wariness in mine; that's our family legacy. I felt it in Švenčionys—stifling in the soft beauty of kitchen gardens and thick grass. A silence, an absence.

BY THE TIME Aunt Karina's passport photo was taken, her mother had already left a transit camp in western Siberia (today, Novosibirsk)—endless swamp, then another destination point, another camp after that. No one told Aunt Karina where her mother had gone. Perhaps she asked my mother. Silence, because my mother had no answer for her, silence that becomes its own habit, its own poison.

I felt myself pushing against it in New York. Every week or so, more translated material was coming from Anastasia. I was a student again; and just as I was in my student days, I constantly diverged. I found myself late at night stumbling on to dubious websites with swastikas in the header that nonetheless quite often contained detailed information about tank maneuvers and other aspects of Operation Barbarossa in the summer of '41. (Battles were discussed with an odd familiarity—I never waded far enough into the sign-up process to find out what else was obsessively chewed over among members who identified themselves with German military insignias and, every once in a while, a thumbnail photo of a bulldog or a tiger.) My father once described my reading habits as a "vacuum cleaner"—I collected anything in my path.

Over and over, I watched and listened to a video of a musician I'd made on our last day in Vilnius, right outside our hotel, across the street near an ATM of a recently defunct bank. In the sunlight the young boy played a *cymbaly*, a hammer dulcimer, the traditional Belarusian music so beautiful it seemed to heal the air around it.

Late autumn colored my study window, quick brilliant dusks over rooftops in the distance, the trees of Riverside Park gone deep rose and brown-gold. The image, in the testimony given by Khone Zak, of the woman with her paralyzed husband on her back faded a little. Now, walking in the chilly streets, it was Rose's unruly brown hair I saw, her purposeful stride quickly past a row of ailanthus trees. I followed her for a block once, almost called out to her. Then, like my father, not her.

I watched footage of KGB postwar show trials I'd gotten on disc during one long afternoon Rose and I spent at the Department of Image and Sound Documents at the Lithuania Central State Archives. The day was hot, the room where we met the archivist close and a bit rank. A table littered with books, a kind of take-home library donated by staff for other staff, gave away the reading habits of at least a few of the archivists. Some of the books were about film and society, film and history, but others were series about secret kingdoms and drawn-out battles in lands with long, fanciful names where heroes and heroines gifted with extraordinary power fought valiantly or betrayed one another or vanished, *never to return*.

The grainy clips of trials of "Fascist collaborators" that might have included my grandfather had he not fled the country were like advertisements for the new Soviet regime. Amid the grim faces in the prisoners' box were empty seats with placards carrying the names of those under indictment but who had gone into hiding.

The archivist—diligent, friendly, deep dark half-moons under his eyes (he liked to read into the night, I surmised)—had a Tolkienesque screen saver on his large desktop, hills and castles, magic and dragons. While he searched files for what we were after, I glanced at the current read he'd downloaded on the screen, the book his distraction during a long, rather uneventful day. Over his broad, rounded shoulder, a small portion of dialogue: "My son, you carried that dagger for months. I believe we dug every trace of it out of you, but if we missed even the smallest speck it could be fatal."

(I scribbled the dialogue on a torn-out day from the archivist's desk calendar, saved for scrap paper. "Spalis 20, 2011." October, from the Lithuanian word *spaliai*, or flax shives, after the breaking and scutching during the harvest—it's over now, for the most part, in the new Lithuania of cheap imports and small independent farmers priced out of their livelihoods.)

The son and the poisoned dagger would make me think of Artūras Karalis, a man stained by the place and business of his day. His belief in the danger of memory had stayed with me. The October of Poligon—my grandfather; he hadn't helped Mirele Rein, but according to my mother and her sister had let dozens of others out of the Švenčionys jail in 1943. Was it true? A lie? I had pieces, mentions, hints, and contradictions. At one point my mother called and said to me, "I don't care what the truth is; it all hurts."

IN A CROWDED café near NYU, where I did my graduate work, I met with a Polish writer whose books, like the translated work of Arunas Bubnys, I'd read many times. Travel marked him. Each expression—a half smile, a studied interest, a laugh—raised a half dozen new angles of worry and love and regret and boredom and surprise across his face, all private. His large eyes looked tired.

"If you're lost, you know you're getting someplace," he said.

He wore a kind of trench coat/overcoat and was politely interested in my questions and also clearly eager to escape—back to his own work perhaps, or to some stretch of quiet at the end of the day. I felt stupid for contacting him and immediately forgot all the questions I'd wanted to ask. I thanked him as quickly as I could and wished him well and good-bye and good luck with your latest project. I promised myself this was the last person I would meet in order to try to find the next archive to tap, the next book to open, the next route to more clarity about Senelis.

I slouched over my coffee. Pulled out a notebook and pen. If anyone looked at me, I didn't want to look lost. In a café with a notebook you can stare for hours at the progress of a day out the window: the plum sky losing itself in the false dark of Manhattan between the Bobst Library and student housing and the Citibank.

I rarely think of my heart surgery, but I thought of it then; I thought of the cab with the broken air conditioning on the way home from the hospital, the heat wave that lasted and lasted (Tammuz—Hebrew for the month that spills over from June into July). Outside the hospital, everyone seemed to move in slow motion. People bunched up at the crosswalks; an old woman with her handy cart, a new doctor in scrubs (was he all of sixteen?), a woman with gleaming chestnut-colored skin crossing the street in gorgeous lime high heels. Strollers stalled at the red light; a mother—her cheeks wide and flushed—fanning midsummer from her baby's hidden face.

A handful of days earlier I'd woken at dawn, startled from a dream, and gone into A-fib. Members of my surgeon's team on call needled vial after vial of different medications into my IV to try to restore my heart's normal rhythm. As the moments dragged on, a nurse got the crash cart ready. My gown was opened, the pacing wires threaded into the zone of my chest straightened out as if for a new sewing project my stepdaughter had concocted. Finally, some combination of drugs worked.

Out the cab window I sent a silent message to every person I saw: *take care of your heart.*

At the café, I thought of my girlhood, as if it were an object outside of time; an apricot the sun hasn't given enough hours to—hard, round—inviolable when I imagine it that way. I thought of the lives before my life—my grandfather in wartime, Uncle Roy as a child, figuring out the logistics of Švenčionys when he returned late in his life for a visit—here is the church, here is the corner where men with their salvaged Mosin rifles took away other men—and then the noise. It happens over and over. When he arrives in Švenčionys in his sixties, he won't go near the small local shooting site, can't even look in that direction, it appears he remembers the most, even if he never spoke of it. But he's gone now; he can't wrap me up in a massive hug. I can't ask him what his father told him about the war.

During my trip to Lithuania, I made a follow-up visit with Arunas Bubnys and had told him about the desecrated Jewish cemetery in Švenčionys. He had quite rightly commented that cemeteries are vandalized all the time—and that it is a municipal problem, one "the West" magnifies into a symbol of ongoing anti-Semitism. I'm not a historian. When he had said "the West," I felt like he had been talking about me.

I remembered the beautiful, pristine Catholic cemetery in Švenčionys. I remembered the birdsong breaking the stillness and the overgrown grass in the Jewish cemetery. The cigarette cartons and liquor bottles, the coil of shit. Someone had taken a heavy, blunt instrument to the gravestone Lili Holzman had paid for and arranged from Israel, to be placed there in memory of her father; the granite was only partially shattered, broken lines running in diagonals past the engraved face of her father, with his glasses on, in the soft light of the summer day. Whoever performed that act of destruction was nameless. Maybe was drunk. Maybe did it on a dare. But knew there would be no repercussions, no local police knocking on the doors in the houses across from the cemetery to ask if they'd seen some of the boys from town on their way in or out. A matter for the town, at any rate, and don't all towns have their lost bored, disenchanted youth?

IN 1926 A thirteen-year-old Lithuanian boy, Edvardis Genaitis, apprenticed at the Jew Shamuil Broyd's bakery in Novo-Švenčionys (Švenčionėliai, in Lithuanian). He had grown up in nearby Terpezhys, a village ten miles north of Švenčionys, in a peasant family that owned one cow, one horse, and a small portion of land. (Similar to what Senelis's father, Kazimieras, had been able to accumulate in his truncated lifetime.) He went to four years of elementary school—but only partial years; he had to take time off to graze other peasants' cattle to help support his family.

Under Broyd's tutelage, Genaitis went from apprentice to master cake maker, learning first how to keep the sour starter alive, to work the rye dough that clung to his hands like gum, how to turn and knead and turn and knead. How the resting dough at a certain point felt under the palm like the new belly of a pregnant woman.

Shamuil Broyd must have seen something in Genaitis, if he was going through the trouble of training him: an appetite for learning, or maybe just an appetite, just hunger. For Genaitis, to go from herding neighbors' cows to learning a trade was a leap forward. He worked at Shamuil Broyd's bakery for nine years. Nine years of passing by the sounds and smells of Friday nights in a certain quarter of the railroad town a handful of miles from Švenčionys. The white tablecloths. The two candles. Did Alta Broyd cover her eyes when she recited the blessing over the candles? Did Shamuil explain the clear Friday-night soup of the poor to Genaitis? The noodles and meat and schmaltz and egg scent of the braided bread that might, after nine years, have permeated his dreams.

In March 1935 Genaitis entered the Polish army (his village was located in Polish territory), and after Poland's defeat he returned to Lithuania, where he was interned briefly at Polonga (Palanga) on the Baltic coast. When the Red Army began its incursion into Lithuania in 1940, Genaitis was released and went to work at a bakery by the Švenčionėliai railroad and then finally as the secretary of the Švenčionėliai police. According to his postwar testimony to the KGB, he initially went into hiding in Švenčionėliai when the Red Army fled the German advance. But when his wife reported to him that men he knew from the police station were walking the streets of Švenčionėliai without fear, he emerged.

Two local policemen—friends—told him to take his Walther pistol and report to the Lithuanian White Guerrilla (white band) headquarters. In fact, according to his testimony, they walked him there in case he had second thoughts—which makes me think, if the testimony is true, that perhaps he was a man uneasy about what was occurring in his town. There, suddenly, the sons of farmers, teachers, railroad workers, carpenters, tannery workers, and ordinary police acquired extraordinary power. They could search dwellings and drag men out of their homes. They could pick a pistol from a weapons cache and walk the dirt street with it stuck in their belts.

At headquarters, he's smacked on the head for some report he wrote up about one of the men present. He's thrown into a basement jail at 50 Vilenskaya Street in Švenčionėliai and urged to join the white bands to secure his release. He's not a stupid man. In '43, when the Germans begin dragging Lithuanians into their army, he forges a Polish passport for himself and changes his date of birth so he can avoid service. When the same "friends" who had escorted him to headquarters tell him his luck will change if he joins up with the rest of them, he understands what unlucky means. He signs up, and so in late June of '41, he becomes one of those who conducted searches and seizures.

Again, according to his testimony, his tenure is brief. He claims it ends right before a group of local Jewish men, young and old, are rounded up and shot on July 22. The men, roughly fifty of them, are told they are going to work "on a phone line"—even though many are taken out of their homes barefoot or in their underwear. They are taken to the same headquarters where Ginaitis signed up for his brief service, only on this day, two SS men are there with paperwork, and the men are asked to sign on a line on a page where one of the SS points and commands "Unterschreiben"—sign. One of the white bands in attendance translates or mimics the signing of a name on a paper written in a language none of the Jewish men could read, a paper that Yankl Velvl Shvartz, "head bookkeeper of the Jewish community bank before the war," warned them all was not a work agreement, not a missive about a phone line or some kind of census or an agreement that their wages would be sent to their families; it was a paper that meant their death.

Stuck for hours in the basement jail, the men are brought upstairs in groups of sixteen, led out into the light that, for a moment, causes them to blink or their eyes to water a little. They are made to sit low in an open truck so they won't be seen, a truck driven perhaps by Bronius Cieciura, who often did the transport in this interim time, from jail or capture point to execution site. The truck bumps and scrapes gears into a thin forest; the men are forced out of the truck at gunpoint and shot where a grave has already been dug. Among them is the baker's son, Hirash Broyd, eighteen now and working for his father, a boy who has grown up around Genaitis. Grown up around the man who speaks a different language and whose legs must have seemed, when Hirash was a child, impossibly long—so perhaps when it was permitted he sat on a stool to watch the master cake maker at work, perhaps even creamed the butter or helped spread the poppy-seed paste between layers.

The reason a record of this slaughter survives is that Fayve Khayet was with one of the groups of men to be executed, a group that included the town's Hasidic butcher and Shloyme Volfson. As the men stand in line, waiting for the white bands to shoot, the Hasidic butcher cries, "Shma Yisroel." He runs one way, and Shloyme Volfson runs another, both drawing mortal fire in the hope that someone will get away. Shots aimed for Khayet miss him, and he runs without looking back.

It's an event that would have been talked about by the shooters; a hunt would be organized for Khayet. Perhaps the family of Volfson and the butcher would be targeted for "revenge." And Genaitis—what did he think when he heard that the boy, now a young man, who grew up around the wooden boxes of flour and sugar and rye and jams Genaitis boiled down, the boy who was tasked with going after the raspberries and came back to the bakery kitchen with his hands stained and scratched, was dead in a pit in the thin woods a mile from the town center?

I was not surprised when I read about the Hasidic butcher and Volfson inviting death to save others. The idea of the passivity of the Jews had always made me feel stupid; I'd never believed it, never understood it, never found confirmation of it in the books I read or the stories I was told. Perhaps I have a different definition of action and resistance. A boy who will become Yitzhak Arad watches his older sister read a letter from home, a home that is burning. His parents plead with him to return, suggest that an escape route is in the offing, a chance to be together in a new place with a new life. Perhaps he studies his father's handwriting on the envelope and thinks of his father's voice, the blisters on his hands from trench digging before the German blitz began. He's observed the goings-on about him; he draws on his intuitive powers; he separates his longing, the terrible hunger he has to see his mother and father, for that which at fourteen seems the best decision to make. Even thinking of this exhausts me; the effort required to save your life and the life of your sister by, for a while at least, remaining where you are, away from the family you love.

AND GENAITIS? DID he warn Shamuil Broyd, his wife, Alta, and Zalmen, the other son? Did he pass the empty bakery and wonder where they'd gone?

In his testimony Edvardas (aka Shoostik) Genaitis describes a date in early July—he can't quite remember it with exactness—when he and several other white bands/white guerrillas were ordered by a Captain Kurpis to conduct searches among Jewish people in the *więzienie* (shed; my Russian translator first thought the word was Ksenzi—perhaps a last name—but she suggested it might be a misspelling of a Polish word for shed, and so it seems it could be). There, according to Genaitis, "We confiscated a lot of money, watches, golden rings, and other valuables, which were handed over to the headquarters."

I looked through the documents I had for events in July in Švenčionėliai/ Novo-Švenčionys. I could not find any other record of this confiscation. Practically speaking, it would have been a waste to round up fifty or so Jewish men from Švenčionėliai or recent refugees from Poland and not, first, relieve them of their material wealth before killing them. Does this mean Hirash Broyd was among them? I don't know.

So much of this narrative is speculative. The service dates Genaitis gives could be factual or convenient. Did Genaitis see Hirash Broyd during the confiscation process? Did the shed trap the musky odor of fear as the men gathered there were robbed without explanation or warning?

What I do know is that Edvardas Shoostik Genaitis worked for nine years in the bakery of Shamuil Broyd. What I do know is that Hirash Broyd was gunned down on the twenty-second of July. The same day the bravery of the Hasidic butcher and of Shloyme Wolfson (who had a bad arm—perhaps it was broken as a boy, perhaps he was born that way) saved Fayve Khayet, bravery that should be marked with a plaque at the killing site, should be recorded in Lithuanian and Polish and Russian and English and Hebrew in the kind of multilingual audio guide the Metropolitan Museum uses, so that I or you or the descendants of the Wolfson family or the family of the butcher or the grandsons and great-grandsons of Edvardas Genaitis can stand where the trees have matured somewhere in the unmarked vicinity of this particular shooting and imagine themselves coming barefoot off the truck, outmanned and weaponless, about to run into oblivion, in the heart of their final summer, without the German reconnaissance planes that will later fly over Poligon, without one of the German military PK (Propagandakompanie) photographers or filmographers capturing their images.

No Germans at all were present. They had left with their signed documents, of which multiple copies would be made, stamped TOP SECRET, one copy making its way to Horst Wulff, the Gebietskommissar of the Vilnius region, who, among other powers, had the authority to determine in difficult cases who was a Jew and who wasn't.

(Yitzhak Arad, in his first interview, said that as a boy in Warsaw, when the city was overrun and he had to wear the Jewish star for the first time, he felt only pride.)

BOTH CHAYA PALEVSKY and Lili Holzman remember Horst Wulff at Poligon, not by name but by deed. He was born on October 28, 1907, in Mulheim, the same year Hitler's mother Klara died of breast cancer despite the best efforts of her Jewish doctor.

Wulff grew up in a city on a river and at twenty-three joined the Nazi Party. Before he married and began fathering four children—one a son who died young—he worked undercover at the Hotel Terminus on the rue Saint-Lazare in Paris.

For a time I confuse his Hotel Terminus with the hotel by the same name in Lyon, where in the 1940s the Gestapo settled in and Klaus Barbie tortured, among many others, the famous French resistance fighter Jean Moulin. I draw senseless parallels between a younger man whose pathology is just beginning

GRAND HOTEL TERMINUS · 108, RUE S!-LAZARE · PARIS

to reveal itself in the early 1930s and that of Barbie, who liked to stroke a small cat before torturing his captives. The time I waste teaches me something; raw cruelty is less frightening if it can be set in a frame. Perhaps that's why, for a time, certain theorists proposed all sorts of connections between the death of Hitler's mother under the watch of a Jewish doctor and the ideology Hitler cleaved to.

Wulff's cover name is Ollritz. He's also the Nazi Party's representative for propaganda in Paris, where the fascist right is a willing audience. The hotel is a perfect place to practice being someone else, to monitor conversations while he pretends to follow the waiters and the *commis débarrasseur*, who clears plates and smells faintly of the lemon juice he uses on his hands to cleanse them of work.

All sorts of people come to the hotel. Wulff takes in lectures at the Sorbonne—maybe he hears Marie Curie lecture right before her death. He's smart and stupid. He cooks the books later at Ordensburg Krössinsee, a large educational facility for young Nazi recruits—still new when Wulff arrives in '36, a huge place of dramatic angles and sharp points. He commandeers his butcher brother to write up fake receipts so he can skim from the supply budget. Perhaps while still at the Hotel Terminus, he develops a fondness for quantities of expensive wine that he continues to indulge in to excess. Imposing at roughly six feet, he becomes mean and threatening when questioned. He writes a letter during a court case brought against him for thievery. It is a partial confession and also an enumeration of all he has done for the party.

With all this, Theodor Adrian von Renteln, the general commissar of Lithuania, talks Wulff up for his appointment there: "He is a good comrade, always ready to help and modest . . . can give a good aural presentation . . . in economically difficult areas . . . complicated with regard to different peoples located there . . . balanced judgment, skill and special readiness for duty."

By mid-August 1941 Wulff orders that all the Jews in the Vilnius region be confined. There are several meetings leading up to Poligon. He attends a meeting in September, according to one source, with all the heads of the county. That logically would include police chiefs like my grandfather and also the white band/partisan leaders in Švenčionėliai—but I've not been able to find a record of who was at the meeting or where it took place.

A letter is also written to the area police chiefs from District Police Chief

Januškevičius, who instructs them to gather the Jewish population for removal to Poligon and to collect their belongings once they are taken away. It's a vast operation. It requires local participation. Wulff shows up at Poligon at a crucial moment, but before that moment, much has been accomplished.

FROM A JULY 2, 1941, memorandum by Reinhard Heydrich to top-level SS and police officials:

> All the following are to be executed:
> Officials of the Commintern (together with professional Communist politicians in general); top- and medium-level officials and radical lower-level officials of the Party. Central committee and district and sub-district committees;
> Peoples commissars; Jews in Party and State employment, and other radical elements (saboteurs, propagandists, snipers, assassins, inciters, etc.).

Then just under two and a half months later, this report from the Einsatzgruppen, death squads composed mainly of SS, local collaborators, German security police, and members of the Security Service: "The principal targets of execution by the Einsatzkommandos will be: . . . Jews in general . . ."

Ads begin to appear in newspapers for translators and secretaries.

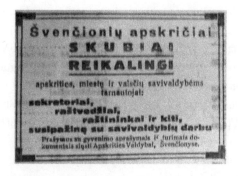

Most of the Germans speak no Lithuanian, and the Lithuanians, if they speak German, will—if they are like my grandfather—use that to their advantage. *The black-market marmalade discovered in the wagon of so-and-so should be inventoried and immediately transported to Gebietskommissar Beck's place. Heil Hitler!* My grandfather nods vigorously to whoever gives the order and tells his deputy Garla to divide a portion of the booty between Garla, himself, and perhaps others he works with—Breeris and Jonas Maciulevičius—and deliver the rest to the resident German in command, Beck, and his subcommand, Gruhl, forthwith. The Germans may have occupied the country, but without the Lithuanians to translate and operate, they can't confine, control, or kill with expediency.

Among those who rely on Lithuanians is one Joachim Hamann. He worked in a drugstore after high school (not as a pharmacist, as some initial sources I looked at implied, but as a stock boy, a clerk). A rather unpromising start to a career trajectory that, with the opportunity of war, placed him at the head of the Rolkommando, a killing unit composed of roughly eight to ten Germans, approximately thirty Lithuanians who were regulars in his detachment, and large numbers of different locals who joined his squad for pay when Hamann or his subordinates arrived in town for a job.

Joachim Hamann

As part of his training, in September 1940 Hamann studies with fellow SS security police recruits at the Einsatzgruppen Training Center at Pretzsch, near Schönebeck, Germany, on the banks of the Elbe River. There the training is less about physical endurance than about the need to undo the aberration that created the Untermenschen. Hamann literally parachutes into this new part of his career. He's a man unafraid of heights, a man who had done at least six jumps, belly to the faraway ground, arms and legs out, a Fallschirmjäger—a parachuting *jäger* (hunter), a man who looks too young for the work he is about to take on.

But before the meetings in September, before the roundup, there are the rumors Arad spoke of. There are attempts to please the Germans and Lithuanians, to impress upon the German Metz (mentioned early on in the Koniuchowsky testimonies) or Gruzdis or my grandfather that one is very good with shoe repair, the building of fences, the slathering on of soap before a shave. Fear is as viral as rumors; every day a humiliation, a killing.

Ruvin Chekinsky is tasked with cleaning out the public toilets (for Gentile use only). His bosses demand that he use his bare hands, but he refuses; he's seventeen after all, the age of refusals. Would they let him use a cloth and water? They'll kill him, they thunder, gather the firing squad. They stab at him with something sharp; the testimony I have about this event calls the sharp object an awl—but what would a tool for leatherwork be doing in the hands of German soldiers? Did they shit in the toilets first, and then call him in to clean? After he's bleeding, they relent. He can use a cloth and water. Even bleeding from his hand or wrist, he accomplishes his job. The detail of the awl nags at me; in each testimony, KGB interrogation or otherwise, I look for embellishments or vagaries, especially if the event didn't happen to the person describing it. *Awl*, an old word; *āla* in the antique high German. A photo of the gear a German foot soldier carries is illuminating; the men take little factories with them—needles, thread, scissors, awls—a kit for each soldier in case a shoe needed to be fixed, a jacket mended, a wound inflicted, quickly, without the waste of a bullet, for sport.

At home, Chekinsky's wounds are dressed, perhaps by his mother, Pesia, or his father, Yitzhak. The iodine stings as they wrap the wounds tight. He's quiet, won't talk even to his brother, won't take food. A day passes, a night. The wounds crust over, but something has happened to him. He can't dress himself. He can't touch his body with his hands, can't put food to his mouth or be touched. Disgust and rage reach so far down inside his teenage life, nothing his parents say soothes him. He smells like German shit. There is stale urine in his soup. Even with the disinfectant, he gets blood poisoning, but he isn't sick enough to die before Poligon. So perhaps he is in a fever when they take him in the cart. Perhaps red welts of infection run from his wounds up his arms. His face flushed with heat. All he wants is to smell nothing, to not be touched, to find his old self somewhere, on Schul Street, singing with his brother.

By THAT TIME in Švenčionys the commandant of the field police had arrived on his way to the front: "a very decent German from Vienna," some who survived Poligon pronounced him. He professed his lack of allegiance to the Nazi doctrine, had dire predictions for the Jews, though he didn't enumerate them. Things would be bad. Better if they had all fled in time to the Soviet Union. Perhaps he found out about the toilet-cleaning escapade and disciplined those involved. Maybe, in the preparation for the heavy fighting, before the mud and outrageous winter conditions became part of his nightmares, he heard about a squabble, inquired—*Well, did you kill the boy?*—and let it go. Maybe he looked in his small shaving mirror and saw that his honor would be his first personal casualty in the war theater; then, perhaps, his death.

Perhaps he gathered those involved and tried to shame them, saw, among the various genuflections, acknowledgments of command chain, personal allegiance, even awe—a look exchanged among them. These boys with fathers broken down by previous war, the aftermath of profiteers, wheelbarrow money—marks printed on one side to save money, the cost of your omelet jumping from the first rancid bite to the next, cocaine and shame and then the crash in the United States that pulled the rug out again. A price must be paid for the cliché of the loaf of bread that sold for two hundred billion marks in 1923, for the overcrowding in the Berlin barn quarter; the Eastern European refugees, poor, needy, in a country sick of need. Jews control and ruin the world, but they also are the poor scum of the world.

This is what the commander (whose name I have not been able to find) sees in the faces he surveys; a schoolboy's flawed equation. And it's all around him, in this lovely country—the bombed rail lines out of sight, the field poppies at their peak; *aguonų laukas*—a local pointed out to him in a drive down a road of fields dotted with the soft red riot of flowers. He's surprised he's remembered the name for the flower; he's forgotten everything about the man who pronounced it for him except for the man's hand gesturing from the half-track (half car, half military vehicle) backloaded, able to head off-road to explore the woods or fields on the way to Švenčionėliai or Łyntupy or Ignalina.

And at any rate, field commanders of Army Group North and Army Group Centre were not to be bothered with trivialities. The designations of army groups will change; commanders will be reassigned, promoted, sustain injuries, die. Those who traveled through the lake country on their way to the front or who were stationed for a time among captives and beetroot farmers and black marketeers and white bands will pass a man in uniform in the street, pushing fifty, the cigarette he holds dwarfed by his large hand. A destination on his mind, apparent in the determined way my grandfather moves, the end of the cigarette mashed between his large thumb and index finger, and then tossed to the dusty curb.

Old door to Švenčionys police station and prison

In mid July 1941, the labor divisions . . . became clearer. Political
investigations, house searches, and detentions . . . were now,
without exception, under the authority of the Lithuanian
Criminal Police and Security Police [Saugumas].
                                                —Cristoph Dieckmann

Q. Did you never receive a report on the shooting of Jews?
A. I did not receive a report on the shooting of Jews. I once heard a
rumor of it.
                —Field Marshal Erich von Manstein, Nuremberg Trials

THE SCHOOLS ARE, of course, shut down—for the Jews. In the fall, my mother
will go to a one-room Lithuanian school.

In my favorite children's book, Madeleine L'Engle's *A Wrinkle in Time*, a
young girl named Meg, her small brother Charles Wallace, and their friend
Calvin travel through time to rescue Meg and Charles Wallace's father, a scientist,
from an entity known as IT. IT is not a person. IT is a brain gone mad with evil
and power. Ultimately, with help from various quarters, IT is defeated.

I think of the Jewish children in Švenčionys with their bikes, perhaps
Chaya's youngest brother or Lili Holzman's little sister—of the parents who
had to explain to their children that their bikes must be given up (a bike a child
has perhaps named as if it's a horse, pedals it fast to the lake with friends, parks
it in front of the Jewish School where Fyodor Markov—soon to be an important
part of the town's war story—worked, hired as a result of a campaign by the
parents' school committee). A bike a boy wheels slowly, a bit unwillingly, to
Nakhum Taraseysky's pharmacy on an errand instead of out to play.

The bike must be given away to the police, the authorities, the Germans,
someone other than you. IT wants your bicycle. IT means hushed conversations your parents have when they don't see you outside the door.

In Švenčionys, as in many other Lithuanian towns, there is a story of the
"great fire" (often several fires, several stories; towns had been vulnerable to

fire through the centuries because of the preponderance of wooden dwellings and shops). The "great fire" in Švenčionys devoured the buildings around the square, the swift, infernal heat of it like a fallen sun right near the community baths. But the lost town was rebuilt again. As in *A Wrinkle in Time*, the story of the fire is one a child might recognize as destruction and loss, followed by a community effort that allowed for repair, for the town to live again, to be whole again. But now no one is predicting when IT will depart, when the Lithuanians or the Germans will leave, when the town will be as it was. Your family home has been requisitioned, and you are not allowed to walk by it, or look in the window of your old bedroom.

On September 19, the Pole Valerish Lukaozewicz is arrested for being a Communist, and then killed on the second of October. Edward Miktas, from Švenčionys, thirty-one years old, who has a gun (illegal, as he's not a white band or police) and is also allegedly a thief, is also killed on the second of October. IT is eating time. People are dying, and you are forced to stay in the house. Even the cat can't go out.

Iozas Breeris, warden of the prison, a forty-four-year-old Lithuanian man, who worked before the war, as Senelis had, in a rural outpost as chief of border police becomes, in the second week of July, one of various police chiefs in Švenčionys—head of "Švenčionys District Police," in his own words. He testifies after the war to the KGB that among his early duties was the return of material goods and land the Soviets had taken from the wealthier peasants and doled out to the poorest farmers of the region. In addition, nationalized businesses could become private enterprises again, though they were configured to serve the war effort. He also mentions court verdicts (there was no court), the arrest of civilians, and their transport to other prisons. The investigation of "robberies and murders." *But it all happened so long ago, details are hard to remember.*

In addition there is the confiscation of radios and bicycles. This is one of the men who worked, in part, under the jurisdiction of my grandfather.

Forty-seven-year-old Ionas Kurpis (who had, like Senelis, been in the Lithuanian reserves) was the leader of the white bands in Švenčionėliai during the time of Poligon, and so was acting, in the fall of 1941, on orders that came down the command chain of which Senelis was a part. (Unless my grandfather was out hunting, as he liked to do. Unless he'd been called, in the fall of '41, down to Vilnius. Unless he'd taken his small son on an extended fishing trip or was laid up in bed with scarlet fever, nursed by his sister, whose heavy tread announced the arrival of tea with, of course, a little whiskey in it.) Unless.

It is kurpis who organizes and supervises the digging of the pit at Poligon. Kurpis with a pistol and a military uniform; no reserves for him anymore. He likes moonshine, is from one of the several small villages outside of Švenčionėliai, Buivydžiai. It's dark when he shows Vitold Savkovsky the perimeters of the ditch that is to be dug. A Lithuanian army officer is with Kurpis. The ditch behind the Zeimena River is vast. Another digger/witness says there was a "technician" on hand—someone to mark the width and length, to eye the land and gauge bodies and pit size. The digging went on all night. It was raining. (Rain pelted the barracks roofs where the captive thousands waited, thirsty, cold.)

The men, three hundred or so of them, had to dig into brush at least three meters deep. The problem with rain, steady fall rain, is that it fills up the hollow you've made in the ground, so you're standing in water as you lift the mud out. And lift it out again. In the bushes, Vlad Ankyanets testified, there were approximately thirty policemen milling around, ten to fifteen local Lithuanians (white bands), and two Germans. The diggers had been ordered to show up at the Švenčionėliai magistrate's at 9:00 p.m. with shovels the magistrate's secretary had thrust into their hands at their own doorstep. Ankyanets and the other diggers were "lined up in groups of four" and went across a bridge over the Zeimiani River to the site where the pit needed to be made ready by morning.

Pavel Petkeevic remembered a town meeting in Švenčionėliai after the shovels were handed out. The "secretary of the town council with the involvement of the German authorities" announced to those who had been gathered "from jobs and farms" that Poles, Lithuanians, and Russians all had to be Lithuanian now. Jews had to be exterminated.

CHAPTER 27

DEVIL IN A GLASS JAR

Gedmino Nr. 11, my grandfather's address; I finally discovered it in a 1942 German census of Švenčionys.

I wish I could bend time the way Madeleine L'Engle made it seem possible in her book. Senelis isn't in the elder care facility in Kansas. The dementia hasn't set in. He's not buried under the open Midwestern sky. The questions I have are more detailed than they were a year ago, and perhaps less bifurcated. *Were you enemy or hero?* No, that's not the way I think of him anymore. I want to ask him about certain names: Beck and Wulff, of course. But others, too. The Polish translator my mother remembers—he must have heard of her, maybe knew her, would know her name. Mirele Rein. I won't accuse him. I won't shut him down. I'll say, "There was a girl who spoke perfect Lithuanian." Pause, add, "She was beautiful."

He's tough, my grandfather, even with all his sweetness and smacks of kisses on my cheeks. The best I'll be able to do is look at his face for the tell:

Does he look down? Does he shift in his chair? The historian Christoph Dieckmann notes that almost every movement of the Germans in Lithuania can be traced through records kept, scrupulous reports that document, minute by minute, who was where when, what they were doing, documents that were carbon-copied ten, fifteen times, sent to the Ostland command and back to Germany to all the various departments whose job it was to issue a status report and perhaps make another copy of a copy and send it to someone else. Or if the document or circular was top secret, burn it, or consign it straight away to a lockbox to which only a few possessed a key.

But there are no such records in the micro world of Švenčionys and Švenčionėliai. There are memories, histories, burned-down houses, a dinner in the one café in town held after a funeral, the soup I ate (made in the same way, I wagered, since the café opened decades ago) in a cordoned-off part of the small restaurant, where I put the potatoes aside and Rose took them, shaking her head. *It's a good potato. What's wrong with you?*

I have four hundred pages of archival material from different sources. Each tells a different narrative, a different truth or half-truth, a different lie. There is a set of thin files in the Lithuanian archives, created by the KGB for those who escaped Lithuania at the end of the war, those, like Senelis, for whom an investigation would be a waste of time. (Though you could torment his family members; send his brother and his family, for instance, to a work camp in Siberia.) I have to create my own record of him, my own file, my own murder book, the cold trail, a dead end at every turn. It's impossible not to try. Impossible in a way I don't understand.

I WATCHED, AGAIN and again, my interviews with Lili Holzman and Yitzhak Arad. After my first interview with Arad, he introduced me to some of his friends at his residence, saying something like, "The Jewish side and the Catholic side of you fought it out, and the Jewish side won." Then he laughed and gave me a brief hug. "It doesn't matter."

At one moment, in my interview with Lili Holzman, when she was talking about the Lithuanian guards and their hatred of the Jews, she said to me, not in apology but as a statement of fact, "At least half of you is that, part of that country."

The more I read about the history of Lithuania, so I could place my grand-father in some kind of context, the more I felt complicit in something—as if trying to understand a place where the Poligons of this world exist was in itself a way of looking for rationalizations. I didn't have the distance of an academi-cian. As glad as I'd been to leave Lithuania, the music of the language stayed in my head. *Laba diena. Aš alkanas.* I wasn't reading *The History of the Jews* my father had given me. I fell asleep over books about empires and small nations.

One night I dreamed that I held a glass jar, the kind with a lid that I punched holes in when I was a girl up-island at my grandmother Rachel's on Martha's Vineyard. Barefoot in the mossy grass, in the dark lit up with the short-lived sparks meant to attract the female firefly to the male, I tried to catch a lightning bug or two for my jar. I stuffed some grass into the bottom, but of course the firefly—destined ordinarily to live three or four days—would glimmer out in less than a day in my jar. I felt both cheated and destructive. When the firefly died, it became just an ordinary bug, and I was the one who'd killed it.

In the dream, the lid was off, and instead of a firefly, a small cartoonish devil with scepter and pointed ears screeched at me as I tried to shove him into a jar he was too big for.

"I hate you I hate you I hate you," I screamed back as I tried to force the strong, wriggling evil thing into the jar, to contain it.

Then, in the quick shifts peculiar to dreams, I said, instead, "I love you I love you I love you," and the devil got smaller and even smaller and finally slipped into the jar. He looked pathetic then, closed in under the tight lid, powerless, his evil diminished. The dream didn't feel like a testament to forgiveness. Did I love my grandfather? Did I want to kill him? I couldn't answer either question. I was trapped.

A FEW DAYS before Halloween, when the fake devils and ghosts and witches of New York City are shepherded carefully through apartment buildings and three or four blocks of a familiar neighborhood, I went shopping at Fairway, a cramped two-level grocery store on the Upper West Side with an interminably slow freight elevator and small aisles taken up almost entirely by employees restocking shelves from big loads of boxes. The store is a kind of joke in the neighborhood, known for the pushing and shoving and boxes of stock blocking the aisles and a gloves-off shopper mentality; every woman with a stroller, every man with a shopping list on his cell phone, for themselves.

Pumpkins lined the outdoor vegetable stands, tomatoes, oranges so orange they looked fake. Such abundance. In the grocery store near our hotel in Vilnius, the vegetables were tired—old lettuce, potatoes from the year before, a soft onion, but several different kinds of mushrooms.

Inside Fairway, sawdust was littered on a wet spot on the floor near cut up melon in plastic packages. "We ate bread made with sawdust," I remembered my mother saying, then something about horsemeat.

"A lump of fat," Aunt Karina had added.

This was in Germany in a border town as they fled the two front lines converging toward the end of the war; fled for my grandfather's life, their own lives.

I NEEDED SOMETHING on the second floor, and for the first time since I'd shopped there, the freight elevator was empty. The rule in Fairway is: move fast, try not to crash into other people's carts, and get out as quickly as you can. The heavy metal elevator door was closing when an elderly woman approached, her aide in tow. I put my hand on the door to stop it so they could get in. I didn't really look at the two women, one very old, the other young, in a familiar home health aide smock.

The old woman gripped my arm. I glanced at her face, then looked again.

"Thank you," she said.

The folds and creases, the large, penetrating eyes—her face was the Ashkenazi face of my grandmother. It startled me. She looked at me hard, dead on, from the long time of her life. I said something like "No problem" and stood aside so the two could enter. The old woman gripped my arm harder, ten seconds, fifteen seconds, looked at me, looked into me. Maybe this was just something she did. Maybe this was a kind of dementia, for she repeated, "Thank you." And once again, I said, "You're welcome," or "No worries, can I help you in?" I was starting to feel trapped, about to break from her grasp and just get off the damn elevator and take the stairs in the crush of those coming down and those heading up, with canes, with bad legs, with too many other packages.

Finally she let go of my arm and we all went up a flight and then went our separate ways.

What did I buy that day? A squash, garlic, out-of-season blueberries, a jar of Hellman's? My grandmother Rachel liked to put whipped honey on the cream cheese of her bagel. She smelled of seaweed, of the sun. Her hands, gnarled by arthritis and her unending work on the land around her cottage, were like claws. Often she gripped my arms when I was near and she wanted to make a particular impassioned point—never my hands, always my forearms—and she'd hold on and on.

CHAPTER 28

THE TRANSLATOR

What is a waste of time? I have no idea. I don't sleep a lot. Some blogs about heart surgery say this happens after your chest is cracked—your sleep cycle is broken and never resets itself. I don't care. I like the middle of the night. It's Tuesday, early spring 2013, a few hours before dawn. I open my laptop to read through more of the scholar David Boder's interviews with Jews and non-Jews in the strange nowhere/somewhere land of DP camps in Western Europe.

Boder was born in Latvia, reinvented himself—left behind, among other things, his original name, Aron Mendel—and did graduate work in the psychology of language at the University of Chicago, where my father earned his doctorate in political science. Boder borrowed off his life insurance policy to help finance a post–World War II journey to interview an extraordinary number of refugees before they resettled, forgot, or went silent because they wanted to forget. He asked many of them if they would sing a song reminiscent of home for the tape machine. Most of those recordings have disappeared, gone like the people who sang the songs.

A journalist interested in Boder noted that some of the refugees he interviewed found him to be aloof. Perhaps part of that aloofness was a protection against the intimacy of the moment—a song sung by a stranger who has lost most of what composed her life, sitting across from a stern man with a well-trimmed beard who listens but at the same time can't help thinking of his next appointment, a train time, a certain breathlessness that has started to overtake him when he walks upstairs or quickens his pace on the platform at the Gare du Nord.

A refugee without a last name—Boder puts a "Mr." in front of his first name, as in "Mr. Joseph"—speaks in Yiddish about a day in Przemyśl, Poland, when all Jews were ordered into the street. Mr. Joseph remained hidden with others in a synagogue. German soldiers poured benzene inside, ignited the fluid with a pistol shot.

Bronė Skudaikienė, Lithuanian, had a milkman husband who was gagged, burned, his face "boiled away" by NKVD and Red Army soldiers who imprisoned him, along with dozens of other men who were then tortured and mutilated in the woods of Rainiai in Lithuania. The massacre is known throughout Lithuania, a manifest tragedy. But when Boder was interviewing Skudaikienė, he was listening to one woman talk about her husband, the husband's expertise in agronomy, the cabbage the Soviets boiled into a burning compress and then laid upon the mouths of the man she loved and the other captives, engines running in the background to override their screams.

I have to stop reading for a minute, look out our two large living room windows. Three lights are on in the floor-to-ceiling windows of the new apartment building at a diagonal from ours, across West End and Broadway. A huge television gives off an eerie blue aura—someone can't sleep, or needs company while they're dreaming.

After my father's death, on a yellow legal-size pad of paper in his study, I found, among other words in the ancient Greek he was trying to learn, $\iota\sigma\tauo\rho\iota\alpha$ (historia). His minuscule handwriting already looked a little like Greek, so he was a step ahead of the game. But he still didn't get very far with his language project since, by the time shortly before his death, no new set of reading glasses or hand-held magnifier could help him write or read even a sentence from a page of a book he loved.

I have that piece of my father's yellow-lined paper. What I'm reading in these transcripts wasn't yet history when Boder was questioning his interviewees. I'm not sure when "history" begins—only that among the names and events people spoke about to Boder, some are now part of a common lexicon of evil and bravery and everything in between that didn't exist in 1946. And today, what is "history" in one part of the world is often largely unknown in another, or diminished or distorted. I wish my father were alive and I could talk to him about this. Though we wouldn't really talk—he would lecture, and

I would listen. The cliché is true: what drives us crazy about a person is also, sometimes, what we end up missing the most.

Boder's transcribed interviews are broken down into various categories. I began using "Language" as my category of choice and first tackled the thirty-two Yiddish-to-English transcriptions. Each is powerful in its own right, but of course I was looking for witnesses to events in the Švenčionys region. In an hour I read through the three Lithuanian-to-English transcriptions, Skudaikienė's among them, then click for the entire list of interviewee names.

Though not included in the list of Lithuanians' interviews, one name sounds Lithuanian: Vladus Lukosevicius. He speaks to Boder in Russian, but is a Lithuanian from, as best as I can make out, Łyntupy, the town where the Švenčionys German convoy was headed on the day it was ambushed in May 1942.

Before '42 Vladus Lukosevicius had been conscripted into the Polish army, and he was in a unit outside Warsaw when the Germans overtook the city. But his answers to Boder's questions are somewhat confusing, and only when he begins talking about the ambush can I make more sense of the events he haltingly relates.

"The translator, Rakauskaite," Lukosevicius says, as he recalls who was in the ambushed vehicle with the Germans, who died, and who survived. *Is it her?* Is this the translator my mother remembered in her white nightgown in my study? In Lukosevicius's account, the translator survives. It must be her. I keep reading. Lukosevicius was caught up in the reprisals immediately afterward, a man in the wrong place at the wrong time—machine guns, bayonets, a group of terrified victims with no prior knowledge of the plan to throw a grenade under the German car. They are dragged from houses, fields, roads, but one among them in the terrified group, a man Lukosevicius doesn't know, makes a choice, throws himself at a machine gunner as the other shooters rally to the gunner's side.

"So, I ran away and [stammers] and I myself don't remember anything how, what . . ."

It's hard for him to find words for his blind race away from the bullets. Is there a song for that? A song for the bullets, for the man whose intestines took a clip of rounds while others shot him in the back, took bayonets or knives to his kidneys? And the man's identity—will I find out who he was along the way?

Rakauskaite—was she Lithuanian? Polish? This is a Lithuanian version of her name, but that doesn't mean she was Lithuanian. She walks out of a story, out of my mother's memory. Night is still night outside my window. The skyline hasn't changed, but I'm changed—shaken by the testimonies I've just read and elated that I've found the translator's name, a strange mix. It occurs to me that the German presence in Švenčionys was so small that Rakauskaite might have worked for several officers—maybe worked for them all, not just Beck. I make a note about this on a blue three-by-five card in my own small, crabbed handwriting.

If I knew Polish or Russian or Lithuanian, I would have stumbled across her name months ago.

It doesn't matter.

Two of the three lights in the other building have gone out, sleep defeating insomnia or loneliness. No one may ever understand what it means to me, this human detail from the paucity of my mother's memory.

A name; a small bit of vanished music. I've found her.

AND THEN, A day or two later, I found her again during yet another read-through of Leib Koniuchowsky's Švenčionys testimonies in my three-ringed white notebook: Miss Rakowska. She, who I'd wanted to discover so badly, had been there all along.

On that same day, the day of Miss Rakowska, Rose sent me an e-mail: a journalist in Poland had found a contact in Lithuania who knew some eyewitnesses to the Poligon massacre, elderly people who might be willing to spend an hour or two with a woman from the United States.

Rose doesn't ask if I'll make the trip, only writes, "Your date of arrival my dear, please give to me."

And so I do.

CHAPTER 29

RAILROAD TOWN

At the airport, Petras smiled when I walked out of the doors from the few luggage carousels. Rose was in the van. She got out to hug me, her twists and curls of thick hair the same.

"You will go to hotel now and sleep," she said.

I asked her where we were going to meet our contact.

"We will meet him in the gas station near Švenčionėliai." As was her way, she spoke deliberately, with a certain elegance that made "gas station" sound like "embassy." Jetlagged, I wondered for a minute if the man we were going to speak with worked there. He did not.

The next day, to the side of the gas pumps, Vaclav Vilkoit is waiting in his car when we pull up in the van. Stocky, with graying hair, blond eyebrows, capable hands—like my grandfather's hands—he speaks quickly and thoughtfully. Among other things, he is the elected president of the Union of the Poles in Nowo-Święciany (in Lithuanian, Svenčionėliai) and also the president of the Association of Minorities (or "Kuna," after the Kuna River in Švenčionys).

Vilkoit has a book in Polish that again links my grandfather to the massacre of local Poles in 1942. My grandfather's name is misspelled.

I look at it, for a second dissociating, there near a curb and vacant back lot with the smell of fuel in the air. Then feel stupid. Despite all the variations of names I've found during my research, it never occurred to me to search for my grandfather's name with different spellings. I scribble a note to myself, and we all get in the van with Petras. I can't quite jump to 1942 yet. Vilkoit knows elderly people in Nowo-Święciany (the Polish name) who remember Poligon. He'll make calls, arrange for meetings on our behalf.

We make several different stops with him before those interviews, the first at the restored Jewish cemetery in Nowo-Święciany. Someone from abroad paid for the restoration, but Vilkoit's pride in the work done, in the return to some quotient of dignity there, countermands all I've heard about the Poles' hatred of the Jews. There are exceptions to every generality. I'm hoping Senelis will be an exception to the slow accrual of information circling around him. Is he inside the circle or outside? Or, more accurately, just how far inside the circle was he?

The next day will be hot, but today, on this morning, August feels like spring.

Rose, her hair hiding her face, bends down to touch a small tangle of white flowers. "Beautiful," she says.

The formal wrought-iron fencing, the care given to the grounds, makes me think of the Jewish cemetery in Švenčionys, the broken granite face of Lili Holzman's father. It makes me want to stay here, just here, among the dead and the mowed green and the tended graves, and stop thinking for a while, stop searching.

Vaclav Vilkoit stands in the middle of it all, and through Rose asks me, "What is the meaning of this life?" He spreads his arms open a bit. The wind picks up.

I ask him to tell me.

"To honor the dead and love the living."

And just then, in the moment, it seems possible to do this—far from my grandfather's past and not yet at the houses of those I'll meet and sit with and talk with, off the main road in Nowo-Święciany, down small arteries, in other near towns.

Nowo-Święciany. The railroad town, Lili Holzman had explained. Which is why, she said, there was a "New" Święciany, because where there are rail lines running to Berlin and Leningrad, there will be people and shops (most of them run, before the war, by Jews). There will be trade and inns and greetings and good-byes.

During my layover in Frankfurt, I watched for the fourth or fifth time the Poligon section of my interview with Lili. The first few times I'd watched the video, I'd misheard the name of her street in Święciany: Pilsutzky instead of the correct Piłsudski (the name of the Polish statesman Józef Piłsudski, who was born in a manor house near, in fact, the borderland where I now sit in the van with Petras and Rose and Vaclav).

Poles and Jews and Russians and Tatars and Lithuanians and Belorussians. Different languages, different foods, different gods, different enmities, but everyone, unless their teeth were rotted out, with molars and wisdom teeth and cavities and a chip, an infection. It was this commonality that ultimately saved the life of Lili and her mother and grandmother and sister and, for a time, a cousin and a neighbor's son. As we drive away from the small cemetery, I remembered Lili saying, "We were so certain this was our end we didn't even take our packages off the cart."

In the packages: Lili's mother's dentistry diploma—a prized item, a practical item once it was possible to work again, to live again—as well as food wrapped in cloth and paper, changes of clothing. They left it. The driver of the cart perhaps took it home as extra pay, and once he'd exited the woods rifled through his booty and let the diploma fall, to be shriven back to pulp in the rain about to descend, though more likely anything left in the carts was immediately confiscated by the authorities of the moment, the day.

Like Chaya, Lili had her own version of the place:

> A huge shack with no windows but there were openings in this shack. They pushed and pushed and pushed us in and we couldn't even stand, then people were already going to the bathroom . . . vasser . . . people begging and screaming for water. We had spent the day not eating and drinking and we had walked far. Thirsty.
>
> The guards were at all the openings of this huge shack . . . three thousand people . . . you couldn't go out. A corner where a woman gave birth . . . I don't know the fate of the child.

I remembered watching her face—wide cheekbones, her red hair, her memory working. I thought, as she spoke, *Of course the child must have died*, but didn't say it. And Lili didn't say it because it could only be deduced; it wasn't something she actually saw with her own eyes.

> People crying out. We were holding each other . . . If we had separated we wouldn't have been able to find each other. Maybe someone had a candle or lit a match but this is how it went all night long. We all knew that no good was coming. We thought they would pour lighter fluid and burn us.

Like Vaclav, she asked me a question: "Why did the Lithuanians hate the Jews so much?" Then she answered it. Yes, perhaps there was jealousy, but even long before, even when all this was Russia, there was a slogan: "Kill a Jew, save Russia." She called Polish her mother tongue and explained that for her, *Żyd*, the Polish word for Jew, had never been an insult, just a common respectful identifier. Only in the Lithuanian tongue and in the mouth of the Germans did this change.

> The morning light comes and we are still alive and doors are open. We can walk out but surrounding the land is barbed wire and we can walk but only to this wire. And it was the end of September, a beautiful summer day, and children being children—they were playing.

Lili spoke about looking around and slowly realizing the scope of their entrapment, not one shack, but several. Not three thousand from Święciany, but thousands more, from all over. Friends and relatives started finding one another, calling out. The bread cart trundled and bumped along the uneven road, and it was announced that people could line up for a ration. The bread was sent from those Jews still left in Święciany. With the bread, a little hope. "Maybe it was a game or a trick and they would take us back."

A few pots were passed around. (One brought by Chaya's mother.) Potatoes, grains, a bit of rice for the children.

There were one or two water spigots outside of the barracks. Lines for water were long; there was quarreling, exhaustion, terror, confusion. *Vasser.*

And every day they let a few people leave; a little shack where guards strip-searched them before they were allowed to go. (Most only to be subjected to another roundup, then brought back.)

> I have to praise myself. My mother was, at this point, in a state of despair, but I was fifteen and my mind wouldn't rest—how could we get out of here? After about a week local Lithuanians would come and take some people to work . . . again hopes were raised. I told my mother: we don't have a father who is going to come for us . . . so we are going to have to do something on our own.

I asked her where she had come by her ferocity. She said she couldn't answer me. She didn't know. She had lived a sheltered life, she said. She'd never had to fight for anything.

So she watches. She looks around. She sees that in the strip-search shack there is a man carrying out body searches (visited upon Chaya and her sister) who was a dental patient of her mother's. The man's name is Urbonas. She approaches him.

"Mister, do you remember my mother took care of your teeth?"

"What do you want?" he asks sharply, impatiently. (His hours are long, and the work is, well, taxing. The shacks stink of confusion and the smoke of small fires everywhere.)

"Let us go," Lili says.

She thinks he will push her away but he considers. "What will you give me?"

She offers up her gold watch, a watch of unusual quality, and he says no, not enough. She goes to her mother, who takes off her diamond engagement ring. She returns to Urbonas, who pockets the ring in the same place where the gold watch now shines inside the green fabric of his uniform. He tells them to stand in the line of people who are lucky enough to have family bribe them out or have the means to bribe themselves out, or have suddenly been claimed as "useful."

So there is a gap in the barbed wire; an egress without mines. Before they go there, Lili tells her mother to explain to the white band in charge of the exit line that she has four children, so the cousin and the neighbor's son can come out with them.

At fifteen, she is in charge. Her mother does as she asks. Incredibly, they are among the lucky ones. The line is moving, but in a few moments or a half hour or a second or two, everything stops.

Among the noise of thousands of people the engine of the Opel Admiral with the canvas top rolled back can't be heard, but people can see it. A car has arrived. Orders are shouted. All the Jews must gather near the car to hear Horst Wulff give a speech. He stands on the back seat for his "good aural presentation." A back seat someone, perhaps he himself, will wipe off before he sits down again. It's the fifth day of his birthday month, October. Maybe he'll be lifted in a chair, glass in hand, and sung to by his underlings. Maybe he'll feel old at thirty-five.

> He's standing there and gives the Heil Hitler and says, "Jews, we want to save your lives, we're not the ones who want to hurt you. We want to save you but you have to pay us. I'll be back in two hours and you need to gather a quarter of a million marks."
>
> People believed it. My mother was the first to convince everyone to give because she believed. I remember her sitting on the ground, a big bucket in front of her. She called out "Jews, Jews, whatever you have throw in here." I saw people throw things in the bucket. They thought they were buying back their lives. This was years before Auschwitz and crematoriums. They themselves [the Germans] didn't know what they were going to do.

In the Frankfurt airport, I'd stopped the video. I was back in the long, dark apartment, talking on the phone with Jonathan Boyarin, Konischowsky's translator, about the difference between the living moment and the look back; history that has the luxury to organize, make assumptions, analyze.

Lili remembered a friend from school who was there, a girl who thought she was smarter, worldly in a way people like Lili and her mother were not, as they gave up their rings and furs and shoes and hats and rubles and marks and bracelets. More worldly than those who could only unroll their socks and twist a wedding ring off or unbutton a shirt and throw that in the bucket for want of something of more value.

"In my girdle I've sewn some money, so I'm not giving anything," the girl said.

A girdle she would later have to unhook or untie in the cold air and leave on the ground beside her.

IN EXACTLY TWO hours Wulff comes back. Buckets and buckets have been filled.

"Jews worked their entire lives for these valuables," Lili said.

And it was then, truly for the first time, that I saw the pain in her face as she recalled the swift dismantling of all a man and a woman could build or dream of one day building. A small store. An education for a daughter. Passage away, to another, better place. Or maybe the dream was more meager; one night a real Shabbos dinner, the means to fix a roof full of holes, money to pay farmers enough to load up a cart with potatoes and cabbages that could be driven down to Vilna to sell at city prices.

Wulff stands up again in the car. "I thank you. You have brought even more than I asked for and I will fulfill my promise."

(Other testimonies give different versions of his words, but this is Lili's recollection.)

Did she remember his face?

No. Only that he drove off, and everyone was certain he would fulfill his promise.

Wulff sits back. His driver commandeers him free of the haggard crowd. An announcement is made. The lines that had been lines before began again, the lines for water, the line for exit, the strip-search line. Lili, her mother, her grandmother, her sister and cousin and the neighbor's son, clamber into a cart that is waiting for just such an occasion—she doesn't remember what the driver charged them—and leave Poligon behind.

When he was interrogated by the KGB after the war, Urbonas, who was a senior policeman in Švenčionys, spoke of his skill as a mechanic. "When there was no driver available I would drive the motorcar for the chief of police; he was armed and I was not . . . The day of the shooting I was on duty and had to stay by the phone in police headquarters of Švenčionys."

One witness testified about Urbonas: "Once I saw a Jewish woman, and she was carrying a dress. He arrested her and took the dress away from her. He was carrying a gun."

I think about that phone he was very busy manning during the shooting at Poligon. The phone for the policemen who were not high enough in rank to have a secretary take and make their calls, a secretary like the woman who ran between my grandfather's office and the office of the Chief of Border Police—a man who is still vague to me. A ghost with a name: Jonas Maciulevičius.

CHAPTER 30

ELENA STANKEVIČIENĖ
NÉE GAGIS

AUGUST 8, 2013

She is eighty-nine. Polish. Her husband is very ill, but she has agreed to speak with us. Her son, whose house in Platumai is large and cool and surrounded by green, stands near and once in a while helps her remember. She has glasses on, two small braids of her white-and-gray hair drawn back from her face, braids that make her look much younger as she talks.

> It was a terrible time. It's very hard for the human being to survive this. It was in Sodo Street, very close. In the street of Sodo. They were driven through our street. In the morning. We had the soldiers staying with us. The people who were shooters stayed in our house. They came and said that they will kill the Jews. Lithuanian. Six of them. They did not ask permission. Scary to have them stay. My mom was a widow. She was asking, if you occupy this home of ours, where will I put my children? [Elena and two older brothers.] She was asking them to close the door. No, they ate elsewhere. They went to live with the neighbors, left our house. No, in this town they were not drunk. On the other side of the river there was a burrow and my brother was very inquisitive. And he lay down on his stomach and he was curious to see what was going on. And he reported to Mom: "Mom, you don't know what terrible things are happening over there." Three rows. Children. Women and men. And they were asking them,

pleading . . . "What did we do to you?" . . . and then [the reply],
"You will see what you did to us." It was Poligon over there. And
they were driven over there. And my older brother came and he
said to my Mom, "Let us go to some village farther away because
we will not survive what's going on, it's impossible." And the
younger of my brothers said the whole barrel of vodka is over
there and a ladle. They were drinking and shooting. Pits
prepared already. Everything was prepared. It's very impossible
to tell. I'd walked through there before . . . all men were digging
the pit. My brothers hid so they wouldn't have to dig. Normal
person would not be able to suffer this whole scene. From Novo
Švenčionys and Švenčionys the shooters. It was all prepared. My
mom put some towels on our heads so we wouldn't hear the
shooting. We heard anyway. It was the shouting of the children.
"What did we do to you?" It was terrible. My mother's name was
Ana, and in Poligon where the [Polish] soldiers earlier stayed and
afterward they left and when we needed firewood we collected
the firewood there because in our family we have a lack of men.
It was the Zeimana the river and it was a bridge and it was the
forestry department behind the bridge and he [from the forestry
department] tells us, "Ana, leave this firewood, look how many
people are coming, throw away this wood," and we threw it
away. And it was the forestry department. And we hid ourselves.
And we lay down and we saw all of them marching by. My
brother was a worker in Ignalina. He was forced to bring
someone from there in a cart. He did not want to go but there
was an order. When it was over, the shooting, it's impossible to
tell, and my brother told to me, and I told him, "Janek, please go
and eat, you did not eat for two days." "If you would see it, you
would not eat for the whole month," he said. "They were
brought by car, it was a woman who just delivered the newborn
baby and they took the child and they threw the child." It's
impossible to tell. Not far from the Zeimana, a little frozen in
October, I told my friend Wanda, and the brother of Wanda was
very bold and he took some boys with him and they crawled on
their bellies and they came back all in blood. The blood seeping
out. God forbid. Terrible. They had their own shops. They were
very good. They were very nice people. It was Olga. We had a

cow and Olga was very nice. And she asked my mom to bring
the milk and my mom used to bring to her the milk. It was Easter
and she asked my mom, "Mrs. Ana, why do you come to me to
buy the flour and the sugar? We are like sisters. I am widow, you
are widow. Whatever you need, please take. I trust you, you are
an honest person." She gave us three kilos of flour and sugar. My
mom gave her whatever she needed from dairy products. What
has kept my faith? I can't tell you. It's impossible to tell.
Impossible.

CHAPTER 31

BUCKET

AUGUST 6, 2013

As soon as Viktorija—my young translator and assistant, back with us again—Rose, and I sit down with Vanda Pukėnienė in her small living room, Vanda moves her large palms across her eyes. It's wilted and hot outside, a bit cooler inside, but we are all sweating, so I can't tell if the palms are for tears or sweat. She was born in 1937 and now, at seventy-six, has a strong face that at first glance is not beautiful, but becomes beautiful. Like Lili and Yitzhak Arad and Chaya, she moves her hands while she talks.

Her father was warned that the Germans were coming, war was coming, so he "was putting everything out from the house and hiding it in a dugout under the lilac tree." Vanda, so young, was worried where they would sleep.

Vanda throws her hands over her shoulders. "One side of the Zeimana River, Russians, on the other, Germans . . . cross-shooting."

Her family had a small flock of three geese. Two sat on their egg clutches. Germans fried the third goose in her family's kitchen. "The whole city burned. Novo Švenčionys. Because when we went to another village we could see the smoke. Dad commented on it."

Her father worked on the railway but left before the Germans arrived to avoid conscription. As the German front moved and the Russian army retreated, he moved his family—Vanda, the only child, and her mother, Veronica Usiene—from one small village to another. From their barn, she watched the German army push through—perhaps those who had stopped for a time in Švenčionys before they shouldered their gear and drove north.

Vanda's dress in some small way matches the gray/silver pattern of her wallpaper. She has on black stockings—I wonder if she put on the dress and stockings for the occasion of our meeting. Her arms and face are tanned.

> I lived on the other side of the [Zeimana] River. It used to be our land there and we came to dig the potatoes. All the Jews were collected in the barracks near the lake [where the river pools and widens]. My father plowed the field so we were going to collect the potatoes and I came with him and there was someone who came on a white horse. He spoke German and gave us the order: "Disappear, leave for home." Three hundred meters from our house was the ditch for killing the Jews. And the trees were all young. We saw people gathered. Young pine trees, now they are bigger.
>
> From the city, men came to make the pit and afterward . . . Thank god my father was not digging or covering . . . no one from our village . . . we were hiding.
>
> And within one or two days, we got the Jewish girl. [Her eyes fill, she wipes them.] She embraced my mom and started to cry. How she embraced my mom. My mom was short and very dark. The girl was taller than my mom and also dark. It was toward evening.
>
> Father prepared strong straw, the kind usually used for a roof, and hid her behind the straw in our barn. Our neighbor warned, "Don't hide anybody because if you will be found, you will be shot." I remember her. I brought to her food. Mama gave

her babushka and her own dress . . . potatoes, milk, eggs . . . She spoke Lithuanian language. Yes, she was beautiful. To me. She used to kiss me when I was giving to her from the bucket. We went to dig potatoes and we prepared the food and when I went to the hiding place in the barn she was gone. Probably she crossed the river or someone took her . . . no one knew. She probably left herself so she would not be found and my mom was very often remembering her, before she died my mom was wondering what happened to her. [Now Vanda is openly weeping.] We were afraid of our neighbor. We did not have a good neighbor. My mother's name was Veronica Usiene. She had pity on people; she was compassionate. Before she died . . . she was asking the question . . . what happened to this girl?

And sitting across from Vanda, thinking of how close her house was to the pit, of Mirele Rein, who was beautiful and spoke perfect Lithuanian, I briefly interrupt her story and tell her about the girl a Lithuanian policeman hid under a pile of brush during the shooting. I ask her if she remembers the name of the girl they sheltered. No.

"Do you have a picture of her?" Vanda asks, intently.

The question, which is logical—I know a girl's name, after all, a version of her story—makes me think of the hours I've spent online, the people I've e-mailed about Mirele Rein, the absence of an image of her hands, her face. I haven't spent enough hours. I'm sure there are contacts I've missed, a follow-up query I've neglected. A chasm. All the Reins were beautiful.

"No, I don't," I say.

Vanda's face falls a little. She's stalwart; her disappointment is greater than she lets on.

I ask her if she could perhaps draw a likeness, but she shakes her head. She can't draw.

Then she gives a mini history of the pit at Poligon—those who came to dig for gold teeth, and the dirt piled around the corpses fell down. And much later, in the 1950s, a lot of people came to the area from Leningrad for vacation because the area was so quiet and so beautiful, and then the authorities covered it with a mound. But earlier, when Vanda was eleven years old or so . . .

Afterwards, I was a cow girl . . . I herded cows. I was with the cows and the cows came over to the ditch and I couldn't control them. The cows were crying, shouting, screaming, mooing . . . they found bones and kept pawing the ground, digging, and I couldn't call them back. [She moves her hands in the air as if they are hooves working the earth.] I couldn't control them, I took one cow back, but the other cow would go. I never went there again. We were so frightened during the shooting, we thought we would be killed too. Jews were forced to dig the pit bigger. We heard talk of it. They were making it longer and people who were alive were falling down. In our closest milieu we did not know these people who were anti-Semitic. We were all . . . the Jewish people stayed with us after the war, they were very nice. When we went to church it was all Jewish shops on the way. The Jews invited my father by name and he would say, "I do not have the money," and they would give him credit. I remember a pharmacy in a Jewish house, Kaltenai Street, there were a lot of Jewish shops . . . I remember the different scents.

There was just a small window in the hiding place in the barn. I would take the bucket in the morning and evening so no one would see. Pancakes. Here is my mom, short as a fence, going with a bucket. For my mother, the bucket had a lot of sentiment.

CHAPTER 32

DEVIL'S AUCTION

We sit on a side porch. A strand of flypaper buzzes from the ceiling. There is the smell of a cat. The poet Zenon Tumalovič, ninety-one years old, holds a green notebook. Behind him, a red geranium adds its blaze to the August afternoon. To his left, his wife Jadyga sits and often contributes, elaborates. Jadyga is Polish. Zenon's father was Lithuanian, his mother Polish. Vaclav Vilkoit—our initial contact who made these interviews possible, President of the Union of the Poles in Švenčionėliai—is with us this time, but frequently goes into the shade of the house to take a call or make a call.

I ask Zenon Tumalovič about his green notebook. I can see pages and pages of handwriting, some smaller, some larger. Poems? No. He is writing out all the wars of the world and their dead, "all the millions of people, the ones who were suffering; the Jews, the Poles, the Germans who didn't want to fight, the wars in North America, the wars from ancient times."

> We have friends and they were forced to dig, young men, Norbert Uzela (he died already). He told how it was . . . not everyone was killed immediately. It was cries and movement of hands, terrible. We were afraid too. They were absolutely innocent. The ones who were shooters had a sign of a corpse, a skull on their uniforms, and bones. Šhaulists. Everything was organized beforehand. It was the ditch, local people were forced to dig in the evening before. People in the town knew. The ones who dug told to their families. They explained to everybody. And they knew that the Jews were over there. And it was the local people who were covering the ditches, a function like some

people were bringing the dirt, others were putting in corpses, like a conveyor. And they were putting lime on.

I was born in January of 1923. I was nineteen. When they were over with shooting all the shooters went to Švenčionys and they were singing Lithuanian songs . . . they were very joyful. They were drunk beforehand. In Švenčionys there was a big long table in the open air with food, like a holiday. The mood was supported by the orchestra. They got drunker. They took from the orchestra two men with beards, old believers, Russians. They took them away, and they were found killed as well. And the people buried them. It was a duty for them to shoot. They signed that they will shoot. It was a service. But the two people from the orchestra—instinct.

Over here there were two wooden synagogues and these were used as warehouses. All the belongings of the Jews were put over there, and afterward there was a sale, an auction. "Who would give these marks, who would give more. I'm partisan, I'm not standing in line." It was like euphoria. I saw it. People were very excited. It was after the killings, so everyone knew. Later they figured out that the best things were already taken. Cicenas was in charge. The clothes, the dress, he would give the price, and they were selling. Underwear. Some people were very upset that there was nothing good. There were war shortages so people wanted what they could get. When the Jews were taken from their homes, they carried suitcases. Suitcases were left, so people went to look for them. People from the villages used to come. Children used to sneak over to Poligon. One Polish man told me sometimes they would find a coin. Villagers who found suitcases were hiding them. I do not know. I do not care. When the Jews were killed . . . some people would go and dig and find the gold . . . near the houses.

Tumalovič's face and the face of his wife blend together: both thin, scrappy, like two birds, two ancient storks. When he talks about the two synagogues where the auctions were held, he gestures beyond the screen, where a field runs between small houses and some scrub and working land. Wooden synagogues. Sweat runs into my eyes—I can see it: the press of the crowd for a pair of socks, poverty shoes with the front soles flapping open, in want of stitching, in want of the feet of their original owner.

When I rise to leave, Tumalovič offers me his green notebook; his record of horror, his list of what it is to be human. Something is lost in translation; since I'm writing a book, it seems he thinks I can take his list into the world with me. I don't take it, and I'm not sure if he didn't want me to just sit with it for a while and go through the pages, different wars and names separated by a line pressed hard into the paper—his project, his burden. His, still.

IN A POLISH testimony, Maria Korecka, born in 1931 in Nowo-Święciany, remembered, "I think it was September when they began to shoot them. People came to us to listen to this, because in our house you could hear everything better."

In a KGB interrogation Petras Gudonis, a Lithuanian white band from the Datynyany area about two and a half miles from Švenčionėliai, describes how he heard about Poligon: "We wished to earn money, so we decided to go there."

For sixteen marks and seventeen pfennigs he guarded the crammed barracks and moved groups to the killing site. "After one group was shot we would replace it with another group. They would make Jews take off their outer clothes by the trench and then push people." Along with his pay he got from the auction "a scarf, three or four sets of underwear, a bench and a trough for [a] piglet."

CHAPTER 33

LUCKY BIRD

We stop in Švenčionys, en route back to Vilnius. Vaclav has gone his own way in his car. The town green, strewn in large uneven patches with shade, seems like a placeholder, a stage set, a made-up town center—the real one in a vanished autumn with dust flying up from the road and wandering dogs and cats barking or mewing their hunger beside doorsteps, next to a vacancy in a wooden side wall where a window had been knocked out as soon as the carts began to take away those who would have set the bowl of milk out, the plate of scraps. I try to imagine a long table laid out in the open, try to imagine an orchestra, the noise of it rising into the night, the strings and singing and shouting. I can't. Zenon is a poet; it's in his nature to make things up: two musicians with beards, a white tablecloth.

I can believe that the night before the shooting, the men and then the women and children were put in separate barracks. I can believe that the few Germans on hand were not simply there to film and photograph, for various reasons, the two-day slaughter, but to send down the command to begin and provide trucks and give the directive that fifty people at a time be brought a certain way beyond the barbed wire, through the sparse woods, and then, at a turn in the dirt road, forced out of the trucks and ushered to the sideline of the pit. I can believe that the shooters were stone drunk and cigarette butts littered each man's perimeter and that they positioned themselves so many feet apart to spare their eardrums during the firing. I believe that between one set of fifty wounded or dead and another set, a piss had to be taken—and why not aim right there at the mess in front of you—and that infants were swung by their legs against the tree, toddlers too, because a bullet would pass too quickly through such a small, dense mass with two eyes and two hands and ribs and elbows and fingernails and the heart of all the cosmic matter that accrues inside the very young and slowly ebbs out of the very old. But I can't believe there was a party on this very town green with food and drink and the local authorities, the shooters, police, my grandfather, eating and singing and feeling the liquor burn the back of their throats, their breath a distillery. I can't believe anyone could be that full and that empty.

It's late in the day. Even so, beyond the green, summer remains a long, bright, hot stretch across near-empty streets. I had wanted to see if the sidur was still upside down in the museum, but the museum was closed. "Topsy-turvy," Lili had said about the town she and her mother and grandmother and sister returned to.

IT WAS NEAR dark when Chaya Palevsky and her family made it back to their house on Schul Street and saw, through a window, a faint light. Poles? Peasants? Germans? They didn't know. They didn't know anything anymore. Chaya's father tried the front door, his door—it wouldn't open. He made his way to the side of the house, where the basement window with the small latch could be opened. Chaya's brother, who had been away in New Zealand and returned to the empty family home, was hiding in the deep, dark basement with two friends. He'd left a candle lit upstairs to alert would-be looters that someone was inside, would hear the split of wood from a broken doorframe, the sound of broken glass.

When Chaya's brother heard noises at the front door, he hoisted himself out through the basement window to confront, from the back end, the intruder. It was his father, who took his son into his arms. That night the whole family slept together on the basement floor, held one another in the refuge of the moment, of their luck.

In the hired cart, Lili and her family arrived back in Švenčionys at dusk and went to the area designated as the ghetto, though not sealed completely off yet. They knocked on the door of a house, and a woman who in an earlier time, when the Swirskis still had use their wealthier relatives' car and Romanavsky, their attentive driver, might have seen them passing as she trudged by with a basket or bundle, let them into her home and, in her new, elevated stature as one of the "useful Jews," pointed to a very small corner on the floor where they could sleep.

In the morning, Germans and Lithuanians announced that everyone in the ad hoc ghetto should send a family representative to the synagogue at such and such an hour with their papers.

"No, you can't go," Lili insisted to her mother, who was a professional woman, who was used to talking to people of importance, allowing them the opportunity to reconsider, pressing her agenda. "If you go, they'll take you right back to the woods. We don't have any papers."

Again, Lili's mind was working. They had to get to Świr, in Belarus, where a grandfather lived; Świr with its mountain and old houses and the smell of the lake and the sound of a pebble thrown at a tin roof, down a cobbled street. A walk through the center of Švenčionys was impossible. Police were milling about. A neighbor might recognize them, and in exchange for a bit of food or money—or just because the Swirkis had had it good once, had lorded over so many, hadn't they now?—turn them in.

Lili led her mother and younger sister through the back fields that abutted the Kuna River (a stream, really) to a house on Ignalina Street with a pharmacy in front, run by a Gentile family friend, Mr. Symansky. He was afraid to take them in, but he did, showed them where to lie down in his bedroom between the bed and the window.

"I knew," Lili said, "there was no hospital or pharmacy in Świr." Which meant that someone from Świr or nearby might have cause to come into the shop for medicine, something from the dispensary. (Before the roundup to Poligon, all Jewish doctors and pharmacists had been told, when they were forbidden to continue working, to carefully label their supplies and leave them, each amber bottle of powder, each liquid vial, each tub of salve. Symansky had little competition, so his own pharmacy would be well trafficked.)

Lili told the pharmacist Symansky to ask whoever came into the shop where they were from, but in the end it was she who asked when a farmer wearing a rough gray greatcoat walked through the storefront. He was Belorussian, from Świr. He knew her grandfather. His daughter was in the hospital, back through the main street of Švenčionys and off a side street where his cart and horse waited for him, waited to clatter off again and head away from the strange town, go home, and be fed. It was midday. Because the farmer was fetching his daughter, he would only take one other passenger. It was decided that Lili would go—better that Lili's little sister have her mother with her. Lili would go, and her grandfather would send someone from Świr to collect the rest of the family. Symansky was not happy with the plan, afraid of getting caught hiding Lili's mother and sister, but he agreed. He had given them food and drink. He treated them well, Lili said.

The farmer brought one of his big coats, and Lili put it on. Her head was swathed in scarves so no one would recognize her. They walked from the pharmacy to the hospital, walked through the middle of town near the police station and the ghetto and the Catholic church, past the street where my grandfather lived. The farmer slung his arm about her, and when they got to the wagon he put her in the back and covered her with straw, then went up two flights in the hospital and brought his daughter down and laid her next to Lili and covered her also with straw.

"It was dusk by then," Lili remembered. "I heard the birds calling and thought each of those birds are luckier than I am."

She made it to Świr. Her grandfather at first didn't recognize her in the bundle of felt and wool. He sent a cart back for her mother and sister. They had all left the open ghetto in Švenčionys just as the boards were being hammered into place and the barbed wire uncoiled. A half hour later, they would have been stuck there, behind the spiked fence on the northwest side of the town.

IN *THE PARTISAN* Yitzhak Arad described how the night before the Poligon roundup, his sister, Rachel, had returned from a German work detail and urged him to leave for Byelorussia with other Švenčionys Jews who knew by the sight of armed Lithuanians and Germans amassing in town, knew from rumors and outright warnings, that trouble was coming. No one could imagine the exact nature of the trouble ahead, but Arad, with a group of his friends, did his sister's bidding. Rachel remained behind with their extended family. She had work. Perhaps she imagined, since they had been targeted before, that the men and boys of the Jewish community were in greater peril than the women.

Days later, Arad would find himself listening, in Głębokie, Byelorussia, to a girl who had escaped Poligon and hidden with a Polish family. As she described the massacre he took in her words with horror, "in my mind's eye I saw my sister walking quietly to the pit . . . my two grandmothers . . . my grandfather . . . aunts, uncles, cousins . . . beautiful Bebe with the two blonde braids whom I had loved with such youthful ardor . . . mowed down."

Though he believed his sister to be among the dead, she had in fact left Švenčionys to come find him in Głębokie; two young people running beside a sled in the snow, crossing a frozen river, still alive in October of 1941, now about to head into another winter.

TWO DAYS AFTER Chaya's family—the irreplaceable felt-factory workers—returned to Švenčionys, they heard what had happened to those they left behind at Poligon, what would have happened to them. A peasant told them, "It was like a big bloody mountain moving and you could hear the crying inside the mound."

IV

CHAPTER 34

BAD MAN/GOOD MAN

I'm exhausted. Glad for the quiet the next morning in the large, bright breakfast room of the new hotel in Vilnius where I'm staying this trip: a big lobby with glossy floors and carefully placed sofas to sink into. No vague smell of cigarette smoke in the hallways, just tasteful new carpeting, a soundless large elevator. I'm about to take my first bite of thin, sweet pancakes when two men amble over to the table at my near left. A floor-to-ceiling tinted window mirrors the three of us, reveals the quiet street—someone checking a map in the sun and already sweating in a suit; a girl in shorts making time on a hefty bicycle.

The men catch my eye because they are not Eastern European, and even more than that, have the middle-aged look of the American Midwest—a paunch, pullover knits or a checked button-down shirt, not quite leisure wear and definitely not for a business meeting, a bald patch, a bit of a sunburn. No wedding rings. I can't imagine what's landed them in Vilnius, Lithuania. They're speaking English. When they talk, I listen, and—out of habit, prurient curiosity, a way of avoiding the documents I've brought downstairs—I open my laptop and transcribe.

"What does it feel like when it cycles?"

"It happens so fast."

"Lasers . . ."

"The cigar thing."

"It's a whole separate expertise . . . I subscribe to . . . and the rifle thing . . ."

"It's a whole lifetime of . . ."

"Are they arms sellers?"

"Guns with lasers."

"It's not like I'm on a SWAT team."

"Breaking it down is simple."

"Yeah, you didn't need any special rules."

"Nothing more frustrating than break a gun down and it won't shoot. I had the darnedest time when I first broke down the model 1900. Put the slide back down, and I thought, what the hell am I doing?"

"Gotta give it to Glock . . . a simple one . . . even a blind man could do that."

"Amateurs who go out on the range . . . fifty-cal sniper rifle shooting at a target two hundred and fifty yards away. Cinder blocks . . . boom . . . richochet tore off his earmuff . . . didn't kill him, but you can imagine . . ."

They pause. One digs into an omelet; the man nearest to me focuses on his over-easy eggs—yellow centers leaking onto a toast wedge.

". . . custom gun that guy uses is made in Texas."

"How does he get it here?"

"I don't know . . ."

"How's his English?"

"Pretty good . . ."

"If they're gonna be tight with their information . . ."

"That's we . . . all guys are interested in that . . . one guy had a Walther P5. Shortened barrel. Wrapped in a rag . . . in his pants . . . I had a guy in Costa Rica telling me . . . wanna make this guy your best friend . . ."

"What's very hot to them? It's a hundred and four in Fairview, Texas."

THE WALTHER P5 is a semiautomatic, a safer and lighter handgun than, for example, the workhorse of World War II, the Walther P38—its parts made at Walther's factory in Neuengamme, the sprawling work/death camp on the Elbe River outside Hamburg proper, whose prison population included a large quotient of Soviet POWs, some destined to be gassed with Zyklon-B.

I suspect my breakfast mates, defense trainers of some sort or another, are charged with expanding the skill set of the young Lithuanian military. They need it, given the maneuvers I saw last summer on June 14, when they paraded in front of Gulag survivors on the green in front of the KGB Museum. Not that the honor guard wasn't crisp and proud and in step, but they all seemed thin and so young, too young. In the pictures I have, my grandfather seems older than those boys; certainly more of life had come at him by the time he began his studies at the military academy in Kaunas. There, one of his classmates was Jacob Gens, destined to become the Jewish head of the Vilna ghetto.

The men next to me have nothing to do with World War II. Nothing to do, most likely, with the closed U.S. black ops site functional after the invasion of Iraq but shut down for a long time now; a gated compound with blocked-up windows just off the Vilnius Highway on the way to Švenčionys. But their gun talk, potholed with gaps when I couldn't catch a word or phrase, gave me a slightly sick feeling. There will always be, somewhere in the world, people comparing more lethal versions of a Nagent to a Walther, or lovingly dismantling, cleaning, and reassembling a Glock 42, or furtively, in an effort to stay alive, scanning a weapons cache under guard, as Yitzhak Arad would do after he and his sister Rachel returned to Švenčionys from Głębokie. And my search for my wartime grandfather—wasn't it more or less like listening to a potholed conversation, spying on the past when the past wasn't looking, trying to fill in gaps that would forever remain blank?

It was 104 in Fairview, Texas. It was hot on the curb when I went out into the blast of the sun in front of the hotel where Petras and Rose were waiting. We were off to meet, once again, with Arunas Bubnys, the director of research at the Genocide and Resistance Research Center. The summer before, I showed him a letter I'd found in the archives written by my grandfather to one of his subordinates. Arunas had actually quoted it at length in the important compilation *The Ghettos of Oshmyany, Svir, Švenčionys Regions; Lists of Prisoners*, published by the Vilna Gaon State Jewish Museum, without assigning an author to the letter. (Signatures on archival documents are often hard to decipher.)

Security Police
Švenčionys Region

CHIEF [of Police]
February 24, 1942
No. 250

Sir:

Under the orders of the German government, Jews must live in ghettos in closed neighborhoods and can only leave the confines of the ghetto with special permission, further, there is a food ration set for them and they are forbidden to purchase privately, the movement [activity?] in the ghettos is regulated. But in Švenčionys Jews follow none of this, the ghetto is not closed, Jews freely walk wherever they like, and it happens that Jews flood [government] agencies with all sorts of requests.

On the street they walk on the sidewalks, they buy food from speculators and so on. Furthermore, the Jews who are given to agencies as workers and specialists are used for personal matters, for example, [female] Jews stand in line with other citizens to buy their boss one or another item. It even happens that agencies and [private] enterprises transport a Jew to other Lithuanian cities as an irreplaceable specialist, but the specialist Jews in making some item for someone demand as much as they like from citizens including even food items, and nowhere are the norms established for them adhered to. Jews make fine use of this and have already begun spreading different rumors and terrorizing people.

This sort of imprisonment of Jews is intolerable and I request that the Commander take the appropriate measures.

Senior officer Pranas Puronas
P. Puronas

It was winter when I'd had the letter translated. As with the selection of the doomed men from the Švenčionys prison yard described by Iozas Breeris, in which my grandfather, with other authorities, calls out names from a list and indicates who is to go back to his cell and who is to die, my first thought was that someone had made him write it. The letter is about hunger and the black market (how dare the Jews buy off the best or the last or anything, when the whole country needs a good meal?) and bribery and the gap between centralized German orders and borderland "negotiations" — a trade, for instance: half a life's savings to get out of a work detail with a sadist who beats you, for a job at the Tatar tannery instead.

The letter is about need, about wanting more than wartime poverty or anytime poverty—even if the more is only a pair of underwear or a corset with ripped stitching because someone (senior police, or burgomaster, chief) was the first to look over and take note of the extra padding in the bodice, thread a girl forgot to nip off with scissors or her teeth after a knot was made, after the money was safe inside the intimate garment she could not envision being commanded to part with.

The German historian Joachim Tauber added more context when I met with him in Berlin, helped me to look at who had power, even slight advantages of power, who was needed, who was in conflict with whom:

> Early on, the Nazi hard liners had the upper hand; always freak groups of players on the German side. Then there was a Jewish Civil Administration, they used the Jewish workers—they got money from them. The Jews worked better than the Polish and Lithuanians. They were better educated. Lithuanians drank. The Jews did not. These groups interacted. You always have to look at the specific region—who was strong? Who were the local forces, were there many ideologically motivated guys?

After meeting with Dr. Tauber, I looked again at Chaya Palevsky's sketch of the Švenčionys ghetto. There exists a more precise schematic, but because she was there, her drawing, with the roils of barbed wire and the darker circles and scrawls of the gate, brings to mind her effort at the table outside her kitchen, her large eyes, the movement of her pen across paper. When I look at her drawing, I see her young, on one of the winter streets, with her gray-haired father, her younger brother who she has by the hand. I see Yitzhak Arad and his closest friends, Gershon and Rueven. I see the unofficial "black gate" where, when conditions allowed it, black-market trading went on between the ghetto inmates, and the peasants and townspeople. Sometimes gifts were passed through, or an offering was made to a Lithuanian policeman who happened to observe a transaction and was duty bound to report it. The latter most likely an ongoing arrangement, renegotiated when the police rotation changed.

Before he made his way to the Švenčionys ghetto, Shlomo Ichiltzik described how he tried to hide from a Lithuanian policeman he recognized on a street in Widze, Poland (now part of Belarus, about thirty miles from Švenčionys). The policeman had been friendly with his grandmother, and Ichiltzik himself used to play volleyball with him before the war, but it was 1942 now, and even a dead Jew hauled to the local police station could fetch a bounty. For all the eighteen-year-old Ichiltzik knew, he would be spotted and killed. Instead the policeman, riding on his horse, caught his eye—"Shlomka, do you know me?"—and threw him a pack of cigarettes.

Later, at a Todt work camp (Todt was a German company that went from garnering huge military contracts to full absorption into the Reich) in Švenčionėliai, a friend from school (under Russian rule, Jews and non-Jews had been in school together) brought him food and one day handed her guitar over the fence as a gift. Ichiltzik was building rail for track to be laid in Russia. The workday was punishing, but with the gift of the guitar, he remembered "no matter how tired or broken we were, we would have nightly sing-alongs."

Yitzhak Arad, in one of our interviews, said that without the aid of non-Jews in Lithuania, no one would have survived. For more than two decades at Yad Vashem, he signed off on the certificates for those listed as Righteous Among the Nations, like the aunt and uncle of Teresa Krinickaja, who took in the small Jewish girl before her parents were killed.

After I found the letter my grandfather wrote about the ghetto, I discussed it with several friends, most of them Jewish. They separately brought up the same paradigm, and it surprised me: "Well, I don't know how brave I'd be if my family's life was at stake or if someone was holding a gun to my head." A pack of cigarettes. A guitar. A shampoo of peroxide to dye a little girl's dark hair blond, roof thatching to make a false wall in a barn behind which a beautiful young woman can hide. I tried to explain that especially in the borderland things weren't that cut and dried. Yes, there were many subtle and brutal ways my grandfather could have been "encouraged" to cooperate or collaborate or participate. In my search for details, for elusive facts about him, I was slowly compiling examples of risk and compassion, small as a potato or large as life.

This particular letter of his had come to me via e-mail with a large trove of fairly short arrest reports (often paired with release reports) from one of my translators in Lithuania. Maybe Wulff or the Lithuanian head of the Saugumas stationed in Kaunas, Stasys Čenkus, had sent up a missive to Senelis: tighten the reins, crack the whip, look like you're running a tight ship. Maybe there had been complaints, rumors. Perhaps Čenkus was one of the visitors to the house vaguely recalled by my mother. Perhaps he urged my grandfather to show some muscle, demonstrate allegiance. It was Čenkus, after all, who convinced his German superiors that an independent Saugumas would function better than a security police folded into the Gestapo, without autonomy.

Before the war, during the Russian takeover, Čenkus had left for Germany where he was trained by the Gestapo. He returned to Lithuania during the German invasion, both a collaborator and a staunch nationalist. Postwar, after a stint in a DP camp like my grandfather and the inexplicable receipt of permanent nonresident status in the United States, he settled in Queens, New York. As his family grew, he became the grandfather of the tennis champion Vitas Gerulaitis, known by sports fans as the Lithuanian Lion. In 1980, angry at a call by linesman Lee Gould, Gerulaitis suggested to a journalist that Gould be burned to death in a crematorium. The profoundly gifted and much beloved athlete died young in a freak accident involving carbon monoxide. Had he lived, he might have looked back over his shoulder at some point with the perspective age affords and wondered why certain outbursts came easily to him. He was quoted after his attack on Gould as saying that some of his best friends were Jews. When I read about this, it reminded me not so much of Aunt Karina standing in my mother's kitchen and saying of Senelis, "But he had Jewish friends, so go figure," but of myself, of the years in which I adopted the family habit of asking no questions, and by not asking, accepting a certain version of the past, making it my own.

"A GENUINE NATIONALIST hates everyone," Arunas Bubnys said during our first meeting, when we were looking at Senelis's letter about the ghetto and talking about Lithuanian collaboration. Later that same trip, rumbling along in the van with Petras, Rose, and me, Viktorija took one of my notebooks and in it wrote, "Lietuviai džiaugiasi, kai kaimyno namai dega" —which she translated as "A Lithuanian is only happy [or celebrates] when his neighbor's house is burning down." She wanted to leave the country as soon as possible. Lithuanians were insular. They hated everyone, and they hated themselves. (*Ah, the absolutes of the young,* I thought then—as if I wasn't full of my own absolutes.)

I had known my grandfather as a joyful man, but what did I really know? By the time of my second trip to Lithuania, his reprimand to his subordinates about the liberties taken by the Švenčionys Jews seemed no longer just an expression of duty but a snapshot of his own mindset. I didn't know yet whether he had been at Poligon, but he wrote about the small population of Jews left in the town where he lived as if they were already dead, as if they were abstractions made real only by the restrictions ultimately meant to kill them.

The more I read the letter, the more I hated him. "On the street they walk on the sidewalks." I wasn't even sure this was true. The ghetto had tightened up in the winter of '42. Was there an understory, a subplot, here? A bribe meant for him that went to someone else? A black-market source he used, tapped out by wealthy Jews able to send proxies to buy goods or, by some risky enterprise, purchase them without a proxy, at great risk, to be lugged back to the ghetto, past the police who would have to be bribed, and smuggled in through a break in the boards and wire?

The paltry wartime food ration for non-Jews included 125 grams of sugar a week, 1,750 of bread, 200 of flour, 400 of meat, 125 of lard, and 150 of grits. But for the Jews, the weekly ration shrank to 875 grams of bread, 100 of flour, and 75 of grits or grain. No sugar. It was a bad harvest year in Eastern Europe in 1941.

Rations for the German army were low. If you were a Jew, a few slices of bread, and there went 200 grams of your allotment. You could not fish or set rabbit traps. You could not go with my grandfather into the woods and take down an elk or a bear, then to the tannery for degreasing or else living with the stink of the hide.

PERHAPS A MONTH after I read my grandfather's letter about the liberties taken by the Jews of Švenčionys, another translator sent me another letter, originally written in Lithuanian but translated into German in 1943 so my grandfather's superiors could read it, and then translated again in 2013 into English for me.

The day I got the translation, even the pigeons looked cold, pecking around the litter of fast food by the subway exit where I emerged after a day of teaching. Home in New York City, I turned on my computer and saw a new e-mail from my German translator. I didn't want to look at it. I was sure it would be another damning report, or even if it didn't mention Senelis, another shooting would be described—a crime over and done with, no redress, only disgust. In the early dark, I felt a little lost. And then I opened the e-mail and downloaded the translation.

Aleksas Malinauskas, then the local head of the Švenčionys police station, had sent his letter by courier on March 16, 1943. It was a long complaint against several men, but primarily against my grandfather, who was his superior. Malinauskas, a thirty-seven-year-old Lithuanian, had much to say about the way my grandfather and a man named Kukutis—the area's Lithuanian political leader—had ganged up on him to the point of endangering his life, and even more to say about my grandfather's disgraceful behavior. To support some of his claims, he included in his diatribe two orders written and signed off on by my grandfather. One gave a Jewish woman, Elena Las, permission to live outside the Švenčionys ghetto. Another order, written up, according to Malinauskas, after their families petitioned my grandfather, changed a work detail for three Jewish men from forest labor in the Todt camp to work in a felt factory, a slaughterhouse, and one other unspecified place in Švenčionys. The order, in effect, released them from the Todt camp.

My grandfather, who wrote about the self-serving agenda of the defiant Švenčionys Jews, was at the same time brave enough, bold enough, to help them openly. I was stunned. A small, unbidden joy took hold of me. It was such a strange feeling, that joy. It wasn't intellectual. It took me by surprise. All my early questions came flooding back from the moment, in the café, when my mother had told me Senelis had worked for the Gestapo. Was Senelis good? Was he bad? Was he a killer? Was he courageous? Didn't these two orders prove, well . . . something? And wasn't that something good?

"The chair of the ghetto committee, the Jew Gordonas [Gordon], is Puronas's permanent guest," Aleksas Malinauskas wrote.

> He drinks with Puronas and hears the news from Moscow in Puronas's home. Gordonas told me this himself. Puronas also informs Gordonas about the political situation and about the situation at the front. A 'drinking evening' was organized by the Labour Department during which Puronas made an anti-German speech. He told me the same evening that I would be put to death by the Lithuanian court if I didn't change. The head of the Kripo [criminal police] Maciulevičius recently carried out a search of a leather factory and discovered 18 different skins that had been given by Puronas to be tanned. This is the kind of person Puronas, the head of the Sipo [a German abbreviation for "security police"] is. No one has killed me as yet . . .

There was my grandfather: stirring things up, drinking, talking war with "the Jew Gordonas," hoping for war's end. There was my grandfather—with Elena Las, another name in need of a backstory, who comes to him and for whose sake he defies all the decrees about aiding Jews, openly, with a written order that can be copied and circulated and used against him. (I think of my mother and her sister's story—"He let a lot of people out of jail, he knew he would be arrested for it.")

The Gordonas mentioned in the letter was Moshe Gordon, a butcher by trade and one of the heads of the Švenčionys ghetto who came to my grandfather's house in 1941 to plead for Mirele Rein's life.

Moshe and Basia Gordon

"A good man," Chaya Palevsky said of Gordon, and she was not one to generalize about those she knew during her time in the ghetto. "He thought about what was good for the people, not himself." Long before I'd gotten this latest letter about Senelis, when I was researching the Švenčionys ghetto, I'd found a prewar photograph in the U.S. Holocaust Memorial Museum archives of Gordon and his wife, Basia. I pulled it back up on my desktop and kept it there, looked at it, at Gordon's face, the set of his mouth, the seriousness of his eyes. During the Poligon roundup he fled with his family to Svir as Lili and her mother and sister had. He returned to the Švenčionys ghetto just before the sequestration of Jews in Svir.

Week after week, I reread the long complaint written by Malinauskas. Much of it was a harangue that had to do with prewar political leanings and Malinauskas's transfer from a police job in Utena, Lithuania, an hour's drive northwest of Švenčionys, because he was not a Smetona supporter (Smetona, recipient of one of Senelis's letters about a wish to return to active duty, and more importantly, the nationalist dictator who fled the country in 1940).

Utena, as noted in the International Jewish Cemetery Project, was the oldest Jewish settlement in Lithuania. An Einsatzgruppen report from August 29, 1941, details the shooting of 1,460 Jewish children there, in addition to hundreds of men and women—part of the context of the place Aleksas Malinauskas is compelled, by his superiors, to leave. The accountings from the Einsatz report of Utena are, of course, not mentioned in his diatribe, his list of personal humiliations. Why would they be? Yet, these narrative gaps, certainly not confined to one letter written by a man with a grudge against my grandfather, seem more than just evidence of the fact that people are often concerned with the small dramas of their own lives and not much else.

The woods smell of blood; the town of Utena (Utyan, in Yiddish), where you just lost your job, is missing two thousand residents. You accept and perhaps participated in their disappearance. They appear only as a suggestion, in the way—in the letter you send off to the German authorities about Puronas—you stress how faithfully you have upheld the German cause.

Maybe the truth about that which is "unspeakable" is simply that it is not spoken of but left out, unmentioned, or encoded. Like the vague signage at the turnoff to Poligon.

WHEN HE ARRIVES in Švenčionys, all of Malinauskas's old bosses from Utena, all members of the fledgling Union of Lithuanian Freedom Fighters (the beginnings of a coalition against the German occupation, but not necessarily against the extermination of the Jews) come to stay at my grandfather's house, and Malinauskas is shut out. His old bosses and his new bosses see him as a lackey for the Germans, a man who can't be trusted, a man who might report bribes or try to upend the local Lithuanian power structure, such as it is, for some personal gain.

> From this point on, Puronas and the district chief Kukutis, who is
> a supporter of Smetona and persecuted Germans in Memel,
> began to persecute me. I felt that many people were avoiding me
> for fear I would report them to the Germans . . . Puronas warned
> his deputy Garla to be wary . . .

Then Garla warns someone else, and so on, and so forth.

Moshe Gordon would eventually lose his life in the Klooga concentration camp in Estonia. His wife would be shot to death at Ponary. Those nights by the radio, the drinking and singing at my grandfather's house on Gedmino, didn't save them.

Over time, I started to read the Malinauskas letter differently. My grand-father's job in Švenčionys was intelligence. It would have behooved him to engage with the head of the ghetto, see what a little drink might bring forth, share a hatred of the devilish Germans; *they've made a mess of things, haven't they?* In early 1943, anti-German partisan activity in the woods of the border-lands was becoming more organized, more lethal. My grandfather's job was to investigate sabotage and ferret out information. If he got to have a few rounds of drinks in the meantime, and sing and rail against the Germans, all the better. I wondered—if there were any truth to the letter—what Moshe Gordon brought to my grandfather's table. What request and what payment? Perhaps he shared with my grandfather a tidbit of information, useless, really, or utterly misleading, about partisans afoot in the woods. Or maybe he worked my grandfather for war news with the hope that ghetto news would slip out. The order to shut down the ghetto could come at anytime, and then what? Everyone was desperate to know: would the remaining Jews be transfered to another ghetto, a work camp, or would they be slaughtered?

As for Elena Las, she either bribed him or was his lover or both—a different kind of exchange. I have no proof. It's a hunch. She might have been eighty years old, for all I know. Still I followed my hunch, right into Arunas's office, with Malinauskas's letter and Viktorija to translate for me.

It's cool in Arunas's office. In his plaid shirt and wire-rimmed glasses, he immediately goes about the business of trying to be helpful. The letter is long, as are most diatribes sent to the superior of someone you'd like to get rid of. I try to tell Arunas he doesn't have to trouble himself with the translation, I already know what the letter says; but he carefully translates the German into Lithuanian for Viktorija, and she repeats it in English to me.

Finally, when we reach the part about the radio and drinking, Arunas smiles and Viktorkija smiles, and we are all laughing a little. It's funny, kind of. But it's not.

We talk about the permission my grandfather gave to Elena Las, and also the work release, perfunctory, without detail, for the three men.

Translated into German by my grandfather's secretary, the document about Elena Las gives her formal permission, from my grandfather, to live outside the Švenčionys ghetto. The other document requests the three men named below be allowed to leave the Todt labor camp. Two of them, Motel Gotkin and Ilel/Gilel Šulheferis/Šulgeifer, appear in a 1942 census of the Švenčionys ghetto with their family members. I have not been able to find Icek Bres, the third, in any ghetto census or victim database.

"Certainly it would have been enough to get him arrested," Arunas said. "It would have been taken very seriously. He was supposed to be doing the opposite—enforcing the incarceration of the Jews, not letting them go free."

He asks if he can make copies of what I've showed him. After he steps out of the high-ceilinged room, with its books and desks and the cabinet where the internal wartime directory with my grandfather's phone number is locked away, I think about my grandfather's arrest. Could the Las permission and the work releases be the reason for his incarceration? "He was gone so long," my mother had said. But the record from Lukiškės prison indicates ten days' imprisonment only—a small punishment for a serious infraction. Once released, he went back to work for the Saugumas under the Germans in the city of Panevėžys. Ten days. It didn't add up.

Arunas returned and mused a bit more about the letter. "It's very unusual to see this—someone in a position of authority taking a risk like this."

I tell him I'm having trouble finding any specific leads about Elena Las. I haven't found any trace of her yet in the Lithuanian archives. Four people with the last name Las are in the 1942 Vornyany ghetto census: a father, a mother, and two young sons. The father works at a felt factory; the mother is at home in the ghetto with her sons. Have they paid to keep Elena Las outside the ghetto in Švenčionys? Does she even know them?

Arunas mentions a particular area of Poland where my search might be more fruitful. While we talk, I wonder . . . did she come to my grandfather with a bundle of marks wrapped in a scarf? Did he see her walking out of the ghetto on a work detail—beautiful, tall? Make an inquiry? I pull myself back to the present.

When I mention that I'm heading for Poland next, and then to Berlin and London, Arunas gives me another lead.

"Have you come across the name Vincas Sausitis?"

I haven't.

"There was a long criminal case in Poland against Jonas Maciulevičius. Many of those who testified were in the Švenčionys region during the war. Some of the testimony was very incriminating in regard to Sausitis. He'd been tried once in Lithuania and done some prison time, but he was tried again on the basis of material that came to light from the Maciulevičius case in Poland and given a capital sentence. There might be material in the case files in Poland about your grandfather."

Jonas Maciulevičius was in Švenčionys during the same time as my grandfather, but I'm confused. Why would a Lithuanian collaborator be tried in

Poland? It's someone else, I think, not the Maciulevičius mentioned in Malinauskas's indictment of my grandfather. Not the Maciulevičius whose office was across the hall from Senelis's and who was the head of Criminal Police. Somehow I can't quite take in what Arunas is saying. Fatigue makes me stupid, but part of my confusion comes from the not infrequent occurrence in the testimonies I've read of the same surname cropping up.

It all seems like a long shot, but I ask him how to get access to the file.

"You need to contact the IPN," he says.

He explains that IPN is the Instytut Pamięci Narodowej, or Institute for National Remembrance, in Poland. The case file will be in their archives. I scribble IPN in my notebook next to the names Vincas Sausitis and Jonas Maciulevičius. Right before I thank Arunas for his time, I mention I've heard that after the killings at Poligon, there was a banquet in Švenčionys for the shooters.

I wait for him to give me a slightly exasperated, tired shake of his head. He is meticulous in his work, and so much in testimonies and even official documents of war is false, must be carefully examined. Who is remembering the memory? What, in the official document, is officially kept opaque?

"It was quite common for there to be"—he pauses, looking for a word— "parties afterward for those who participated. It happened in many places." His face is flat, readable and unreadable at the same time. A rather slight, gentle man, he is not the person you would expect to find trudging through the violence of his country's past.

Zenon, the angry poet, in the heat with his book of war, was he right after all? If so, where exactly was the table laid in Švenčionys, in late fall of '41? Who came with the shooters; who stumbled through a door or across the town green and shouted a request to the orchestra, sat down in a sprawl or casually took a seat, not yet blind drunk but eyeing the food? Who reached for a hunk of bread and the platter of herring swimming in cream as the music began?

It was one of those dishes, at our Lithuanian family dinners, I always thought I liked until the first salty bite. It didn't matter. Senelis, Uncle Roy— anyone at the table would give me a hug, push the tin of cookies my way, bend over the milky fish on my abandoned plate.

CHAPTER 35

SHOOTER

On a wooden table at the Lithuanian Special Archives close to my hotel, Viktorija, Rose, and I open up the file on Vincas Sausitis, the man Arunas mentioned. He was retried in Lithuania for his collaboration with the Germans, partially on the basis of the court case in Poland against Jonas Maciulevičius, who was indeed, it turns out, one of the men my grandfather worked closely with in Švenčionys. Free for twenty-two years after doing his time in a Gulag labor camp for collaborating with the fascists, Sausitis was in prison again. In the statement he wrote after his capital sentence was pronounced, he railed about his superiors. They were shooters, just as he was; they organized it all. (My grandfather?) Why weren't they in jail? Why were they all free? He spent most of his time as a shooter at Ponary, but testimony at his trial placed him at Poligon as well.

He claimed to have killed only ten people in total and to have actively aided others who were imprisoned, of every nationality, whenever he could— passing messages, sending letters. He had to make his own shoes when he was a boy. He didn't want to be sent to the German front. He was uneducated, unwise to the ways of war and cities. He didn't know what he was getting himself into.

"If someone tried to run away, I would have no choice but to shoot him, otherwise the fascists would say I let him go on purpose."

The man who ran the lunchtime food concession during the Poligon massacre (food for the shooters was provided near the train station in Švenčionėliai) didn't remember seeing Sausitis among the thirty-odd shooters who arrived bloody and hungry and sometimes drunk before going back for the rest of their day's work. But at least two other shooters—one sentenced right after the war—were with him at Poligon, and placed him at the pit with his army gun.

The file holds letters he received during his incarceration. I touch the envelopes. The old paper is rough. There are children, a wife. I go back to a section of the statement Sausitis wrote to the court after his sentencing: there weren't many "runners" at the pits at Ponary; one "young and strong Jewish guy tried to run and a guard shot him in both legs." I close the file.

CHAPTER 36

INSIDE/OUTSIDE

When Lili's grandfather sends a man with a cart back to Švenčionys, Lili's mother and little sister are not at the pharmacy. Fearful of being discovered, Symansky, the pharmacist, with the help of a nurse, has moved Lili's mother to the isolation ward in the hospital. Lili's sister Khanale is in a regular ward, wearing a cross, instructed not to let a word of Yiddish come out of her mouth—no *Ikh hob moyre*, "I'm afraid," to a kind face ministering to the small, sick girl. Symansky fetches them at the hospital, and they travel by cart, as Lili had done, back to Belarus, where the German presence is established but the incarceration of the Jews has not yet begun.

At the grandfather's large house, Lili's mother has somehow managed to hold on to her dentistry case, her knowledge of dentum, the pulp, cementum, the remarkable practical intelligence of her eldest daughter in the terrifying crush at Poligony, her late husband's absorbed concentration in the lab, the razor-sharp loss of her first love, after which she might have believed no one else would be taken from her again. Now she's got her hands on a drill, a foot-pedaled drill or an agonizingly (for the patient) slow electric, but a drill, nonetheless. She has curved and straight extraction forceps, Novocain (invented by a German scientist), probes, and filler. There is no dentist in Svir; she makes her case to the German authorities.

Yes, she may open a clinic. She separates her patients; a German soldier doesn't wait his turn while a Jewish man comes upstairs with a swollen cheek over an infected back molar. Most of her business comes from Belorussian farmers and their wives and children, and locals from town—grateful not to have to bounce for miles in a cart, a rag tied around their heads, a tooth gone pulpy overnight, pain like a nail hammering from gum line to forehead.

All this in a war: her town dead, her future rotting out around her. First the yellow star, next a small ghetto is erected around Rybnaya Street with the smell of the lake, Shkolnaya Street, the wooden synagogue.

Because of her clinic, she and her daughters are allowed to live outside the rather flimsy barricade, but Lili's grandfather and aunt and uncle are incarcerated. Lili and her sister and mother bring them food. The clinic does well, and since money is essentially worthless, pay comes in foodstuffs; a chicken, eggs, milk, cheese, flour that Lili's aunt works into warm loaves before she is rounded up and taken away.

When a German comes for an extraction, Lili has to hold the man's large, sweaty head as still as she can, holding him as if she is older than fourteen, as if she has been trained as a dental assistant, as if he is not the enemy who now groans and thrashes as her mother twists the forceps. Each time her mother calls her to help, she's certain the soldier will bolt from the chair and attack her, strike her down because of the bloody mess her mother has made of his mouth. It doesn't happen. They're a team, mother and daughter, responsible now for the younger daughter/sister and for the rest of the family trapped in the ghetto.

When the large house is requisitioned and they are forced to move to a small two-room house—one room for the clinic, one for their lives—Lili cooks her mother lunch on the little stove—beans and carrots, white beans that keep their shape while the sugary carrots break down. It's their favorite dish. A bit offered perhaps to Dominika, their landlady—hair a mess, a large woman who has let herself go but is glad for the rent and puts in a version of a boiler so they can have hot water for a bath, a luxury they can't share with the rest of their family.

Yes, they knew what was happening in Švenčionys, knew about the ghetto that Chaya described as she drew its boundaries and the center of town—the part that was inside the ghetto, the part that was outside the ghetto—using the Yiddish *gas* for street. Cloister Gas, Łyntupy Gas. Chaya talked while she sketched:

> The ghetto is near the center of town, on one side of the church
> . . . two synagogues . . . here were some houses . . . mostly brick.

Here, this was like an entrance to the city and from here . . .
different kinds of lanes and around the lanes there were houses,
a little river and near the river was the gate. In the back of the
synagogues is already the marketplace and all the stores around
it. The marketplace was beautiful with trees around and grass,
and here were the big stores . . . two, three stories high. [Chaya
laughs at her drawing.] The street of Vilnius is large, very
modern. Sventsian was a very cultural city. So much to tell . . . so
much what's going on. After Poligony we knew that our time
will be up because little by little they were killing everyone.

At a certain point I asked my mother, as I asked everyone I met who had
been young in the Švenčionys region during the war, what her hopes as a child
had been. Did she have a dream? An aspiration? My mother looked at me, her
face a veil not so much of bitterness but of surprise at the ignorance of my question. "I wanted the war to end," she said. She wanted food. She even wanted
her parents back together, fighting again. The sack of potatoes from the farmer
just over the Latvian border dumped near the stove, her mother's familiar pull
on three strands of her hair worked into a perfect braid—Babita's small victory,
a little order imposed upon the dissolute, smelly, wild beauty of life and her
oldest child. Would this predilection for order save my grandmother in the
camps, or get her beaten into the snow like a stiff heap of rags? Impossible to
know.

Lili Holzman, in Svir, had "the will to live."

Chaya Palevsky and Yitzhak Arad did not expect to live.

"Death escaped me. I didn't escape death," Chaya said.

Before the war, Arad had been utterly consumed by the desire to get to
Palestine. Now, once he returned with his sister to Švenčionys from Głębokie
(which was no longer safe), it was how to get out of the ghetto. At fourteen he
was already a tactician, measuring off distances in his mind, thinking of snow
that would allow footsteps to be noticed, taking stock of the Judenrat or Jewish
Council—who might help, who might protest.

In the months following Poligon, a small group began to hold meetings in
the ghetto. Chaya was the only girl. A boy in the group was in love with her
and wanted her with him at all times, and Chaya abided. *Wither thou goest, I will*

go, Ruth said to Naomi in the Hebrew version of the Bible. My Jewish grand-mother bestowed it as a nickname upon my mother. "You are my Ruth," she would say.

But for Chaya, romance was the least of it. Quickly, as the group cohered, she became committed to the formation of a plan, hashed out over many weeks, primarily by the young (with the exception of Chaya's mother, who was apprised of everything, who, in Chaya's words, was not only her best friend but "one of us"). So—a few adults, but mostly teenagers who wanted to avenge the dead, regardless of the cost.

But in the beginning, they were stuck. In the beginning they took stock. What was possible, what was not? Could a secret be kept in the ghetto? Who, among those outside the ghetto, might help you or kill you? Dvora Goldhirsh's best friend in school—a Polish girl—had turned on her in 1941, "never so happy as to see Jewish blood spill."

Karina Margolis, with the peroxide-blond hair, had a different story.

Her parents, perhaps better informed than most or shrewder than some, understood when they heard through rumor or official announcement about the roundup for Poligon that they would probably be killed or taken to a camp, where their four-year-old Karina would have little chance of survival. They begged a man named Sylkovsky to take Karina and raise her. He agreed. One of the few memories Karina has of her birth parents is of the piano in their house that her mother, who did not work, sometimes played. They seemed to have been well off, so they would have offered whatever they could on behalf of their only child.

Sylkovsky grew frightened. It was hard to disguise a little Jewish girl. Perhaps the fact of the slaughter at Poligon terrorized him. First the Jews—who would be next? He decided he couldn't keep the child. It was simply impossible. He began asking, discreetly, this person and that person—*take the girl, I beg you.* But one after another, those he asked refused until finally, Anna and Piotr Miksta at 112 Strunaicha Street said yes. They'd just lost a twenty-year-old son to war. They opened their hearts to Karina.

"What did you make of your life then?" I asked her.

I had called her at her home in Moscow from New York City.

"I missed my dolls and my toys," she said matter-of-factly, and then told me that under the watch of Anna and Piotr (Mom and Dad to her for a long time), despite the fact that she was a child and that her life before them was a near blank, she was aware of everything that came after.

Her new mother and father were at constant risk. Inevitably, someone informed on them. Karina was hauled to the police station with Anna Miksta, who was put in a separate room, down a hallway, behind a closed door, out of Karina's sightline. Karina was five. She was led into a room where a red-haired German officer waited to interrogate her. Perhaps it was Metz (helpful according to some testimony, brutal and a shooter at Poligon according to others). Perhaps Horst Wulff had red hair; I can't tell from the photographs I have of him.

A female translator, well dressed, well spoken, was in attendance. Was she Rakowska? One source indicates that the translator was from the ghetto, but the way Karina described the skill with which the translator mediated this encounter seems to fit Rakowska. Her métier, after all, was translating for the Germans, for Beck in particular. And in a crisis situation she might be called in to assist elsewhere, might actually have made sure of it, for reasons not yet apparent when I interviewed the grown Karina.

Crammed into the office with the translator, the officer, and the girl under scrutiny were all the women of the Švenčionys ghetto of childbearing age. Rachel, Hana, Ester, Mira, Genia, Riva, Frieda, face after face, hands nervously pulling at the fabric of a shawl or chafed and white and still.

The German began his interrogation abruptly. He wasn't going to slip a sweet to the girl to disarm her. He wasn't going to pat her on the head and instruct the translator to reassure her.

He tipped his head or motioned with a large hand toward the cluster of women sitting and standing, some in near rags, others wearing the well-made clothes of their former lives: a blouse, a dress, a sweater that had not yet been bartered away. "Look at them. Look," he commanded the blond Jewish/ Catholic girl. The translator quickly translated his German into Polish. Did she know it was a lie—this girl, her Polish "mother" down the hall? She must have known. The informer had some sort of proof, others to confirm his story. But then, it was a time of informers, a consumer enterprise that brought every liar, every local with a private jealousy or old wretched grudge, every man or woman hungry enough and/or mean enough or frightened enough, to the buyer's table.

The women's faces were turned to the floor. Some wept. At least a few had known Karina's mother or father or both before the couple were summoned away from their piano, their only comfort the fact that their daughter was, they hoped, safe. Which meant that they had lost her, that they were lost.

"Which one is your mama?" The German officer made it clear that the women from the ghetto must show their faces to the child, all headscarves off, no shifting behind someone taller.

The translator repeated the officer's words again in Polish for the Jewish girl. *Który z nich jest twoja mama?* Perhaps she used her hands, pointed to the women, touched her own chest, a hand laid atop her blouse where underneath her own heart beat. *He means Mama, who you love, who is in your heart.*

"My mama is in the other room," Karina replied in Polish without stumbling.

How thick the air must have been. I've seen the old offices at the police station in Švenčionys; the industrial gray, only new then, constructed for occasions like this one.

"Look at them," the German screamed in his frustration. He pointed at the women summoned without forewarning, their lives resting on the ability of Karina to withstand the German officer's threats.

Karina didn't know Polish well, but her adoptive parents had made the most of the little time they had to teach her a few words about her mama, to drill into her that this was all she must say, whatever question she was asked. So she, who "understood everything," did. Her only mother was outside the room, down the hallway, in another room. She was terrified to look at the ghetto women crowded together. Among them there might have been a familiar face—a neighbor, an aunt, a family friend, even her real mother—and she might have given them all away. Longing compelled her to risk; she looked. Among the distraught group there was no one she recognized, no mother.

The red-haired German had had enough. He undid the large buckle of his belt, a practiced move—he'd used it before, though perhaps not on his own children.

"Which one is your mama?" As he spoke, he slapped the belt down on the edge of the desk. Maybe a sheaf of papers fell, the uncapped Edelstahl pen rolling off to the floor, fat as a cigar with a sharp tip. He turned to Karina with the belt.

"Mama," Karina cried.

He grabbed her arm, bent her over for the first blow, but suddenly the translator from the ghetto or Rakowska intervened, began speaking to him quickly, softly. Karina, today, has no idea what the translator said to him, what mollification, what alternative—a better way to find the truth, or perhaps a very carefully worded suggestion of what the little girl might be worth to her "family."

The women from the ghetto were there for all of it. The little blond-haired girl was one of them, belonged to them, but she didn't. She ate bacon and potatoes with Piotr and Anna. She slept outside the ghetto. She'd been baptized at the Catholic church. She would survive, and as an adult she would never be sure of the day or the year in which she was born.

Whatever the translator had said on the day of the German and the belt and the weeping women, relatives of the Mikstas who had a farm gave away a prized cow, and with the Mikstas, put together a huge sum of money in addition to the cow—both impossible to recoup in wartime—and in this way paid off the German officer, the informer, and whoever else could have taken Karina away.

For the moment, Karina was safe. She was allowed to go down the hall and find Mama and go home.

On the phone I asked Karina what she believed accounted for the bravery of Anna and Piotr Mikstas.

She didn't know. She didn't even know if she would call it bravery. Maybe they just wanted a child to love them and to love.

Yitzhak arad's sister had survived Poligon because a "useful" tailor in Švenčionys claimed her as his daughter. Perhaps it was Yakov Wexler, who knew how to extract information from the German Metz. Or perhaps another tailor, unnamed in a testimony I have, who worked past curfew one night on a vest for a Gentile customer, insisted on finishing the delicate, beautiful fit despite the trouble it could cause for both of them; moving a button, straightening a seam until—perfect—and his client snuck back into the world outside the ghetto through a secret exit between the boards and wire, the tailor's pride tucked in a package under the frightened man's arm.

After Poligon, when Arad and his sister returned to the Švenčionys ghetto from Głębokie (which had quickly become too dangerous for them), he noticed first a preponderance of children whose parents were dead in the pit, taken in by those who could manage it or who couldn't manage it but did it anyway. Among the men and women, instead of utter despair or the blank faces of mourning, there was a resigned workaday attention to life in the moment—as if Poligon had been only a bad dream. No looking back, no looking ahead.

In Israel, at our first meeting, I asked Arad how he felt in those first weeks and months.

> Look, we were young, and when you are young you are quite
> optimistic. And especially when all the time you are active—I *have*
> to escape, I *have* to cross the border, I *have*—you don't actually have
> time. I even asked myself during the war, with the ghetto—did I . . .
> was I in a bad mood, did I have the pessimistic approach? No—
> because all the time I was active. I never had time just to say, okay,
> what am I going to do? Let's say, when the Germans came, yes? . . .
> all the time, always I had some aim, something to reach, to do . . .

Behind the couch where he sat there was a large abstract painting, framing a man who was only just now (in an evolution that had nothing to do with my questions) starting to look back, not as a soldier or a scholar but as a man aware of the boy he was and what that boy had lost.

In Warsaw, he said, "There was a choir in the synagogue, and I was singing in the choir. We have now here a choir and I'm singing. Since that time, all my years, I wanted to go back to singing. So now I returned. There's a Russian saying—'In the old man is the child.' "

He smiled a little, not so much at me as at time. And then we spoke of the past again.

* * *

Moshe gordon, chairman of the Judenrat, is aided by Khayem-Hersh Levin, Dr. Binyomin Taraseysky, the tailor Yankl Wexler—men who have connections in one way or another outside the ghetto, who can speak Lithuanian or German or both, who are thoughtful and pragmatic. A finance committee periodically has to put out the call for candlesticks and bracelets and rubles and marks, a fur hat, a diamond hat pin—anything that can go into the ghetto war chest so that, at a moment's notice, a crucial bribe or "gift" can be given to Metz or Maciulevičius or Skrabutenas or Kenstavicius or perhaps Puronas—perhaps. For a long time these names, except for Senelis's, blend together for me; *vicious*, I keep hearing, thinking; a name from a fairy tale, each individual conflated into one bad man.

A small Jewish police force is established in the ghetto. According to Chaya, one of the ghetto officers is caught raping ghetto children. (Her face collapses in horror, but only for a few seconds—we must press on, and it's another story, she tells me.) The ghetto inhabitants, living under constant threat of death, are still a spectrum of humanity like any community.

The all-important labor bureau sends workers out as demanded or presents orders to those manning the few workplaces left inside the ghetto. There is a sanitation crew—a difficult task under the cramped conditions, with water often in limited supply. A painting brigade goes out each day from the ghetto. A street brigade keeps the sidewalks clean, shovels snow, chips the ice off the steps of Josef Beck's office, the post office, the mess hall for the police on Vilenskaya Street. An observant, quiet girl mops the floors in the police station. A few women give themselves to a German or a Lithuanian big shot who, under the right conditions, talks too much. The women offer themselves up and return to the front gate of the ghetto with information and hair that smells of cigarette smoke and a mark of what was taken, what they gave, on a neck or a breast, what they will wash away from between their legs.

Some people work harder than they have ever worked in their lives, as if work will guarantee their lives. Others are lazy. Some are wealthy and lazy, but at least hire proxies to fill their slots. Moshe Gordon works some expensive magic with the authorities, and a horse and cart are allowed in the ghetto, making it so much easier to bring foodstuffs—the rationed allotment and perhaps a black-market sack of flour hidden underneath—through the gate, along Schul Street, in and out of the small lanes that, but for the satellite dishes, to this day remain somewhat of that moment: unpaved, though the original wooden houses were torched at the end of the war, bombed into dust.

Like Yitzhak Arad, the teenager Tuvia Brumberg saws wood in his first job after the ghetto is established. His grandfather's old house, a felt factory in the basement, lies close to the perimeter of the ghetto. Strangers live in it now, but the factory is still in operation, and after the forest, he's assigned there for a time. He and some of his coworkers "stay and work late . . . intentionally sleep outside the ghetto" in case the Lithuanian police and a handful of German officers and gendarmeries (as Yitzhak Arad calls them) are given a middle-of-the-night order to kill off the five hundred or so Jews of the Švenčionys region. The last ones.

Adolph Jurkovenas is the cook at Švenčionys prison. The isolation cell, roughly two meters wide and long, flooded before winter. Now ice waits on the floor for the next prisoner.

To sleep and wake with that fear, to thread a needle, to hold a match to the cigarette of a man who doesn't speak your language and tomorrow might kill you but tonight wants you, to vomit one morning and realize you're going to have a belly to hide (one small son already given away to a Lithuanian family for a king's ransom, and now this), and not simply go mad or surrender to grief or become mute, to read hidden books, sing and survive the worst among you, and find those who will be your teachers, your guides, your better halves, the whole time captive in a captured town, is an existence that requires a verb that hasn't been invented yet. Or perhaps exists in a language I don't know.

There is gossip and rumormongering, the washing of socks, the watchers and the one being watched as a woman walks back a little behind the rest of the crew charged with cleaning the public baths, and in her isolation, endures contempt mixed with a bit of wonder because one of those taking note of her progress in the gutter lives in her house now and sleeps in her bed and eats off her plates and has found, in a cupboard, stewed fruit she put up a week before the war began, stone fruit under a paraffin seal, small dissolved suns in sugar syrup slurped and sucked down.

And who is the new woman of the house? I imagine her. She's Lithuanian, with a son who might be called to the front. She's overheard the Germans mimic her mother tongue. In autumn, she admires the late-blooming flowers dead people planted in the garden next door. She doesn't speak to the men who shovel snow from her wrought-iron gate to the curb; she's just a housewife who goes to church, whose husband is important in some temporary way. It wasn't her idea, any of it. "War is a beast for sure," she might say, but she's grown from it, born in Kaunas or Panevėžys or Trakai. Who knew she'd be gifted with a better life? Though a poor cousin down in Vilnius, married, has just been picked up in a sweep—accused, of all things, of giving sex to soldiers so her family can eat. She'll speak to her husband about it tonight; they'll hire a driver if he can't be spared, he'll call down to Vilnius without her even asking—that's the kind of man he is, her husband—and then her cousin will be free. The dumb criminal police should have better things do to. She'll bring a food parcel and won't say a word to the rest of the family; money for her cousin to fill the cupboards, to last at least until spring.

1942 mugshot of a Lithuanian woman arrested in Vilnius on the charge of prostitution

CHAPTER 37

A GAME OF LIFE
AND DEATH

Some things I know are true: my Lithuanian grandmother learned to freeze the lice out of her clothing by burying some of what she wore in the snow at night. In the based-on-a-true-story-that-wasn't-true movie *The Way Back*, a Gulag inmate who was a Polish cavalry officer also learns this small but crucial part of Gulag hygiene. It's easier to think of him than it is to think of my mother's mother: the scarf she tied around her head, her thinly padded jacket.

She was a meticulous, intelligent woman; she must have quickly learned to find the right burial ground outside her barracks, one less likely to be spotted and pilfered by a fellow inmate. In the Siberian winter, a strange conversion: 40 below is the same in Celsius or Fahrenheit. Each night she dug a grave for the rags wrapped around her delicate feet. Each morning saw a resurrection in the barracks while women's clothing thawed and stank. Outside, there were dozens of small burrows in the snow, littered with dead insects—fat with the blood of my grandmother and her fellow prisoners, the tenacious little claws at the end of each of their six legs hanging on to nothing but the winter dawn.

Snow was a stopgap measure; the lice were never-ending. Still, it was something. I wonder if she thought of her children in those frozen moments outside at night, after her food allotment was measured against the work she and her barrack mates had done. Motherhood brings with it routine, and in her old life she must have gathered the clothing of her son and two daughters— pants and dresses and blouses and shirts alive with the scent of them—and decided what to scrub clean with the board that night or the next morning before her work at the library. Or maybe one day a week was washing day. Maybe she forced her children from her mind entirely, or found that amnesia torture had brought on during her time in Lubyanka periodically returned, until coughing and thin in her bunk, all she could remember before sleep was the sound of the broad saw she and another woman took to the fir tree, the cut smelling of turpentine. If you chewed a small chip and spit a bit of pulp in your hand, you could rub it on an itchy lice trail and let the camphor in the wood give you a few seconds of relief from the need to pick and scratch.

ANOTHER THING I know is that on February 6, 1942, my grandfather interrogated Kazimeras Czeplinski, a seventy-one-year-old Polish resident of Nowo-Święciany, about the whereabouts of his son Zigmuntas in regard to an act of sabotage at the railroad. (Senelis on the same date ordered his other son, Juozas, to be held in the Švenčionys jail; he hadn't been able to find Zigmuntas.) Among the family members who lived with Czeplinski, he listed his wife Jozefa, son Zigmuntas, daughter Kamile, and an "orphan child," Jonas Gabis, who was twelve years old. Gabis is not an altogether uncommon name in Lithuania, but Nowo-Święciany is not far from Belarus, where the Jewish Gabises on my father's side of the family were from. My grandfather wasn't interested in the orphan child; where he came from, who his parents were, or how they had been killed. He was conducting a sweep: pulling in men and women, Polish and Lithuanian, to question them about the mining of a train and to prove his mettle as an investigator in one of the first significant partisan attacks in the area.

I wonder about that orphan child with my family name—a name spoken in the presence of my grandfather, almost as if a whisper of the future had presented itself to him. According to my grandfather's interrogation of Czeplinski as it was recorded by his secretary, Czeplinski could barely keep track of how many children he had. He was nervous—probably for his son, who my grandfather, at least temporarily, was interested in as a suspect. But maybe he had even more reason to worry—a small riddle I'll never solve. Gabis. Today, in the United States, the *a* is long as in "hay," although Czeplinski might have pronounced it differently. For centuries surnames for the Ashkenazi were like the Lithuanian names of the months—they weren't fixed. A man might keep his father's name and tack on a surname after a nearby river or a town or a mountain or a profession and then change jobs and change his name. Aunt Shirley, my father's sister, told me that once the writer Isaac Bashevis Singer explained to her that Gabis, as a patronymic, was from the Hebrew for Gabriel. But there is a more modest derivation: Gabis from *gabbai*, one who assists at synagogue or perhaps oversees the upkeep of the local cemetery or, in the event of fire, heads the collection effort for those whose houses burned down.

IN THE ŠVENČIONYS ghetto ("twenty to thirty small wooden houses," recalled Yitzhak Arad at our first meeting) the whisper of a future came primarily to the young. The ghetto elders had to organize ghetto life around the demands of each day, split between a belief that work and bribery would keep the ghetto functioning and an awareness that it was all temporary—even with the Germans' miscalculation about the quick, glorious victory they now knew would not be theirs. ("I would give up God and my own Humanity for a piece of bread," wrote the young German soldier Willy Reese from the frozen, undersupplied eastern front.) A longer war meant an ongoing need for felt boots, panje supply wagons drawn by one or two horses, seats for motorized military vehicles, wheel rims, barbed wire, furs remade into soldiers' coats in Kalis, a labor camp adjacent to the Vilna ghetto . . . But at some point it would all end, a candle burned down to a dark stub of nothing. There would be no victory over the Seleucids, no Hanukkah miracle with a light that defies diminishment.

On a freezing morning in early February 1942, a hastily assembled work detail of a dozen or so men, most of them teenagers, walked through the gate of the Švenčionys ghetto, the small cluster of wooden houses falling away while they trudged in the street, as required by restrictions initially laid down locally by my grandfather's cohort Mykolas Kukutis. From the sidewalk, their Lithuanian guards barked into the quiet: "Faster," a curse delivered, the prod of a stick or rifle butt. In the street, Itzhak Rudnitzky/Yitzhak Arad, Moshe Shutan, Arad's friend Gershon Bak, and the others went as they were directed. The Jewish cemetery loomed. Was today the day they were going to be shot? Arad wondered.

Švenčionys Jewish Cemetery, 2014

This was how it happened: men called for work, men vanishing. He began gauging any exit. If he were to run, would it be down Ignalina? Gedmino, past my grandfather's house? The cemetery was now a kill zone, winter snow piled up, a field on one side of the tumbled stones.

It was going to happen this morning. His sister Rachel would find out. The shot in the back of the neck, a nick in his spine if he ran fast enough. The blue sky broke open, daybreak to daylight. The group was ushered past the cemetery. To another death? They were moving farther and farther away from the ghetto.

There were several munitions dumps in Švenčionys. The same Gudonis who helped lead the Jews to slaughter at Poligon worked as a guard for a time at one of them, "at the end of Godutishkaya [Godutish] Street by the milk factory." He was one of three police officers who rotated in three shifts to protect the stocks of ammunition and confiscated weapons.

Several other storehouses were loaded with Red Army functional or busted (purposefully in some cases, so the Germans couldn't make use of them) revolvers and rifles and machine guns and grenades, as well as more arms the locals had been required to turn over. The mess needed sorting, fixing if possible, cleaning. The DP machine gun with a round magazine—I saw scores of them in the old Soviet war movies that played at my first hotel in Vilnius— was light, but liable to break down. Stick grenades were jumbled alongside *otrezankas*, a version of the sawed-off shotgun favored by bank robbers and bootleggers during Prohibition in the United States. The wooden buildings were originally part of the Soviet infrastructure before the Germans came in; now a small crew of older (and thus possibly less rabid) Germans who had seen action in the first war kept watch on the dim interiors of metal, dust, and cold.

Arad and Tuvia Brumberg and Chaya Porus and her brother Itzik and Gershon Bak and Reuven Miadziolski and Shaul Michelson had heard the future whisper something they couldn't quite make out, know only that it wasn't, if they could help it, month after month of handing over "gifts" or slave labor until one day they were locked in the old synagogue, windows smashed and benzene poured in.

At Poligon the ground was littered with rags, caps, headscarves of family and friends. Frost heaves opened the earth. Nearby farmers must have dreaded the coming spring, a thaw and washouts that would carry bones into the rye and flax fields. They had crop quotas the local "headmen" handed down from the Germans—unmet the last half of the summer of '41 and after the fall harvest of the same year. And now spring would mean corpses of Jews showing up like a nightmare, Jews who had a way of wreaking havoc, even dead Jews, even the Jews who were your friends.

The little convoy stopped in front of the large Soviet barracks. A German older than the oldest boy's father, his eyes still crusty with sleep, fumbled a little with the locks while the Lithuanian police moved off. The doors swung open. The teenage boys who dreamed of sports and Palestine, who knew how to sing, how to bind a book, how to make a pair of boots, walked into their future.

In an interview in 1996, Tuvia Brumberg said, "Now I will tell you that those eighteen-year-old boys would leave [the warehouse] with gun parts under their coats. And I was one of them."

Arad wrote: "I tried not to let either the Germans or the Jews see the impact this abundance had on me, knowing that in matters involving life and death, one must be aware of Jews too." Not everyone in the group could play the part of the moment—one word, one gesture or telling look, and it would be over.

Late in the workday, their guard followed his superior out the door, just for a moment. The hours had been uneventful—a quick cigarette maybe, a few words together that the Jewish boys inside shouldn't hear. They had been diligent, quiet; and anyway, who but a trained soldier would be brazen enough to shove a sawed-off shotgun into his pants, under his shirt, and then quickly put on his jacket?

The workday spent, the corporal ordered the crew to line up in front of the barracks, light snow in the yard crunching under their heels like stale *kichlach*, the sweet cookie of dreams, of that other life that didn't belong to them anymore. Would it happen? Would the corporal give the order to the soldier at hand to take them back to the ghetto, but then "Warten," wait—some equation slowly taking shape in his mind, guns + Jews. And almost as an afterthought, touch the tip of his Karabiner to Arad's jacket, say with intent but without urgency "Ausziehen," or simply "Aus," and watch as Arad, his face gone flat and empty, slipped off his jacket, let it fall to the ground. The rifle wasn't so good with distant targets, but a teenage boy at close range—*poof*. Or torture to start with, as this was thievery of the first order. Chief of criminal police Maciulevičius would call the chief of security police, my grandfather. What would happen next—it didn't pay to think of it. Arad could only wait. His friends, who knew what the jacket hid, looked ahead, frozen, impassive.

It didn't happen. The Karabiner remained slung over the corporal's shoulder. He was pleased with their work, ordered them back to the ghetto under German guard, told them they would be returning. They retraced their steps, Orion a fixed searchlight, the constellation a scattered battalion in the indigo sky—in service of whose fate, impossible to know. The one Lithuanian guard at the ghetto gate, lower on the food chain than the German, waved them along.

Arad, the smallest among them, brought the first stolen weapon across the threshold, hid it in the family home in the room that had been his grandparents', before a shooter took them down at Poligon.

CHAPTER 38

MISTAKES

As Chaya remembers it, the oldest member of the budding resistance group in the ghetto had been a student of Fedka (Fyodor) Markov before the war. Markov, a Russian Communist, had been the mayor of Švenčionys during the Soviet occupation as well as a history teacher at the Jewish secular *folkshul*. Alexander Bogen, a survivor of the ghetto, described him as handsome and blond and tall.

Now he was in the Naroch forest, where Polish kings once took their hunting parties; a forest of alder and swamps, oak and pine, the huge lake where, after winter, long-lived eels slithered out of the mud. Markov was just beginning to fight the Germans in single acts of sabotage with a small band of fellow partisans—the train investigation my grandfather was conducting.

Markov's ex-student spoke to the group about joining him and fighting. More weaponry had to be collected. A reconnaissance team would have to sneak out and come back. Guns were useless without ammunition—they had a few bullets, but most of the boys (and Chaya) couldn't shoot yet. Unlike my uncle Roy, none of them had had fathers who hunted and fished and trapped. Their fathers had been readers or cantors. They had managed small factories or run apothecaries. They played the violin. Even if they were not "religious," they observed Shabbos, made sure to invite someone without a family for Friday dinner, went to synagogue.

The group had to wade through every angle of every possible plan; any choice they made would affect the rest of the ghetto. Was it better to stay and fight in the event of an action against the entire ghetto? If they took to the woods, what kind of retribution would their families—or for that matter, everyone still alive in the few blocks and lanes left to them—face? A gun stowed under a floorboard in a cramped storeroom endangered everyone. Was it fair? What did "fair" mean, as the food supply shrank and the "gifts" purchased less, the demands for them unending?

IN JUNE OF 2013 I sat with Yitzhak Arad in Ramat Gan, in the same large common room where we had met the year before. He spoke of Markov, and the young group he was part of in the ghetto.

> Markov was a small team at that time. Ten, fifteen people, no more. The Soviet partisan movement was still very weak in the area. It was a game of life and death. At that time, we were aware that our fate was to be killed. We definitely thought that. Germans aren't going to leave. Yes, we took all the money from the Judenrat [to purchase more weapons] by pressure and threats ... In my research I justify the policy of the Judenrat to prolong life in the ghetto, as long as they could. People believed that an uprising in the ghetto did not offer survival.

He reminded me that he had written the first half of his book about the Švenčionys ghetto and his life as a partisan when he was only nineteen. As soon as he landed, illegally, on the shores of Palestine, he wrote it straight through, until the next chapter of his life took him over. Again I found myself watching his hands; delicate, even elegant. In the struggle for Israeli independence, he had served in the Palmach, an underground army of expert fighters, demolition specialists, bomber pilots, supply convoys that took heavy casualties.

He coughed a little from the dry air. He often spoke like a teacher to me. Images—sensory particulars of his own past—did not come easily to him, unlike Lili Holzman and Chaya Palevsky, though his scholarly work is both erudite and gripping. He was a military man, had been at the head of Yad Vashem for many years.

Suddenly he changed topic. "I had a terrible thought the other day."

He looked at me, his face holding the surprise of the moment in the recent past when the terrible thought had come.

"The forest was only open for young people like myself. To be honest today, it's good that my parents remained in Warsaw. If they had come, I would have stayed with them. In Švenčionys I couldn't have taken them into the forest. I'd never thought about it before."

Tears rimmed his eyes. For once, after all my questions for him and others I'd interviewed, my prodding, my intrusion, the interruptions while I changed memory cards or slipped a new battery into the video cam, chattering so the thread of the conversation wouldn't float away, I couldn't speak.

"It's not a terrible thought," I finally said. My words sounded stupid, though I meant them. I should wrap it up, I thought. His reflections seemed private, spoken to me only because I happened to be there.

My stepdaughter was with me, taking photos. Irit Pazner Garshowitz, my keen, compassionate researcher and translator in Israel, went for water. It was a hot day. Desert wind had hit Israel. The taste stayed in my mouth, chalk and sand—the Khamsin wind that slammed open the long unlatched windows of my hotel room, thrashed the orange trees in the courtyard below, then disappeared at night—an uninvited guest I somehow missed when the stars came out. A last question. Could he describe his two closest friends in the ghetto, Gerson Bak and Reuven Miadziolski?

"I can see them now; Reuven was a sportsman. Gershon had a better sense of humor . . . a little smaller . . . both very smart . . . happy, joyous. Youngsters . . . exactly my age."

Yitzhak Arad, 2012

It has been said to me that there were no secrets in the ghetto, but in any small community, the closer you are to an event, the more hard knowledge you have of it. In order to stay under the radar, Chaya and Arad and their partners in their embryonic enterprise took precautions. They didn't often walk through the ghetto together. It was rare that one member of the group would visit another's house. Ultimately, they became known—they had to in order to succeed, but it was an accident that initially raised their profile. In different testimonies, one person remembered that a boy shot himself in the foot. Someone else declared that the secret group was never a secret to anyone.

Spring of 1942: the time to start mushroom hunting, time for the three-toed woodpecker, whose pecking mimics the sound of a round going off—loud, and then diminishing, then quiet, then starting again, *rat-a-tat-tat*—so that someone might look up at the sound from a newly thawed garden in the chilly sunshine and remember the powder burn on the right hand, the heat of the chamber.

According to Yitzhak Arad, late in the day on April 13, Chaya's brother, Itzik Porus, came to Arad's house in the ghetto, violating the group's dictum that they keep their distance except for clandestine meetings. Something had happened, something so bad the group code had to be forsaken.

In the attic of one of the empty buildings outside the ghetto, three of their group members, David Yochai, Reuven Miadziolski, and Gershon Bak, were sewing makeshift holsters for guns they had risked their lives to collect, for their soon-to-come life outside of the ghetto in the forest. Reuven Miadziolski did what boys do; for one second, gun in hand, he was aiming at a German or Lithuanian partisan. He brandished the gun at Gershon Bak, and it went off. The bullet caught Gershon in the throat.

A boy lay bleeding on the attic floor. His parents were alerted. Dr. Taraseysky was brought to the scene. According to Shimen Bushkanetz and Khaye Ginzberg, interviewed by Leib Koniuchowsky in 1948, Dr. Shabad, a Jewish eye doctor from Vilnius, also arrived. The consensus was that Gershon would live, but the bullet needed to be removed.

In Arad's account, the bullet was removed by Dr. Taraseysky. Bushkanetz and Ginzberg described events differently:

The doctors were urged to remove the bullet and keep silent . . .
Dr. Taraseysky refused to operate. Shimen Bushkanetz personally
heard Dr. Taraseysky proposing that the incident be reported to
the head of the criminal police, the Lithuanian Maciulevičius.
Bushkanetz proposed . . . there was no one to be afraid of, and no
one in the ghetto knew what happened. Taraseysky responded:
"I'm afraid of you!" That meant that [he] was afraid that any Jew
might happen to report the incident to the Lithuanians or the
Germans.

There was a ghetto resident who was close to Jonas Maciulevičius, had an
allegiance to him that could possibly put them all in danger, make the keeping of
a secret impossible. Dr. Taraseysky consoled Gershon's father; his son, via a bribe,
would be taken to the local hospital, then returned home after the interrogation
at the police station. A story was floated to the powers that be about boys fooling
around in an attic, stumbling across a gun, and so on. No one believed it.

Arad wanted to gather his group together, hide Reuven, and at the first
opportunity sneak him out of the ghetto with the rest of the group and into the
woods. The ghetto elders refused to sanction Arad's plan of escape; the reprisal
would be calamitous. All the arms the group had managed to hide inside the
ghetto, where in an event of a German action they could be immediately put to
use, now had to be smuggled to a ruined synagogue beyond the wire. Arad's
closest friends faced torture. Gershon Bak's last words to Arad were "Keep it
up, and take revenge."

"So the two young men went to clean up," Chaya recalled,

and one of the guns went off and shot Gershon Bak in his throat.
He was so scared . . . in the ghetto in the attic of his aunt's house.
They told him not to go out to the Germans or police and wanted
to hide it and went to the Jewish council. And Dr. Taraseysky. He
could take out the bullet, but he wasn't sure and didn't want to.
"No, we have to take him to the hospital outside the ghetto." I
will never forget it. I shudder to think of it. They tortured him so
much. The nails. The fingers. In the door. "Is there a group?" "Is
he a partisan?" Mozart in the background. Squeezed the fingers
in the door. Both of them, he couldn't talk, the other one who was

shot . . . he could, but he made believe he couldn't talk. They never gave out. They said they went up into the attic to look for clothing and it happened that they found a gun and they didn't know how to handle it. And after torturing both of them so much they killed them.

There were twenty people living in our house, in every room six, seven people . . . In the middle of the night my mother and my sister Rachel put a lot of dirt in two big water pails and put the bullets [we were hiding] in the dirt in the buckets and took them out of the ghetto to a burned house so no one would find them.

Sonderbehandelt on the boys' arrest cards meant "special handling" by the Lithuanian police. The quiet, industrious Jewish worker who pushed her mop down the hallways of the police station was there when Reuven Miadziolski was dragged past her, bloody, swollen. He managed a whisper in Yiddish: "We will not reveal a single name."

IT WAS A spring for killing. Not that that was unusual anymore. It's the logic of war, the logic of slavery. War does not devolve into peace. Murder's aftermath is ruin. And who knows what is set in motion, how one killing alters something we can't quite see or touch or hear. My grandfather would have been at work during the few days the boys were tortured at the police station, a quick motor-cycle ride from Gedmino. He lives a few streets away from Josef Beck, Gebietskommissar of the Švenčionys region. Spring, even a cold spring of fits and starts and more snow and boys tortured and killed, along with a Jewish girl named Sorele Levin, a young woman whose only crime was refusing work duty; he can race around, now that the roads are clear, in his motorcycle with the sidecar. He can ride it to a meeting at Beck's, though Beck's is a brief walk from his house and a waste of petrol. Still, it's something to be seen revving a motor, arriving in style; it feels powerful. It feels like freedom. Perhaps he'll simply wave at the assembled group and gun it on by, just because he can.

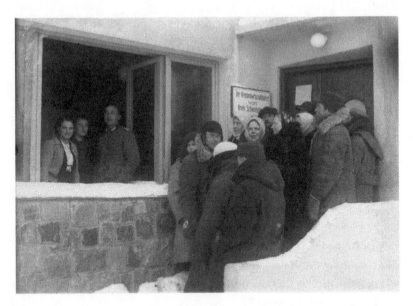

Josef Beck's office window

HORSE MOBILIZATION
People tell about a German, a Lithuanian, and a few officials who recently went through the villages confiscating livestock and haven't come back to this day.

—Diary entry of Herman Kruk in the Vilna ghetto, May 20, 1942

A LITTLE MORE THAN a month after the killing of Miadziolski and Bak and Levin, on the morning of May 19, Josef Beck, his deputy, Walter Gruhl, and Schneider/Schmidt (one source has him as Beck's replacement, another as a new commandant for a nearby Soviet POW camp), along with the translator Rakowska, set off on the road to Ignalina. They were going to commandeer local horses. More and more horses were dying, and since horses pulled the panje wagons, they were an absolute necessity in the supply chain to the north, as well as the regional fortifications. There are dozens of versions of what happened on that road.

A simple, unadorned version is this: Markov's small band is informed about the requisition trip for horses and hides in the brush, not far from Švenčionys. They spot the Opel and toss a grenade—it lands in the middle of the undercarriage of the car and explodes. The blast throws Rakowska, bloody and unconscious, from the vehicle. Beck, Gruhl, and Schneider/Schmidt (the unlucky replacement) are immediately dragged from the burning vehicle and shot. Their genitals are hacked off. Caps worn by ground troops in the Polish army are thrown down next to each dead German, though neither Markov nor his men are part of the Polish Home Army. Rakowska's eyes flutter open; she's shocked to see Markov, who she taught with at the *folkshul* before the war, standing over her. With cuts on her forehead, her stockings ripped, a gash in one leg, she walks, dazed, back to town to police headquarters to report the ambush. She is immediately arrested and placed down in solitary, where, since spring has arrived, the plank floor is a dirty flood. Her apartment is searched. She is interrogated and interrogated again.

Immediately, a list of suspect local Poles is produced by the Lithuanian authorities, including my grandfather. A hunt for Poles from the entire region ensues, some on the list my grandfather will soon hold in his hand in the prison yard, some not even Polish (like the man who stammered out the Lithuanian version of Rakowska's name to his interviewer, David Boder, after the war), but just there in the sight line of the hunters who worked quickly and asked few questions of those they encountered on paths and roads and fields.

My grandfather is with Maciulevičius and Gestapo from Vilnius at the scene of the crime. A bloody, grotesque mess, a taunt—the mutilation meant to humiliate: *You think you're all powerful, you think your balls are so big. Look at this.*

Word of the killings traveled quickly, and Poles began to hide. "You're on the list," someone would tell a frightened man he ran into in front of the Catholic church in Švenčionys. Maybe someone from the police, maybe a Lithuanian partisan who for whatever reason leaked information—money, or a crush on the pretty daughter of a man about to be dragged out of his house while his wife takes refuge in the dank well in the back, where raspberries grow in summer.

I HADN'T PLANNED on going to Poland but in New York, in the spring of 2013, I met my friend who led our *Odyssey* reading group (years ago now) for a quick coffee at a rather sterile café in the sprawling Time Warner Center—a fancy mall that always makes me feel like a tourist. The indoor café seemed like it could be anywhere. I felt rootless. I wanted to stay home.

We talked about my research.

"Of course you're going to Poland," he said, blowing on the foam of his cappuccino. It wasn't really a question.

"Of course," I said, on autopilot. Our time was too brief to lay out my latest intentions: continued research at the Holocaust Museum, translating and studying more than two dozen testimonies from the USC Shoah Foundation.

The reprisals for the killing of Beck had taken place in the Švenčionys region. I'd already inquired when I was there about local descendants of those killed, or elderly friends who might remember them. I'd come up empty except for Teresa Krinickaja's account of her best friend's mother hiding in terror in the family well. Beyond that, there had been a brief exchange in front of the Jewish cemetery in Švenčionys. On the road right outside the green, among uncut grasses, in a breeze I can hear now in the mic when I replay the few moments, a woman holding an empty cardboard box—Jadwiga Rakoska, born in 1943—told us that her sister had been an eyewitness to the exhumation of the Poles shot in the Jewish cemetery after Markov's ambush. Her sister had fainted dead away. There were Soviet "doctors"—perhaps forensic workers. The stench of cadaverine and putrescine (the names of the proteins sound like their odors) after the top layer of dirt was shoveled away was overwhelming. A few more words, and then, as we were walking into the cemetery, a friendly warning from Jadwiga to look out for ticks—they were especially bad this year.

A FEW DAYS after coffee with my friend, I realized I had to go to Poland. I hadn't tried hard enough. I'd mixed up my frustration at how little I initially had been able to find with defeat. Maybe descendants had moved from Švenčionys to Poland after the war. It stood to reason that wartime archives in Poland would have a greater depth of material about the killings—wouldn't they?

My entire search was beset by the inexplicable, the disappeared. Mirele Rein. A list from the Lithuanian archives of names and addresses of Švenčionys Poles, the list dated several weeks prior to the attack on Beck—men and women my grandfather wanted brought to the police station, his signature on the bottom, little check marks next to a dozen of the names. Why? Elena Las and the fate of Icek Bres, one of the three men my grandfather "released" from the Todt forestry camp; it went on and on.

I did go to Poland, but in the end, it was in Lithuania where I met descendants of those killed during the Beck reprisals. In preparation for the Poland trip I'd contacted Johanna Berendt, a smart young Warsaw-based journalist who did initial research and made inquires for me. It was she who found contact information for Vaclav Vilkoit, with his excellent overview of the minority Polish population in Lithuania. The people I ended up interviewing were in Vilnius—each a fifteen or twenty minute trip from my hotel.

CHAPTER 39

ANTON LAVRINOVICH

AUGUST 12, 2013

He has the slightly grizzled look of an old soldier: working hands, a shyness that makes his smile at first seem like the embarrassed smile of a schoolboy who, though he knows the answer, hates being called upon. He only lives in his Vilnius apartment (today taken over by the heat wave) part time; otherwise he is in Adutiškis, one of several small towns in the Švenčionys district. He was born in the village of Gudeli in Belarus in 1930, eighteen miles or so from Švenčionys.

He was nine years old in 1939 when war broke out; Adutiškis, the birthplace of his mother, was still a Polish territory. He is third in line in a large family, has a twin; his father was a teacher at the elementary school. His mother, Veronica, was his father's student, sixteen years younger than the teacher she would marry. (Veronica's own mother was a janitress at the school at the time.)

His memories of the German arrival in their area are sharp, in part because the family home, on a high hill, was used for the German telegraphist—with communication equipment that had to be powered manually.

> They were carrying cannons with horses, and they put immediately this communication person [in the house] to use the power engine, and they unharnessed their horses—and it was actually the oats which were planted next to our house where they let the horses eat the oats. My mom came out and said, "What are you doing!" and they said, "It's war." She did not know yet what that meant. When the Germans came in 1941, Russian schools were closed, and a Lithuanian school was opened.

He recalls working the handles of the telegraph machine for the Germans. Were they nice to you? I ask. "It was not a very big animosity; there was not big fighting." Our talk turned to the Jewish population in town.

> In '39 there was a Jewish school. When Bolsheviks came, schools were connected and the Jewish school was closed. I would not say they were different [his new Jewish classmates], but there were many people who were talented. Math—I remember there was a girl whose name was Gritskea. It was me, also, who was not—like—stupid. We were competing to see who would get the right answers on our homework.
>
> When the Germans came in '41, there was a ghetto in Adutiškis. It was one street that was separated where Jewish houses and Jewish stores were. Everybody moved to this one street. And in September they were forced to bring the carts and wagons and everybody was put on them—like old people, women, and children were put onto the carts and wagons, and they were brought into Švenčionėliai, where the barracks were. It was a—like Poligon before. From the whole region, they were all brought over there, and they were all murdered unfortunately. The ones who were able to walk, they marched on foot.

He was not allowed to go down the hill from his house to the ghetto, nor did he witness the carts and people marching. His parents would not speak of what had happened. The local authorities were now Lithuanian, and in town, after Poligon, people would speak about the murder of the Jews—"a bad feeling in the town, the houses empty."

I ask if he can describe himself as a boy. I'm sitting on what serves as his bed. The open door to a small balcony refuses the breeze from outside. He's embarrassed again, smiles.

"I was as everybody, nothing special." Then adds, "We had very strong ties between ourselves in our family." (Six children, one named Yanuck, who died in 1932.)

As soon as I bring up the subject of the Lithuanian authorities, he begins to speak about the Beck reprisals, starting with what is most painful for his family.

My father [Kleofas Lavrinovich] was killed in '42. He was like a
hostage, because on the eighteenth of May, Gebietskommissar
Beck, he was on his way to Ignalina from Švenčionys. It's
fourteen kilometers. The Belarus partisans came, and Beck was
killed. Yes, a translator was with them; she was not killed, she
was local. And it was the order after that—five hundred people
should be shot. And "local authorities—please, whoever you
know, please collect everybody." And on the nineteenth or the
twentieth, at night, at two in the morning, in our house, there
was Dewejkis, the policeman, vice chairman of the police, and
Kuczinskas. He was the local nationalist. He had been a student
of my father. He knew him very well. Algis Kuczinskas. He was
approximately ten years older than I, so he was born around
1920.

They were collected—the men. Thirty-three from Adutiškis.
And even women were collected. It was in all the towns around
Švenčionys. In many of the other places, the women were not
gathered, but over here, the women were collected. The nationalists of Adutiškis—they somehow figured out that they should
collect the women as well. The family of Bravolski—it was father,
two sons, and two daughters living in one house, and the
daughter-in-law. All these six people—they were all collected.
Only mom was left behind, the old lady and one grandchild who
was one year old.

I ask if he had any idea of how, in his town, the list of who was to be taken
was created.

It was just the meeting of the local activists. And they put
together the list. The people who compiled the list, they knew
everybody's address. [This was crucial in every roundup. Many
testimonies make the point that only a local could identify the
ethnicity of another local—a Pole instantly knew who was a Jew.
A Lithuanian could spot a Pole a mile away. Germans, particularly in the rural areas, ceded to local authorities considerable, if
ultimately limited, power because of their need for this most
basic information.] They mostly collected the local intelligentsia;

teachers, the clerics, people who were working at the main
offices; they were all told they would be taken to Švenčionys.

Could he describe the moments when his father prepared to leave in
accordance with his ex-student's demand?

> He did not wake up the children who were asleep. He kissed
> those who were not asleep. And my mom is asking Kuczinskas,
> "You are taking him away, will he be back?" And Kuczinskas
> said, "Of course he will come back—it's not like the Bolsheviks;
> they took people and sent them to Siberia." My mother prepared
> breakfast for my father. My father took off his wedding ring and
> watch. It was his watch since he started out in St. Petersburg. He
> said, "I will probably not need that."

Hear it? The sound the ring makes when set down on the table by the dish
of half-eaten food prepared in the middle of the night. The twelve-year-old
son's eyes follow his father's movements as he takes off the watch that perhaps,
on special occasions, when Anton was younger and still climbed onto his
father's lap, he was allowed to wear for a few minutes—put it to his ear.
There—his father's time.

And then his father held his wife, and perhaps kissed again the top of his
son Anton's head, and was gone.

> [By morning] the rumors started to—the rumors that these
> people will be shot this day, and the rest of the families shot the
> other day. And the shooters came—a special group. The Einsatz
> [short for Einsatzgruppen, the killing squad], they were
> Lithuanian. It was called the Kuczinskas regiment. When they
> saw the women, they wouldn't take them, they let the women go
> home. The mother of Kuczinskas sent someone to my mother to
> tell her she should go to Kuczinskas and beg him to let her
> husband go free. So Mom took the youngest child in her hands
> and she took the youngest twins along and she ran to the elders'
> office. She ran and she passed the church. Burokas was standing
> over there at the office; he was a guard, a farmer, a partisan. He

wouldn't let her inside, so she ran to the church, she went inside
and started to cry in the church. She fell onto her knees. It was
the time of the special May prayers, every day at six o'clock the
prayers started in church. It was then that the men were taken to
the truck and they shot them just at the outskirts [of town]. When
the people were praying, they started to shoot.

Afterward, Anton's mother was afraid to stay with her children at the
family home. No one wanted to give them shelter. Finally a woman named
Maria Unton, with three daughters, let them sleep on the floor. There were so
many fleas, they were "dreaming about sunrise" so they could leave.

"Did you know what had happened to your father at that time?" I ask.

Anton Lavrinovich, 2013

"I understood that Father was killed, yes, I understood."

They did not allow us to go and get our father's body. When they
were all killed, one person tried to escape. There was a retired
sergeant—they were letting three of them out of the truck and
then shooting them in the back. They were let to run, and then
the shooters were shooting them in the back. He actually died
in the truck—the sergeant. And Józef Polhalski, Kazimierz

Dobrowolski, and Stanislaw Nowak; they did not run, they just turned around to them and they said, "You shoot us," and so they lay together. This is from the words of the people who guarded. And afterward they put dirt on it. Afterward they dig a pit, four meters by two meters, and they were all thrown out and covered with dirt. And it was a plowed field and they actually planted oats so it was not to be noticed where the grave was.

But his mother knew; everyone knew. He gesticulates—a burial mound collapses. "And then it was a kind of pit over there. There was not dirt and it was forbidden to take dirt from the surrounding area. The family members used to bring dirt in the wagons to make this a proper grave."

"Did the family members have to live with the nationalist partisans who had done this, afterward?" I asked him.

"Yes, we continued to live side by side."

In 1944, when the Soviets reoccupied, a commission was established to study this particular crime. There was the opening of the grave, and in anticipation of it, family members paid to have coffins made or made the coffins themselves. "But two years passed, and they decomposed, so it was impossible to know who is who. Ludvic Bravorski, he had long white hair so they recognized it's him. And the others were—they were unable to identify them, so they left it as is. They burned the coffins and they buried the remains."

We speak briefly about his life after the war. He was a "day worker"— whatever was needed, in the Soviet Army for three years, a shop assistant. Afterward he was elected as a deputy for the local council in the same area where his father was killed.

"In this region it was twenty-two villages, and every village knows it doesn't matter—all the changes of rule. They all respect me. I'm not ashamed. I was working for all those thirty years."

Although the documents I have about my grandfather's role in these reprisal killings place him, thus far, primarily in Švenčionys, he was chief of security police for the entire region. I turn off the video and stand and apologize to Anton Lavrinovich.

CHAPTER 40

JOSEF BECK

Josef Beck

He is mentioned in the compulsory war diary kept by Hauptmann Klöpfel, stationed in Kaunas. On April 2: "The note I already sent you on Josef Beck and the instruction to him to change the construction of panje cars, farmers' horse cars from two to one horse."

April 19, 1942, a month and a day before his death: "Kreislandwirt Beck from Schwentschionys informs that 1,419 pairs of felt boots have been completed and are ready for pickup." And then an entry on April 20: "Roll call in honor of Hitler's birthday." The small German command in Švenčionys would have marked the day just as the Germans in Kaunas did.

Josef Beck was born on September 2, 1910, the second-oldest son in a family of five children. He married into a farming family, but fate dealt him successive blows; his first son, Gerhard Josef, died on the day he was born, and a year later Beck's wife died after a surgery. The heritage laws of the Reich required him to enter into military service. For a time, before he was called up, he worked shoveling hay in the Hamburg-Hagenbeck zoo. A box of his civilian clothes arrived at his parents' door, and in June of 1941 he was in Švenčionys.

On October 23, 1941, when he was thirty-one years old, he wrote home to say he had been promoted to Kreislandwirtschaftsführer, the country agricultural/supply official. As the oldest officer in Švenčionys, he was now the commander of the town as well.

The killings in May and early June of 1942 throughout Švenčionys and the surrounding areas after Beck's assassination were reported in the two main "newspapers" that served as propaganda machines from the first day of the German occupation.

From *Ūkininko Patarėjas* 21, May 29, 1942 (also appeared in *Į Laisvę* 120, May 23, 1942):

Two Reich Soldiers Cowardly Shot
Harsh measures taken — 400 people killed
Kaunas, 22 may

In the eastern Lithuanian region two Reich soldiers, namely Joseph Beck and Walter Gruhl, were cowardly killed while on an official business trip. Four hundred Communist saboteurs, most of them Poles, were shot in response to this abominable crime.

The crime, committed against German soldiers, who were working on the restoration of regions severely affected by bolshevism, was so brutal and barbarous that it had to be responded to by taking the harshest measures possible. The crime is considered very serious since it was committed by the criminal element in the region, which during the enormous fight on the eastern front was experiencing the benefits of peaceful and creative work . . .

The Lithuanian nation was given self-government. It also just recently has acquired municipal government in its regions, cities and villages. And this all has happened while the war still goes on. The Reich minister Alfred Rosenberg, during the meeting of general councilors in Kaunas, declared that restoration works will be required to overcome all internal difficulties. "If there is a lot required from the people of the eastern regions, there also has been a great deal more required from the German nation, and for many more years."

Thus the harsh vindictive measures that had been taken are equivalent to the barbarous character of the murder itself. It can be certain that any crime of similar scope and influence to the peaceful work of others will receive similar unequivocal response. In this regard, the warning has been passed not to confuse nobility with weakness . . .

THE NEWS OF this foul murder of Reich soldiers in the eastern region of Lithuania, of course, surprised everyone . . . Terroristic banditry is alien to our nation . . . It was committed not by one of us, but rather by those provoking elements that aim at disrupting our peace and work, and turning us against our German saviors who rescued us from bolshevism.

We completely understand the harsh measures that the German government took in retribution for this treacherous and low crime . . . it is not only Germans who should fight against such banditry. It is also a Lithuanian matter.

Through Konrad Beck, one of the family descendants, I learned that the family had never been told about the violent aftermath of Josef Beck's death. Konrad Beck wrote to me through my researcher in Berlin: "The whole family was very shocked to hear of the massacre killing of all those innocent people as a result of our uncle's death . . . It was good and had a healing effect to relive the . . . past from a distance of almost three generations and to hear that the fate of strangers so far away from each other seems to be tied so closely by the historic events."

I had imagined the Reich would have wanted the family to know the scale upon which Beck was avenged—a perverse matter of honor. It shocked me that from 1942 on, no one in Beck's family had any knowledge of the nod the

Germans gave to the Lithuanians in and around Švenčionys, using the occasion of Beck's death to pay back the Poles who had once been the majority in the region and who, so many years ago, had stolen Vilnius in World War I. (I was shocked, even though I myself had only recently learned about my grandfather in the Švenčionys prison yard with the infamous list in his hand—the varying accounts of numbers of victims; ten, twenty, fifty-four, thirty-five—and that was just in Švenčionys proper.)

But then again, the Reich was obsessed with posterity. The killing of noncombatants had to be blamed on locals or burned and ground down into nothingness, into a poorly kept secret. As for Konrad Beck, who had studied history and German philosophy—his uncle and my grandfather probably drank together and ate together at least a handful of times, and of course, there were other occasions, less innocuous, when their paths might have crossed.

Whoever he had been in the intimate scheme of his own life, Beck came to be different things to the different constituencies of Švenčionys. To the Poles, he had been something of an ally, tamping down Lithuanian aggression against them. (His death would unleash the same.) The Polish/Lithuanian problem bedeviled the Germans constantly, only because it interfered with a reliable, cohesive work force. For the Jews, Beck was a German who had been at Poligon. Perhaps he was one of those, as Vincas Sausitis suggested, who tried his hand with his pistol, caught up in the alcohol vapor and scent of blood, a boss who never put his name down on the pay sheet because it was sport after all, as far as he was concerned— or perhaps not. Testimony also places his second-in-command, Walter Gruhl, at Poligon. Of my grandfather's whereabouts during those few weeks of the Poligon massacre, I was still unsure. I had a suspicion, though, that if Beck made a point not to be present on at least one day at the crowded barracks or by the pit dug in a single night even with the troublesome rain, Senelis, almost twenty years Beck's senior, would have thought him weak. He would have known from the outset that Beck wasn't military material—just a farmer with grief in his heart, sent up north of Vilnius to be a cog in the supply chain, nothing more.

CHAPTER 41

ILLEANA IRAFEVA

AUGUST 13, 2013

She was born December 15, 1942. A lovely (red hair, delicate cheekbones), thoughtful woman, she points to an old photograph framed on the wall of her apartment in Vilnius: a picture of her father wearing the uniform of a Polish soldier. Pieter Kulesh, formal, eyes straight ahead in the photograph, was born in 1910; her mother, Usefa, was born in 1913 in a small village in the Švenčionys district. She was pregnant with Illeana when her husband was killed, and when Illeana was roughly five years old, she told her how her father had been murdered.

> They knew about it. [Beck's killing.] My father was working on the railroad, so he said, "I am innocent, I didn't do anything." And he was taken from the bed during the night. My mother knew who came for him; she knew everybody in the village. Somebody once came from America for her to identify him. It was in the court, he was brought over here, she identified. It was during the Soviet time. It was an announcement that if you know something, if you remember, please come and identify him. She knew all of them.

She returns to the story of her father's disappearance.

> They were inviting him, as if for an interrogation. He quietly dressed and he went. Whoever was found at home—the men—

everyone was taken out. My father was not Polish. We're all Belarus people. Nobody made any difference whether you are Belarusian or you are Polish. Many, many Jews were killed over there. The Jews also lived over there. My mom knew all of them.

Mom was actually telling that they were—when they [her father and others] were marched, their killers would say, "We will kill you, we will kill you." The place where they were all gathered—nobody was allowed to go there. It was wartime. My mom and all my uncles would say that they were not afraid of Germans, only Lithuanians. They were asking for vodka. They were drinking all the time, the Germans. And the Lithuanians were all in the forest.

They knew where the bodies were. This they knew. Guards were over there and nobody was allowed to go. They lay like that several days and afterward the Germans forced somebody to dig up the pit, and they put everybody there.

She shows me a photograph taken by someone who risked his or her life, who snuck out in the bitter end of dusk to make a quick record of the carnage, to prove that it happened.

During this time, one woman, she actually stole the body of her husband and she buried him in the courtyard of her house. And she was betrayed, and she was forced to dig him out and to bring him back. The priests—they were actually watching and they were killed also, on the road from Švenčionys to Švenčionėliai. [Vaclav Vilkoit and I had gone to the priest's graves in Švenčionėliai several days earlier.] It did not make any difference. They wanted to kill any man in the radius of twelve kilometers from the place where Beck was killed.

I ask Illeana if her mother was aware that the Germans had ordered the killings. She says that her mother believed the Germans "allowed" the killing, but the "order"—the decision as to who should be killed—was made by locals. Illeana also remembers talk of Beck being a very cruel man, which was why he was killed.

As our conversation continues, it turns out that all three of her father's brothers were partisans with Markov's brigade. One, Sergei Kulesh, was killed "in the first days of the war as a Communist youth by the white bands." Boris and Alexander Kulesh, her other uncles, were with Markov during the attack on Beck.

"Is this perhaps the reason your father was taken?" I ask.

She doesn't think so, doesn't think her uncles' connection to Markov was known. And then she corrects one of several versions of Beck's killing: the road was mined, there was no grenade. Markov and his men mined the road and then ran away. She asks me about my research: "But you probably know that the people who were killers, they were turned into heroes. They were not pure fighters for freedom; it was cruelty, and cruelty causes cruelty."

Her mother continued to live among those who had killed her husband, frightened all the time, giving aid to Illeana's uncles in Markov's brigade. Of her father, her mother often spoke to Illeana of his kindness. He had a good heart.

"I never knew him, my children never knew their grandfather. But people say that my youngest, the one who plays the piano, he looks exactly like him."

The švenčionys policemen who were interrogated by the KGB after the war and speak of my grandfather all say that only ten to twenty men were taken away by car that May in 1942, after my grandfather culled them from the list he held.

In Zdzisław Chlewiński's book *Groza i Prześladowanie Polaków i Żydów na Wileńszczyźnie* (*Terror and Persecution of Poles and Jews of Wilno*), he lists thirty-seven Švenčionys victims. The numbers of those killed in the entire region range from four hundred to over a thousand.

In Švenčionys, Alfons Romanowski was a printer; Julian Sierociński, a teacher—of what, the list doesn't say. (Recently my mother recalled that the father of the family of Poles who lived in the other half of their house on Gedmino until the time of the Beck reprisals, when they disappeared, was a piano teacher.) Czesław Dubowski was a clerk. Stiepan Markow was the seventy-year-old grandfather of the partisan Fydor Markow(v). Michał Walulewicz had at one time been deputy mayor of the town. Among those marched or driven to the Jewish cemetery to be shot, two women were pulled from the group by Germans on the scene; one of the women was a German officer's paramour, and she fled with him to Germany when the Soviets returned to take over "Ostland."

Three of those shot, hands bound behind them, bodies beaten, were Jews from the ghetto who had worked industriously for Beck. (Perhaps, if one worked hard for a German in command, your chances might be better for food, information, or even your life.) Khayem Sheytl was one of Beck's drivers. Dovid Ginzburg was an electrician. Gurvitz, who on Chlewiński's list is identified as a shopkeeper, shined Beck's shoes, ran errands, fetched his jacket, helped the cook, watered the garden. These men died simply because their work duty had been at Beck's office and house.

CHAPTER 42

WORK

In 1943, my grandfather will be arrested. His wife, my Babita, will be moved to yet another Siberian camp, near the Ural Mountains, where she'll come upon a field of peonies that spread out before her and her fellow prisoners on a work detail. When they bend down to the large half-open blooms—the unexpected profluence of beauty—the flowers will have no scent, as if the perfume has been stolen.

But before these events—after the killing of Beck and those murdered because of his killing—work continued. Work was a requirement of war, it was the penance of the prisoner; sometimes it killed you, other times it could save your life.

In nearby svir—now home, at least temporarily, for Lili, her sister Khanale, her mother, and their extended family—the Germans ordered all young people to leave for an undisclosed work site at a Todt camp. From the ghetto, Lili's grandfather convinced a farmer to hide her, but when her grandfather was thrown in the ghetto prison because Lili couldn't be found, she—with her best friend Nihamah, who would be by her side for the war's duration and aftermath—joined the transport to the camp.

"What seemed like a tragedy—that they were going to take me and send me somewhere, to work somewhere unknown—in the end, and I'll tell you the story, this was my winning card. This was the way I stayed alive." Her eyes flash.

She's resolute, a little triumphant, when she tells me this on one of two long afternoons in Israel in June of 2013—my second visit to the country and to her cool house, where photographs from her travels, newspapers, and books mark her as a woman engaged with the world. Irit is with us, as is my stepdaughter. As usual, there are cakes on the table and offers of juice.

Lili is both welcoming and workmanlike; we have a lot of ground to cover. On the first day, after several hours, she says *Enough*. It's exhausting and painful, this story. She sees us out; the next afternoon, nothing of her fatigue will be in evidence. She is only slightly frailer than the year before; a sprained ankle, a cane.

Her grandfather was released from jail, and shortly after, Lili and Nihama and the other young Jewish residents of Svir walked for many hours to a depot, then rode a long way in regular train cars back to Lithuania. The Todt camp living quarters were in Žiežmariai (not far from Kovno), in an old wooden synagogue. There were bunks with straw: girls and women downstairs, men upstairs.

On Sundays the women washed their clothes in the nearby mikveh, then sat on the ground and picked the lice out of the waistbands and seams and collars—"We were covered with lice," Lili said. Unless the water was hot enough, simply washing the clothes did nothing to get rid of the infestation.

When she returned to Žiežmariai several years ago, the synagogue had become a tourist site. She paid a dollar or two to walk again through the dilapidated quarters where, when she was incarcerated, as luck would have it, an older German commander "was okay." They nicknamed him Hezeriker— "hoarse," in Yiddish—for his rough voice. He gave them their work assignment: to pave a road.

> My job, along with some of the others, was to use a big
> hammer to break rocks into gravel. They didn't have
> any gravel, so we had to make it and then spread it.
> After that a machine would come by and flatten it out.
> I don't think there was cement. It was very hard work,
> very hard.
>
>   One German, older, a foreman, liked me and said in
> German—I was redheaded, really, I had flaming red hair [she
> laughs at the memory]—he said, "The girl with the red hair is the
> best."

Unsteady carts on a track, carts not meant to carry a group of young women and men, transported them partway to their work each day. One day the cart Lili was in tipped over, and when she fell, her head hit a rock; the scar remains on her scalp today.

The foreman—suddenly she remembers his name, Miller—

> kept saying, "The girl with the red hair is dead. She's dead."
> They took care of me. There were no antibiotics. They sewed it up, but it was oozing infection so they had to even take me to a German clinic. It was several months before the gash healed. Then back to building the road, each day of work, each day closer to finishing the ten-kilometer road, we were terrified. As more of the gravel was flattened, with each kilometer, we wondered if we would be killed at the end, when there was no more road left.
>
> It was a good road. We did a good job. When we were done, we thought, *We're not necessary anymore*. But as you can see, they didn't kill us.

Even though she is sitting across the table from me, it takes me a moment to register the fact of her survival when the road was done. Her story has lodged an image—an instant nightmare—in my mind: the end of the road, those who spread the gravel dead in a nearby newly dug pit.

> In the winter of '43, an epidemic of typhus broke out, and we lay there in the hay and the filth. No medicine, only Gordonovich, the doctor, would walk around and take everyone's temperature, which reached 42 Celsius [over 107 degrees Fahrenheit]—as high as it could reach. So he would take your temperature and say, "Full"—the thermometer has gone all the way up.

The lice created a typhus epidemic in the camps and ghettos, the same disease that was the scourge of Napolean's army, traces of the infection found in the tooth pulp of bodies uncovered in Vilnius in just the last decade.

The lice infects once the unbearable itching starts and the stricken human host starts scratching, breaking the epidermal barrier; it's not the lice itself, but their feces, infected with a strain of the Rickettsia bacterium, that causes illness. The first time I scrolled through the captured German records at the Holocaust Museum in Washington, I found document after document noting the presence or absence of illness in the ghettos; kept, of course, not for the benefit of the prisoners but because of the Germans' fear of *Fleckfieber*.

Žiežmariai Synagogue that served as the Todt barracks

We felt we needed to hide the epidemic from the Germans, so they wouldn't destroy the barracks and kill us all. Afterward, we were crawling to work. The illness did something to our brains. We were very—[she tries to think of how to explain it]—we were not the same. One girl was impacted so badly that when we would go out to work, she would lift up her dress and walk around; she wasn't in control of what she was doing. The high temperature had given her some sort of encephalitis or something. And through it all, for food, we got a slice of bread before work. If you could bear not to eat it all at once, you would try and divide it and then have it during the day. In the middle of the day, they would come with a plate of very watery soup that was really flour and water.

The illness with the raging fever, without any antibiotics to treat it, while she was subsisting on starvation rations—supplemented from time to time by packages from Svir—did not damage Lili permanently. She notes her own soundness of mind—all the translation work she still does, the acuity of her memory.

From the head of the camp we learned that the smaller ghettos were being liquidated. Hezeriker said, "Make me a list of family members that you have left and I will try and bring them here." So you see, what seemed to be a tragedy worked out to be a good thing.

TYPHUS ALSO STRUCK the ghetto in Švenčionys. During that time, my own mother suffered a long, bad bout of jaundice, one possible manifestation of the illness; perhaps she, outside the wood and wire, was also infected.

In October 1942 the ghetto in Vidzh (Yiddish; Widze, Polish)—part of Poland as Švenčionys had been, and then, in 1939, Belorussian until the Germans, with their "Ostland," ceded it to Lithuania—had been liquidated. Upward of a thousand former residents of the Vidzh ghetto traveled the thirty-eight miles to the few, already crowded blocks of the Švenčionys ghetto. Hundreds of Vidzh residents were crammed into the old synagogue, now airless and fetid. Dwellings that had barely contained the Švenčionys Jews became incubators for disease. The small ghetto medical staff, managed to a large extent by Dr. Taraseysky, couldn't begin to keep the epidemic at bay. This was at a time when the Reichskommissariat Ostland, led in Lithuania (Litauen in German) by Theodor von Renteln, was reconsidering what, from the beginning, had been a controversial policy: retaining a labor force of Jews rather than finishing them all off in the pits and/or deporting them to camps outside Lithuania.

In short order, Chaya Palevsky was working with her sister Rachel in a secret hospital behind a false wall in a house in the ghetto. Yitzhak Arad, sustained in part after the death of his two friends by his older sister Rachel's love, continued to make plans with the determined band of soon-to-be partisans. The Narocz forests waited.

(In Great Britain, in 1843, the Society for the Diffusion of Useful Knowledge published a volume of the *Penny Cyclopaedia* in which the Narocz appeared: "East of Wilna, the climate . . . more temperate than . . . north, but the winters, though short, are very cold; the spring is long and humid; the autumn and summer wet and foggy." A few paragraphs later: "These Jews, wherever they insert themselves, are a scourge." A century after the type was set—the same deep snow, the enmity of much of the local population, and a new element: discrimination from non-Jewish partisans who had already established bases in the woods. No end of ways to break the hearts of the young who wanted to avenge the deaths of those they loved, the young who at every turn were forced to discover new strategies for survival.)

ACCORDING TO TESTIMONY in the Koniuchowsky record of the time, Yankl Levin and his painting brigade, after their own long day of work outside the ghetto, grabbed tin, wood, glass—anything that could be used to extend a small house or make a shack livable for the influx from Vidzh. The Sventsian Judenrat contacted the Vilna ghetto administration as typhus infection rates soared. A medical team from Vilna, where the ghetto was large enough to have more infrastructure and also more resources, arrived and helped strategize. Instructions were given; the painting brigade jerry-rigged a disinfection station to stem the spread of disease.

Every effort related to the typhus outbreak, including ministering to the sick, had to be kept from the Lithuanian and German authorities. Life had to appear as normal as possible. When secrecy failed, a bribe was presented to whoever threatened to spread the news that inside the ghetto, scores of people lay in fever sweats. If you could, you went to work, a jacket covering the pink and then dark spots and blotches on your arms, on your neck underneath your scarf. Somehow Levin managed to bring "a 200-liter boiler from town" and set it up in a quickly renovated smithy. There, with a stone oven and water, the impromptu disinfector "was heated to exactly 120 degrees centigrade."

After a stop at the bathing station, people put their lice-ridden clothes, their blankets, their scarves and socks, inside the hot disinfector. Every day a team went to each ghetto residence to see who had been infected, who was well. This was a war inside another war. Most of those on the front line got sick themselves, got better, kept soldiering through.

* * *

OUTSIDE THE GHETTO, Markov's partisan band grew larger and more active. Patrols along the Švenčionéliai rail line increased. The police were given schematics for mining trains and roads so they would know better what to look for, hidden in barns and under false floors of those in league with the partisans: melinite, fuses, blasting caps or traces left behind in hastily abandoned forest digs, wire, a bit of yellow powder. Locals complained of robberies—a cow, a chicken, bread, milk, a rifle, blankets, homebrew—asked for or taken at gun- or knifepoint. The Germans tried to frame the fight against "banditry" as a Lithuanian cause, but the war dragged on. The hope of Lithuanian independence gone, animus toward the Germans increased.

What was my grandfather doing in the fall of 1942?

He was riding his motorcycle and sending his "agents" into the countryside to see who had noticed something odd about a neighbor; who, for a drink or a few cents, had a story to tell. He was hunting. He was dictating reports for the Germans he loathed. He conducted sweeps like the one that brought in the elderly father of the orphan "Jonas Gabis." Those who harbored a Jew had to answer to him (ironic, of course, given the privileges he'd extended). Interrogations were frequent. Just as in the sizable cities of Lithuania (Kaunas, Vilnius) and in Germany itself, war brought with it a culture of informants, self-appointed spies. It was a liar's holiday, bribes greasing clean hands and dirty hands. Senelis let some prisoners go, sent some prisoners down to Lukiškės in Vilnius, to the Gestapo, to death or a labor camp or—infrequently, when officials in Vilnius found there was no case—to freedom.

Blackmarketeering, making and selling moonshine, stealing, carrying an unauthorized weapon, murdering (in an unofficial capacity), were crimes that fell under the purview of the criminal police, the Kripo, not my grandfather's security police (the Sipo or SD). But law and order was a fiction. Right in front of the Švenčionys Catholic church, fifteen hundred people lived in a cage.

In Lublin, Poland, a man who was born in Švenčionys, Romuald-Jakub Weksler-Waszkinel, told me that the placement of the ghetto was deliberate, meant to force the Jews who "killed Christ" to look out, from their confinement, at the holy structure that survived defilement.

After my meeting with Weksler-Waszkinel, before packing my bags for Germany and London, I followed a suggestion from my fixer in Poland, Maciej

Bulanda, and looked up the backstory of a family who had lost the man of their house in the Švenčionys killings after the murder of Beck.

Zofia Walulewicz, with her deaf daughter, hid a young Jewish girl after Michał Walulewicz, Zofia's husband, was called out of the lineup by my grandfather at the Švenčionys prison and killed. Like Anna and Piotr Miksta, they joined the ranks of Yad Vashem's Righteous Among the Nations.

But there is, as Chaya Palevsky would say, another story within this story. Michał and Zofia Walulewicz's son Zdzisław played the drums, and at nineteen was asked to perform in the small orchestra at the Švenčionys Kasino for the banquet after the Poligon killings. With him was a thirty-one-year-old piano player, Alosza Żaniewicz-Podaszewny (was *he* the piano teacher on Gedmino my mother remembered?). At some point in the evening, the two musicians were dragged out of the Kasino and killed because they didn't drink and were overheard speaking Polish instead of Lithuanian.

The Kasino (pictured on page 119) was at the corner of Jadkowa and Vilenskaya Streets. Lithuanian officials were in attendance as well as the Šauliai, members of the Rifleman's Union. My grandfather fell into both categories, as did his fellow police chiefs.

Yet another banquet was held at the Kasino after the killings of May 20, to celebrate the death of the local Poles. The story Zenon Tumalovič, the poet with his notebook of war, told me is gaining heft, dimension, as is his rage at all of it.

When there were no banquets, no birthday parties, there was always a card game, always liquor—a welcome stopover after a day at the office, or on an evening when your older sister was a nag. A place to drink, a place to sing— even without musical accompaniment.

My POLISH FIXER, Maciej Bulanda, with his father, designed the mezuzah mounted at the entrance of the stunning new Museum of the History of Polish Jews in Warsaw, on the site of what was once the central thoroughfare of the Warsaw ghetto. Maciej had been a critical member of the museum team from the ground up. I contacted him just when he had a stretch of time to join me in my research. With the aid of the Polish journalist Johanna Berendt, he cleared up, after a visit and some phone calls to the Warsaw branch of the Institute of National Remembrance—Commission for the Prosecution of Crimes against the Polish Nation (IPN), my uncertainties concerning Jonas Maciulevičius.

The Jonas Maciulevičius whose office was across the hall from my grand-father's in the old, now defunct part of the Švenčionys police station and jail was, in fact, the same Maciulevičius Arunas Bubnys had told me about. He was extradited from France to Poland after the war and tried there as a war criminal because of the killings of Polish noncombatants after Beck's death, as well as other acts deemed to be genocide by the Polish Supreme Court.

At the IPN archive in Gdansk, Maciulevičius's prosecutorial case file filled ten volumes. As soon as permission came through, and Maciej's studies allowed it (he was starting graduate school in London in the fall), we agreed that he would go to Gdansk and get copies of anything about my grandfather in the ten volumes. There might be nothing in the volumes, or perhaps only a mention of Senelis's name. The massive file had only an elementary index, so it was impossible to get a cursory sense of the contents beforehand.

Jonas Maciulevičius

I WAS HITTING the three-year mark in my search. My deficit in terms of languages—not to mention the destruction, right at the war's end, of German documents and Lithuanian security police records—left me not exactly hopeful, but I was resolute. Where was the film the Germans took at Poligon? In what vault, in whose attic or home safe in Germany? I made inquiries when I was in Berlin, without success. I hoped that in the images of the shootings there might be glimpses of the ones in charge, "the ones giving the orders"—those Vincas Sausitis pointed a finger at. Men who didn't bother to put their names on a pay list, who took a shot after a certain amount of vodka, or because camaraderie and a demonstration of authority demanded it.

Through my researcher and now friend in Berlin, Almut Schoenfield, I stumbled upon a curator in possession of hundreds of photo albums of German soldiers. Did one of them contain snapshots of Poligon or of the Švenčionys ghetto?

Several weeks later in London, I got access to the same collection, in the process of being digitized.

A pair of boots upright in a small autumn field, military issue, the owner of them, like Khone Zak's father, buried headfirst off the side of the road, his legs sticking out; only this was not Khone Zak's father in Podbrodz, but an unnamed man in an unnamed village. And those bodies slumped against the wooden siding of a barn—whose barn? Who were the dead, and what were the circumstances of their deaths? The absence of narrative made the images grotesque mysteries with no way to honor those in the frame. Beyond that, the lack of a cohesive story made me acutely aware of all that was missing in the information I had so far about Senelis.

Motive, means, method, opportunity, or some variation thereof: these create narrative. Senelis's expressed anti-Semitism, KGB testimony that linked him to the selection after Beck's death, a plethora of other research, a town and its surrounds starting to come to life through interviews and travel—I called it all, to myself, "ghost knowledge." It was enough to haunt you, but not enough to flesh out one man's actions in an area under his partial wartime jurisdiction. Not enough to get a clear grasp of his thoughts and feelings regarding the small and not-so-small decisions he made when he lived there.

CHAPTER 43

JUMP

CHAYA PALEVSKY NÉE PORUS, FEBRUARY 2012

Švenčionėliai train station

[In April 1943] they announced that Sventsian ghetto and all around would be evacuated to a larger ghetto—either Kovno or Vilna. Did people believe it? They wanted to believe it. In the ghetto they always made you believe there will again be a future. The reason given was that there were a lot of partisans in the area and they wanted to take everyone to a "safer place."

You had no choice, no place to run. It was before Pesach; they told you take whatever you can, you will be there, you will need it. Already, they were preparing lists and unfortunately our family was put on the list to Kovno. We had family in Vilna and there was a room for us there, we'd been on that list. But someone bribed their way on, so we got taken off. We didn't have anyone in Kovno, but okay—this had happened.

This was typical of Chaya in the small chunk of our time together, an attitude modeled perhaps by her mother—be prepared, stay "intact." The winds shift; shift with them.

It happened at that time (the Germans didn't know) we had a hidden hospital in a big house in the ghetto. One of the front rooms was a library with books and shelves, but the shelves opened, and behind there were two rooms with beds and people sick with typhus. If people outside knew there was typhus in the ghetto, they would burn it down instantly. So my sister Rochl and I worked day after day, hidden, and no one knew. My other sister took sick and then I took sick with typhus at the time when you had to leave for Kovno.

Malke Porus

They took me home on a stretcher. I told my mother, "I'm not going. I cannot move"—104-degree fever. "Leave me here because I will be a burden to you. I cannot walk."

My mother said: "Chaya, you are going with me. I will dress you and take you along. Or I will undress myself, lie down in bed with you, and we will both be killed."

"Mother, I don't want you to be killed because of me." So I promised her I will be there.

"There" was the train station in Nowe-Święciany (Švenčionėliai), where ghetto residents had been assigned trains to either Kovno or Vilna. According to Yitzhak Arad, thirty-three cars for Kovno, only two for Vilna.

> The Chief of the Partisans arranged it; a few of them had found out about the repatriation from the ghetto, so they came to take the rest of the Sventsian ghetto partisan group to the woods. They didn't know that I was sick and couldn't go—then they came and saw me in bed with a high fever. I promised my mother that the two partisans would bring me later to Nowe Sventsian. I told her, "Mother go, don't worry—I will meet you there." She dressed me and left.
>
> Yeschik Gertman and another partisan took me under their arms and carried me twelve kilometers to the station. The train cars were already closed up. When they carried me I felt so wet—maybe the temperature broke—I felt a little better. I could stand. A few minutes before the train was to leave, Gertman stepped up on the steps of the train and I after him . . . on the steps, not even inside the train.

At the request of the Germans, Jacob Gens, the head of the Vilna ghetto, had helped to organize the repatriation. He was actually in one of the two train cars bound for Vilna, in a cabin for police that was the only one not locked from the outside. Residents of the now-forsaken Švenčionys ghetto were surprised and alarmed when Jewish policemen from Vilna slid the train car doors shut and bolted them, but the presence of Gens at the outset was reassuring.

> On the steps all of a sudden, Gertman said, "Chaya, please jump. Jump!"
>
> I jumped—and he jumped after me just as the train started moving.

He said, "I had a premonition. I don't want to go on this train. We will find another train and go to Vilna, and then find a way to Kovno and meet your parents."

I wasn't wearing the star, and we began to move a little farther from the station so people wouldn't notice us. I was blond in those days, and he was tall—we were like Gentiles. We laughed and spoke Polish, as if we were two young people without any cares on a sunny spring afternoon. When people looked our way, one of us would say, "Oh, we wanted to say good-bye to our friends."

Gertman had a train worker's shoulder band with a particular insignia, and sometimes on his missions, he would use it. Now, still near the station, we waited. In the evening a commercial train came through; cattle cars—one car with straw, the other with cattle. He helped me jump into a car without cattle, then he jumped in after me and we crawled deep into the straw. The train was headed for Vileika, a station not far from Vilna, maybe ten miles away or less. In Vileika, the train would stop and we could crawl out.

Yeschik Gertman had a brain. I knew him from our time in the ghetto, but we were in two different environments: mine was Polish; his was Yiddish. He was like an open encyclopedia, full of common sense. He knew everything. In the dark, the train car opened, and before we could be noticed, we jumped again. We rolled, with hay on us, down the incline from the track and lay there until early morning. From the Vilna ghetto, a group would be coming to work on the Vileika train tracks, and Gertman knew the leader. We would be able to pretend we were workers with that group and make our way to Vilna.

We both had guns—I had a small Belgium. No one noticed. The leader of the work group hid it for me. We had trained to shoot in the ghetto in Sventsian. So we came to Vilna.

IT HAPPENED THAT, already, there were a lot of friends from different towns that we knew from the ghetto in Sventsian in the Vilna ghetto. Some of them belonged to our group, and we were in touch with the FPO [Fareynikte Partizaner Organizatsye—the partisan group from the Vilna ghetto] underground. And so we told them what our aim is. They wanted us to stay.

"No, no—we are looking to go to Kovno because my parents are there." They looked at me like I was from another planet.

"Chaya, you did the right thing. You are in the right place. Don't think about going to Kovno."

They told me everyone on the other trains was killed at Ponary.

I became a stone. I couldn't say a word. Couldn't cry, couldn't understand. All of a sudden I thought: It's impossible. It's not true. I was numb.

They took me to an apartment and inside, into the kitchen. They put a curtain up in the kitchen with a cot behind it—a place. You know, I wasn't myself. I didn't know what to think. I felt I am all alone; I have no one now. [She puts her hand over her mouth.] No tears. Everything upside down. And I thought, my goodness, my mother wanted to save me by going with her and she was so worried I will be killed and here they are all killed and I am alive.

Chaya dabs at her eyes with a paper napkin. It can't be described, she says, the feeling—her family dead, with the exception of her brother Itzik (also a partisan) and Bronia, the oldest of her sisters. "The feeling," she says again, and then is very quiet for several moments. We both sit.

Then Chaya leaves the reverie behind us.

I became my own mother. "What should I do, Mom?" For me, the moment was unforgettable. I felt like her spirit turned in me. She was with me. I became her. For myself, I became my own mother. That's what I felt. "What should I do now?" I thought, Mom, whatever you tell me to do—I always listened to you. You were very smart, so show me the way, show me what I should do. I talked to myself. I talked to my mother. Until now I have episodes that my mother is with me; she is always with me. Whenever I have to decide. She is with me, my best friend.

This was in April. In May, the Vilna ghetto used to have

special theater events . . . They had a concert on May 1. They
were not allowed to call it "May day" because of Communism, so
they called it "spring festival." At that time, in the ghetto, I found
friends of one of my oldest sisters; one was Avrom Sutzkever [the
poet], and they said to me, "Chayale, come with us to the concert,
come, it will do good for you." One young man, I learned his
name later—Rabinovich—he played the violin and he played
Pablo de Sarasate's *Zigeunerweisen* (*Gypsy Airs*). This is the last
thing my father played in the ghetto before he gave his violin
away to be "hid" upon his leavetaking. I broke out in such
hysterical crying, no one could stop me: there was a doctor there
and he came to me and said, "Take her home. Let her cry."

I cried all night.

In the morning, I felt so at ease. The tears had been pressing on
me—I let them go. With the other partisans of my group—we were
prepared. The FPO wasn't ready to go, but we decided we will take
the rest of the partisans in the ghetto; we knew they had some
ammunition from our group that came from Sventsian. We decided
that, on our own, we would go out together [to fight, as clandestine
partisans, on behalf of the murdered and incarcerated Jews] with a
group of working people on the highways, and that's what it was
and we went out of the ghetto. Forty people and we made it.

Sarasate composed *Zigeunerweisen* in 1878; Sir Arthur Conan Doyle made it a great favorite of Sherlock Holmes. In the face of the unsolvable, what better than a bow on the strings, a piece that is wild, and sweet, and sad? I listened to it after my interview with Chaya. I'm listening to it now.

V

Puronas ancestral grave in Gindviliai—the writing is in Kupiškis dialect and Latin letters

CHAPTER 44

JANUARY 2014

Back to Lithuania again. Sixteen degrees below, breathing the night air was like inhaling dark, pure oxygen.

On the first hop of my flight, from JFK to Frankfurt, the flight attendants woke us in the middle of the transatlantic night; we were turning around—far out to sea already—for an emergency landing in St. John's, Newfoundland. A woman had had heart trouble. An hour or so later we landed at the small airport. Several medics in dark blue ferried the woman on a stretcher down the aisle opposite mine and out of the plane. Would she die that night? Would she tell the story for years to come with just a tinge of embarrassment, or simply gratitude and awe: *They turned the whole plane around to save my life!*

Instead of empathy, I grumbled with other grumblers—the long delay, connections missed, etc. Others were gracious, concerned, asking the flight crew about the condition of the sick one. I flashed on my sudden return to the hospital in New York when things went bad for me postsurgery, each breath a knife between my shoulder blades. I pressed my face against the dark window, searching for an ambulance. Would the woman get the right medical care here? I wasn't grumbling anymore. She'd frightened me. I was frightened for her.

My airline had only two flights out from Frankfurt to Vilnius each day. I watched the day draw down out the lounge windows. Intermittently I cataloged what the ill passenger's situation might be: pulmonary embolism, heart attack, clots in her arteries, a thoracic aneurysm like me—no, if she had a bursting aneurysm, she might have been dead before the plane made it back to St. John's. Another stranger whose fate I'll never know. Too many now.

Almost midnight that night, our small plane from Frankfurt landed in Vilnius. There was no heat on in the airport; most of the staff had gone home. I blew on my hands until the baggage tumbled onto the short track, then out the double doors, and there was Petras bundled in a heavy jacket—the first time I'd seen him with a hat on his head. I was glad to see him, to be here, glad to be alive. I'd come for more archival work and to do what I'd not done in any of my previous trips: meet with some of my Lithuanian family.

CHAPTER 45

ŠAKOTIS

They had been waiting for me: Marytė with her flushed cheeks and warmth and cutlets and the gift of the blue knitted shawl; Danute's family with the gift of *šakotis* ("branch"), a cake in a waffly tree shape, sweet and long-lasting. The Lithuanian national cake, it is sister to a Polish version, if you follow the trail of recipes and time. It's a cake made on a spit, rich and yolk yellow. *Take it back to New York with you!* They'd all heard I'd been traveling in and out of the country over the past several years, but why hadn't I come to visit?

I'd been afraid to meet them.

I was afraid they would hate me for the research I was doing. More and more, my mother's terror had grown: "something" I might find out about Senelis, if it came to light, would shame her in her community. Since she did not want to know what I was actually discovering, there was no way for her to mediate her anxiety. Senelis was her father, and I was dismantling part of her hold on him, her memory of him. Any fear she had, any enmity toward me, was legitimate. On my end, it was in part what I thought to be her outsize fear that made me keep digging. Under her nonmemory, what was there a memory of? What was brutal enough and big enough to make her imagine someone would paint a swatiska on her front door, friends shun her, a revelation undo her?

I never wanted to experience again, as I had at Ruta Sepetys's reading at the Lithuanian embassy, the feeling of being both split apart and erased. Still, I was sure Senelis's relatives would have their own important stories about him and Babita, but I also wanted to tell them of my search for details about Senelis during wartime before they found out indirectly.

It was Aunt Karina, several years earlier, who, after our meeting on the Vineyard, had thoughtfully sent me a letter with contact information for my relatives in Lithuania along with detailed descriptions of who was related to whom. Before this winter trip, I unfolded the two-page list of names and descriptions, grateful for my aunt's effort and struck by the irony that it was she, who'd been out of my life for so many years, who was helping me get in touch with the Puronas branch of the family.[*]

I took a dumb chance and phoned my mother to see if she might make a few advance calls to Lithuania on my behalf, to say I was coming. She spoke tersely. "No more."

My first visit to Lithuania, I'd called her in the bright northern evening as soon as Petras dropped me at my hotel.

"I'm here, Mom, the place you talked about all those years!"

She was excited and moved and spoke about flax and the smells of the countryside, a homemade sauna at an aunt's house, juniper branches, a hand-woven sash a cousin gave her as a welcome gift, the beauty of Vilnius. In some strange way, I felt like I'd found her for the first time. Since then I'd been finding and losing her over and over.

Rose and petras picked me up in the blue, dark morning at my hotel the day after I arrived. Because she knew I wouldn't think of it, Rose had somehow found and bought, an hour earlier, a bouquet of fragile roses tinged with faint lavender. I brought the dry frozen air into the van with me, and she handed me the flowers—divided into four small bouquets, three roses in each. In Lithuania, she explained, you don't give an even number of flowers unless someone has died.

The tiny bouquets seemed too small to give, even in their beauty.

"You don't understand very well," Rose said. "This is your family. They will be very happy. You will see."

She was right.

Instead of Vilnius Highway, we took another road outside the city—everyone's headlights on because of the early hour, the late dawn, and long night of the northern winter. The snowpack in the field was a fingertip layer of ice

---

[*] Please refer to the Puronas family tree on page 47.

crystals. Petals and tissue paper soft in my hand, I went over the names of my relatives with Rose so I would pronounce them correctly. At each stop, I instantly forgot her brief lesson.

Česlovas (pronounced "Cheslŏvahs") and Bronė (pronounced "Brana") in Panevėžys were our first stop. Bronė's father Danielius, born in 1910, had been eleven years younger than his brother, my Senelis.

Recently recovered from a stroke, Česlovas was gray and spry and thoughtful. He'd been an architect, and it was he who had drawn the marvelous family tree that Aunt Agnes had sent me a copy of. Bronė took the gift of flowers, and the couple ushered us into their light-filled apartment. In the living room, a table was laid with special glasses and cakes and meat and cheeses and the fancy plates for the guest from America.

I could not see my grandfather in Bronė. She'd been less than a year old, according to Aunt Karina, when Senelis fled the country with the children. In her sweater and skirt, with her lovely hands, Bronė reminded me of my mother more than anyone. She loaded up my plate with more food than I could eat in two days, and Česlovas, after our meal, made me a good copy on thick paper of the family tree.

In bits and pieces they told me part of the family history, beginning with the fate of Bronė's father, Danielius, and her mother, Vaclova, after the Soviets retook Lithuania before the official end of the war.

Bronė's father, "a well-known chorister" at his local parish had inherited the Puronas family house and farm in Gindviliai. The fleeing Soviets torched it at the beginning of the war, the cattle stolen along with the furniture, china, and clothes. All they left were the clay walls of the barn. Due to the "goodwill of the people," timber and other building materials were donated for a start at a new life. So when the Soviets returned in 1945 and began conscripting men into the army, Danielius refused to join. If he went, who would run the farm? Who would take care of his wife and two children, Bronė and her brother? Danielius was arrested and sent from prison to prison, before eventually ending up in Lukiškės in Vilnius.

There Danielius suffered from a terrible hernia—perhaps the result of work on the farm, or from a beating by a guard. Finally, he was taken to a Vilnius hospital for surgery.

Bronė sets her plate back down on the glass table. The sun warms every corner of the room as if the cold outside is a fiction. She mimics her mother putting food and warm clothing into a carryall, something she could hold on her lap, with the food carefully wrapped so as not to spoil or spill. Bronė looks at me, then down at her lap and shakes her head. Her mother was traveling with her carryall to see a dead man. Blood poisoning had killed Danielius during the long-delayed surgery before Vaclova set foot in Vilnius. He died on April 29, 1945, right before the end of the war and of the Soviet conscription.

Before her death, my great-grandmother Barbara made sure that Bronė and the rest of the family knew how Danielius's widow, Vaclova, and the two children struggled. A doctor had told her that Vaclova, weak from grief and work, should eat cabbage for strength, but that year—the horrible year of her husband's death—their cabbages would not grow. "The women from the village were bringing many pots of sauerkraut for her. That shows how good and sensitive were the people of Gindviliai." Vaclova regained her strength. She worked her land. She could slaughter a pig on her own. So went Bronė's history, passed down from my namesake.

We are all quiet after the story of Danielius. The cakes and homemade cookies sit on the table. To break up the sadness, I reach for a cookie, buttery, rich. "Good," I say.

Bronė smiles. She'll give me some to take with me later. In the moment, in the bright room, they're the best cookies I've ever eaten. I want her to be happy. I want the story of my family to contain happiness.

"What about Kazimieras, Senelis's father, what kind of man was he?" I ask.

Česlovas and Bronė look at each other and smile. Then Česlovas leaves the room for a minute and comes back with a copy of the Puronas family history that Bronė had written. He points to a word I can't understand. It was Senelis's father's nickname: *skersai*. Česlovas translates; as a nickname it means "he who walks crosswise or not in a straight line"—bestowed upon Kazimieras because he was stone drunk most of the time.

"Alcoholic," we all say together, and my hosts nod and laugh, and I laugh with them, even as I think of the barrels of vodka at Poligon and the smell of cherry wine on Senelis's breath and the dark, deep green of the bottles he'd bring to the Vineyard on his summer visits.

Coffee is poured. We pile the desserts on our plates. On the wall across from the table hang several of Česlovas's and Bronė's immediate and extended family trees, full of leaves and branches and birds and graves and broken offshoots, all drawn by Česlovas. I try to say something about my research and Senelis, but Bronė plants herself next to me on the couch to talk about Babita, who had stayed with Bronė's family for quite a while after she was freed from the Gulag and came back to Lithuania.

Babita was very kind. (*Kindness* was a word my mother and her sister had reserved for their own Babita, Barbara.) She was very malnourished when she returned, and it took her a long time to get any strength back.

It is from Bronė that I learn about the needlework done from bandages and my grandmother's chain-smoking. It is also from Bronė that I learn what others would repeat later in the day: the match with my grandfather was no good— everyone knew it from the start. They were too different.

"She didn't have any clothes," Bronė said of my grandmother upon her return.

The family dressed her and fed her, and no, my grandmother would say very little of her time in the Gulag.

On one of my earlier visits to Lithuania, Rose had found a woman who claimed she'd known my grandmother in Siberia, had met her briefly in some holding cell, shortly before Babita was allowed to return to Lithuania. I had interviewed the woman at her home; she spoke rapidly, without making eye contact. She said my grandmother had obviously had a nervous breakdown, since she shook so much. I shared this with Bronė who assured me that the shaking was a motor disorder. There had been no breakdown. Tuburculosis, torture, typhus—but the woman who came back to them in the mid-1950s had all her faculties and baked wonderful sweets. She endured.

Babita was kind.

At first she had no notion of the lives of the family she'd lost, or the possibility of joining them. For the first time in my life I wondered if she had any idea what Senelis had done and where he had been during the war, if she had wanted to know when she returned from Siberia.

When I look closely at the first picture taken of her after the Gulag, one hand behind her back, something is out of joint in her posture. I can't stop staring at her ankles. Her hands are much larger than I'd imagined, long fingers good for work with a small crochet hook or a threading needle. There is a slight

Babita in 1956

vacancy in her smile. I wonder what shape her teeth were in, how many times in fifteen years she unwrapped the rags around her thin ankles to freeze out the lice. A librarian. I vaguely remember someone telling me that there was a protocol for the photograph of the re-educated prisoner come home: a particular backdrop, the best (one's own or borrowed) shoes, and a new dress—a healthy, good Communist. Perhaps that's the reason for the hidden arm, why she faces forward, though her body turns away.

When we leave, Česlovas slyly disappears for a second, comes back with a large accordion and makes music out of our good-byes. When the music ends, after they have wrapped up cookies and chocolates for me, Česlovas and Bronė tell me to e-mail, to stay in touch now that we have met, after all this time.

THERE ARE TWO Marytės I see on this winter day. The first Marytė also lives in Panevėžys not far from Česlovas and Bronė. Her father was Senelis's brother Povilas, seven years younger. Widowed in 1975, Marytė ushers us into her roomy house with her sister, a new nephew, and her lively daughter-in-law. She takes my face in her hands many times. Smart, she is a retired teacher like Aunt Karina. Petite, yet sturdy, she wears a lovely scarf around her neck and a pin on her sweater. I wish I'd worn a nicer dress, cleaned my boots.

"Teach," we say together when I tell her about my own teaching.

We laugh then, and hold hands. The younger sister Marytė cares for is silent. A bit like a stunned child in my presence, she is shepherded gently to each place we sit, each room we walk through. She is a casualty of the cruelty inflicted upon the family by the Soviet secret police after my grandfather fled Lithuania, and the Soviets were again in power. Night after night, for fifteen years, the secret police came to Marytė's childhood home. The head of the secret police in that region was actually a Latvian, notorious for his brutality. Marytė speaks of those years, describes the horror of it animatedly, moves about the room as if the police were here now, here again.

"Puronas was commandant, and you too stole from the Jews," was one of the accusations the Latvian head of the NKVD made.

A rote accusation? I wonder.

"Jews came to your grandfather with propositions, but he never took anything," she says.

How do you know that? I want to ask, but don't. This is what she was told, and very little else. The NKVD chief would drag her father into the yard and tell him to run so he could be shot in the back—run in the snow, run in the night, run in the late light of summers. After fifteen years of it, his health went. The secret police only went after family members with the Puronas last name.

On the night of one of these visitations from the secret police, Marytė's very pregnant mother was struggling to climb down a ladder from the attic when one of the secret police screamed at her to hurry. Startled, she fell and later gave birth to the child who is now the silent, slow-moving woman who walks with us into a room off the living room, her face shiny, her eyes, when she looks at me, without curiosity or comprehension.

Marytė and her daughter-in-law, who has donned a brightly woven traditional dress to show part of the past to me, lead me into a side room where a huge hand-painted dowry chest, given to Marytė by Great-Grandmother Barbara's sister, Ona, sits. It's magnificent. I touch the raised dots of paint on the old wood. Is it big enough to hold all I carry from both sides of my family? The mix of sweetness and confusion is overwhelming; for a second I send up a silent prayer to Great-Grandmother Barbara that she lay a soft spell on me.

The gift of the chest was a rarity, she tells me, for Ona was as parsimonious as Barbara was kind. Yes, Great-Grandmother Barbara was a spell caster. She had a spell for snakebite. She had other spells. Ona knew them too, but unlike her sister, Barbara, she did not gift them to any of the family. This, I learn, is what you are supposed to do with a spell: pass it down to the younger generation, treasure the old knowledge, keep it alive.

We go back to the living room. Even with the language barrier it feels as if there is so much to say. Marytė bestows her own gifts upon me. First is flax woven by my great-grandmother. I hold the fabric up to my face, the linen scratchy and soft at the same time. I wish I'd known her, Barbara who would not let someone in need leave her house without some trifle, a bit of food, a coin.

After the linen comes a gift of amber. After the amber, the rest of the cakes and chocolate.

My grandfather was beloved, Marytė tells me, but he was not spoken of very often over the years. Except for a mention, of course, of his fondness for a good card game and the fact that Ona, his wife, in her day was a beauty and spoke Polish and German along with Lithuanian. I had not known my Babita was a beauty. The trouble Marytė's family experienced at the Soviet's hand after the war appears to be directly connected to Senelis's "criminal activity," but she doesn't say so. She was a child, after all, when her mother fell from the ladder and her father ran, his back a target.

It's hard to leave the warmth of this gathering. The small narrative I present to them about my research is, as with Česlovas and Bronė, less important in the moment than our meeting. They actually know very little about my grandfather during the war, but they know the Jews were massacred. "Everywhere," Marytė acknowledges. But it is time for family pictures. It is time to hold hands again, time to walk with waves and tears out the door.

"Ah, what a nice family you have!" Rose says.

It is so much easier to be the stranger from afar, welcomed briefly into the family fold, than with my Lithuanian family in the States. I grew up knowing my mother's story, but knew nothing of these people who are part of me through Senelis.

At our next stop there will be much more talk about Senelis. Everything I hear about him I immediately compare to all the archival material I've waded through: myth and fact, lived experience and KGB inventions, survivors' statements, photographs. I feel alternately like a double agent and an idiot. I feel strange unto myself. I feel unknown but loved.

THE FACE OF a young woman peers through lacy curtains at the cold and the sound of the van's engine. What is she looking at? I take her in through the back-seat window. A few seconds later, a well-fed, intrepid cat leads the charge. Kristina, the woman in the window, and the rest of the family come out to the gravel driveway; they are the family of Danute, a widow whose husband, Petras, was the son of Senelis's brother Danielius, the one who died of blood poisoning in 1945. (That is a story I'll hear again in summer, when Danute's grandson sits at our dinner table in New York City and tells me he wants to know everything I've learned about Senelis.)

There is a version of *cepelinai*, Lithuanian dumplings. There are meats. There is fish and chicken. There is sweet layered pastry with custard. To my right, dark-haired Kristina, Danute's daughter, begins to cry when we start to talk about the family. Her face goes red, and the tears fall onto her plate. They all remember Uncle Roy's visit. Afterward Kristina visited him and Aunt Aggie in Kansas, and they would talk on the phone, and she misses him so much; now there are just phone calls with my aunt. "We cry together," Kristina says.

I hadn't seen Uncle Roy for several decades before he died. I should be crying too at the loss of him, along with my lovely young Lithuanian relative. But I am the one who left the family when I was still a girl, and part of the price of that leavetaking is, oddly enough, an absence of tears at a moment like this. The gift of remembered closeness.

Danute, her son, Egidijus, and Kristina, recall how they all drove with Roy to Švenčionys, how the large, slow-moving man my uncle was got out of the car and ran as soon as they came to Gedmino Street (where he and my mother and her sister and Krukchamama lived when Senelis was chief of security police), and then stood in the place I stood the last summer, and stared at the patch of green, the vanished past.

"But one part of town, he wouldn't go near," says Egidijus, round-faced, with quick eyes.

His sister and mother echo him. It was a part of town where shooting regularly took place.

When I begin to talk about my research, about being half Lithuanian-American, half Jewish, Egidijus and Danute begin to tell me bits and pieces about the family during wartime. Danute tilts her head a bit and smiles when she looks at me, as if looking for part of her own past. Egidijus talks in bursts, trails off, and then his mother or sister fills in what comes next.

"Your grandfather warned the Jews in Kupiškis when it started," Danute says.

(So he was there, near Skapiškis—Commandant Puronas—when the Soviets fled and the Germans trampled in.)

She continues, remembering what was told to her by someone in the family, perhaps her husband, who had heard it from Bronė or the Marytė we haven't visited with yet today.

"Jews came to Senelis's brother Petras and his wife in Gindviliai for help. It was a young couple, and they gave a pair of long white socks and a gold watch, but our family said we don't want to take it and told them not to go back to Kupiškis. Someone had told them there was an escape route through Kupiškis, a way to get to Palestine. They were pleaded with not to go, but they went, and they insisted on leaving the socks and the gold watch."

"And they were killed," I say.

"Yes, all the Jews in Kupiškis," the matriarch Danute confirms.

Again, I'm told that the family didn't want the socks and the watch, and that soon enough white bands came banging at the door and demanded the family hand over anything Jews had given them.

Where was my grandfather? According to Danute and her family, he was in the area warning the Jews to leave, warning them that death was coming. He was, I was told, the only commandant in the family.

Egidijus speaks rapid fire: "I got the worker list [of those employed during the Poligon massacre] from the archive to see if his name was there."

I tell him I got the same list and looked for Pranas Puronas.

I make a gesture of wiping sweat from my brow. What a relief, Egidijus says, that he wasn't on it. I nod and smile back at him. I'm impressed that Egidijus did his own micro search about Senelis, but I'm remembering the passage in the shooter Sausitis's statement where he elaborates on the fact that the higher-ups never signed anything, never put their names on paper, but were shooters too—roaming free.

I mention the massacre of the Poles in 1942.

Egidijus clears that up too. "He just had to sign some list. He had nothing to do with it. Ramute [my uncle Roy] told us about it."

Danute clears her throat. "Your Senelis wrote us when your mom and dad married. All he said was that your mother had married a Jew. Nothing else."

I'm dazed by all the meetings. I keep drifting off to those white socks and the gold watch. Why did the couple leave them, when they might have been needed to secure passage to Palestine? The long white socks the mark of the observant male, worn to synogogue. Precious. Perhaps the couple were newlyweds. Did the young man unroll his socks in front of my long-ago relatives? Were they stashed in a quick bundle? How did the white bands know to come knocking on my family's door? Probably they went everywhere.

I take Kristina's hands and tell her if she keeps crying, I will cry too. She stops. And starts. And finally smiles.

With Rose translating, I begin a small narrative about Senelis: how his job gave him a modicum of power, how there was a huge massacre of the Jewish population under his watch in Švenčionys. How my mother does not want to know any of the details, anything I've dredged up in the archives. So I won't speak of it to her, and won't speak of any of it to them if they prefer.

Danute sits straight, her chin high, looks in my eyes. "I want to know."

Rose gives me a look—*So go on, speak*. But I don't know how to begin. There is not yet any way to clarify the information I've found. How do I speak about Chaya Palevsky? I briefly tell the story of Mirele Rein, and then quickly, guiltily—for they have been so kind to me, all of them—I talk about Senelis drinking with Moshe Gordon and how he hated the Germans who reneged on their promise of Lithuania for Lithuanians. Egidijus nods, though I can see he knows there is more. Perhaps not more that is "true," but more than the brief outline I've given them, like one of Chaya's quick sketches, though without her local knowledge. Maciej Bulanda and I are still sending official requests to the IPN in Poland; I am still reading archival material.

I don't know how to describe the years of research. I don't even know how to talk about the day before, when Rose and Viktorija and I, at the Lithuanian Central State Archives, went through roughly four thousand arrest cards from Lukiškės prison to separate out the ones from the Švenčionys region.

The cards of those sent down from Švenčionys to Vilnius to be killed do not say who made the arrest. It could have been Senelis. It could have been Jonas Maciulevičius. The first card I found was for one of Yitzhak Arad's closest friends, Gershon Bak. I smell Senelis's breath and feel the heat of the porch in summer when he asks me not to be like my father. I mention Poligon, and the faces of my relatives turn toward mine, waiting, but I have no more words to talk about any of it.

I hate myself for trying to be ingratiating, not saying too much, not wanting to be cast out. It is my own private fear. It isn't put on me by Danute and her children, who are, just as Rose says when we are back in the van, "a very wonderful, very intelligent family."

And even as I agree with her, I'm thinking of what, according to Egidijus, Senelis told my Uncle Roy: "I never took anything from the Jews."

And one last detail about my grandfather, shared with a mix of seriousness and levity. His motorcycle with a sidecar—yes, it was German, they confirmed. He buried it in Lithuania before he fled the country because he loved it so much, was so proud of it, was sure he would return one day to dig it out of the ground and speed away.

"Where did he bury it?" I ask.

No one knew. It was my grandfather's secret.

THE OLDEST MARYTĖ, who lives in Kupiškis, is the only family relative I met before this trip. Her father is Peter—or Petras. The previous summer, in a local hospital with heart trouble, she had checked out for the day to see me. Her wide face flushed easily. We sat that summer under an umbrella at a little café, stopping between spoonfuls of soup to hug. *Her heart,* I kept thinking, astonished and also worried that she had left the hospital for just our brief visit. In her seventies, smart and magnanimous, she exuded both frailty and strength. I hurt her feelings when I picked up the small café bill and paid it while she was inside washing her hands.

This winter visit, she is well. Flowers bloom on one sill of her neat apartment. In the living room a low table is covered with dish after dish. Rose, Petras (our driver), and I eat again. Candy in shiny wrappers fills a bowl. The potatoes are huge and steaming. We settle back. There is time now to talk.

She brings out several albums of photographs, some sent to her from my family in the States. It's somehow jarring to see those faces here: myself as a child, Aunt Karina by a Christmas tree, my father holding a newspaper. I never knew those photographs had made their way to Lithuania. There are other photographs, taken at a Siberian logging camp where Marytė's whole family was deported after the war for ten years.

(Marytė too, does not speak about it in my presence, but the experience of her family fills out the picture of how Senelis's collaboration and his disappearance at war's end brought suffering to the family he left behind. The Soviet administrative units under whose directives the secret police operated wanted my grandfather. If they couldn't get him, they would get his relatives.)

Marytė describes the sight of fifty or perhaps seventy freight cars, how everyone being deported to work (not to prison camps) made and then dried bread that would last. Their freight car was number 50, sixty people or more crammed inside, her mother breastfeeding in the chaos. When the Soviet secret police had come to send them away, Marytė remembers one of them was a woman who kept taking out a little mirror to touch up her lipstick.

At the logging camp in the Altai region of Siberia, whenever packages of bread and pork fat arrived from their family, Marytė's father Peter shared it with the others who lived in their barracks. The barracks was made of wood;

there was no lock on the door, for there were no thieves. Marytė remembered the felt boots they wore, and her father falling in the cold, loading wood. Even so, young as she was, she came to feel at home there—it was what she knew, and so returning to Lithuania was very hard.

We leave Marytė not having eaten enough of her feast to please her, but with embraces all around. As Petras blasts the heat in the van and backs out of the parking lot in front of her apartment complex I ask Rose how close we are to Skapiškis, where according to the Lithuanian history published by a Soviet writer after the war—a bit of which my journalist friend from Vilnius had shared with me some time ago—Commandant Puronas sat behind a desk while a woman waited for the verdict on her husband to be pronounced by him. The husband was shot.

"Maybe twenty minutes from here," Rose tells me, winding and unwinding a thick strand of her hair.

On a map I'll look at back at my hotel, Skapiškis makes a scalene triangle—no side equal to another—with Gindviliai, the Puronas ancestral home, and Kupiškis, where we were so warmly greated by the oldest Marytė. It was in Kupiškis where my mother and her sister and brother stayed with Krukchamama for a time during the war, before my grandfather got his job with the Germans, and then again, right before before Senelis fled the country, the machinary of the German occupation crumbling as he ran.

CHAPTER 46

GONE

It takes a long time to drive back to Vilnius. The strange roads are mostly empty.

"Lithuanians don't usually drive in the dark," Rose says.

I ask her why.

She shrugs, as if to say, *Why would anyone want to drive in the dark*? "They don't like it."

A quarter moon glazes the white field stubble; then woods and a scrim of shadows I can't see beyond. I imagine my grandfather, digging in the dark, digging and digging—a hole big enough for his BMW motorcycle. I have the branch cake wrapped in crinkly see-through paper. I have the printout of the Puronas family tree. Hands I've held, farewell embraces, long individual and group hugs with promises of return. Lovely, inquiring faces that will come to me often, in memory, in the photographs I go back to again and again. Lili Holzman was right: half of me is this. I'm not sure what that means, not sure that if or when I can create a coherent timeline of Senelis during the war, I will be so welcome in the homes I've just visited. But that seems churlish. "I want to know," Danute had said. A few weeks later in his office in D.C., Michael MacQueen will mention that it is much harder, in some ways, for those who leave the home country. Perhaps not materially, not in terms of freedoms offered or denied, but something deeper, more complex—a dislocation that wrecks the heart or creates an emptiness that time only partialy remediates.

In the dark I wonder if all the silence imposed upon my Lithuanian relatives who stayed behind during the Soviet era makes them value "truth" or openness more—silence like a long shadow that stretched out over the country, into phone lines, under the carefully licked flaps of envelopes: oppressive, dulling, dangerous. Like Vaclav Wilcoitz in the Jewish cemetery in Švenčionėliai, the conversations with my Lithuanian family eluded the easy categories; the Lithuanians who refused to fully recognize the role their own population played in the decimation of the Jewish population of their county, those who argued for the equivalency of the Soviet occupation and the Jewish Holocaust.

In the small booklet about the deportations to Siberia I bought a few years back at the KGB Museum in Vilnius, one passage had stuck with me. "No one has been called to account . . . The West has chosen to forget these horrors . . . There is no grand museum in Washington, D.C., dedicated to those whose lives were destroyed by the communists." *Well, then build one,* I'd thought. A thought as facile as any generality about the West or the East or, for that matter, the road I was traveling on—too full, wired from all the cakes and cookies and coffee and a cosseted sense of belonging equally matched by the absolute difference between the forces that had governed my own personal history up to now and the history that had dictated the postwar lives of my Puronas relatives. Except for one common denominator: silence.

I ask petras how much longer to Vilnius.

"Not too long," he says. Then, "Far, I think, maybe."

He's like me, trying to mollify and say what he knows at the same time.

Every so often wisps of low, stratus clouds hide the moon, and the only light is the front beams of the van. I can't see the forest. The fields are dark gray. I have my own simple equation about wartime. It only goes as far as the borderland, the life of my family, and the families whose stories have been unspooled for me over time. It's this: who ends up dead, who ends up alive.

At the hotel there was another e-mail from Maciej Bulanda. I had hoped to go to Poland, to the IPN, from Lithuania this trip, but we were still held up by paperwork and permissions. There was yet another "official" letter I had to write. The ten-volume court case of Jonas Maciulevičius felt like a last stop for me. I was running out of archives to consult. I opened the curtains to the night and looked out. Cathedral Square, empty and lit up.

Why is it that the unobtainable takes on magical properties? I turned the light on again and wrote Maciej a strident e-mail about how critical it was that we get access. His "reading break" at grad school was coming up; once it passed, he would have no time to leave London for Poland to be my proxy at the IPN.

I thought of all I hadn't said to Danute and Egidijus about Senelis. How his crony Malinauskas's complaint traveled for several years up the Gestapo food chain. Copies are signed off on by Ostuf (short for OberSTUurmFührer) Paul Müller of the SD, the security branch of the SS; Hschaf (SSHauptscharführer) Rauca, the staff sergeant who for a time worked under Joachim Hamann with his shooting squad; and the deputy commander of the Gestapo in Lithuania, Heinrich Schmitz. (The same Rauca, along with Schmitz, took part in the selection in the Kovno ghetto on October 28, 1941.)

But during the many months in which different ranks of the Gestapo and other branches of the SS reviewed the Malinauskas complaint—which included proof of Senelis's permission to the Jew Elena Las to live outside the ghetto and his decree that three Jewish men should be given the right to leave the Todt labor camp, where beatings were frequent and rations were even scarcer than in the Švenčionys ghetto—Senelis kept working as chief of security police in Švenčionys, until his brief stint at Lukiškės prison and a demotion and transfer to Panevėžys, where he was a member of the security police under the Gestapo.

The next afternoon, a small plane carried me over Vilnius and the winter woods beyond. What had they looked like in 1943? As the ground shrank beneath me, I thought of Chaya and her partisan group and Yitzhak Arad with the Chapayev unit commanded by Markov, of the order from the Soviet partisan leadership that required Arad and his mates from the liquidated Švenčionys ghetto to hand over all but a few of the weapons they had obtained with such daring and risk. But before the plane even took off, before we bumped our heads on the low ceiling above the seats and squeezed through the narrow aisle with our carry-ons, I had asked our driver Petras, as we made the turn to the airport, if he knew anything about a wartime labor camp nearby during the war.

He didn't.

It was such an important destination in Lili Holzman's journey during the war, and Petras knew so much about local wartime geography. I wondered, not about the veracity of Lili's testimony, but about the many structures of work and death—prisons, really, even if they were not officially called that during the war, nor labeled "concentration camps"—that have simply vanished.

In ŽIEŽMARIAI, DUE to the kindness of their "hoarse" German commander, Lili's little sister Khanale and Lili's mother were given permission to join Lili in 1943. They have news. Lili's grandfather is gone, starved to death in the Svir ghetto.

> He was a man who liked to eat—a big guy. We would always laugh that he would eat soup out of a serving bowl and that his fruit compote he would eat also out of a big bowl. So imagine, he was almost eighty and he had nothing to eat. When I was a young girl I would imitate my grandfather burping, three burps and one big one.

Lili's Aunt Manya, who baked such wonderful bread, has been mowed down with her husband at Ponar (Ponary). People know about the shooting pits at Ponary. "The news traveled . . . it just moved."

As she has done before, Lili's mother is allowed to function as a dentist for the workers, with Khanale beside her, but shortly after their arrival another change: trucks appear, to take them to Ponar, they think. They're loaded on and driven not to Ponar but to the Kovno ghetto, which to Lili seems like civilization. "Look—we saw that there was life, and that people were dressed, and we even saw new hairstyles." Two cousins of her father invite them to their house to bathe and get organized. "I remember very clearly walking into their house, and in one of the rooms they had a light fixture that was pink, and I was astonished. I said to myself—well, people are still alive. And a bed. I saw a bed."

In the recent ghetto past, ten thousand ghetto prisoners have been taken to the Ninth Fort and shot. (My grandfather still has his job in Švenčionys at this time, still hasn't been arrested for a crime I haven't been able to pinpoint, still hasn't been driven past the Ninth Fort in Kaunas/Kovno, aware of the killing zone it has become and afraid for his life.)

Lili works for a time digging peat outside of Kovno and starts to write poetry. Her shrewd mother finds her way to the Judenrat and is given the job of assistant to the head of the orphanage for children whose parents have already been exterminated. "And this [the job] was very important because there was food at the orphanage and she could bring little Khanale every day and Khanale could have food from the orphanage." Work—where, for how long, what kind—was, as the historian Joachim Tauber said to me, everything.

They eat a soup they nickname *yushke*—a Ukrainian word for a fish soup with many variations. For them, "watered-down—tasteless, with little bits of things floating in it, peels and vegetables." There are also very small portions of horsemeat: diced, cooked with onions and made into meatballs, one hundred grams every two weeks. (Lili—unusual for her—left her narrative of the past briefly, mentioned a current scandal in France about horsemeat being passed off in restaurants as, well, some other meat. She smiled a smile full of irony: "I remember the taste of it today as though it was a delicacy.")

Through her mother's connections in the Judenrat, Lili gets work at a sock factory called Silva outside the ghetto. She works at night, checking the socks for defects, first bland silk, then dyed. (Today she gets compensation from the German company for her work there, but only because when the paperwork came from the company regarding the compensation, she agreed not to write "forced labor." Otherwise, no compensation.)

Older workers, particularly those emboldened by their knowledge of Lithuanian, steal socks by wrapping them around their bodies under their clothes, and then sell them in the ghetto.

Then—"a smell," Lili calls it, that this isn't going to continue, something is going to change.

> So we're at the end of 1943. It's after Stalingrad and the German defeat . . . There was one job at the airport that was a very, very hard job, but people feared . . . with the Germans, your fear was always not to work—so people went anyway to the airport. There was an old kind of base outside . . . It had been used as a prisoner-of war camp, so the Kovno Judenrat decided that instead of moving people every day, because it was a far walk, they would put two thousand people that work in the airport to live in the base because it was only a kilometer away. Because there is a sense of some kind of doom, everybody tries to organize a job for themselves that they feel is necessary. There was a feeling that they were going to close the ghetto.

But once again Lili's mother was able to convince the camp authorities to let her practice dentistry at the base near the airport instead of going out each day for the punishing work. When they arrived at the base, her mother claimed that Lili, at sixteen and a half, was a certified nurse, and the "Germans were so stupid they believed it." But then, she *had* worked with her mother before. She knew how to hand her mother a piece of equipment or hold the head of a patient undergoing an extraction. Because they were part of a very small medical team at the base—a doctor, his mother, and a nurse and her mother— they were spared sleeping on the floor in the big halls. They had bunk beds. They treated only the two thousand workers, not the German personnel.

Lili told me several times that the base was near the Vilnius airport. In fact there was a Soviet POW "stalag" in Vilnius, but it appears more likely that the airport was the S. Darius and S. Girėnas Airport/Aleksotas, closer to the Kovno ghetto. The Germans sent ghetto workers there to break ground and build out the small runway for a functional military aviation center. Airport workers were known as "aerodromshchikes"; theirs one of the most taxing, dirty jobs.

This one day—I remember because we stayed within the camp, we worked in the camp—it was the twenty-seventh of March [1944]. So there was a building that was used as a laundromat. That's an exaggeration . . . that's where we all went to wash our clothes, in these big pots where you could boil clothes . . . You know, by hand we washed clothes. So I went to wash and the door was open, but suddenly I see a German soldier and he closed the door and locks me in the laundry room, and says, "Don't go out." And my mother is in [a separate] building with my sister. I could look out the window . . . saw that they were leading the old people and children outside of [that] building. I remember very clearly that they organized them near the gate.

I saw my little sister Khanale walking hand in hand with Mrs. Rubincheck, the mother of Frieda, the twenty-year-old camp nurse . . . Mrs. Rubincheck . . . has her arm around my sister. The gate opens, and I see a big black truck pull up. The doors of the truck are open and I see them start to throw the old people and the children in—I'm watching it all from the window in the laundry. All at once a German soldier walks into the laundry room. I hid, and from my hiding place I see him take his gun and with the gun's bayonet start puncturing the big washing vats in case somebody was hiding a child there.

Several trucks had come. They pulled away and about two hours later the laundry was finally opened up. I got out and ran to my mother [who was in the room with bunk beds in the adjacent building]. The first thing I did was hit my mother. I yelled, "Why did you let them take Khanale?" And my mother explained that she had hidden my sister underneath the bunk bed, but they had a large dog and the dog had smelled her sister and the soldiers pulled her out. My mother told them, "Take me with my child." But they had unleashed the dog on my mother and the dog jumped up on her and knocked her down. She must have lost consciousness, she said, for maybe just under a minute. When she opened her eyes, Khanale was gone, the dog was gone, and the Germans were gone.

Our girl was gone.

They took all the children, not only my sister.

The arrangement they had then—because everybody had to work, and there were families there with children—they organized little day-care centers for the kids, and an older woman would take care of the children. That day at four in the afternoon when the women were done working, they came to pick up their kids—they didn't know. I remember today the screaming and crying of those mothers who came back and found out there were no children left.

CHAPTER 47

GIVEN BACK

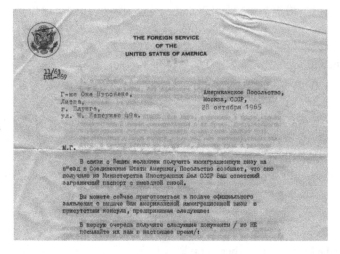

Part of the first page of a three-page procedural for Babita's emigration to the United States

The way I remember the story—which, since I wasn't there at the time, is probably inaccurate—is that Aunt Karina, who would never, as my mother and Senelis and Uncle Roy had at least partially done, accept the fact that her mother was lost to her, got a phone call one day. It was a friend from the Lithuanian-American community. Someone her friend knew had received a letter, and in the letter the writer had casually mentioned seeing Ona Puroniene walking down a street in Lithuania. Aunt Karina nearly dropped the phone.

As quickly as possible, contact was made. In discreet written communiqués—no point calling, my mother had said, since all the phones were tapped—Babita listed goods she could give certain Soviet officials, their underlings at first, then someone with greater power. And so the boxes of bribes were packed up and sent. Beautiful fabrics, velvet, I think Aunt Karina mentioned, were particularly sought after, yards and yards of it. Silk, children's toys, aspirin. Canny, Babita would find out what a local politico might be yearning for, what his wife might thank him for a thousand times over (and perhaps be convinced to forgive a few sins), the date of his childrens' birthdays. The energy of my Lithuanian family gathered around the return of the lost one. Because I was a child at the time, the whole enterprise had the feel of a strange and magical turn of events that would give back to my mother and her sister and her brother what I had had all my life. I do not know how Senelis reacted to the discovery that she was alive. On his certificate of naturalization from 1962, he lists his status as married; his wife "apart from me."

As Anne Applebaum notes in *Gulag: A History*, it had become clear to the reform-minded Soviet leader Nikita Khrushchev that the vast Gulag system was draining the country's coffers rather than expanding (with slave labor) the agricultural and industrial enterprises modernity required. Had Khrushchev not come to power, Babita might have lived out her days from camp to camp to camp. (In fact, my mother—always slow to remember/divulge family particulars beyond her own personal set of losses—ultimately told me, Babita was offered a job at a camp when her release was pending.) As a prisoner, she had won an "award" when, under her direction, her barracks was recognized for being the cleanest. She turned the offer down.

When the bloated Soviet bureaucracy in Lithuania made the decision to let Babita go, she was given twenty-four hours to ready herself and was then flown out of the country in the middle of winter in her summer clothes. She was only allowed to take her travel and emigration documents, the money for the fees to be paid, and the outfit she had hastily thrown on before boarding the transport at the end of December in 1965, first from Soviet Lithuania, then from Moscow into her childrens' arms.

I WAS EIGHT years old on the night in late December 1965 at Chicago O'Hare when a blizzard kept her plane circling above us for hours. Hotel rooms had been rented to spare Babita the drive back to Hammond after her long flight, a drive the weather would have made impossible anyway. The snow fell like goose feathers, blanketing the tarmac as soon as it was plowed clear. The night swirled with the storm. Senelis was there, eyes red-rimmed from a complex of emotions I can't imagine, along with my regal Aunt Karina, her husband, and my father, who had volunteered to welcome Babita on my mother's behalf because she felt compelled to leave the airport to care for my year-old brother, who, with a babysitter in tow, was sick with a high fever at the hotel.

Our part of the terminal was mostly empty. Uncle Alan, short, animated, told jokes, got us candy from the snack machines. My father, of course, had a book to read and mark up with tiny hieroglyphics in the margins. The snowy dark outside the long windows seemed limitless, endless. I thought, *It won't happen, the plane won't ever land.*

Finally, the wild weather broke. I can't remember if the passengers entered through the terminal doors or my family went out to meet Babita once the stairs, folding open and down under the spell of some invisible force, revealed the open door of the plane. It seemed a very long time before the small, shaking woman who was my grandmother appeared, helped by one of the flight crew. Aunt Karina, the first to reach her, placed a fur coat, a gift from Babita's children, over the thin shoulders of my grandmother. I remember thinking she might collapse under the weight of the fur.

I do not recall whether she and Senelis embraced; they would not live together until the very end of their lives. Babita took my face in her trembling hands. Her voice quavered, and she spoke to me in Lithuanian: *Dear one. Hello. Granddaughter.* Exhausted from the long trip, her excitement and trepidation, she was fragile and wan. I'd expected another grandmother like Nana; Babita, with her quivering voice, was a ghost.

Even though it was the middle of the night, a Lithuanian feast covered the long table the hotel staff had set up in one of the rooms. Babita was matchstick thin. Was there a ham? A goose? I know there were dark breads and meats, perhaps octopus, maybe a turkey. There were candies wrapped in different colored paper. There were toasts, the pop of a bottle of champagne.

So many of Aunt Karina's hopes had circled around her lost mother, but she didn't really know the woman the Soviets had ripped from our family and then given back. The woman who had said, at one camp within sight of the Manchurian border, when one of the guards let her know if she walked toward the border he wouldn't stop her, "Where would I go?" Broken down by imprisonment, elderly though she was not yet *old*, how could she find a life in a strange Asiatic country without money or family or language or a vision of hope that is, most often, the domain of the young?

Of course, she did, in fact, find a life, crossing many borders and settling in a place where the urban lifestyle, the language, the culture, were not her own.

During my recent visits with my Lithuanian relatives, they spoke of the letters she wrote them from America. She would have been happier in her home country, she told them. It was too different, the new home of her children. She (with the gifts of many languages) never learned more than a small bit of English. She hardly ever wore the fur coat.

When she first arrived among us, being young and improper, I was fascinated by her tribulations and asked questions. The only tidbit I was given was the word *torture*. During my reunion with Aunt Karina at my mother's house, she described how the physician, at the excellent hospital my aunt took her mother to straightaway, couldn't believe how much scar tissue Babita had on her upper arms, "where the skin was pulled out with pliers."

She gave me intricate pieces of needlework that all looked like doilies. She made amazing desserts: twists of fried dough served with powdered sugar, a cake decorated in the shape of a log, like one of the branches on our family tree. When I was visiting, I regularly snuck into her room at Aunt Karina's and Uncle Alan's where she lived the first years of her arrival. Her bed was made with the tight corners of a barracks. Except for a few pieces of amber, some of her needlework, and a cross over her bed, it was a spartan, empty space. I couldn't understand why someone who had lived with nothing for so long, someone who had eaten snakes and rats and grass, someone who had expected death to come each day, wouldn't want a pretty blanket and lots of pillows, furs, and shag rugs (they were all the rage then). Only now can I almost imagine how important a well-kept, sparse sanctuary must have been for her, and how lonely she was.

Of her time in the Gulag, she said, "If I thought about what the next day would bring, I would have slit my throat." She was always something of a marvel to me, and remains so today, for her toughness. She never forgave my mother for not being at the airport.

In the prewar and postwar Soviet sweeps to Siberian prison and labor camps, the Lithuanian Center for Genocide and Resistance (where Arunas Bubnys directs research) numbers the deportees at approximately 132,000. Eighty thousand did not come back, dead or forgotten by the Gulag administrators in faraway Siberian work villages.

My Babita, who flew down to land among us like an angry sparrow, her fingers always stained with nicotine until her lungs were close to ruined and she quit her chain-smoking ways, lived in and through each minute of her travail. She did not endure by imagining a future of freedom and loved ones. She endured by entering each moment without thinking of the next, except in the most utilitarian terms. Cigarettes were her great luxury. She liked to clean.

She of the parquet floors, who appeared to me in a dream years before I began making inquiries about Senelis. I sat at a long plank table, and she walked over to me, holding in her shaking hands a white bowl of fresh raspberries, which I refused at first. She pressed me. "Eat," she said in English in my dream. And then her hands stopped shaking, and I took the bowl, and I ate.

CHAPTER 48

ROBIN FISH

Since I first learned about Senelis's time in Švenčionys, I'd wanted tangible evidence of what he had done or not done, what he had participated in, what he had walked away from, whom he had helped, whom he had hurt. When I returned to New York from Lithuania in January 2014, Maciej Bulanda contacted me. With the generous help of Dr. Monika Tomkiewicz, a senior historian at the Gdańsk branch of the Institute of National Remembrance—Commission for the Prosecution of Crimes against the Polish Nation (IPN), the errors (all my fault) that Maciej and I had made in our attempts to gain access to the Maciulevičius case files were corrected.

In a few weeks Maciej would travel to Gdańsk, where Dr. Tomkiewicz had graciously offered to lend him a hand. To our astonishment, it turned out that she had actually known the elusive translator Rakowska (Eleanora was her first name) quite well in Rakowska's later years. During Maciej's time at the archive, Dr. Tomkiewicz would make herself available for an interview about the translator who had drifted into my mother's memory what seemed like a very long time ago.

That I would, through Maciej, be able to ask questions of someone to whom Rakowska had spoken of her time in Švenčionys was miraculous to me. Whether or not the case records of Jonas Maciulevičius would answer any of my questions about Senelis was a complete unknown. Nonetheless, in the days leading up to Maciej's arrival at the archive, a brew of hope (for something conclusive) and dread (of anything conclusive) wound me up. I watched videos of interviews I'd done, read and reread testimony, looked at the faces of the dead and the living in my own stills, in photographs from archives and family photographs survivors had thoughtfully made available to me—a photo of my grandmother Rachel with her mother and her sister Klara, both girls ravishingly beautiful, Babita in her elder years, Senelis as a boy. I couldn't sleep.

During those few weeks, someone who had heard that I had been in Lithuania researching the Švenčionys region contacted Rose and asked her to pass some information along to me. He wanted to remain anonymous since he still lived in the area and didn't want to suffer the enmity of those who had known him and his family all of his life. Not surprisingly, Maciulevičius still had family in Lithuania, clustered together in some of the villages that, if you are ignorant of their history, seem simply lovely, delightfully antique— especially when the flax is a sheen across the fields and the days are warm, with a good breeze.

Among his Lithuanian descendants there was the general opinion that he had been a sadist, a man capable of many crimes of great brutality. (Rose had already sent me some information about his arrest in 1920 for impersonating another officer during his army service. Convicted by a military court, he spent eight months in prison and was stripped of his rank. "The inventor of identity theft," Rose wrote.) It was unusual for a Lithuanian family—for any family, for that matter—to readily describe one of their own in such a way, but there was more that my anonymous source wanted me to know. As treacherous as their relative Jonas Maciulevičius had been, as many crimes he might have indeed committed, the slaughter of the Poles in Švenčionys—*well, that one was on Puronas.*

Perhaps what struck me most about this "tip" was simply that my grandfather's name was remembered, at least in some circles, outside of his Lithuanian family. Through another source I learned that Maciulevičius had a son who was alive and living in America. Because his father had been Senelis's co-worker, I wanted to talk with him. I knew how old he was. It was quite likely that he would have attended the same small Lithuanian school as my mother in Švenčionys. I was given the new name the son had taken and tracked down a phone number and left a brief message. He never returned my call. Given the trajectory of his father's life, why would he? His father had been executed by the Polish government for war crimes, not something a son would be eager to talk about with a stranger. Still, I had to try.

During those same, strange few weeks, I pulled out some notes I'd made a year or so back, when my brother called me out of the blue because he had suddenly remembered an experience he'd had with Senelis and wanted to share with me. I'd had a partial memory of it all along but had forgot the totality of it. As soon as he started talking, my own memory resurfaced.

"Remember how we used to go fishing on the pier in Oak Bluffs with Senelis?" my brother said.

Of course I did. The pier was a popular spot for solo fisherman and families. I'd forgotten that my much younger brother had made his own trips with Senelis to the pier, but I'd loved them. We fished for baby blues that swam in the shadows near the pilings. When we'd caught enough of them, Senelis taught me how to knife off the rainbow scales. Filleted, thrown in a pan with butter, salt, parsley, a bit of lemon—they tasted like all the goodness of summer by the sea, of the sea itself.

"There was this one kind of fish everyone threw back. I think it was called robin fish. Maybe they didn't taste good. I don't remember now why, but if you pulled one up, you unhooked it and let it go back into the water. Everyone did it, except Senelis."

As my brother spoke, I was there again with the smell of the planking, the squid we used for bait, the long stretch of the pier, as long as summer, different gradations of green and, farther out, a blue shimmer of water.

"When Senelis pulled up a robin fish, he never threw it back. He unhooked it and let it flop on the dock and then started stomping on it, blood and guts everywhere, stomping until the fish was dead. It embarrassed me. People would be looking at us. I asked him why he didn't just let the fish go. He said it was dirty. He said it had no right to live."

And then I remembered turning my back on the people who watched while Senelis ground the dying fish under his heel with vigor and not quite disgust but a kind of righteousness, as if he was ridding the waters of a pestilence. As I recalled it with my brother on the phone, it had seemed to take a long time for the killing to be done with. But then, I was a child during those hot summer days on the pier, and like all children, experienced time in a measure commensurate with my age. July lasted a year, at least. My grandfather would live forever.

CHAPTER 49

WITNESSES FOR THE PROSECUTION

O n February 17, all afternoon, as I moved through the city, I checked and rechecked my e-mail on my cell phone. Maciej was six hours ahead of me in Gdańsk on the Baltic Sea, at his first day of work at the IPN.

My frame of reference for that city, until Arunas Bubnys mentioned the file at the IPN, had been limited to three names and events. It was in Gdańsk that Lech Wałęsa founded the Solidarity movement in the famous shipyards. Lili Holzman, at one point in her wartime journey, was nearby when the city was known as Danzig—a "free city" by order of the Treaty of Versailles, then taken by the Germans in 1939. Lili's story also intersected with that of one SS-Sturmbannführer Max Pauly, who directed the execution of the Danzig postal employees and locals who fought off the SS occupation of the Danzig post office for hours with a paltry stock of weaponry. An amazing story, though they were overcome—another story within a story, as Chaya Palevsky would say.

I was all the way downtown, on Spring Street in SoHo, when I heard from Maciej. "Good news! Skype as soon as possible." I skidded on the slushy sidewalk, King Street to Houston, a block north to the subway. Out of the subway uptown, I ran home.

Jonas Maciulevičius was extradited from France for war crimes against the Polish nation. He was sentenced to death by the appeals court in Olsztyn, Poland, on May 2, 1950, and then executed. The investigation was reopened on August 18, 1997, and closed eight years later, on January 1, 2005. Once Poland was no longer a puppet nation of the Soviet Union, it began re-examining war crimes cases to ensure that proper juidicial standards had been met. This was crucial to me. This was not a case built on testimony from tortured witnesses. So many decades on there was far less political capital or revenge to be gained by those who had had wartime contact with the defendant. Witnesses—Jewish, Lithuanian, Polish, and Belarusian—came forward, first in the postwar occupation zone in Germany, then in Poland.

Through Maciej, I had queried Dr. Tomkiewicz about the focus of the case. Neither my grandfather nor any other chief or village head or Lithuanian district commander who had worked with Maciulevičius had been under scrutiny. (During Maciulevičius's original prosecution, my grandfather was in the vast system of DP camps, then on his way to the United States with his children and his oldest sister, Ona.)

Dr. Tomkiewicz had explained that the IPN's investigations (among them the Katyń massacre of Polish officers, committed by the NKVD but blamed on the Germans) both prior to 1989—the year of Poland's emergence as a democracy—and currently, fell into two categories: "against" and "regarding a case." The first was direct and narrow, the other much wider, focusing on an event. Although the Maciulevičius case was underpinned by an event—the killing of Polish citizens during the Beck reprisals, which by its nature tasked the prosecution with an examination of the massacre of the Jews of the Švenčionys region—his prosecution and the evidence gathered to support it fell into the "against" category, limited to his culpability as a war criminal.

ONCE HOME, I unwound my scarf, shut my study door behind me, and Skyped Maciej.

It was nine at night in Gdańsk. Maciej was wired, close to his computer screen, his face serious, expressive, repeating for me when I asked, when I couldn't understand.

Yes, my grandfather was mentioned almost immediately in the case files as one of the "three pillars" of authority in Švenčionys, directly under Maciulevičius.

Yes, testimony placed Senelis at Poligon with Maciulevičius.

Maciulevičius himself, along with other witnesses, placed Senelis at the meeting with Januskevicius and the Gestapo representatives when plans were made for the killing of the Jews and the creation of the ghetto: who would be responsible for what and when.

Another witness had heard Senelis complain that Maciulevičius was so power hungry and overzealous that he was usurping his role as chief of Saugumas, though according to a bystander, they were often "seen together" walking the streets of Švenčionys. (Maciulevičius, long before the German occupation, had a history of engendering conflict which lends credence to Senelis's complaint.)

From the veranda of the Švenčionys post office, a witness named Aleksander Bilakiewicz had seen, from five meters away, "how the defendant Maciulevičius with a rifle in hand, dressed in a uniform, together with Puronas walked next to the column of arrested Poles led to the site of execution . . . After . . . about 4:00 P.M. the police organized themselves a party at the school [the Lithuanian gymnasium turned Kasino] near the post office."

A man who worked in the housing office in Švenčionys, headed by one Żukowski, spoke of my grandfather's friendship with Żukowski and how, several weeks after the killing rampage against the Poles, my grandfather paid his friend a visit to vent. Senelis could understand the destruction of the Poles, but not Maciulevičius's willingness to go after Lithuanians as well. "That's why we don't like him, Kukutis told me the same," my grandfather reportedly said. (Mykolas Kukutis, chief of the local white bands, had became "the district governor" and in that role in 1941, helped commandeer the workforce of local shooters and diggers and guards at Poligon.)

Mieczysław Szuchowski testified that he "became the commandant of the ghetto . . . I shall also state that Puronas the chief of political police often called me to his office, beat me and demanded a ransom. Once I had to give him my wife's golden watch."

A watch that perhaps belonged to someone else's wife, either still alive in the ghetto or in the pit in Švenčionéliai, or maybe a watch that Szuchowski had given his wife as a present, or maybe a watch my grandfather knew was stolen from a Jew and so he pocketed it and paid a visit to Moshe Gordon to make sure it was returned, or perhaps a gold watch and other ransoms too, because unlike Szuchowski's, my grandfather's job did not put him in daily proximity to a captive population that could be ordered to pay up at a moment's notice.

(Maciulevičius, apparently, was infamous for his visits to the ghetto to beat and rob. Before his arrest, he was spotted in France with his wife, who was wearing a fur coat that belonged to the wife of one of the few survivors from the Švenčionys ghetto.)

Bohdan Polak, a boy at the time, remembered the fear "Puronas's death brigades" inspired.

In his own testimony before the court, Maciulevičius claimed that during his tenure as chief of criminal police in Švenčionys, he brought my grandfather up on bribery charges that ultimately cost Senelis his job and landed him briefly in Lukiškės prison. This is somewhat supported by the Malinauskas complaint, which describes Maciulevičius's discovery of a large number of hides my grandfather had dropped off at the local tannery to be worked on, presumably at no cost. But then, Maciulevičius was, by many accounts, a sadist and a liar and was deeply involved, as many were, in extorting the ghetto inhabitants and the locals outside the ghetto.

CHAPTER 50

THE COMPANY WE KEEP

Maciej and I spoke every day that week but one—a long day and night he spent organizing and translating the material that was important to me. At the IPN, he was given the desk of a secretary on holiday. He was given cookies and help with the ten unindexed volumes he searched on my behalf. Because of his efforts, I have every mention of my grandfather, with its context, in the Polish, accompanied by an English translation. Another translator worked on the long (130 pages or so) case summary.

Most often, the damning mentions of Senelis are off the cuff—the subject is Maciulevičius, but the witness remembers my grandfather in passing, almost as an afterthought: "Other officers also arrived at the scene of the attack [on Beck], Puronas as well . . . I don't know whether he [Puronas] was sentenced."

My grandfather's presence at the Poligon massacre is confirmed by two different witnesses. Three people confirm his presence at the meeting to plan the killing of the Jews and the creation of the ghetto from which, one day, Yitzhak Arad and his fellow partisans would flee into the forest to fight, and where Chaya Palevsky would spend the last days with her mother, Malke, her father, Eliash, and her youngest brother, Hirshele, before they were shot at Ponary on April 5, 1943. (Her sister Rivke had attempted, early on, to escape to the Soviet Union, but the family knew that she had met her death along the way.)

The IPN court summary stresses that Maciulevičius was the engine behind the killing of the Poles and that yes, a list of those to be executed had been made up by a "committee" that included the defendant, my grandfather, the local Reverend Budra, and Dr. Rymas, the school principal. The committee had made up the list in advance, waiting for the opportunity to use it.

I was able to Skype with my tipster, and he clarified. My tipster believed that because my grandfather was relatively new to the area, Budra and Rymas would most easily have been able to provide the names and locations of the Poles. He also surmised, as did the IPN court summary, that the slaughter of the Poles was in part political revenge for the Polish incursion of 1919, which had, among other humiliations, robbed Lithuanians of Vilnius. It was only 1942, after all; if you lived in the Švenčionys region and you or a member of your family had been in the Polish Legions, you had a death sentence on your head.

Yet, as with many, though not all, mass killings, the documentation suggests a randomness to the violence. People were gunned down working in the fields. You might flee to another town, but a list would be waiting there as well. According to the IPN court summary, the Germans had originally given the Lithuanians a week to wreak their vengeance against the Poles. But the killing got out of hand; after two or three days, they reined men like Maciulevičius and my grandfather in. The victims of the Beck reprisals— the Poles, a few Russians and three Jews who had worked for Beck and were shot in the Jewish cemetery in Švenčionys—were lying facedown, each with a bullet to the back of the head. But before they were shot, either in prison or at the cemetery, they'd been beaten; there were cracked skulls, broken ribs.

The massacre of the eight thousand Jews at Poligon was, oddly, more contained. One witness in the IPN files states that the Germans there were only documenting the killings, not giving orders about trucks or lining up shooters or winding up the killers over bonfires with a barrel of vodka. Liquor was given so freely to the guards and shooters during the genocide that the words of a witness named Dionizy Blicharski, thirteen at the time, seem likely to be at least partly hyperbolic: "At the time when the crimes against the Jews were committed, drunk Lithuanian policemen were walking through the town, and in exchange for the rings, earrings, and gold teeth, sometimes still covered in blood, they wanted to buy vodka."

Saugumas members were in attendance at the shooters' banquet after the killing. Since my grandfather was their chief, it is hard to imagine that he wasn't there when the musicians Zdzisław Walulewicz and Alosza Podoszewny-Żaniewicz angered the Shaulists.

Among the drunken band of Shaulists were the Poligon shooters and those who performed tasks other than shooting—making sure the trucks were loaded up at the barracks as quickly as possible, directing the swift clearing away of the victims' stripped-off clothing at the pit's edge before the next terrified group was unloaded from another truck. No doubt some at the banquet were simply there to take advantage of free food and drink. Multiple testimonies concur that a group of the enraged banquet attendees, fueled by blood and liquor, turned on the musicians because they wouldn't speak Lithuanian with them, and so dragged them out and killed them (acting out of "instinct," as the poet Zenon Tumalovic had said).

The killings of Sore Lewin, and Yitzhak Arad's friends Gershon Bak and Rueven Miadziolski are mentioned frequently in the court summary and in witness statements, several of which claim that Maciulevičius directed their executions and, in fact, buried Gerson Bak while he was still alive.

AND THEN THERE is Eleanora Rakowska, who was there for all of it, until, of course, her arrest in late spring of 1942. Her interview as a witness in the Maciulevičius file is succinct. She was, she said, a member of the Polish Home Army with the code names "Hajduczek" and "Magda." So it was as a spy that she became an interpreter to Beck, whom she described as "apolitical, he snored during Hitler's speeches on the radio." To my ear, her comment about Beck demonstrates one of the oddities of the borderland—a Pole working for the underground calls one of the few German commanders in town "apolitical," though he was part of the machinery of Poligon. Even if he wasn't eager to be there, I found no evidence that he intervened on behalf of Jews in Švenčionys or the region as a whole.

Because Rakowska is the only survivor of the Beck attack, I include her testimony at length.

> On May 19 in Świr [where Lily Holzman's grandfather died in the ghetto] a horse overview to which Beck, Gruhl, and Schneider [who was, Rakowska confirmed, head of a POW camp near Švenčionys] were invited by Beck's counterpart in Świr about 30 km away . . . I was asked to come by at seven o'clock, we departed at eight. We drove the road toward Łyntupy. Beck was

driving, Gruhl next to him, Schneider behind Beck, and myself behind Gruhl. I don't remember what kind of car, but it was small with two doors.

A woman walked on the road, she stopped and she was waving at us. Beck did not stop. Actually she had waved just before the road was coming into the forest. We've entered the forest and we've got a petard that set the car on fire. The shooting began on the right-hand side. We've all jumped out of the car. While still in the car a bullet went just by my head. Germans began to escape to the right . . . I crawled for some time. At some point I could hear a gun being loaded over my head . . . I looked up and I saw the Soviet partisans.

Then Markow [Markov] came and recognized me. He told me to go home. Markow used to live in Święciany under the Soviet occupation. He was the school principal while I taught there. Markow was surprised, he asked "Razwie eta Beck?" I think Beck was not their target. I did not see the killed Germans. Only the Gestapo showed me the pictures. On the same day the Gestapo came to us [her mother and sister lived with her] and arrested me. They first took me for interrogations in the HQ of gendarmerie of Święciany . . . a cell in prison, in water where the rats were . . . On the next day I was beaten again, interrogated by Germans, Gestapo . . . also by Maciulevičius. Later I was transported to Lukiškės prison in Wilno, where I found out that my mother and sister and myself . . . got a death sentence. We were bailed out by the Home Army, [our] death sentence was changed for the labor camp in Prawieniszki [Pravieniškės in Lithuanian; the site of a camp not far from Kaunas].

But Eleanora Rakowska and parts of her testimony are a puzzle, even to Dr. Tomkiewicz, who came to know her well. Her documents claimed that she was born in Wilno, yet her family had an estate in "Old Święciany." Rakowska told Dr. Tomkiewicz several stories about her father, who perhaps, at some point during the war, had fled to Belarus. But when Dr. Tomkiewicz attended Rakowska's funeral, a family member contradicted Rakowska's narrative about her father. (Dr. Tomkiewicz did not want to elaborate on the nature of the contradiction.)

Rakowska arrived at nineteen in Švenčionys with a "degree" in the German language from Batory University in Wilno, yet no such course was given there. According to Dr. Tomkiewicz, the Germans had been "operating" in Lithuania from the 1920s and in greater numbers the following decade, probably recruiting informants and gathering intelligence.

That her former colleague Markov appeared at the moment one of his attack team was going to take her life is rather miraculous. Perhaps *miraculous* is too strong a word, but Markov must have known her well, if he believed she might hold up under torture and not give him away.

Tomkiewicz has spent years of her professional life studying Lukiškės prison. To her knowledge, no one charged with a capital crime ever had a sentence reduced during the war, not even with a big bribe from the Home Army. Rakowska's sentence reduction is as strange as my grandfather's reassignment to Panevėžys under the Gestapo, assuming that the story that he released fifty or eighty prisoners or more from the Švenčionys jail in the fall of 1943 is true.

At the camp in Prawieniszki, instead of doing hard labor, Rakowska was installed in the chancellery, where she was often left alone with prisoner files. She used the opportunity, when she could, to let prisoners know of changes in their status. If a file was marked "Karcer," for instance, it meant a trip to a special solitary cell where inmates were tortured. Her relatively easy work duty and her access to records were, according to Dr. Tomkiewicz, unprecedented. Why did the Germans allow it?

ELEANORA RAKOWSKA WAS, according to Dr. Tomkiewicz, "very bright, and had this talent, ability to find herself in every situation." There is no evidence that while at Prawieniszki she aided the Home Army in any way. When the war ended, she went back to Warsaw with her mother and sister and began to work for the postwar regime of the day.

There is perhaps more to Rakowska's story, but Dr. Tomkiewicz is protective of her memory. Rakowska suffered greatly. During her torture in Švenčionys, she was choked and battered to such an extent that she never fully recovered her physical stamina. Whatever she did, and whoever she may have done it for, she was devastated by the war she survived.

Dr. Tomkiewicz offered to share a few pictures of an elderly Rakowska with me. After looking at them for a few days, I realized with a small shock that I'd had two pictures of her during wartime, the ones that Konrad Beck had been gracious enough to share with me. In one of the photos (shown earlier on page 195), undated, but obviously taken before May 1942, Rakowska is behind the typewriter with a map, presumably of Ostland or the borderland, above her. Fitting that in the photograph of her, much older, she also appears to be holding a map. She, like Senelis, crossed borders, becoming what her nature and her circumstances required.

CHAPTER 51

ONLY GOD KNOWS

Romuald-Jakub Weksler-Waszkinel

Yitzhak Arad told me in Israel, in June 2013, that I should speak with a man who became a Catholic priest in Poland, only learning at the age of thirty-five, on February 23, 1978 ("the date of my second birth," he calls it), that he was Jewish—alive because his Jewish parents had found a home for him before they perished.

Romuald-Jakub Weksler-Waszkinel was born in the Švenčionys ghetto to Batya Weksler and her husband, the tailor Jakub Weksler. (In the Boyarin translation of the Koniuchowsky testimonies, Jakub Weksler's name is given as Yankl Wexler—the gifted tailor who, with his language skills and intelligence, became a ghetto leader, able to gather crucial information from the German and

Lithuanian command and interact with them when a crisis required it.) He was not, it turns out, the tailor whose customer had to slip terrified out of the ghetto past curfew. Until the liquidation of the ghetto, Jakub Weksler was allowed to work in his shop, which stood outside the walls and the wire.

Romuald-Jakub Weksler-Waszkinel, Arad said, was living in Israel, working in the archives at Yad Vashem. But I had only two days left in the country, both reserved for meetings with Lili Holzman. And besides, much has already been written of Weksler-Waszkinel. He has been interviewed at length, and in 2011, the filmmaker Ronit Kertsner made a documentary, *Torn*, about his life as both a priest and a Jewish scholar of the Talmud.

IN AUGUST, WHILE I was in Warsaw, Maciej Bulanda sent me a link to the same "incredible" documentary. He was excited to tell me that, as it happened, Romuald-Jakub Weksler-Waszkinel was back in Lublin for a few days to give a talk. Should he contact him on my behalf to set up a meeting? I said no. People get tired of being asked to repeat their story. I had combed the web and read a lot about him, had seen the photo of him as a young boy, standing with his "Polish parents," Emilia and Piotr Waszkinel, who are honored as Righteous Among the Nations by Yad Vashem. Like the woman who bore the Ashkenazi face of my grandmother at the freight elevator door in Fairway, the young Romuald had clearly Semitic features.

He was a fragile child who began intuitively questioning his identity early on. A story in the *New York Times* described the intense fear and confusion that accompanied his suspicions that he might be Jewish. He would stare at himself in the mirror, trying to find physical similarities to his Polish parents. In a time of intense postwar anti-Semitism, the family repatriated to Paslek, a Polish town away from the settlement area chosen by most of the Poles who left the Švenčionys region for their home country. His parents were horrified when Romuald decided to become a priest. It was a choice utterly contrary to his lively, social nature—better to live a regular life like any young man, choose a profession, take a wife.

Ironically, it had been Batya Weksler's appeal to Emilia Waszkinel's Catholic faith that had finally convinced her, childless and frightened, to take the infant, born sometime in 1943 when pregnancy was illegal in the ghetto and liquidation was on its way. "You believe in Jesus, who was a Jew. So try and save this Jewish baby . . . and one day he will grow up to be a priest." Emilia Waszkinel willed herself to forget the names of her son's Jewish birth parents, lest she give away his identity under torture.

When I turned down a meeting with Weksler-Waszkinel, Maciej momentarily became a young, blond Polish version of Rose, who in Lithuania frequently commanded me to do this or see that or speak with someone when I was reluctant.

"You must have this meeting," Maciej said. And so I did.

Romuald-Jakub Weksler-Waszkinel surprised me at every turn with his quick wit and openness as we talked in his apartment at the Convent of Ursuline Nuns in Lublin. His father had died of a heart attack shortly after his son began his studies for the priesthood; so, despite his own conflicts, Romek, as he was called, pressed forward to honor his father. All of Eastern Europe had lockjaw. Certain topics—the fate of Eastern European Jewry and Polish complicity among them—were never to be discussed.

After Weksler-Waszkinel was ordained, he took a degree in philosophy at the Sorbonne. It was after he began teaching that a colleague steered him toward a history of World War II that broke through the rhetoric of suffering Soviet citizens and presented a more inclusive and complex narrative.

In his third decade, he began to press his mother, who, still afraid, still traumatized by war and the effort to keep her son safe, asked him to stop asking. He didn't stop, and finally she told him that his first parents had been Jews from the Švenčionys ghetto.

"It felt like I was dropped from a plane into no-man's-land," he said.

His mother could not tell him his Jewish parents' names, though she was certain they had died.

"I was really afraid to tell anyone that I'm a Jew. To be rejected. In Poland, in my generation, Jews are not liked. So Pope John Paul II, before he was chosen, was cardinal and my teacher, and he was the first person I told I was a Jew."

He gave Pope John Paul two reasons why he had chosen him: "First, you are a successor of a Jew because Peter was a Jew, and secondly, you are Polish and I have been fortunate to have amazing Polish parents. I thanked him for the Polish part of who I am and asked John Paul for a prayer that I might find a trace of my biological parents."

He also wrote that he would keep his identity secret until he found out his real name. "I didn't want to be *some Jew*, I wanted to have a name, a mother and a father."

The letter he received back from John Paul began: "My beloved brother."

Some time later, Weksler-Waszkinel was in summer residence in a school for blind children in the suburbs of Warsaw. He took the confession of a nun there, and in the course of the confession used a Polish idiom—"To be born five minutes before midnight"—in the context of believing in faith over fear, of being saved. He had no way of knowing that the nun, who helped save Jewish children during the war, had another very specific context for the idiom: the Jewish child who is snatched from death at the last minute.

"She left me a note in my room—'If you have anything you want to tell, you can tell me.' "

The message confused and angered him. He confronted the nun: "What the hell do you mean? Do you think I have big eyes, big nose, big ears . . . is this racist?"

"Don't be angry. I've seen more Jews in my lifetime than you have in yours," she said. Taking her confession, his use of the idiom had felt like a miracle to her.

In her presence, Weksler-Waszkinel began to weep. "I only know two things: my father was a tailor, and I had a brother, Samuel."

Ultimately, the nun, ninety or ninety-two years old, would be his first emissary. On a trip to Israel she made inquiries. Yes, people knew about the tailor Yankl Wexler in the Švenčionys ghetto who had given up his son to a Gentile family. In 1982 Romuald-Jakub Weksler-Waszkinel traveled to Israel for the first time. He purposefully didn't wear his clerical garb, for his father's relatives were Orthodox. After he went through security in the Tel Aviv airport, a "group of elderly people started running toward me. They hugged and kissed me. 'How did you know it was me?' I asked. One of my relatives said, 'You walk just like your father.' "

In the Yitzkor book for the Švenčionys region, there is a photo of his Jewish mother, Batya. He has never seen an image of his father's face. When he said this, with tears that came easily to him during our time together, it struck me that most likely my grandfather had seen the face of Jakub Weksler, who knew Lithuanian and who was the resident tailor for the occupiers—until, one day, he wasn't.

I told Weksler-Waszkinel I would try to find an image of his father in my archival work; I have tried and, so far, failed. In the moment, he listened carefully and spoke with detailed eloquence—the windows closed against a barrage of motorcycles, the day waning. I felt a hatred of time itself. My grandfather quite probably had once had a gift the man in front of me might never find—a memory of the face of a tailor with his needles and threads and fabrics, and a shrewd ability, even under the duress of his day, to establish relationships with the enemy, one of whom would have been Senelis, unreachable behind the wall of time.

There is another remarkable story: how, by accident, luck, fate, Romuald-Jakub Weksler-Waszkinel, in Israel, where he ultimately gained permanent residency status, happened to get a ride home from Yad Vashem with a stranger who turned out to be part of his mother Batya (Kovarski) Weksler's large clan.

In Arunas Bubnys's compilation about the Švenčionys region during the war, the 1942 Švenčionys ghetto census reports that Weksler-Waszkinel had an older brother. It gives his name as "Kolya," born in 1940. In fact, Weksler-Waszkinel's older brother was named Samuel and the Wekslers had given all their wealth to a Lithuanian family to take him in, take him out of the ghetto. And Kolya? Perhaps he was an orphan they claimed as their own, both to help him and to divert suspicion should any authority question them about a son born in 1940, before the Germans arrived. Or perhaps "Kolya" is simply some record keeper's error.

Sometime before the liquidation of the ghetto, the Lithuanian family who had agreed to take Samuel came back to Batya and Jakub Weksler demanding more money, more valuables. But there was nothing left to give, and the family returned Samuel. Later, when Batya Weksler approached Emilia Waszkinel with her pleas, she gave the Waszkinels the only thing she and her husband had left: a samovar. The Wekslers survived the liquidation of the ghetto in Švenčionys and made it to the Vilnius ghetto. Most likely Samuel was killed during the same "Children's Action" that took the life of Lili Holzman's little sister. Weksler-Waszkinel believes his mother met her death at Majdanek, the vast camp outside Lublin.

Today, in one of the surviving wooden barracks along a dusty old camp road, a new air-conditioned, digitized exhibit commemorates Poles who were displaced or killed during the war. In the others, there is only the stifling heat; the scent coming off the wood; the decaying leather of a mountain of shoes; the old displays providing the slightest embodied experience of what it might have been for those worked to death instead of being killed outright as the lives of the locals continued on just outside the massive complex, which was fenced by a system of trenches and barbed wire and guard posts so that it was possible to take notice, if you cared to, of the marching and counting and the arrivals, of the pit shootings that accompanied the gassing by Zyklon B or by carbon monoxide from truck exhaust.

WHEN BLUMKE KATZ, the resident historian of Švenčionys, was still alive, Romuald-Jakub Weksler-Waszkinel, ordained by then, came back to Švenčionys. He asked the priest at the Catholic church if he might speak before the congregation.

"Okay, but make it quick," the priest advised.

Weksler-Waszkinel smiled when he related this detail to me, irony, sadness, and a bit of his shrewdness perhaps all part of that smile; he wasn't as quick as the Švenčionys priest had hoped. "I told the story of myself and who I am and the story of my brother and the family that took him and then brought him back demanding more money and that my brother died because of this. I said I had not come to ask for money but to say that it was absolutely cruel and can not happen again."

I asked if he knew the name of the family who brought Samuel back. He wouldn't tell me.

"Only God knows," he said; again, the same complicated smile.

"What was the response of the congregation?" I asked.

"None, maybe. *We don't know, we are afraid still . . .*"

A few days later an article appeared in a Lithuanian newspaper that defamed his Jewish father: "The tailor—a bad Jew."

Blumke Katz advised Weksler-Waszkinel to get out of the country: if he got into trouble, she wouldn't have much pull to help him. So he left.

Lithuania is probably one of the only countries where perpetrators were not convicted [after the end of Soviet rule]. The policy,
the agenda in Vilna is to divide history into three parts: Nazis,
Communists, and a Free Lithuania that does not bear any
responsibility for what came before. Lithuania entered the EU
and NATO without any responsibility to rehabilitate the
perpetrators; there is no debate like the one that is so present in
Poland today, and this is why I understand the grief and anger of
many Poles. I just wanted to tell the truth. I wasn't naive. I wasn't
counting on them to start crying.

He explained to me that when his young Polish parents first took him
in, someone from Švenčionys informed on them, so they quickly left their
rented room at Grotsky's on Vilenska (Vilnius Highway, which runs directly
through town). "I was already a few years into the priesthood when I got a
letter from this lady, asking for forgiveness. All the kids in Švenčionys were
getting conjunctivitis during the war, and her little girl died and she couldn't
stand that I was alive [with new parents] . . . so out of grief and anger she
reported them. What was it like for me to get the letter? Well, I'm crying
now, so you can imagine . . . This is the bottom line of what it's like. The aim
of the letter was to ask for forgiveness so she knew what she'd done and that
I survived. So I wrote her back that I was alive, and I had to forgive her
because she had asked me to."

"Was it hard to forgive?" I asked.

"Yes, it was hard," he said. Then a long pause.

Walking where the ghetto once stood in Švenčionys, he'd felt a powerful
spiritual connection to his Jewish parents. "I realized, there, that the happiest
time of my life was when I was in my mother's womb. I realized what courage
it took for her to let me be born, to find a way for me to live."

There were tears in his eyes again. He is a man through whom emotions
flow freely now.

"So there is on the one hand punishment, the problem of the past . . . and
responsibility, which is the question of our future. The truth has to come out."

Shortly after, we stood and shook hands, and he ushered us down a maze
of stairs into the now quiet, dusky street and waved us on our way.

CHAPTER 52

MEMORY

In the winter of 2011, during the visit my husband and I made to Martha's Vineyard to meet with my mother, Aunt Agnes, and Aunt Karina, there was a moment at the table in the kitchen when my mother and Aunt Karina began to remember out loud the recurring nightmares that had plagued them both for decades after the war. For my mother, they have ended, though she is still unable to sit through a film in which there is gunfire, pillage, war. Aunt Karina's nightmares, which were just like my mother's, still visit her from time to time. Speaking sometimes in tandem, they described a close version of one of the two dreams I had had all through my childhood. Someone is coming to hunt them down, in the dark—harsh voices, shooting, escape is impossible, running is impossible, chaos, bright lights, boots kicking and stomping. There's a strange dislocation upon waking. Is it safe? Was it real?

My husband, whom I'd told about my two dreams several times, looked at me across the table, astonished at how closely matched one of them was to the one my mother and my aunt were describing in the dreamless morning light.

For them, one continuous attack, coming in sleep for a long time. Neither of them dreamed my second dream: the dream of being the killer, the threat of being found out.

Perhaps, when I was very young, my mother had shared her nightmare with me, and I'd adopted it as my own. I don't remember this having happened, but it might have.

Memory, I have frequently read over the last three years, is an unreliable source for a historical record. "Historia/ἱστορία," my father had scribbled on his yellow legal pad. Perhaps that is true. My experience of late has been that memory is a record of life and of death, of story that is both freed and limited by all the variants that impact how and what and when a dream or a day or a life or the end of a life is recalled.

I REMEMBER SITTING in a chair in the Bronx next to Chaya Palevsky as, from memory, she re-created the needlepoint cover of a photo album, made originally by her mother for a collection of family memories added to, year after year, in their home in Švenčionys before the war. It was strange and powerful to sit with her as she spoke of the dangerous missions she and her fellow partisans, many of whom were killed, undertook during the last deadly months of the war. She returned to Lithuania only once, with her children and in the company, once there, of my friend Regina Kopelevich.

She made a pilgrimage to the pits at Ponary to honor the family she had lost. There were little yellow flowers growing, some grass around the ashy soil, but the trees were bare—"naked," Chaya had said, as if they were ashamed of what had happened there. She sank down, her children holding her, and began to see the faces of her dead mother and sister and brother and father swimming up toward her. Without being conscious of it, she had grabbed at the soil and grass and flowers with each hand. It was Regina who had told her, "Chaya, take these back to your hotel, where there will be newspapers and magazines. Put

From left to right: Rivke Porus, Malke Porus, Hirshele Porus, Eliash Porus, Rochl Porus

these between the pages to dry, and in this way you can take home something of your family."

She did, and from the killing grounds at Ponary made a memorial she calls "A Vision Out from the Ashes in the Pits of Ponary" that hangs on the wall of her apartment to this day.

IN 2007, YITZHAK Arad, serving with great equanimity according to those who worked with him on the Lithuanian Commission for the Evaluation of the Crimes of the Nazi and Soviet Occupation Regimes, found himself suddenly targeted by the Lithuanian prosecutor general's office. Virtually the entire Jewish population of Lithuania had been exterminated during the war, largely at the hands of Lithuanians. Now the prosecutor's office was considering charging Arad and others like him, who had escaped the ghettos and fought for their lives as partisans, with war crimes. It would take several years before a reconstituted commission sent him a written apology, and the letter did not undo the damage done.

In the only photograph Arad has of his family before the war, he is the small, spunky boy to the left of his father; his sister, Rachel, the only other surviving member of his family, is on the far right.

Arad titled some of the personal writing he shared with me, aptly, "Memories: From the Depths of Memory and Before Forgetting." He began by reflecting on earlier work.

> In the memoirs I wrote those years, I tried, subconsciously, to hide the emotional aspect, and therefore my memoirs are more like a military report. I explain this to myself by acknowledging that at a young age I must have seen feelings in regard to my activities during the Holocaust as a sign of weakness as opposed to the image of a combatant against the Nazis . . . With the public atmosphere at that time in Israel, the heroism of the ghetto fighters and partisans was glorified, contrasted with the unjustified feeling of "sheep to the slaughter" in regards to survivors of camps and ghettos who then arrived in Israel . . .
>
> The lack of emphasis and limited reference to the emotional aspect is seen in the places where I describe parting from my parents, the murder of dozens of my family members in the Poligon near what is today Švenčionėliai, and also in Ponar near Vilna and the murder of all the Jews from Švenčionys. Also, in the description of the period after May 1945, when I escaped the Soviet Union and got to Poland and found no trace of my parents, and it was clear to me that they, from whom I parted at the end of December 1939 in Warsaw, were no longer alive. These feelings I hid deep, deep inside my consciousness and in my soul . . .
>
> In recent years, my thoughts go back again and again to my parents and extended family killed in the Holocaust, and to my childhood. My memories take different forms. One of them is that I hum and sing to myself often (especially in the shower) songs my mother sang to me . . .
>
> One of the songs I love singing and whose words express my feelings is a song written by Mordechai Gebirtig, "Kinder Yoren" (Childhood Years) . . .

Lovely childhood years, the years of our childhood
Forever etched into our hearts
Their memory rises before my eyes, my heart is flooded
How fast they stayed behind

I still remember my home
Where I first opened my eyes
The picture of my crib, her coming toward me
Like a dream carried to the sky . . .

(The poet and songwriter Mordechai Gebirtig was in the Krakow
ghetto and was murdered in 1942. He also wrote the song
"Brothers, fire in our town, our town is burning completely.")

IN MID-FEBRUARY OF 2014, toward the end of my meeting with Michael
MacQueen at ICE in Washington, D.C., I detailed for him the discrepancies
on my grandfather's intake form from the DP camp registration in Ingolstadt
and in the paperwork required for the U.S. Displaced Persons Commission.
He had brought his children and older sister with him to Camp C with a
pocketful of German marks and my mother, his oldest, utterly ridden with
what a researcher at the Holocaust Museum described as "a terrible case
of the creepy crawlies"—lice. At the DP camp, he claimed that, during
different time frames, he had been a merchant in Lithuania, in flight school,
and—during the period when he worked for the Gestapo in Panevėžys after
Švenčionys—a farmer. Interestingly, on the extensive form for the DP
Commission he noted his service as chief of security police in Švenčionys.
Perhaps part of the advice circulating was not to lie about what was easily
traceable.

But I have no idea if, on May 12, 1945, he even imagined himself as the
possible target of an investigation that might impede his family's immigration
to Canada, his first choice, or to the United States.

The appeals court that sentenced Jonas Maciulevičius to death based their
sentence, to a large degree, on the application and interpretation of the new
Nuremberg Laws concerning perpetrators of genocide. The court included
my grandfather as one of these perpetrators, along with Maciulevičius,
and also made a case against the Saugumas as a whole, for the substantive role

its members played as deadly agents for the Reich's agenda. Wherever my grandfather went, it had to be somewhere out of reach of the Soviets, who were already looking for him in what was now a Lithuania under Soviet domination, handed over on a platter via the Yalta agreement.

When I brought up the complaint against Senelis—how he had let Elena Las live outside the ghetto, how he had given the three men a work release from the Todt labor camp—MacQueen sat back in his chair.

"How many members of Saugumas do you think were executed by the Germans in Lithuania?"

I had no idea.

"Zip. Not a single one. Why would the Germans bother? They could ship you off to a labor camp instead. The one thing that you could get into big trouble for was gold, money, rubles, robbing the Germans of the bounty they collected from the Jews."

(MacQueen's comment made me think of Senelis's claim—*I never took anything from the Jews*. Was this a wartime phrase meant to inoculate one from suspicion, a phrase that outlived the war, especially in a place like Lithuania where the Soviets, for different reasons from the Germans, prosecuted and/or persecuted people for having stolen from the Jews?)

At the end of our conversation MacQueen stood up and pausing a moment just outside his office said, "You know, I started out with this work years ago thinking I'd catch the bad guys, and all these years later, the bad guys just keep coming."

For a moment he seemed a bit like an old-time sheriff, still sharp, but feeling not so much his age as time itself and the list of the most wanted that never becomes any smaller, no matter how many names get knocked off the top.

"Well, someone has to do it, go after the bad guys," I said.

I felt like I was twelve years old for a second. Bad guys, good guys. But what about all the gray in between? MacQueen shrugged. He was in his own private moment, and I don't know if he even heard me.

We shook hands before he used his key card to open the heavy metal door for me and promised to be available via e-mail if I had more questions. I did, and he answered the ones he could. His case files for the Poligon guard Vincas Valkavickas are still on the specialist's desk at FOIA (Freedom of

Information Act). Perhaps they will provide a clue about how Senelis slipped through the cracks and became a United States citizen. The fact is, when he was being interviewed at the DP camp, the main interest was in the Communist threat, not the Jewish dead or those who had helped kill them.

Until the Valkavickas file is declassified, MacQueen can't speak with me about it. I suspect he may no longer be on the job when a redacted set of records finally arrives in the mail. But I might be surprised, as I have so often been during these last years of travel.

BACK OUT IN the cold, I had one more stop before Union Station. I wanted to find, on microfiche at the Holocaust Museum, Lili Holzman and her mother Rachel's Stutthof concentration camp registration cards. I made my own short pilgrimage in the cold. She and her mother were not, among the horrors they encountered, given tattoos. In Israel, Lili had already given me their prisoner numbers. Lili's number was 41338, her mother's 41339.

The blast of heat inside the museum threw me off somehow. I was exhausted, not just by the day but by all of it. My grandfather should never have been allowed into the country. But he had been. And here I was. I took the elevator upstairs, picked up my microfiche, and sat again at one of the machines to the left of the reference desk. It took only a few minutes to find the S's, and then her maiden name, Swirski.

I looked at their cards and, when I couldn't stand it any longer, did a quick rewind, put the roll back in its white box, delivered it to the larger box for returns, retrieved my blue jacket and bag from the locker, and made the train that outpaced the coming blizzard by a few hours. Home the next day, in the white frozen world, I thought of Lili's account of the trek she and her mother made, past what was then occupied Danzig to one of the women's camps at Stutthof.

Out of the freight car:

> They were doing a selection of the women and we could see that
> they were separating the old women, and my mother, though
> forty-five years [Lili crimped her fingers in quotation marks]
> "old," already had gray hair. But her face . . . was very youthful.

She never had to use any cream. She always had good skin, and it had color to it. So I put a kerchief on my mother's head to cover up the gray and because my mother looked so youthful, she was able to go with me. We were chosen for life—to life.

We were then brought into a big hall, and the German soldiers or officers were sitting behind desks and writing things, and we stripped naked. And we had no sense of shame—I walked around completely naked and so did my mother—it was nothing. My mother was naked in front of a table full of men. I don't know why. I don't know how to explain it. I know that I walked without shame. I was seventeen, and I had a beautiful body.

We put our clothes in a pile. After they registered us, you had to give over any jewelery . . . everything, except you were allowed to keep combs.

Lili laughed. "But later we wouldn't need combs."

Afterward there was another room with a cement table. Everyone had to lie down and have a gynecological check to see they're not hiding anything. It was done by men; they were [again the quotation marks] "doctors." I was young, I was a virgin, but there were older women who had had children. The men dug into them, really dug. They were aggressive. I remember very well there was a young woman with us who had hidden things. She had hidden a watch and some jewelry and in the gynecological check they found them and took them out. She was crying afterward; "Not only did I lose my jewelry, but I'm not a virgin anymore."

After the "exam," the women's heads were shaved. But not all the women; Lili, for some unknown reason, was spared, but her mother was shaved. Perhaps the arrival of a new transport meant the process had to move more quickly, skip a step, a prisoner or two.

It was very very sad for me to look at my mother naked with a shaven head. This is an educated woman, and to see her like that, walking around, to see her face—

Next, the registration.

> I don't understand. They asked us so many questions even
> though their intention was to exterminate us. Height, eye color,
> color of hair, width of nose, of face, of mouth, education, criminal
> record, everything. They wrote it all out and then you had to sign
> at the bottom.

After a quick dribble of water in showers all the women were convinced were actually spigots for deadly gas, they were given uniforms, shoes that didn't fit. Wooden shoes, Lili recalled. The barracks were plain wood, no straw.

> We were there for six weeks. We didn't work, just suffered from
> torture and beatings. And every morning they would wake us up
> very early and have us stand for hours with no food and nothing
> to drink, and it was very, very hot.
>   At nights, there were women—mostly Russian women—
> perhaps with criminal records. They looked well fed and they
> had connections to the Germans. We used to see orgies. They
> were brought in to be a kind of guard of the Jewish women. They
> were prisoners as well, but on a higher level.

Here she interjected, "It's a paradox, because here when it's a little windy or a little cold, people get sick—you get a cold, you get a flu. And there, where it was horrific, we were fine."

It was at Stutthof that the SS Commander Max Pauly, wielding a huge wooden stick, with an empty tin tied to its end, would portion out a thin soup into the women's brown plates. No spoons, so the women just tipped the plate and drank. When it fancied him, if perhaps a woman complained of a short ration or of hunger in general, he would beat her with the same stick used to serve the soup.

After their six weeks of internment, the women were brought out of the barracks before a huge pile of clothes: slips, pajamas, underwear, nightgowns, jackets, pants. They were instructed to take off their prison garb and dress themselves in the leftover clothes of the dead.

> It was funny—we would look at each other and laugh, because a
> fat woman would wear something that couldn't close on her, and
> a thin woman wore something very large. I ended up with a
> nightgown, and my mother also had some sort of nightgown. We
> didn't ask why. There was no why. An order was an order.

They were sent out on trains to dig trenches, moving as the Russian front closed in. In summer, "It wasn't so bad." The women worked from six in the morning until six at night. When the winter of 1945 began, the work, partly under the cruel oversight of a German commander named, of all things, Kafka, became unendurable. Their shovels were blunt. The ground was frozen. They were starving and dying. On Christmas night Lili's mother snuck out into a village and knocked on a cottage door to beg for food. The woman of the house agreed to give her some Christmas cake, but first Rachel Swirski had to sit and darn the family's collection of torn socks.

At one point, sleeping at night on the frozen ground, finding themselves unable to work any longer, they asked their captors to send them back to Stutthof.

Lili's children call it the day she "signed up for the gas chambers."

They waited, inert, for the truck to come and take them to their death, but instead, a few days later, a German officer made an announcement: "We are no longer killing Jews."

All the women were roused. They were not going to be gassed or beaten to death. They were going to be marched into oblivion.

> The night came, and at that point we were near a logging factory.
> They brought us in there and told us to lie down. We were so
> exhausted we just did it. Next day, same thing—walking,
> marching. Where and for what? Night comes, and again we slept
> somewhere . . . we walked like this about five days. Many fell to
> the side and died, and anyone who couldn't walk was shot, and
> my mother and I—really with our last drops of strength we just
> kept walking and walking.

One morning when Lili woke, her thick head of red hair that had been spared at Stutthof was frozen to the ground; clumps and strands of it broke off when she sat up to begin walking again.

> One night they brought us to these Finnish-style round barracks. We heard the Russian front. We understood they were closing in, and yet we were being marched and taken and we didn't understand where and we didn't know why. We woke up in the morning. We were so used to being people that are ordered around, yelled at—not human in our own right. But it was silent. We looked around and realized there weren't any guards. We actually got scared and looked for our guards; we couldn't believe that we were free.

It turned out that Elena Las, a young Jewish widow with a child, with means of some kind, lived—per my grandfather's permission—at the end of Gedmino, half a block from his house during his time in Švenčionys. If they both walked out their doors at the same time in the morning, they could have waved to each other. Under the heading for religion in the 1942 census that lists her by name and provides her address, over an initial, unreadable entry is written "Roman Catholic." I'll never know what arrangement was made between my grandfather and her.

Of Mirele Rein, I have found no trace—just a part of a testimony that anchors her in memory and time. But one day a friend who had visited Denmark said she had seen a remarkable exhibition of drawings by a young Lithuanian artist named Mindaugas Lukošaitis. I looked up his work, and in a collection of drawings he titled *Jews: My History* I found an image that immediately became, for me, one way of remembering the girl who spoke beautiful Lithuanian, who perhaps tumbled into the arms of a short, dark woman in a doorway on a road in Novo-Švenčionys, and who, if the testimony about her is accurate, my grandfather would not save and who lost her life when the Postavai ghetto was liquidated; another shooting, another pit.

And then she vanishes.

WHEN MARTYNAS, THE twenty-year-old son of my Lithuanian relative Egidijus Puronas, came to New York for job training, he visited us twice for dinner.

At the end of one evening, he spoke of the story he had been told about my grandfather, about all the people Senelis had freed from jail, the lives he had perhaps saved. I watched his face as he spoke and saw there what I've felt inside myself, the power of the family narrative as it is handed down to us, our desire to believe in the simplest way, that those we love or have loved are good, even heroic.

He asked me many questions about my archival work, and I tried to explain to him as carefully as possible that I had looked for evidence that Senelis had performed this courageous act but had not found it.

Martynas, pragmatic, quirky, bright, said, "Maybe someday the relatives of those he saved will come forward." He couldn't let go of the truth as he knew it, as it had been given to him, like a spell handed down by my great-grandmother Barbara. He was optimistic.

"Maybe they will," I said, and felt, for just a second or two, the pull of that particular narrative, a bit of hope.

It was a steamy city night, and the open window, a small whirl of a fan, didn't alleviate the heat. I cleared the table, and perhaps it was the close air and the summer shirt sticking to my back and the Lithuanian accent of Martynas that made me think of the afternoon when I had stood in the heat outside of Lukiškės prison with the man at the top, Artūras Karalis.

There he is again, stocky, handsome (like Senelis was at his age), as the shadow of the afternoon divides the street—cautioning me about entering the prison and about the perils of memory in general. He makes a sweep of his arm, as if gesturing beyond Lukiškės to the whole of Vilnius and the country itself.

"This is a place of tears," he says. He is right.

EPILOGUE

Try to look . . . if you don't find anything, don't regret your efforts. There's little
hope, but there's still some sort of tiny crystal of hope.

—Ona Šimaitė in a letter to Marijona Čilvinaitės, December 17, 1957

When i first began to learn about Lithuania during World War II, Ona Šimaitė—who
in addition to having the same first name as Babita was also, like Babita, a Lithuanian
librarian—captivated me.

Employed at the Vilnius University Library, Šimaitė continually risked arrest and
death as she smuggled food and supplies into the Vilna ghetto under the cover of participating, with Herman Kruk and others, in the decimation of Jewish literary culture by
finding and sequestering important books for the Germans.

Yad Vashem lists eight hundred Lithuanians as Righteous Among the Nations,
Šimaitė included, but Lithuania keeps its wartime secrets. In the countryside especially,
there is still a fear of saying too much, fear of a bad neighbor, a reprisal from one quarter
or another, some of the fear left over from the Soviets who, directly at war's end, immediately executed roughly the same number of Lithuanians honored today by Yad Vashem.
And then after that, year after year, killed or deported more.

Members of the same family are often deeply divided about the past. On a trip to her
home country, my mother was told by a Lithuanian relative that "we got rid of both of
them, the Jews and the Russians." A few days later, a cousin drove my mother to a small
memorial for local Jews massacred during the war.

I am sure that many Lithuanian families have as yet untold stories of grandparents
and great-grandparents, fathers or mothers, uncles and aunts, who brought butter to the
"black window" and refused to be paid, who thrust bread into the hand of someone
marching from work or to a labor camp, who gave shelter, or simply saw and did not
report someone running for his life.

There were Germans also—not many, but some—like the well-known Major Karl
Plagge, who through a factory in Vilnius offered extra food, protection, and life-saving
permits to many of the Jewish workers there.

Some people both hurt and helped. Some people *collaborated*—the inadequate
word—and then stopped, for reasons that might have had nothing to do with horror at

the massacre of the Jewish population of Lithuania. Some helped those in need for a price that kept getting steeper.

As I read through the interrogations of those who worked with or under my grandfather and Jonas Maciulevičius, certain tropes repeated themselves. Many witnesses insisted that they provided aid to "Soviet citizens" trapped under fascist (German) rule. Iozas Breeris, warden of the Švenčionys prison, claimed that he had released a significant number of prisoners close to the end of the war, and had witnesses to back him up. No one my grandfather worked with ever mentioned under interrogation that Senelis had been arrested by the fascist Germans for freeing prisoners, even though they might have attached themselves to his efforts—he was their superior, after all—to win some slight mercy at the Soviets' hands.

Certainly there were Lithuanians who abandoned their work on behalf of the Germans without repercussion. Joachim Hamann's killing squad, for example, had its share of Lithuanian defectors, who were allowed to walk away from the carnage without any punitive measures. My grandfather might have been horrified to find himself at the meeting in early fall of 1941 that mapped out the killings at Poligon and the creation of the Švenčionys ghetto, but if so, it had not been enough to make him request another posting.

Still, as a historian I interviewed and questioned via e-mail several times noted, my grandfather was never put on trial. Though he lied on his naturalization and immigration forms, the lies were not picked up by the U.S. Justice Department. He never had the opportunity to address questions about his wartime life and answer them in a court of law, even an immigration court. According to my mother and her sister, he never mentioned either Poligon or the 1942 Beck reprisals to them, so again, in the end, there is no direct account of his role (or lack thereof) in these events.

I recently received a pro forma letter from the FOIA unit of the Criminal Division of the Justice Department regarding the case file and notes for Vincas Valkavickas, the Poligon guard. His extradition case still intrigued me. Why, I wondered—and still wonder—had a Poligon guard living in the United States been located and prosecuted, while Senelis, chief of security police for the whole Švenčionys region, had been left untouched?

Perhaps, the letter suggested, since my FOIA request has taken so long to fulfill, my interest in the material might have waned. If I no longer wanted the material, the harried specialist—who, as she told me during several phone calls, is short on staff and constantly pulled out for meetings and has a pile of requests on her desk that has mounted at a steady twenty cases in CD format, month after month after year, with mine close to the bottom of the stack—perhaps could pull my files out of the pile and send them back to storage. "If you are still interested . . . and wish for the request to be processed, please respond . . ."

"Yes, I am interested, yes, I wish," I write back right away.

ACKNOWLEDGMENTS

I HAVE MANY people and institutions to thank for their contributions to this book. Before I recognize them here, let me first say that all missteps and errors in these pages are my own.

In Israel: Yitzhak Arad answered my many questions with patience and the same scholarly precision found in his many books. It is my great hope that his book *The Partisan: From the Valley of Death to Mt. Zion,* currently out of print, will be available to a wide readership again. In addition to the crucial Holocaust history it contains, it is an astonishing, universal story of young people torn from their ordinary lives and forced to try to find a way out of an impossible maze of entrapment and death.

Lili Holzman spent hours with me on two separate occasions, speaking, as almost all my interviewees did, of the greatest tragedies of her life with erudition and an extraordinary memory for detail that has been with her since childhood. I count her, as I do Yitzhak Arad, as one of my most valued teachers, for she not only told me her own story but explained the unfolding of local and national events in wartime Švenčionys and beyond with precision. (I add also my gratitude to her daughter, Gitit Holzman, who initially contacted her mother on my behalf.)

Irit Pazner Garshowitz served as my fixer and translator during my interviews in Israel. She made time, despite the demands of her work for the *New York Times* bureau in Jerusalem, to troubleshoot for me frequently, often with little advance notice. Her fine translation of a portion of Yitzhak Arad's private papers is included in this book. Not only has she been a passionate, dedicated, and insightful ally, but she has become a beloved friend whose generosity of spirit has seen me through a dozen small and large crises and encouraged me at every turn. I owe her a debt that cannot be repaid.

Nadav Kersh journeyed through Jerusalem with me twice. His enthusiasm, his extraordinary local knowledge, and the depth of his version of historical context was thought-provoking, his love of his surroundings infectious.

I also wish to thank the Yad Vashem Archives, and particularly Zvi Bernhardt, for last-minute permission to use the Leib Koniuchowsky material so crucial to this enterprise.

Finally, my stepdaughter, Lily Fishleder, joined me on my second trip to Israel, and in addition to her fine company, did the film and photography work for those interviews.

In Lithuania: Rose, Viktorija Bourassa, and Petras, my stalwart companions—you have my love and gratitude.

My extended Lithuanian family offered me their hospitality and affection, and shared many stories about our family, their own postwar experiences, and what they could remember about my grandfather, Pranas Puronas.

Arunas Bubnys, director of research at the Genocide and Resistance Research Center, provided valuable leads and was an illuminating force. As noted in the text, I read much of his translated scholarship before I set foot in Lithuania, and each time we met, I left with a greater understanding of the different forces at play during first the Soviet and then the German occupation of his country.

Rachel Kostanian, who at the time of our interview was still the director of the Green House in Vilnius and has an encyclopedic knowledge of the Holocaust in Lithuania, gave me several hours of her time on a cold day in late spring. Her discussion regarding the politics involved in both the forgetting and remembering of wartime events in present-day Lithuania foregrounded the beginning of my research.

Emanuelis Zingeris spoke with me about the experience of a dual identity and the postwar struggle for Lithuanian independence, encouraging me in my efforts at a time when encouragement was sorely needed.

I owe particular thanks to Dalius Žižys, director of the Lithuanian Central State Archives, for allowing me, during my last visit, to access a large amount of material within a brief time frame. Within the Lithuanian Central State Archives, I also made use of the Archive of Image and Sound. Archivists at the Lithuanian Special Archives and the Lithuanian State Archives provided valuable assistance as well. Petras Kibickis lent a much-needed hand at several of the archives mentioned above.

The Nalšia Museum in Švenčionys graciously gave me permission to use images from their impressive digital image collection. Naderda Spiridonovienė was a helpful guide during my initial visit and copied the Poligon file for me that Giedrė Genušienė used during her own research.

My interviewees in Lithuania spoke of what for many were the most traumatizing events of their lives. Together with Yitzhak Arad and Lili Holzman, they offered me a window without which any part of the dimensional past this book has managed to capture would have remained a blank. To Teresa Krinickaja, Zinaida Aronowa, Anton Lavrinovich, Illeana Irafeva, Vanda Pukėnienė, Elena Stankevičienė née Gagis, Zenon and Jadyga Tumalovič, Artūras Karalis, Vaclav Vilkoit, and my extended Lithuanian family my deepest appreciation.

Though we only met once in Vilnius, Geoff Vasil not only did a superb translation of the bulk of my grandfather's reports and letters but was consistently helpful from afar over the course of several years. He, as others did, gave me an additional perspective on current issues in Lithuania regarding the narrative of its past. I am doubly grateful to him for introducing me, via e-mail, to his wife, Milda Jakulytė-Vasil, who in conjunction with the Vilna Gaon Jewish State Museum created *The Lithuanian Holocaust Atlas*. I am thankful for her permission to use an interior shot she took of what was once the Vilna ghetto library.

In Poland: The gifted journalist Joanna Berendt provided crucial leads and initial, important research for me. Her astuteness, generosity, and willingness to share a small part of her own personal narrative were of great help to this entire endeavor.

Maciej Bulanda was an outstanding companion/fixer/translator. With him, my husband and I toured the stunning new Museum of the History of Polish Jews in Warsaw, whose program director, Barbara Kirshenblatt-Gimblett, stepped in several times with useful advice for us as we navigated various Polish archives. Without his prodding, I would not have traveled to Lublin for an astonishing interview with Romuald-Jakub Weksler-Waszkinel. Maciej translated the interview on the spot, and the emotional courage and immediacy of Weksler-Waszkinel's remarkable story reinforced again for me that the past lives on in us, if only we can bear it.

At the Oddział Instytutu Pamięci Narodowej w Gdańsku (the Gdańsk branch of the IPN), senior historian and researcher Dr. Monika Tomkiewicz was crucial to this project. Maciej spent one long week at the Gdańsk IPN, poring over ten volumes of the Maciulevičius case file during the day and then translating and Skyping with me each night. Dr. Tomkiewicz answered all of the questions different aspects of the case file brought up, as well as allowing Maciej to interview her, on my behalf, about Eleanora Rakowska. In addition, she provided several photographs of Rakowska for use in this book. The staff at the Gdańsk IPN offered help at every turn.

In Germany: Almut Schoenfeld worked her way tirelessly through many different archives. She was a deft researcher who, though it is cliché to say it, left no stone unturned on my behalf. In addition, she often translated useful material uncovered during her work, and when we finally met in Berlin, she quickly became dear to me. She has continued to answer questions related to my work, as well as translate correspondence when a quick turnaround is needed.

Dr. Joachim Tauber allowed me to interview him at length during my time in Berlin. His insights, particularly in regard to work and power in German-occupied Lithuania, have been illuminating. As I mention in the text, the word *collaborator* seemed to me from the start too simple a term. It did not capture the complicated complicities war provides a breeding ground for. Dr. Tauber spoke eloquently about the admission (or denial) of guilt on the part of both the individual and the nation. I am grateful for our time in Berlin as well as his lengthy response to a series of questions I posed after our meeting.

Konrad Beck generously shared both photographs of Josef Beck and the outline of Josef Beck's history as the family knew it, and via e-mail wrote movingly of his own relationship to the past and the strange link between our families.

In London: The historian Antony Polonsky talked through the structure of this book with me and what I hoped it might achieve, less a personal narrative than a close examination of a particular place at a particular time. Both his work as editor of and contributor to the journal *Polin* and his responses during our interview helped clarify a long, complicated history in the borderlands. He invited me to ask more questions, and I'm grateful for our correspondence.

Timothy Prus and his staff at the Archive of Modern Conflict were welcoming and generous with their time. A staff member searched through a monumental amount of material for images of World War II relevant to my book and quickly made high-resolution copies of photographs I was interested in. The archive is an astonishing effort, and I was privileged to see it firsthand.

In Washington, D.C.: Archivist Megan Lewis at the U.S. Holocaust Memorial Museum has been of great help the last several years. (She is just one of several archivists who were always ready to respond to the most remedial questions, speedily responded to all of my inquiries, and made valuable suggestions when I was stumped.)

His contribution to my work is mentioned in the text, but again, in D.C., Michael MacQueen at ICE provided important details and context that helped fill in some of the gaps regarding the particulars of my grandfather's brief incarceration in Vilnius, as well as the information on his immigration and naturalization forms.

In New York: Chaya Palevsky allowed me both to interview her and also to return with the photographer Edwin Torres to take still photographs of some of her most cherished memorabilia, including photographs of her family, as well as a portrait of her. My meeting with Chaya Palevsky was my first interview with a survivor of the Švenčionys ghetto. Like Yitzhak Arad and Lili Holzman, she is one of my teachers. Through her, I began to see a town, a way of life now vanished, the terror that was visited upon her family and others she loved, and her indomitable intelligence and strength as both a young person and the older woman who told me "stories within stories." I am grateful also to her son, Elliott Palevsky, who helped me to establish contact with his mother and made sure that my presence would not be intrusive.

I thank YIVO, particularly head archivist Fruma Moher, for use of the Boyarin translations of the Koniuchowsky papers so vital to my book. Fruma Moher's assistance and encouragement represents the graciousness of the staff at YIVO in general. I began my actual research there, and have thought, many times, of those who helped the institution survive when Vilna was crumbling.

Jonathan Boyarin allowed me to interview him by phone in November 2011. We talked at length about his translation work on the Koniuchowsky material, and his insight about the way the past is reconstructed in the present (represented in the text) proved to be a compass point for my entire endeavor.

Timothy Snyder was one of the first historians I contacted when I began my research. He responded with advice he said he often shared with his students: "The questions you start out with won't be the questions you end up with, but they won't be entirely different either." I have often wondered if this was a sort of professorial koan he invented simply to keep his students asking questions and pressing on. It certainly had that effect on me, and in the end, perhaps, it turned out to be true.

Alexander Stille, on several occasions, gave thoughtful advice about personal historical narrative. Marie Howe and Erica Ferrari offered initial support.

Rita Phelan, William Haywood Henderson, and Tina Harrell have been beloved anchors throughout. Dr. Ellen Pearlstein, my superb internist, literally saved my life. My sisters: Laurie Kutchins, Donna Masini, Regina Kopelevich, Honor Moore, Alice Spitz, and Regina McBride lived through each chapter with me, in one way or another, and they, along with Daniel Mendelsohn, both mentor and friend, carried me forward.

Julija Šukys, author of *Epistolophilia: Writing the Life of Ona Šimaitė*, gave me permission to use a few lines from one of Šimaitė's letters that Šukys translated so beautifully. Thanks also to another wonderful contributor, Ellie Moidel, who provided invaluable translation skills to an important part of the text.

Jason Gallagher began the process of creating order in my impossible filing system. Edwin Torres provided his skills as a photographer and photo editor, and Sara Fetherolf worked tirelessly on the various crucial addendums to the book. A stickler for detail, she has caught mistakes I've missed, raised questions I neglected to ask, and been a steady presence throughout. During the last mile, the vocal range of Justin Vernon and the beauty of Goat Rodeo challenged me to keep discovering.

My wonderful editor at Bloomsbury, Nancy Miller, believed in this book from the start. It is because of her that I plunged ahead. I thank her for her editorial acumen, and her friendship. Also at Bloomsbury, Lea Beresford patiently fielded dozens of questions. With her, Gleni Bartels, Patti Ratchford, and Theresa Collier helped me move from draft to book.

In addition, thanks go to Alexandra Pringle at Bloomsbury UK, Jeffrey Miller, Esq. for sound advice, and the support of my unflappable agent at ICM, Lisa Bankoff.

Finally, to Susan Chira for giving a late draft a keen read; Michael Shapiro for his quick insightful take on what always seemed to be unsolvable issues; Suzanne Daley, David McCraw, Kami Kim, Tommy McDonald, Susan Caughman, Gerry Goodrich, Edie Silsdorf, Nicole Gill, Eli Fishleder, and Gloria Crumrine—thank you for suggestions, encouragement, and most importantly, your steadfast friendship. The rest of the Friday night gang—along with friendship, you gave me continuity week after week, even when I was traveling or at home working.

My family of origin—my brave mother, Aunt Karina, Aunt Agnes, and my aunt Shirley Gabis Perle who championed this work: thank you for remembering . . .

Paul and Lily Fishleder, you are my loves, my anchors, my sails.

LIST OF ILLUSTRATIONS

NOTES

EPIGRAPHS

vii **We were riding through**: Czesław Miłosz, "Encounter," trans. Robert Hass, in *The Collected Poems, 1931–1987* (Hopewell, NJ: Ecco, 1988), 27. Used with permission from Harper Collins.

vii **Sventiány was remembered**: Leo Tolstoy, *War and Peace*, trans. Louise and Aylmer Maude (New York: Simon and Schuster, 1942), 716.

vii **We were dreamers**: Abraham (Avrom) Sutzkever, "The Lead Plates at the Rom Press," in *The Penguin Book of Modern Yiddish Verse*, ed. Irving Howe, Ruth R. Wisse, and Khone Shmeruk (New York: Penguin, 1988), 678. Translated by Chaya Palevsky née Porus.

PROLOGUE

xviii **variously as Tregub, Trigub, or Tregubas**: Kiev Gubernia Duma Voters List Database, http://www.jewishgen.org/databases/Ukraine/KievDuma.htm.

xviii **Vsia Rossiia business directory**: Visia Rossiia Database, http://www.jewish gen.org/databases/vsia.

xviii **Shoah Victims'**: Central Database of Shoah Victims' Names, Yad Vashem, http://db.yadvashem.org/names.

xviii **three-by-five card**: U.S. Naturalization Record Indexes, 1791–1992 (indexed in World Archives Project), record for Wolf Treegoob, ancestry.com, accessed November 5, 2010.

xviii **version of *The Book of Blessings***: *The Book of Blessings: For the Sabbath and Holidays with the Family*, ed. David Arnon and Helli Doucani (Israel: Matan Art, 2010). Gift of the Jewish National Fund.

A SMALL THING

03 **meeting with Michael MacQueen**: Michael MacQueen, interview by author, Office of Immigration and Customs Enforcement, Washington, D.C., February 12, 2014.

03 **Vincas Valkavickus**: "Lithuanian Prosecutor Trying to Show Some Movement in Investigating War Criminals," U.S. State Department, January 2000 (Docno: Vilnius 000148).

04 **a write-up about MacQueen**: David Holzel, "Hunting War Criminals," May 3, 2011, University of Michigan website, http://www.lsa.umich.edu/lsa/archives/ci.huntingwarcriminalsv2_ci.detail.

FAYE DUNAWAY AS AN INVADED COUNTRY

08 **a scene in *Chinatown***: *Chinatown*, directed by Roman Polanski, 1974.

08 **Molotov-Ribbentrop Pact**: Michael Bloch, *Ribbentrop: A Biography* (New York: Crown, 1992), 233–50. For further discussion of the different pacts between Germany and the Soviet Union leading up to World War II, see Yitzhak Arad, *In the Shadow of the Red Banner: Soviet Jews in the War Against Nazi Germany* (Jerusalem: Gefen, 2010), xxv–xxx.

08 **Lithuania lost all independence**: Timothy Snyder, *The Reconstruction of Nations: Poland, Ukraine, Lithuania, Belarus, 1569–1999* (New Haven, CT: Yale University Press, 2003), 83–84.

08 **On June 22**: Yitzhak Arad, *Ghetto in Flames* (New York: Holocaust Library, 1982), 36.

08 **Reichskommissariat Ostland**: Snyder, *Reconstruction of Nations*, 84.

09 **in 1990, when Lithuania declared**: Ibid., 97–102.

11 **"Year of Remembrance of Defense of Freedom and Great Losses"**: Seimas of the Republic of Lithuania, "2011-ieji paskelbti Laisvės gynimo ir didžių netekčių atminties metais," September 28, 2010, http://www3.lrs.lt/pls/inter/w5_show?p_r=4445&p_d=102577&p_k=1.

11 **"Year of Remembrance of Lithuanian Citizens Who Were Holocaust Victims"**: Seimas of the Republic of Lithuania, Public Relations Unit, "2011 Proclaimed as the Year of Remembrance of Holocaust Victims of Lithuania," September 21, 2010, http://www3.lrs.lt/pls/inter/w5_show?p_r=7694&p_d=102309&p_k=2.

14 **displaced persons camps were established**: "Lithuanians in DP Camps," Displaced Persons' Camps, http://www.dpcamps.org/lithuania.html. To identify family members who were in DP camps, readers may consult the International Tracing Service Inventory Search, now a part of the U.S. Holocaust Memorial Museum: https://www.its-arolsen.org/en/homepage/index.html.

14 **in Germany in the deportation camp**: A.E.F D.P. Registration Records, 3.1.1.1/68719292#1, 68719295#1, 68719288#1, 68719286#1, 68719291#1/ITS Digital Archive, Bad Arolsen.

19 **Lithuanian Activist Front**: Kai Struve, "Rites of Violence? The Pogroms of Summer 1941," *Polin* 24 (2012): 264–71. See also Stasys Lušys, "The Emergence of Unified Lithuanian Resistance Movement Against Occupants, 1940–1943," *Lituanus* 9, no. 4 (1963): http://www.lituanus.org/1963/63_4_03.htm; Jürgen Matthäus, "Key Aspects of German Anti-Jewish Policy," Lithuania and the Jews: The Holocaust Chapter (USHMM Center for Advanced Holocaust Studies, 2004), http://www.ushmm.org/m/pdfs/Publication_OP_2005-07-03.pdf.

20 **the Russian occupation of Lithuania**: Prit Buttar, *Between Giants: The Battle for the Baltics in World War II* (Oxford, England: Osprey, 2013), Kindle ed. ch. 1.

20 **Nazis violated the Molotov-Ribbentrop pact**: Bloch, *Ribbentrop*, 334–47.

20 **a pay voucher for local police**: Lietuvos Centrinis Valstybinis Archyvas (hereafter LCVA), f. R-1548, ap. 1, b. 1, l. 226–31. This voucher, submitted to the German command, lists the names, towns, and amounts owed to locals under their employ between September 27 and October 9, 1941. Not everyone who participated in the Poligon massacre is represented on this list.

For the letter that was sent to accompany this voucher, with translation, see I. Guzenberg et al., ed., *Ašmenos, Svierių, Švenčionių apskričių getai: Kalinių sąrašai* (Vilnius, Lithuania: Valstybinis Vilniaus Gano Žydų Muziejus, 2009), 121.

WORD GETS AROUND

25 **The generals of Stalin's army:** Antony Beevor, *The Fall of Berlin, 1945* (New York: Penguin, 2002), 436.

25 **many were executed:** Ibid., 322.

25 **Peretz Markish:** Elie Wiesel gives a brief, informative account of Markish's biography in his introduction to Peretz Markish, *Inheritance,* trans. Mary Schulman (Toronto: TSAR, 2007), xi–xii.

25 **"You'll pay with your head":** Peretz Markish, "To a Jewish Dancer," in *Inheritance,* 26.

BAD STUDENT

28 **confirmed that he was chief of Saugumas:** Lietuvos Ypatingasis Archyvas (hereafter LYA) to Rita Gabis, "Relating to Search for Documents," February 10, 2011.

32 **Mike Plant's boat was found:** Barbara Lloyd, "Solo Sailor Is Presumed to Be Dead," *New York Times,* November 26, 1992, http://www.nytimes.com/1992/11/26/ sports/solo-sailor-is-presumed-to-be-dead.html.

IT'S OPRAH'S FAULT

33 **"You may encounter reluctant witnesses":** John M. Howell, *Homicide Investigation Standard Operating Procedures,* revised March 2001, http://www .policeforum.org/free-online-documents.

FATHERS AND SONS

44 **Darton learned printing:** "Children's Books Published by William Darton and His Sons: A Catalogue of an Exhibition at the Lilly Library, Indiana University, April–June, 1992: A Machine-Readable Transcription," Lilly Library Publications Online, 2005, http://www.indiana.edu/~liblilly/etexts/darton.

44 **Darton traces the Bug River:** The Bug River created the line used to divide Poland's territory between German and Soviet occupants in the treaty of September 28, 1939.

45 **the Pale of Settlement:** For a straightforward introduction to the Pale and its various incarnations over time, see Paul Johnson, *A History of the Jews* (New York: Harper & Row, 1987), 358–62.

AN EDUCATION

49 **Three hundred and thirty-six young Lithuanian men:** *Generolo Jono Žemaičio Lietuvos Karo Akademija,* trans. Laima Grigalauskaitė (Vilnius, Lithuania: General Jonas Žemaitis Military Academy of Lithuania, 2007), 7.

50 **the academy will relocate there:** Ibid., 11.

50 **Soviet-Lithuanian peace pact:** Snyder, *Reconstruction of Nations,* 63.

51 **Nisonas Mackebuckis:** "Žydų Kariai Savanoriai Žuvę Kovose Už Lietuvos Nepriklausomybę" (Jewish volunteer soldiers who died fighting for the independence of Lithuania), Vilna Gaon Jewish State Museum website, last updated January 12, 2007, http://www.jmuseum.lt/index.aspx?Element=ViewArticle&TopicID =179&IMAction=ViewArticles&EditionID=86.

51 **Lieutenant Colonel Moshe Dembovskis:** "Laukiame žinių apie savanorius," *Santaka,* translated by Anatanas Zilinskas on "Moshe Demboski Family Album," *Vilkaviskis: A Small Town in Southern Lithuania Where the Jewish Community Is No More,* http://www.jewishvilkaviskis.org/Moshe_Demboski_Family_Album.html.

52 **"You shall not draw the sword":** *Generolo Jono Žemaičio Lietuvos Karo Akademija,* 9.

54 **"smoked meats all cured":** Adam Mickiewicz, *Pan Tadeusz* (New York: Mondial, 2009), 40.

WAR

64 **a Jewish bank, a separate Jewish library:** Anatolij Chayesh, "Some Historical Facts and Stories About the Jewish Community of Žeimelis," trans. Yuriy Levin, 1997, http://kehilalinks.jewishgen.org/zeimelis/zanatoli.htm.

64 **In 1937 there were nine Jewish tailors:** Yosef Rosin, "Zheimel (Žeimelis)," ed. Sarah and Mordechai Kopfstein, 1999, http://kehilalinks.jewishgen.org/zeimelis/ YosefRos.htm.

65 **was he the famous Rabbi Kook?:** For a fascinating look at the life of Rav Avraham Yitzhak Kook, the spiritual leader, see: Yehudah Mirsky, *Rav Kook: Mystic in a Time of Revolution* (New Haven, CT: Yale University Press, 2014).

66 **"Did he think of them all as Communists?":** Šarūnas Liekis and Antony Polonsky, "Introduction," *Polin* 25 (2013): 34.

THIS KIND OF WORLD

69 **"Life like a dream":** Alexander Harkavy to his brother in the United States, date unknown, from the author's collection.

71 **"Sowgoomas":** MacQueen, interview by author, February 12, 2014.

71 **"Obama does what his Jew owners tell him":** Theo Emery and Liz Robbins, "In Note, More Clues to Holocaust Museum Killing," *New York Times,* June 11, 2009, http://www.nytimes.com/2009/06/12/us/12shoot.html.

72 **records of the Gebietskommissar Wilna-land:** U.S. Holocaust Memorial Museum, Record Group 26.017M, "Records of the Gebietskommissar Wilna-Land," 5 microform reels. I am grateful to Lietuvos Centrinis Valstybinis Archyvas for permission to use these records in the text.

73 **"Perhaps world society does not know":** Ilya Ehrenburg and Vasily Grossman, "From the Diary of Doctor Elena Buividaite-Kutorgene (June–December 1941)," *The Complete Black Book of Russian Jewry,* trans. David Patterson (New Brunswick, NJ: Transaction, 2002), 335–68.

73 **Jakob lives at Maironio str. 18:** USHMM, RG-26-017M.

73 **first major order in German and Lithuanian:** Ibid.

For a full translation of this order, along with a discussion of its historical context, see Arad, *Ghetto in Flames*, 94–95.

75 **Bessemer's Hall of History Museum**: "Special Collections," Bessemer Hall of History Museum, http://bessemerhallofhistory.blogspot.com/p/hitlers-typewriter .html.

75 **"it was very seldom the [slave] huts"**: "O. T. McCann's response to H. C. Nixon's questionnaire about slavery in Alabama," December 5, 1912, file Q31586–Q31603, box LPR91, folder 1, ADAH Digital Collections, Alabama Dept. of Archives and History, http://digital.archives.alabama.gov/cdm/singleitem/collection/voices/ id/3729/rec/1.

77 **a complaint written from one Röhler**: USHMM, RG-26-017M.

78 **I have a small timeline in my head**: Arad, *Ghetto in Flames*, 37. For a further discussion of the German advance through Lithuania, see Richard Rhodes, *Masters of Death: The SS-Einsatzgruppen and the Invention of the Holocaust* (New York: Vintage, 2002), 38–52; Prit Buttar, *Between Giants: The Battle for the Baltics in World War II* (Oxford, England: Osprey, 2013); Erich Von Manstein, *Lost Victories: The War Memoirs of Hitler's Most Brilliant General* (St. Paul, MN: Zenith, 2014); Ehrenberg and Grossman, "Part 4: Lithuania," *The Complete Black Book of Russian Jewry*, 240–375.

79 **Their tanks are too light**: Arad, *In the Shadow of the Red Banner*, 129–39.

A GOOD GET

81 **The handwriting**: LCVA, f. R911, ap. 1, b.1, l. 193, translated by Viktorija Bourassa. A truncated translation of this document appears below.

> Witness Interrogation Report
>
> 1942 April 27, Chief of the Security Police in Švenčionys Region, Pranas Puronas interrogated a witness from Ignalina:
>
> I am Kazys Šuminas, son of Jonas, born 1900 February 15 in Šuminų village, Tauragė district. Nationality—Lithuanian. Religion—Roman Catholic. Literate. No crime record. Lives in Ignalina. In regard to the Town Market Square case No 161 I declare that in January 1942, I cannot remember the exact day, Miciūnas Juozas from Ignalina brought an American watch for me to mend, which in my opinion, was made from American gold. This same year, on the 25th of April, the same Miciūnas Juozas brought me a golden ring which was broken and asked to add the missing parts. I do not know where from did he get that watch and ring. Also, Juozas Miciūnas told me that he had a golden bracelet which he took to Vilnius to mend but it got lost. Where he gets those things, I do not know. He did not tell me. I have nothing else to add.

The subtext of this report was a belated effort on the part of the German Occupation Administration to stop the flow of Jewish goods into the hands of the locals, particularly the police, local headmen, and regional chiefs like my grandfather. To that end, the administration required that in every town a witness "voluntarily" step forward to give an accounting of where the belongings of vanished Jews (particularly gold) had gone. Men like my grandfather and other police chiefs made sure that the police—from a regular officer to a chief—were not implicated by the "witness." Then the reports were submitted to the German authorities for review. Of course, goods, including gold, were also making their way into the pockets of Germans stationed in Lithuanian cities and towns, either through direct thievery or via bribes.

OUR ANNE FRANK

87 **Babita's arrest files**: LYA, f. V-5, ap. 1, b. 40373/5, translated by Anastasia Kurochkina.

88 **file that lists the minimal contents**: Ibid., l. 25.

89 **"Record of interrogation"**: LYA, f. V-5, ap. 1, b. 40373, l. 12, translated by Geoff Vasil.

90 **Jewish family name Jakushok**: For example, this 1920 census database shows 25 people with the Jakushok/Yakushok surname in the Žeimelis area: All Lithuanian Revision List Database 1, LitvakSIG: Lithuanian-Jewish Special Interest Group, http://www.litvaksig.org. Accessed December 31, 2014.

91 **baltaraiščiai and Germans gun down**: Barry Mann, "The Žeimelis Jewish Cemetery," *LitvakSIG Online Journal*, 2001–2009, http://www.litvaksig.org/litvaksig-online-journal/the-zeimelis-jewish-cemetery.

91 **paperwork on Babita and Senelis**: LYA, f. V-5, ap. 1, b. 40373/5, translated by Anastasia Kurochkina.

91 **1,004 members of the Communist Party**: Vladas Sirutavičius, "'A Close, but Very Suspicious and Very Dangerous Neighbor': Outbreaks of Antisemitism in Inter-War Lithuania," *Polin* 25 (2013): 261.

91 **a thick book: *The Last Days***: Herman Kruk, *The Last Days of the Jerusalem of Lithuania*, ed. Benjamin Harshav, trans. Barbara Harshav (New Haven, CT: Yale University Press, 2002).

92 **Alfred Rosenberg, chosen by Hitler**: William L. Shirer, *The Rise and Fall of the Third Reich* (New York: Rosetta, 2011), Kindle edition, 48.

93 **Kruk and others, at great personal risk**: Benjamin Harshav, introduction to Kruk, *Last Days*, xliv–xlv.

93 **"burned the soles of her feet with hot irons"**: Julija Šukys, *Epistolophilia: Writing the Life of Ona Šimaitė* (Lincoln: University of Nebraska Press, 2012), Kindle edition, ch. 12.

94 **"The most accessible scapegoat?"**: Edward Kuznetsov, *Prison Diaries*, trans. Howard Spier (New York: Scarborough, 1980), 110.

94 **"He who does not bow the knee"**: Ibid., 203.

97 **distinguished himself for his brutal service**: "Mikhail Suslov, Chief Ideologist, Is Dead in Soviet," *New York Times*, January 27, 1982.

98 *The Witness of Poetry*: Czesław Miłosz, *The Witness of Poetry* (Cambridge, MA: Harvard University Press, 1983). Although the entire book is remarkable, Chapter 5, "Ruins in Poetry," contains a particularly relevant and profound discussion of poetry in wartime Poland.

99 **about her writing process**: "About," Official Webpage of Author Ruta Sepetys, http://rutasepetys.com/about/.

99 **the grown-up Lina returns**: Ruta Sepetys, *Between Shades of Gray* (New York: Philomel, 2011).

99 **Kazimierz Sakowicz**: Kazimierz Sakowicz, *Ponary Diary*, ed. Yitzhak Arad (New Haven, CT: Yale University Press, 2005).

100 **Approximately eighty thousand people**: "Ponar (Ponary)," Yad Vashem website, http://www.yadvashem.org/odot_pdf/Microsoft%20Word%20-%205747.pdf.

101 **it was several weeks, not a year**: LYA, f. V-5, ap. 1, b. 40373, l. 23, translated by Anastasia Kurochkina. This registration document for a transit camp in the village of Yeltsovka is included in my grandmother's arrest records. Comparing the date of her arrival at this camp to the date of her arrest makes it possible to create something of a timeline directly after her arrest.

THE HUMAN HEART

103 **"torn asunder in all shapes"**: Appian of Alexandria, *The Roman History*, 8.19.129.

EPIGRAPHS, PART II

110 **"The crime scene encompasses"**: James W. Osterburg and Richard H. Ward, *Criminal Investigation*, 7th ed. (New York: Anderson, 2014), 85.

110 **"Of all the places I lived"**: Yitzhak Arad, from personal papers given to author, translated by Irit Pazner Garshowitz.

110 **"Erev Sukes (Sukkot) 1941 returning"**: Khone Zak, recalling events in Podbrodz in the Sventzion region; testimony submitted to the Jewish Historical Institute in Białystok, June 1948, Żdowski Instytut Historyczny, 2014. Translated by Elmar Miller.

YITZHAK ARAD

112 **A boy and his sister in the snow**: Yitzhak Arad, interview by author, May 24, 2012.

115 **"The social elite of the Jewish community"**: Yitzhak Arad, *The Partisan* (New York: Holocaust Library, 1979), 27.

ANIMALS

118 **"On the way to a small island"**: Arad, *The Partisan*, 135.

119 **"This is the one place in all of Belorussia"**: *Defiance*, directed by Edward Zwick, 2008.

119 **a Jewish woman living in Moscow**: Karina Kavina, phone interview by author, July 9, 2012.

119 **a Lithuanian** *gimnazija*: Naderda Spiridonovienė, interview by author, June 11, 2012.

120 **a watering hole for the local German command:** For a description of the wartime use of the *gimnazija*, see chapter 42.

127 **Giedrė did interviews and archival work:** Giedrė Genušienė, interview by author, June 11, 2012.

129 **Leib Koniuchowsky, a survivor:** Ruth Horvath, "A Jewish Historical Commission in Budapest," in *Holocaust Historiography in Context: Emergence, Challenges, Polemics and Achievements,* ed. David Bankier and Dan Michman (New York: Berghahn, 2008), 488–89.

129 **"History is by its nature retrospective":** Jonathan Boyarin, phone interview by author, November 10, 2011.

MIRELE REIN/HIGH HOLIDAYS

132 **in an interrogation on June 19, 1952:** Interrogation of S. Gineitis, LYA, f. K-1, ap. 58, b. 23875/3, l. 97–103, translated by Anastasia Kurochkina.

133 **Iozas (Joseph) Breeris:** Interrogation of I. Breeris, LYA, f. K-1, ap. 58, b. 23875/3, translated by Anastasia Kurochkina.

133 **"Suslov: Who and under what circumstances":** Gineitis interrogation, LYA, l. 101–2, translated by Anastasia Kurochkina.

134 **Is she in one of the two isolation cells?:** LYA, f. K-1, ap. 58, b. 23875/3, l. 32, translated by Anastasia Kurochkina.

134 **"Saugumas Puronas":** LYA, f. K-1, ap. 58, b. 23875/3, l. 101, translated by Anastasia Kurochkina.

134 **"I encountered the prisoners being led away":** Arad, *The Partisan,* 80.

134 **"stop by the prison":** LYA, f. K-1, ap. 58, b. 23875/3, l. 101, translated by Anastasia Kurochkina.

135 **"We did it!":** Joachim Tauber, historian at the University of Hamburg, interview by author, August 14, 2013.

135 **Bronius Gruzdys:** Interrogation of B. Gruzdys, LYA, f. K-1, ap. 58, b. 45561/3, l. 82–83, translated by Anastasia Kurochkina.

136 **"October 5, 1941, when the ditch was ready":** Ibid.

136 **"exactly two days":** Ibid.

137 **In 1925 a center for Jewish history and culture:** "Brief Introduction," YIVO Institute for Jewish Research, http://www.yivoinstitute.org/about.

138 **remarkable collection assembled by the late David Bankier:** David Bankier, *Expulsion and Extermination: Holocaust Testimonials from Provincial Lithuania* (Jerusalem: Yad Vashem, 2011). For a full collection of translated Koniuchowsky testimonials assembled by Bankier, see Yad Vashem, Record Group: O.71—Koniuchowsky Collection of Testimonies from Lithuania.

139 **Shokar had an iron business:** Excerpt from interview by Binyomin Taraseysky and Yankl Levin, page 3, typescript on the extermination of Lithuanian Jewry, 297 pages (total), Folder VIA, Papers of Leib Koniuchowsky, Record Group 1390, YIVO.

139 **"I was a spoiled girl":** Lili Holzman, interview with author, May 24, 2012.

139 **The girl is the cousin of Fayve Khayet:** Excerpt from interview by Fayve Khayet and Rokhl Khayet-Kramnik, page 140, Folder VIA, Papers of Leib Koniuchowsky, RG-1390, YIVO.

140 **Sukkot—a time of joy and deliverance:** Arnon and Doucani, *Book of Blessings*, 55–65.

CHAYA PALEVSKY NÉE PORUS

141 **"This world today—unbelievable":** Chaya Palevsky, interview by author, February 15, 2012.

MESSENGER

146 **"All the Reins were beautiful":** Zinaida Aronowa, interview by author, June 7, 2012.

147 **Teresa was only seven:** Teresa Krinickaja, interview by author, June 7, 2012.

148 **the Jewish girl with the peroxide-blond hair:** Kavina, interview.

150 **Zinaida told us something else:** Aronowa, interview.

LILI HOLZMAN

154 **his classic text on the investigation of unsolved homicides:** Richard H. Walton, preface to *Cold Case Homicides* (Boca Raton, FL: Taylor & Francis, 2006).

157 **sat down for hours with Lili Holzman:** Holzman, interview, May 24, 2012.

157 **"J. Swirski (wojloki/feutre vegetal)":** "The 1929 Polish Business Directory Project," Jewish Record Indexing—Poland, 2000–2001, http://jri-poland.org/bizdir/bd1929.htm.

161 **the list of those "employed" for duty at Poligon:** LCVA, f. R-1548, ap. 1, b. 1, l. 211.

161 **"Mergaitė":** Holzman, interview, May 24, 2012.

POLIGON

162 **starvation and exposure was a purposeful tactic:** Christoph Dieckmann, "Murders of the Prisoners of War," *The International Commission for the Evaluation of the Crimes of the Nazi and Soviet Occupation Regimes in Lithuania*, http://www.komisija.lt/en, 4–7.

163 **"You can feel the souls":** Giedrė Genušienė, interview by author, June 14, 2012.

165 **in the shtetl Ceikiniai's necrology:** "Ceikiniai Necrology," trans. Beryl Baleson, on Shimon Kanc, ed., *Svinzian Region; Memorial Book of 23 Jewish Communities*, http://www.jewishgen.org/yizkor/svencionys/sve1916.html.

165 **Švenčionys Yitzkor book:** Kanc, *Svinzian Region*, http://www.jewishgen.org/yizkor/svencionys/svencionys.html.

166 **"Poligony?":** Palevsky, interview.

169 **"Now we have taken the last path of the victims":** Genušienė, interview, June 14, 2012.

170 **"We ran like a storm":** Palevsky, interview.

DAY OF MOURNING AND HOPE

171 **to Lukiškės prison, where my grandfather spent ten days**: LCVA, f. R-730, ap. 2, b. 168, l. 77.

172 **in a Kaunas newspaper office**: Although I have been unable to document this information through outside sources, both my mother and aunt are certain of this version of events. The drive by the Ninth Fort is included in the narrative, showing he was aware at that time that it was a place to fear.

172 **the Ninth Fort**: For details about the October 4, 1941, massacre at the Ninth Fort, see Rhodes, *Masters of Death*, 192–98. See also the many online testimonies at the U.S. Holocaust Memorial Museum website; for example, USHMM, RG-50.030*0660, "Oral History Interview with Uri Chanoch," http://collections.ushmm.org/search/catalog/irn47192.

173 **Jonas Maciulevičius, his boss**: Breeris interrogation, LYA, l. 20, translated by Anastasia Kurochkina.

173 **where prisoners scratched last messages**: "The Einsatzgruppen: Massacres at the Ninth Fort," Jewish Virtual Library, 2014, http://www.jewishvirtuallibrary.org/jsource/Holocaust/ninthfortpics.html.

173 **remanded into Lukiškės on October 11**: LCVA, f. R-730, ap. 2, b. 168, l. 77.

ARTŪRAS KARALIS

176 **tried to throw their voices over the walls**: "I have now learned that many of those who were snatched . . . were sent to Łukiszki jail . . . Many women gather in front of the prison." Kruk, *Last Days*, 51.

177 **Karalis speaks rapidly**: Artūras Karalis, interview by author, June 14, 2012.

179 **"the country is one big cemetery"**: Rachel Kostanian, director of research at the Green House Museum, Vilnius, interview by author, June 4, 2012.

179 **"The spirit of the old times"**: Karalis, interview, June 14, 2012.

LOST

183 **Heida Lapido**: Testimony of Michael and Hirsh Rayak, Yad Vashem Archives, O-133/4076.

183 **in the necrology for Švenčionys**: "New Švenčionys Necrology," trans. Steven Weiss, on Shimon Kanc, *Svinzian Region*, http://www.jewishgen.org/yizkor/svencionys/sve1903.html.

183 **Hoduciszki necrology**: "Hoduciszki Necrology," trans. Beryl Baleson, on Shimon Kanc, *Svinzian Region*, http://www.jewishgen.org/yizkor/svencionys/sve1929.html.

184 **In 1920 my grandfather joined the Lithuanian Rifleman's Union**: LYA, f. V-5, ap. 1, b. 40373, l. 22, translated by Viktorija Bourassa.

184 **who took to the woods as anti-Russian partisans**: Buttar, *Between Giants*, Kindle ed., ch. 4.

185 **vigorously campaigned for his reinstatement**: LCVA, Army Service File of Pranas Puronas, 1926–1940, f. 930, ap. 2P, b. 156, translated by Viktorija Bourassa.

185 **Bronius Gruzdis . . . also a Shaulist**: Interrogation of B. Gruzdis, LYA, f. K-1, ap. 58, b. 45561/3, l. 54.

185 **"To His Excellency the Minister of National Defense"**: First Lieutenant in Reserve Puronas to the minister of national defense, January 31, 1928, LCVA, f. 930, ap. 2P, b. 156, translated by Viktorija Bourassa.

186 **"In 1927, after the uprising"**: Ibid.

186 **"It is an honor for me to ask"**: Ibid.

187 **"Currently I am serving in the 7th category"**: Ibid., December 6, 1928.

187 **A Captain Stakonis vouches**: Ibid., August 27, 1930.

187 **would be reinstated, but for a dearth of positions**: Ibid., April 16, 1931.

187 **has lost the edge of a military man**: Ibid.

187 **June 28, 1941, the Lithuanian Colonel Jurgis Bobelis**: Yitzhak Arad, *The Holocaust in the Soviet Union* (Lincoln: University of Nebraska Press, 2009), 142–143.

187 **Chief of the Gestapo in Švenčionys**: Gruzdis interrogation, LYA, l. 54, translated by Anastasia Kurochkina.

188 **Arunas Bubnys**: Bubnys, interview by author, June 5, 2012.

188 **Mykolas Kukutis**: Instytut Pamęci Nardowej (hereafter IPN), OK.Gd, S 96/01/ Zn, vol. 1, Investigation Commenced on 18.08.1997, 10–11, translated by Maciej Bulanda.

189 **"the punitive unit which ran rabid"**: *Masines zudynes Lietuvoje* (Vilnius, Lithuania: Mintis, 1973), 215. Selection translated by Geoff Vasil.

191 **"Now I'm going to speak as a historian"**: Arad, interview, May 24, 2012.

192 **twenty-four-year old Ḳlarah Gelman**: Ḳlarah Gelman, Israel, September 12, 1995, Visual History Archive, 2011, USC Shoah Foundation, accessed February 16, 2014. Translated by Mor Sheinbein.

193 **the taking of his uncles and the cleaning**: Arad, *The Partisan*, 35–36.

193 **Ḳlarah Gelman's testimony**: Ḳlarah Gelman, September 12, 1995, USC Shoah Foundation. Translated by Mor Sheinbein.

PLANNERS, DIGGERS, GUARDS, SHOOTERS

194 **"In the beginning of August"**: Arad, *The Partisan*, 38.

195 **"ten men working for the security police"**: Excerpt from Interview by Binyomin Taraseysky and Yankl Levin, page 19, Folder VIA, Papers of Leib Koniuchowsky, RG-1390, YIVO.

195 **"his assistant, Feliksas Garla"**: Gruzdys interrogation, LYA, l. 55, translated by Anastasia Kurochkina.

195 **hiring thirty employees**: Breeris interrogation, LYA, l. 19, translated by Anastasia Kurochkina.

196 **"different billboards and propaganda"**: David Katz, interview by Bina Kutner, Rishon LeZion, Israel, May 21, 1997, Visual History Archive, 2011, USC Shoah Foundation, accessed April 4, 2014. Translated by Mor Sheinbein.

199 **"My son, you carried that dagger"**: Robert Jordan, *The Dragon Reborn: Book Three of the Wheel of Time* (New York: Tor, 1991).

201 **commented that cemeteries are vandalized**: Arunas Bubnys, interview by author, June 13, 2012.

201 **In 1926 a thirteen-year-old Lithuanian boy**: Interrogation of E. Genaitis, LYA, f. K-1, ap. 58, b. 10712/3, l. 71–74, 97–103, 225–228, translated by Anastasia Kurochkina.

203 **"on a phone line"**: Excerpt from interview by Fayve Khayet, p. 127, Folder VIA, Papers of Leib Koniuchowsky, RG-1390, YIVO.

203 **"head bookkeeper of the Jewish community bank"**: Ibid., 128.

203 **driven perhaps by Bronius Cieciura**: Indictment, Feb. 27 1945, LYA, f. K-1, ap. 58, b. 10712/3, l. 289, translated by Anastasia Kurochkina.

203 **Among them is the baker's son**: Excerpt from Interview by Fayve Khayet, page 130, Folder VIA, Papers of Leib Koniuchowsky, RG-1390, YIVO.

204 **Fayve Khayet was with one of the groups**: Ibid., 129.

205 **In his testimony Edvardas (aka Shoostik) Genaitis**: Genaitis interrogation, LYA, l. 228, translated by Anastasia Kurochkina.

205 **Shloyme Wolfson (who had a bad arm)**: Excerpt from Interview by Fayve Khayet, page 129, Folder VIA, Papers of Leib Koniuchowsky, RG-1390, YIVO.

206 **he felt only pride**: Arad, interview, May 24, 2012.

206 **born on October 28, 1907**: SS Party Record Card of Wulff, Horst Wulff Personal Papers, Bundesarchiv (hereafter BA), VBS 286, translated by Almut Schoenfeld.

207 **Wulff's cover name is Ollritz**: Horst Wulff File, BA, R 90/748, translated by Almut Schoenfeld.

207 **He cooks the books**: From the files of the upper party court, BA, VBS 253, translated by Almut Schoenfeld.

207 **"He is a good comrade"**: Horst Wulff File, BA, R 90/748, translated by Almut Schoenfeld.

208 **"All the following"**: "Extract from Guidelines by Heydrich for Higher SS and Police Leaders in the Occupied Territories of the Soviet Union, July 2, 1944," Yad Vashem Shoah Resource Center, http://www.yadvashem.org/odot_pdf/Microsoft%20Word%20-%204036.pdf.

208 **"The principal targets of execution"**: Einsatzgruppen Report no. 111, October 12, 1941, in Yitzhak Arad and Shmuel Krakowski, *The Einsatzgruppen Reports: Selections from the Dispatches of the Nazi Death Squads' Campaign Against the Jews in Occupied Territories of the Soviet Union, July 1941–January 1943*, ed. Shmuel Spector (New York: Holocaust Library, 1989), 185.

209 **tells his deputy Garla**: Interrogation of K. Garla, LYA, f. K-1, ap. 58, 10712/3, l. 144–49, translated by Anastasia Kurochkina.

209 **worked in a drugstore**: Joachim Hamann Personal File, BA, VBS 286-64000 14780, translated by Almut Schoenfeld.

210 **Hamann studies with fellow SS security police recruits**: Ibid.

210 **the training is less about physical endurance**: Rhodes, *Masters of Death*, 3–18.

210 **the German Metz**: Excerpt from Interview by Binyomin Taraseysky and Yankl Levin, page 19, Folder VIA, Papers of Leib Koniuchowsky, RG-1390, YIVO.

210 **Ruvin Chekinsky is tasked**: Testimony of Michael and Hirsh Rayak, YVA, O-133/4076.

210 **something has happened to him**: Ibid.

211 **"very decent German"**: Excerpt from Interview by Binyomin Taraseysky and Yankl Levin, page 17, Folder VIA, Papers of Leib Koniuchowsky, RG-1390, YIVO.

213 **"In mid July 1941"**: Christoph Dieckmann, *Deutsche Besatzungspolitik in Litauen, 1941–1944* (Wallstein, 2011), from selection translated by Martin Schefski.

213 **"Q. Did you never receive"**: Nuremberg Trial Proceedings, vol. 20, Two Hundreth Day, August 10, 1946, Avalon Project, Yale Law School Lillian Goldman Law Library, 2008, http://avalon.law.yale.edu/imt/08-10-46.asp.

213 **Nakhum Taraseysky's pharmacy**: Excerpt from Interview by Binyomin Taraseysky and Yankl Levin, page 4, Folder VIA, Papers of Leib Koniuchowsky, RG-1390, YIVO.

214 **Iozas Breeris, warden of the prison**: Interrogation Protocol of I. Breeris, LYA, f. K-1, ap. 58, b. 23875/3.

214 **Ionas Kurpis**: Indictment of Kurpis Ionas Iozasovich, LYA, f. K-1, ap. 58, b.19712/3, l. 4, translated by Anastasia Kurochkina.

215 **with a pistol and a military uniform**: Confrontation between Kurpis Ionas Iozasovich and Veryk, Edvard Antonovich, LYA, f. K-1, ap. 58, b. 19712/3, l. 219, translated by Anastasia Kurochkina.

215 **He likes moonshine**: Interrogation of Yusefa Felisovna Kulesh, LYA, f. K-1, ap. 58, b. 19712/3, l. 170, translated by Anastasia Kurochkina.

215 **when he shows Vitold Savkovsky**: Interrogation of Vitold Anufrievich Savkovsky, LYA, f. K-1, ap. 58, b. 19712/3, l. 189, translated by Anastasia Kurochkina.

215 **Another digger/witness**: Interrogation of Ankyanets Olgerd Vladislavovich, LYA, f. K-1, ap. 58, b. 19712/3, l. 170, translated by Anastasia Kurochkina.

215 **Pavel Petkeevic remembered**: Interrogation of Pavel Dimentievich Petkeevic, Gosudarstvennyj Arhiv Russkoj Federaciji (hereafter GARF), f. 7021, op. 94, d. 435, 13d, p. 268, translated by Anastasia Kurochkina.

DEVIL IN A GLASS JAR

217 **Christoph Dieckmann notes**: Christoph Dieckmann, "The Holocaust in Lithuania," Yad Vashem, https://www.youtube.com/watch?v=HH2ocwBuFEA.

217 **a set of thin files**: LYA, f. V-5, ap. 1, b. 40343, l. 1–16.

THE TRANSLATOR

221 **David Boder's interviews**: *Voices of the Holocaust*, Paul V. Gavin Library, Illinois Institute of Technology, 2009, http://voices.iit.edu.

221 **Aron Mendel**: Alan Rosen, "Early Postwar Voices: David Boder's Life and Work," *Voices*, IIT, http://voices.iit.edu/david_boder.

221 **A journalist interested**: Alan Rosen, *The Wonder of Their Voices: The 1946 Holocaust Interviews of David Boder* (New York: Oxford University Press, 2010).

222 **A refugee without a last name**: David P. Boder Interviews Joseph [last name unknown], September 25, 1946, Wiesbaden, Germany, trans. Khane-Faygl Turtletaub, *Voices*, IIT, http://voices.iit.edu/interview?doc=joseph&display=joseph_en.

222 **Bronė Skudaikienė, Lithuanian**: David P. Boder Interviews Bronė Skudaikienė, September 21, 1946, München, Germany, trans. S. Peters and P. Gaensicke, *Voices*, IIT, http://voices.iit.edu/interview?doc=skudaikieneB&display=skudaikieneB_en.

223 **Vladus Lukosevicius:** David P. Boder Interviews Vladus Lukosevicius, September 21, 1946, München, Germany, trans. Roy Cochrun, *Voices*, IIT, http://voices.iit.edu/interview?doc=lukoseviciusV&display=lukoseviciusV_en.

224 **Leib Koniuchowsky's Švenčionys testimonies:** Excerpt from interview by Fruma Hochmann, p. 113, Folder VIA, Papers of Leib Koniuchowsky, RG-1390, YIVO.

RAILROAD TOWN

225 **a book in Polish:** Zdzisław Chlewiński, *Groza i Prześladowanie Polaków i Żydów na Wileńszczyźnie* (Płock, Poland: Samizdat Zofii Łoś, 2009).

226 **Vaclav Vilkoit stands in the middle:** Vaclav Vilkoit, interview by author, August 4, 2013.

227 **"We were so certain":** Holzman, interview, May 24, 2012.

229 **The man's name is Urbonas:** Interrogation of V. Urbonas, LYA, f. K-1, ap. 58, b. 24329/3.

230 **"He's standing there":** Holzman, interview, May 24, 2012.

231 **interrogated by the KGB:** Urbonas interrogation, LYA, translated by Anastasia Kurochkina.

231 **"When there was no driver":** Ibid., l. 128.

232 **"Once I saw a Jewish woman":** Ibid., l. 140.

ELENA STANKEVIČIENĖ NÉE GAGIS

233 **"It was a terrible time":** Elena Stankevičienė, interview by author, August 8, 2013.

BUCKET

236 **"was putting everything out":** Vanda Pukėnienė, interview by author, August 6, 2013.

DEVIL'S AUCTION

240 **"We have friends":** Zenon and Jadyga Tumalovič, interview by author, August 4, 2013.

242 **"I think it was September":** Testimony of Maria Korecka, *History Meeting House*, Instytucja kultury miasta stolecznego Warszawy, translated by Maciej Bulanda.

242 **In a KGB interrogation Petras Gudonis:** Interrogation Protocol of P. Gudonis, LYA, f. K-1, ap. 58, b. P-19224.

LUCKY BIRD

244 **"Topsy-turvy":** Holzman, interview, May 24, 2012.

244 **when Chaya Palevsky:** Palevsky, interview.

244 **In the hired cart:** Holzman, interview, May 24, 2012.

245 **all Jewish doctors and pharmacists:** Excerpt from interview by Avrom Taytz, p. 83, Folder VIA, Papers of Leib Koniuchowsky, RG-1390, YIVO.

246 **how the night before the Poligon roundup**: Arad, *The Partisan*, 39.

246 **"in my mind's eye I saw my sister"**: Ibid., 50.

247 **"It was like a big bloody mountain"**: Palevsky, interview.

BAD MAN/GOOD MAN

253 **Arunas had actually quoted**: Arunas Bubnys, "The Fate of the Jews of Švenčionys, Oshmyany, and Svir Regions, 1941–1943," in Guzenberg et al., *Ašmenos, Svierių, Švenčionių*, 91.

254 **"Under the orders of the German government"**: Lithuanian security police Švenčionys region chief of 24 02 1942 to Švenčionys district police chief, LCVA, f. R-911, ap. 1, b. 4, l. 52, translated by Geoff Vasil.

255 **"Early on, the Nazi hard liners"**: Tauber, interview.

256 **Shlomo Ichiltzik described**: Shlomo Ichiltzik, interview by Vladimir Solomon, Givataim, Israel, January 21, 1997, Visual History Archive, 2011, USC Shoah Foundation, accessed May 15, 2014. Translated by Mor Sheinbein.

256 **without the aid of non-Jews**: Yitzhak Arad, interview by author, June 17, 2013.

257 **Gould be burned to death in a crematorium**: "Gerulaitis Threatened After Blasting Judge," *Pittsburgh Press*, May 10, 1980.

258 **"A genuine nationalist"**: Arunas Bubnys, interview by author, June 5, 2012.

259 **Aleksas Malinauskas**: Chief of the Švenčionys Police Station Aleksas Malinauskas to Chief of German Security Police in Lithuania, LCVA f. R-1399, ap. 1, b. 9, l. 180–88, translated by Viktorija Bourassa.

260 **Moshe Gordon, a butcher**: Excerpt from Interview by Binyomin Taraseysky and Yankl Levin, page 42, Folder VIA, Papers of Leib Koniuchowsky, RG-1390, YIVO.

260 **in 1941 to plead for Mirele Rein's life**: Excerpt from Interview by Fayve Khayet, page 140, Folder VIA, Papers of Leib Koniuchowsky, RG-1390, YIVO.

261 **"A good man"**: Palevsky, interview.

261 **he fled with his family**: Excerpt from Interview by Binyomin Taraseysky and Yankl Levin, page 29, Folder VIA, Papers of Leib Koniuchowsky, RG-1390, YIVO.

262 **"From this point on, Puronas"**: LCVA, f. R-1399, ap.1, b. 9, l. 180v, translated by Nick Woods.

262 **lose his life in the Klooga concentration camp**: Excerpt from Interview by Binyomin Taraseysky and Yankl Levin, page 69, Folder VIA, Papers of Leib Koniuchowsky, RG-1390, YIVO.

264 **Motel Gotkin and Ilel/Gilel Šulheferis/Šulgeifer**: Guzenberg et al., *Ašmenos, Svierių, Švenčionių*, 579, 607.

264 **"Certainly it would have been enough"**: Bubnys, interview, June 13, 2012.

265 **ten days' imprisonment only**: Lukiškės arrest record, October 11, 1943, LCVA, f. R-730, ap. 2, b. 168, l. 77–82.

265 **Four people with the last name Las**: *Ašmenos, Svierių, Švenčionių*, 501.

265 **Arunas mentions a particular area of Poland**: Bubnys, interview, June 13, 2012.

SHOOTER

267 **Free for twenty-two years:** Interrogation of V. Sausitis, LYA, f. K-1, ap. 58, b. 47746/3, translated by Viktorija Bourassa.

267 **"If someone tried to run":** Ibid.

267 **The man who ran the lunchtime:** Ibid., l. 115–16.

268 **at least two other shooters:** Ibid., l. 35–37, 100.

INSIDE/OUTSIDE

269 **When Lili's grandfather:** Lili Holzman, interview by author, June 20, 2013.

270 **"The ghetto is near the center":** Palevsky, interview.

271 **"the will to live":** Holzman, interview, June 20, 2013.

271 **"Death escaped me":** Palevsky, interview.

271 **Before the war, Arad:** Yitzhak Arad, interview by author, May 24, 2012.

271 **In the months following Poligon:** Palevsky, interview.

272 **Dvora Goldhirsh's best friend:** Dvora Goldhirsh, interview by Nitza Leelo, Tel Aviv, Israel, June 13, 1996, Visual History Archive, 2011, USC Shoah Foundation, accessed March 26, 2014. Translated by Mor Sheinbein.

272 **Karina Margolis, with the peroxide-blond hair:** Kavina, interview.

273 **Metz (helpful according to some):** Excerpt from Interview by Binyomin Taraseysky and Yankl Levin, page 29, Folder VIA, Papers of Leib Koniuchowsky, RG-1390, YIVO.

273 **all the women of the Švenčionys ghetto:** Kavina, interview.

275 **Perhaps it was Yakov Wexler:** Excerpt from Interview by Binyomin Taraseysky and Yankl Levin, page 29, Folder VIA, Papers of Leib Koniuchowsky, RG-1390, YIVO.

276 **when Arad and his sister returned:** Arad, interview, May 24, 2012.

276 **Look, we were young:** Ibid.

277 **aided by Khayem-Hersh Levin:** Excerpt from interview by Shimen Bushkanetz and Khaye Ginzberg, page 94, Folder VIA, Papers of Leib Koniuchowsky, RG-1390, YIVO.

277 **According to Chaya:** Palevsky, interview.

277 **There is a sanitation crew:** Excerpt from Interview by Binyomin Taraseysky and Yankl Levin, page 58, Folder VIA, Papers of Leib Koniuchowsky, RG-1390, YIVO.

277 **A painting brigade:** Ibid., 39.

277 **A street brigade:** Ibid., 40.

278 **teenager Tuvia Brumberg saws wood:** Tuvia Brumberg testimony, September 26, 1996, Visual History Archive, 2011, USC Shoah Foundation. Translated by Mor Sheinbein.

278 **Adolph Jurkovenas is the cook:** Breeris interrogation, LYA, l. 134, translated by Lina Khentov.

A GAME OF LIFE AND DEATH

280 **movie *The Way Back*:** *The Way Back*, directed by Peter Weir, 2010.

281 **my grandfather interrogated Kazimeras Czeplinski**: Witness Interrogation Report, February 6, 1942, LCVA, f. R911, ap. 1, b. 4, l. 6, translated by Geoff Vasil.

281 **ordered his other son, Juozas, to be held**: Ibid., l. 8.

281 **According to my grandfather's interrogation**: Ibid., l. 6.

282 **"twenty to thirty small wooden houses"**: Arad, interview, May 24, 2012.

282 **"I would give up God and my own Humanity"**: Willy Peter Reese, *A Stranger to Myself: The Inhumanity of War; Russia, 1941–1944* (New York: Macmillan, 2005).

282 **a hastily assembled work detail**: Arad, *The Partisan*, 54–55.

283 **The same Gudonis who helped lead**: Interrogation Protocol of P. Gudonis, LYA, f. K-1, ap. 58, b. P-19224, l. 3578.

283 **Several other storehouses**: Arad, *The Partisan*, 55–56.

284 **"Now I will tell you"**: In an interview in 1996, Tuvia Brumberg, September 26, 1996, *Visual History Archive*, 2011, USC Shoah Foundation.

284 **"I tried not to let either"**: Arad, *The Partisan*, 55.

285 **Arad, the smallest among them**: Ibid., 57–58.

MISTAKES

286 **As Chaya remembers it**: Palevsky, interview.

287 **"Markov was a small team"**: Arad, interview, June 17, 2013.

289 **According to Yitzhak Arad**: Arad, *The Partisan*, 67.

289 **According to Shimen Bushkanetz and Khaye Ginzberg**: Excerpt from Interview by Shimen Bushkanetz and Khaye Ginzberg, page 91, Folder VIA, Papers of Leib Koniuchowsky, RG-1390, YIVO.

289 **In Arad's account**: Arad, *The Partisan*, 67.

290 **"The doctors were urged"**: Excerpt from Interview by Shimen Bushkanetz and Khaye Ginzberg, pages 91–92, Folder VIA, Papers of Leib Koniuchowsky, RG-1390, YIVO.

290 **Arad wanted to gather his group**: Arad, *The Partisan*, 68–70.

290 **"So the two young men went"**: Palevsky, interview.

291 **"We will not reveal"**: Arad, *The Partisan*, 71.

291 **Sorele Levin, a young woman**: Excerpt from Interview by Shimen Bushkanetz and Khaye Ginzberg, page 92–93, Folder VIA, Papers of Leib Koniuchowsky, RG-1390, YIVO.

292 **HORSE MOBILIZATION**: Kruk, *Last Days*, 293.

293 **My grandfather is with Maciulevičius**: IPN, OK.Gd, S 96/01/Zn, Vol. V, Witness Testimony of Bohdan Polak, 932.

294 **brief exchange in front of the Jewish cemetery**: Jadwiga Rakoska, interview by author, June 7, 2012.

294 **A list from the Lithuanian archives**: LCVA, f. R911, ap. 1, b. 4, l. 69.

ANTON LAVRINOVICH

296 **"They were carrying cannons"** Anton Juzef Lavrinovič, interview by author, August 12, 2013.

JOSEF BECK

302 **"The note I already sent"**: War diary of Rüstungskommando Klöpfel, BA, R 91/16, translated by Almut Schoenfeld.

302 **Josef Beck was born**: Information on Josef Beck's background taken from personal letters held by Konrad Beck, gratefully used here with his permission.

304 **"The whole family was very shocked"**: Konrad Beck to translator Almut Schoenfeld, e-mail message, April 11, 2013.

305 **as Vincas Sausitis suggested**: Sausitis interrogation, LYA, translated by Viktorija Bourassa.

ILLEANA IRAFEVA

306 **"They knew about it"**: Illenana Irafeva, interview by author, August 13, 2013.

309 **Zdzisław Chlewiński's book**: Zdzisław Chlewiński, *Groza i Prześladowanie Polaków i Żydów na Wileńszczyźnie* (Płock, Poland: Samizdat Zofii Łoś, 2009). Selection translated by Maciej Bulanda.

309 **Among those marched**: IPN, Ok.Gd, Sn96/01/Zn, vol. 4, Judicial Decision of the Court in the Name of the Republic of Poland, vol. V, page 847.

WORK

310 **my grandfather will be arrested**: Lukiškės arrest record, October 11, 1943, LCVA, f. R-730, ap. 2, b. 168, l. 77–82.

310 **"What seemed like a tragedy"**: Holzman, interview, June 20, 2013.

313 **"We felt we needed to hide"**: Ibid.

314 **Chaya Palevsky was working**: Palevsky, interview.

314 **Yitzhak Arad, sustained in part**: Arad, *The Partisan*, 83–89.

314 **Society for the Diffusion of Useful Knowledge**: *The Penny Magazine of the Society for the Diffusion of Useful Knowledge*, https://archive.org/details/ThePennyMagazineOfTheSocietyForTheDiffusionOfUsefulKnowledge.

315 **testimony in the Koniuchowsky record**: Excerpt from Interview by Binyomin Taraseysky and Yankl Levin, pages 60–61, Folder VIA, Papers of Leib Koniuchowsky, RG-1390, YIVO.

315 **The Sventsian Judenrat contacted**: Ibid., 59.

315 **"a 200-liter boiler"**: Ibid., 61.

316 **the placement of the ghetto was deliberate**: Romuald-Jakub Weksler-Waszkinel, interview by author, August 10, 2013.

317 **Zofia Walulewicz, with her deaf daughter**: "Irena Walulewicz," Jewish Foundation for the Righteous website, last updated 2014, https://jfr.org/rescuer-stories/walulewicz-irena.

317 **Michał and Zofia Walulewicz's son Zdzisław**: IPN, OK.Gd, S 96/01/Zn, vol. 2, account of Bohdan Polak, page 206, translated by Maciej Bulanda.

319 **"the ones giving the orders"**: Interrogation Protocol of V. Sausaitis, LYA, f. K-1, ap. 58, b. 47746/3.

JUMP

320 **"They announced that Sventsian ghetto"**: Palevsky, interview.

322 **thirty-three cars for Kovno**: Arad, *The Partisan*, 104.

322 **"The Chief of the Partisans arranged it"**: Palevsky, interview.

322 **"On the steps all of a sudden"**: Ibid.

ŠAKOTIS

341 **the passage in the shooter Sausitis's statement**: Interrogation Protocol of V. Sausaitis, LYA, f. K-1, ap. 58, b. 47746/3.

GONE

345 **mention that it is much harder**: MacQueen, interview, February 12, 2014.

346 **"No one has been called to account"**: Dalia Kuodytė and Rokas Tracevskis, eds., *Siberia: Mass Deportations from Lithuania to the USSR* (Vilnius: Genocide and Resistance Research Center of Lithuania, 2004), 51.

347 **signed off on by Ostuf**: LCVA f. R-1399, ap. 1, b. 9, l. 180–88.

348 **"He was a man who liked to eat"**: Holzman, interview, June 20, 2013.

349 **Work—where, for how long**: Tauber, interview.

349 **"watered-down—tasteless"**: Holzman, interview, June 20, 2013.

350 **airport was the S. Darius and S. Girėnas**: *The Clandestine History of the Kovno Jewish Ghetto Police*, ed. Samuel Schalkowsky (Bloomington and Indianapolis: Indiana University Press, 2014), Kindle ed., 112–19.

351 **"This one day—I remember"**: Holzman, interview, June 20, 2013.

GIVEN BACK

354 **"apart from me"**: National Archives, Certificate of Naturalization for Pranas Puronas, February 6, 1962.

354 **Anne Applebaum notes**: Anne Applebaum, *Gulag: A History* (New York: Doubleday, 2003), 506–26.

357 **Center for Genocide and Resistance**: Kuodytė and Tracevskis, *Siberia*, 5.

ROBIN FISH

359 **impersonating another officer during his army service**: LCVA, f. 355, ap. 1, b. 243.

WITNESSES FOR THE PROSECUTION

361 **Lili Holzman, at one point**: Lili Holzman, interview by author, June 24, 2013.

361 **Jonas Maciulevičius was extradited**: Maciulevičius personnel file, Ministry of Internal Affairs, LCVA, f. 377, ap. 1, b. 243.

361 **He was sentenced to death**: IPN, OK.Gd, S 96/01/Zn, vol. IV, Judicial Decision of the Court in the Name of the Republic of Poland, 2 May 1950.

361 **The investigation was reopened**: Ibid., vol. I, Investigation Commenced on 18.08.1997.

362 **The first was direct and narrow:** Monika Tomkiewicz, interview by Maciej Bulanda, February 19, 2014.

362 **Yes, my grandfather was mentioned:** IPN, OK.Gd, S 96/01/Zn, vol. I, Investigation Commenced on 18.08.1997, page 10–11.

363 **Yes, testimony placed Senelis at Poligon:** Ibid., vol. III, Protocol of the Witness Hearing 26.04.1948, page 474.

363 **placed Senelis at the meeting:** Ibid., vol. III, From Defendant's Hearing, page 587.

363 **Senelis complain that Maciulevičius:** Ibid., vol. V, Sentence of the Trial, page 852.

363 **"how the defendant Maciulevičius":** Ibid., vol. IV, Indictment/Prosecution Office in Olsztyn, 28.01.1950, page 787.

363 **Mykolas Kukutis, chief of the local white bands:** Ibid., vol. I, Investigation Commenced on 18.08.1997, page 10–11.

363 **"became the commandant of the ghetto":** Ibid., vol. IV, Indictment/Prosecution Office in Olsztyn, 28.01.1950, page 690.

364 **was infamous for his visits to the ghetto:** Ibid., vol. III, Protocol of the Witness Hearing, 26.04.1948, page 481.

364 **"Puronas's death brigades":** Ibid., vol. II, Account of Bohdan Polak, 1994, page 206.

364 **Maciulevičus claimed that during his tenure:** Ibid., vol. IV, Indictment/Prosecution Office in Olsztyn, 28.01.1950, page 673.

THE COMPANY WE KEEP

365 **"Other officers also arrived":** Ibid., vol. V, Witness Testimony of Bohdan Polak, page 932.

365 **confirmed by two different witnesses:** Ibid., vol. III, Protocol of the Witness Hearing Szymon Buszkaniec, 26.04.1948, page 474; Ibid., 435.

365 **Three people confirm his presence at the meeting:** IPN, OK.Gd, Sn/96/01/Zn, vol. III, Fragment of Defendant's Testimony, page 587; vol. IV, Indictment/Prosecution office in Olsztyn, 28.01.1950, page 650; vol. IV, Indictment/Prosecution Office at Olsztyn, 28.01.1950, page 655.

365 **made up by a "committee":** IPN, Ok.Gd, Sn96/01/Zn, Judicial Decision of the Court in the Name of the Republic of Poland, vol. V, page 842.

366 **given the Lithuanians a week:** IPN, Ok.Gd, Sn96/01/Zn, Judicial Decision of the Court in the Name of the Republic of Poland, vol. V, page 848.

366 **the Germans there were only documenting:** IPN, Ok.Gd, Sn96/01/Zn, vol. IV, Indictment/Prosecution Office in Olsztyn, 28.01.1950, page 781.

366 **"At the time when the crimes":** Ibid., vol. VI, Protocol of the Witness Hearing, 7.10.2002, page 1037.

366 **when the musicians Zdzisław Walulewicz:** Ibid., Account of Bohdan Polak, 1994, page 206.

367 **Maciulevičius directed their executions:** IPN, Ok.Gd, Sn96/01/Zn, Judicial Decision of the Court in the Name of the Republic of Poland, vol. V, page 844.

367 **code names "Hajduczek" and "Magda"**: IPN, Ok.Gd, Sn96/01/Zn, vol. II, Witness Hearing, Warsaw, 9.10.2001, pages 287–289.

368 **a puzzle, even to Dr. Tomkiewicz**: Monika Tomkiewicz, interview by Maciej Bulanda, February 19, 2014.

369 **At the camp in Prawieniszki**: Ibid.

ONLY GOD KNOWS

371 **"the date of my second birth"**: Weksler-Waszkinel, interview.

371 **Jakub Weksler's name is given as Yankl Wexler**: Excerpt from interview by Avrom Taytz, page 79, Folder VIA, Papers of Leib Koniuchowsky, RG-1390, YIVO.

372 **story in the *New York Times***: Roger Cohen, "For a Priest and for Poland, a Tangled Identity," *New York Times*, October 10, 1999, http://www.nytimes.com/1999/10/10/world/for-a-priest-and-for-poland-a-tangled-identity.html.

373 **"It felt like I was dropped"**: Weksler-Waszkinel, interview.

374 **In the Yitzkor book for the Švenčionys region**: Kanc, ed., *Svizian Region*, http://www.jewishgen.org/yizkor/svencionys/svencionys.html.

375 **Weksler-Waszkinel had an older brother**: Guzenberg et al., *Ašmenos, Svierių, Švenčionių*, 518.

375 **demanding more money, more valuables**: Weksler-Waszkinel, interview.

375 **The Wekslers survived the liquidation**: "Vilnius Ghetto List," LitvakSIG, http://www.litvaksig.org, accessed December 31, 2014.

376 **"I told the story of myself"**: Weksler-Waszkinel, interview.

MEMORY

379 **the dangerous missions**: Palevsky, interview.

381 **"In the memoirs I wrote"**: Yitzhak Arad, "Memories: From the Depths of Memory and Before Forgetting," personal papers translated by Irit Pazner Garshowitz.

382 **The court included my grandfather**: *Republic of Poland*, 5:861–62, translated by Agnieszka Chęcińska.

383 **"How many members"**: MacQueen, interview.

384 **In Israel, Lili had already**: Holzman, interview, June 24, 2013.

384 **I looked at their cards**: USHMM, RG-04, "Concentration and Other Camps," RG-04.058, "Stuthoff Concentration camp records," reel 96.

384 **"They were doing a selection"**: Holzman, interview, June 24, 2013.

388 **Elena Las, a young Jewish widow**: Wohnungs-Haushaltungsliste Buto-Ūkio, Lapas Nr. 13, LCVA, f. R743, b. 5901, l. 27–28.

EPILOGUE

391 **"Try to look"**: Ona Šimaitė to Marijona Čilvinaitė, December 17, 1957, in Šukys, *Epistolophilia*. Original held by the Mažvydas National Library, Vilnius.

BIBLIOGRAPHY

BOOKS AND PRINTED MATERIALS

Applebaum, Anne. *Gulag: A History.* New York: Doubleday, 2003.

———. *Iron Curtain: The Crushing of Eastern Europe, 1944–1956.* New York: Doubleday, 2012.

Arad, Yitzhak. *Ghetto in Flames: The Struggle and Destruction of the Jews in Vilna in the Holocaust.* New York: Holocaust Library, 1982.

———. *The Holocaust in the Soviet Union.* Jerusalem: University of Nebraska Press, 2009.

———. *In the Shadow of the Red Banner: Soviet Jews in the War Against Nazi Germany.* Jerusalem: Gefen, 2010.

———. *The Partisan: From the Valley of Death to Mount Zion.* New York: Waldon Press, 1979.

Arad, Yitzhak, and Shmuel Krakowski. *The Einsatzgruppen Reports: Selections from the Dispatches of the Nazi Death Squads' Campaign Against the Jews in Occupied Territories of the Soviet Union, July 1941–January 1943.* Edited by Shmuel Spector. New York: Holocaust Library, 1989.

Arendt, Hannah. *Eichmann in Jerusalem: A Report on the Banality of Evil.* New York: Penguin, 1964.

Arnon, David, and Helli Doucani, eds. *The Book of Blessings: For the Sabbath and Holidays with the Family.* Israel: Matan Art, 2010.

Baltrušaitytė, Jurgita. *Lithuanian Dictionary and Phrasebook.* New York: Hippocrene, 2004.

Bankier, David. *Expulsion and Extermination: Holocaust Testimonials from Provincial Lithuania.* Jerusalem: Yad Vashem, 2011.

Bankier, David, and Dan Michman, eds. *Holocaust Historiography in Context: Emergence, Challenges, Polemics and Achievements.* New York: Berghahn, 2008.

Bartal, Israel, Antony Polonsky, and Scott Ury, eds. *Jews and Their Neighbors in Eastern Europe Since 1750.* Polin: Studies in Polish Jewry 24. Oxford: Littman Library of Jewish Civilization, 2012.

Bartov, Omer. *Hitler's Army: Soldiers, Nazis, and War in the Third Reich.* New York: Oxford University Press, 1992. Kindle edition.

Bauer, Yehuda. *The Death of the Shtetl.* New Haven, CT: Yale University Press, 2009.

Beevor, Antony. *The Fall of Berlin, 1945.* New York: Penguin, 2002. Kindle edition.

Blakian, Peter. *Black Dog of Fate: A Memoir.* New York: Basic Books, 2009.

Bloch, Michael. *Ribbentrop: A Biography.* New York: Crown, 1992.

Breitman, Richard. *Official Secrets: What the Nazis Planned, What the British and Americans Knew.* New York: Hill and Wang, 1998.

Browning, Christopher R. *Ordinary Men: Reserve Police Battalion 101 and the Final Solution in Poland.* New York: Harper Perennial, 1998.

Bubnys, Arūnas, and D. Kuodytė. *The Holocaust in Lithuania between 1941 and 1944.* Vilnius: Genocide and Resistance Research Center of Lithuania, 2005.

Buttar, Prit. *Between Giants: The Battle for the Baltics in World War II.* Oxford, England: Osprey, 2013. Kindle edition.

Cassedy, Ellen. *We Are Here: Memories of the Lithuanian Holocaust.* Lincoln: University of Nebraska Press, 2012.

Cavafy, C. P. *Complete Poems.* Translated by Daniel Mendelsohn. New York: Alfred A. Knopf, 2009.

Chaix, Marie. *The Laurels of Lake Constance.* Champaign, IL: Dalkey Archive, 2012.

Chlewiński, Zdzisław. *Groza i Prześladowanie Polaków i Żydów na Wileńszczyźnie* (Peril and Persecution of Poles and Jews in the Vilna Region). Płock, Poland: Samizdat Zofii Łoś, 2009.

The Clandestine History of the Kovno Jewish Ghetto Police. Edited and translated by Samuel Schalkowsky. Bloomington: Indiana University Press, 2014.

Clark, Christopher. *The Sleepwalkers: How Europe Went to War in 1914.* New York: Harper, 2013. Kindle edition.

The Collections of the State Archive of Lithuania: A Source of Research on the Holocaust in Lithuania. Vilnius: Vilna Gaon State Jewish Museum, 2011.

Collins, Larry, and Dominique Lapierre. *O Jerusalem! Day by Day and Minute by Minute, the Historic Struggle for Jerusalem and the Birth of Israel.* New York: Simon and Schuster, 1972.

Cox, Margaret. *Forensic Archaeology: Advances in Theory and Practice.* London: Routledge Taylor, 2005. Kindle edition.

Dambriunas, Leonardas, Antanas Klimas, and William R. Schmalstieg. *Beginner's Lithuanian.* New York: Hippocrene, 1999.

Darwish, Mahmoud. *If I Were Another.* Translated by Fady Joudah. New York: Farrar, Straus and Giroux, 2009.

Davies, Norman. *Litva: The Rise and Fall of the Grand Duchy of Lithuania; A Selection from Vanished Kingdoms.* New York: Penguin, 2013. Kindle edition.

Dawidowicz, Lucy S. *The War Against the Jews, 1933–1945.* New York: Open Road, 2010. Kindle edition.

De Waal, Edmund. *The Hare with Amber Eyes: A Hidden Inheritance.* New York: Farrar, Straus and Giroux, 2010.

Deak, Istavan, Jan T. Gross, and Tony Judt, eds. *The Politics of Retribution in Europe: World War II and Its Aftermath*. Princeton, NJ: Princeton University Press, 2000. Kindle edition.

Desbois, Father Patrick. *The Holocaust by Bullets: A Priest's Journey to Uncover the Truth Behind the Murder of 1.5 Million Jews*. New York: Palgrave Macmillan, 2008.

Dimont, Max I. *Jews, God and History*. 50th anniversary edition. New York: Signet Classics, 2004. Kindle edition.

Dobbs, Michael. *Six Months in 1945: FDR, Stalin, Churchill, and Truman—from World War to Cold War*. New York: Alfred A. Knopf, 2012. Kindle edition.

Dubnow, S. M. *From the Earliest Times until the Present Day*. Vol. 1 of *History of the Jews in Russia and Poland*. Translated by I. Friedlaender. Philadelphia: Jewish Publication Society of America, 1916. Kindle edition.

———. *From the Death of Alexander I Until the Death of Alexander II*. Vol. 2 of *History of the Jews in Russia and Poland*. Translated by I. Friedlaender. Philadelphia: Jewish Publication Society of America, 1918. Kindle edition.

———. *Jewish History: An Essay in the Philosophical History*. N.p.: n.p., n.d. Kindle edition.

Dundes, Alan. *The Blood Libel Legend: A Casebook in Anti-Semitic Folklore*. Madison: University of Wisconsin Press, 1991.

Ehrenburg, Ilya, and Vasily Grossman. *The Complete Black Book of Russian Jewry*. Translated and edited by Davit Patterson. New Brunswick, NJ: Transaction, 2002.

Fallada, Hans. *Every Man Dies Alone*. Translated by Michael Hofmann. New York: Melville House, 2009. Kindle edition.

Forgá, Péter, and the Klezmatics. *Letters to Afar: Exhibition Catalogue*. Warsaw: Museum of the History of Polish Jews, 2013.

Frazier, Ian. *Travels in Siberia*. New York: Farrar, Straus, and Giroux, 2010.

Fussel, Paul. *The Great War and Modern Memory*. Oxford, England: Oxford University Press, 2000.

Geniušienė, Sudarė Gidrė, ed. *Švenčionių krašto žydų tragedija, 1941–1944 m.* Švenčionys, Lithuania: Nalšios Muziejus, 2002.

The Gestapo and SS Manual. Translated by Carl Hammer. Colorado: Paladin Press, 1996.

Ginzburg, Eugenia Semyonovna. *Journey into the Whirlwind*. Translated by Paul Stevenson and Max Hayward. San Diego: Harcourt, 1967.

Gordon, Harry. *The Shadow of Death: The Holocaust in Lithuania*. Kentucky: University Press of Kentucky, 1992. Kindle edition.

Grade, Chaim. *My Mother's Sabbath Days: A Memoir*. Lanham, New York Rowman & Littlefield, 2004. Kindle edition.

Gross, Jan T. *Fear: Anti-Semitism in Poland After Auschwitz*. Random House, 2007. Kindle edition.

——. *Neighbors: The Destruction of the Jewish Community in Jedwabne, Poland.* New York: Penguin, 2001.

Gross, Jan T., and Irena Grudzinska Gross. *Golden Harvest: Events at the Periphery of the Holocaust.* New York: Oxford University Press, 2012. Kindle edition.

Grossman, Vasily. *Life and Fate.* Translated by Robert Chandler. New York: New York Review of Books, 2006.

——. *A Writer at War: A Soviet Journalist with the Red Army, 1941–1945.* Edited and translated by Antony Beevor and Luba Vinogradova. New York: Vintage, 2007.

Guzenberg, I., Olga Movšovič, and Jevgenija Sedova. *Ašmenos, Svierių, Švenčionių apskričių getai, 1942: Kalinių sąrašai.* Vilnius, Lithuania: Valstybinis Vilniaus Gano Žydų Muziejus, 2009.

Hamburg Institute for Social Research. *The German Army and Genocide: Crimes Against War Prisoners, Jews, and Other Civilians, 1939–1944.* Translated by Scott Abbott. New York: New Press, 1999.

——. *Vernichtungskrieg: Verbrechen der Wehrmacht, 1941 bis 1944.* Germany: Hamburger, 1996.

Herbert, Zbigniew. *Report from the Besieged City and Other Poems.* Translated by John Carpenter and Bogdana Carpenter. New York: Ecco, 1985.

——. *Selected Poems.* Translated by Czesław Miłosz and Peter Dale Scott. New York: Ecco, 1968.

Hilberg, Raul. *Perpetrators Victims Bystanders: The Jewish Catastrophe, 1933–1945.* New York: Harper Perennial, 1992.

Hoffman, Eva. *Shtetl: The Life and Death of a Small Town and the World of Polish Jews.* Boston: Houghton Mifflin, 1997.

Howe, Irving, Ruth R. Wisse, and Khone Shmeruk, eds. *The Penguin Book of Modern Yiddish Verse.* New York: Penguin, 1987.

Isherwood, Christopher. *Goodbye to Berlin.* New York: New Directions, 2012. Kindle edition.

Johnson, Paul. *A History of the Jews.* New York: Harper & Row, 1987.

Judt, Tony. *Post War: A History of Europe Since 1945.* New York: Penguin, 2005.

Klee, Ernst, Willi Dressen, and Volker Riess, eds. *"The Good Old Days:" The Holocaust as Seen by Its Perpetrators and Bystanders.* Translated by Deborah Burnstone. Old Saybrook, CT: Konecky & Konecky, 1988.

Kovner, Abba. *Sloan-Kettering: Poems.* Translated by Eddie Levenston. New York: Schocken, 2009. Kindle edition.

Kruk, Herman. *The Last Days of the Jerusalem of Lithuania: Chronicles from the Vilna Ghetto and the Camps, 1939–1944.* Edited by Benjamin Harshav; translated by Barbara Harshav. New Haven, CT: Yale University Press, 2002.

Kugelmass, Jack, and Jonathan Boyarin, eds. and trans. *From a Ruined Garden: The Memorial Books of Polish Jewry*. New York: Schocken, 1983.

Kulish, Nicholas, and Souad Mekhennet. *The Eternal Nazi: From Mauthausen to Ciaro, the Relentless Pursuit of SS Doctor Aribert Heim*. New York: Doubleday, 2014.

Kuodytė, Dalia, and Rokas Tracevskis, eds. *Siberia: Mass Deportations from Lithuania to the USSR*. Vilnius: Genocide and Resistance Research Center of Lithuania, 2004.

Kuznetsov, Edward. *Prison Diaries*. Translated by Howard Spier. New York: Scarborough, 1980.

Larson, Erik. *In the Garden of Beasts: Love, Terror, and an American Family in Hitler's Berlin*. New York: Crown, 2011.

Levi, Primo. *The Periodic Table*. Translated by Raymond Rosenthal. New York: Schocken, 1984.

Levin, Dov. *The Lesser of Two Evils: Eastern European Jewry Under Soviet Rule, 1939–1941*. Translated by Naftali Greenwood. Philadelphia: Jewish Publication Society, 1995.

Liekis, Šarūnas, Antony Polonsky, and Chaeran Freeze, eds. *Jews in the Former Grand Duchy of Lithuania Since 1772*. Vol. 25 of *Polin: Studies in Polish Jewry*. Oxford, England: Littman Library of Jewish Civilization, 2013.

Lowe, Keith. *Savage Continent: Europe in the Aftermath of World War II*. New York: St. Martin's Press, 2012. Kindle edition.

Lower, Wendy. *Hitler's Furies: German Women in the Nazi Killing Fields*. New York: Houghton Mifflin Harcourt, 2013. Kindle edition.

Lown, Bella. *Memories of My Life: A Personal History of a Lithuanian Shtetl*. New York: Pangloss, 1991.

Lukacs, John. *The Last European War: September 1939–December 1941*. New Haven, CT: Yale University Press, 2001.

Lukas, Richard C. *Forgotten Holocaust: The Poles Under German Occupation, 1939–1944*. New York: Hippocrene, 2001. Kindle edition.

Lukša, Juozas. *Forest Brothers: The Account of an Anti-Soviet Lithuanian Freedom Fighter, 1944–1948*. Translated by Laima Vincė. Budapest: Central European University Press, 2009.

Lusseyran, Jacques. *Against the Pollution of the I*. Sand Point, ID: Morning Light Press, 2006.

———. *And There Was Light*. 2nd ed. Translated by Elizabeth R. Cameron. Sand Point, ID: Morning Light Press, 2006.

Maass, Peter. *Love Thy Neighbor: A Story of War*. New York: Vintage, 1996.

Margolis, Rachel. *A Partisan from Vilna*. Translated by F. Jackson Piotrow. Brighton, MA: Academic Studies Press, 2010.

Markish, Peretz. *Inheritance (Yerushe)*. Translated by Mary Schulman. Toronto: TSAR, 2007.

Mendelsohn, Daniel. *The Elusive Embrace: Desire and the Riddle of Identity*. New York: Vintage, 2000.

———. *The Lost: A Search for Six of Six Million*. New York: Harper Perennial, 2006.

Mickiewicz, Adam. *Pan Tadeusz; or, The Last Foray in Lithuania: A Story of Life Among Polish Gentlefolk in the Years 1811 and 1812*. New York: Mondial, 2009.

Miłosz, Czesław. *Beginning with My Streets: Essays and Recollections*. Translated by Madeline G. Levine. New York: Farrar, Straus and Giroux, 1991.

———. *The Collected Poems, 1931–1987*. Hopewell, NJ: Ecco, 1988.

———. *The Issa Valley*. Translated by Louis Iribarne. New York: Farrar, Straus and Giroux, 1981.

———. *The Land of Ulro*. Translated by Louis Iribarne. New York: Farrar, Straus and Giroux, 1984.

———. *The Separate Notebooks*. Translated by Robert Hass, Robert Pinsky, and Renata Gorczynski. New York: Ecco, 1984.

———. *The Witness of Poetry*. Cambridge, MA: Harvard University Press,1983.

———. *To Begin Where I Am: Selected Essays*. Edited by Bogdana Carpenter and Madeline G. Levine. New York: Farrar, Straus and Giroux, 2001.

———. *Unattainable Earth*. Translated by Robert Hass. New York: Ecco, 1986.

Mirsky, Yehudah. *Rav Kook: Mystic in a Time of Revolution*. New Haven, CT: Yale University Press, 2014. Kindle edition.

Nagorski, Andrew. *Hitlerland: American Eyewitnesses to the Nazi Rise to Power*. New York: Simon and Schuster, 2012.

Neitzel, Sönke, ed., *Tapping Hitler's Generals: Transcripts of Secret Conversations, 1942–45*. Translated by Geoffrey Brooks. St. Paul, MN: Frontline, 2007.

Némirovsky, Irène. *Suite Française*. Translated by Sandra Smith. New York: Alfred A. Knopf, 2006. Kindle edition.

Nikžentaitis, Alvydas, Stefan Schreiner, and Darius Staliūnas, eds. *The Vanished World of Lithuanian Jews*. New York: Rodopi, 2004.

Oksanen, Sofi. *Purge*. New York: Black Cat, 2008.

Olive, Michael, and Robert Edwards. *Operation Barbarossa, 1941*. Mechanicsburg, PA: Stackpole, 2012.

Pilecki, Captain Witold. *The Auschwitz Volunteer: Beyond Bravery*. Translated by Jarek Garlińksli. Los Angeles: Aquila Polonica, 2012.

Piotrowski, Tadeusz. *Poland's Holocaust: Ethnic Strife, Collaboration with Occupying Forces and Genocide in the Second Republic, 1918–1947*. Jefferson, NC: McFarland, 1998.

Poddębski, Henryk. *The Eastern Borderlands*. Edited by Leszek Dulik and Waldemar Golec. Lublin, Poland: Ad Rem, 2010.

Polonsky, Antony. *The Jews in Poland and in Russia*, vol. 3, *1914–2008*. Oxford: Littman Library of Jewish Civilization, 2012.

Polonsky, Antony, and Joanna B. Michlic, eds. *The Neighbors Respond: The Controversy Over the Jedwabne Massacre in Poland*. Princeton, NJ: Princeton University Press, 2014.

Potašenko, Grigorijus, ed. *The Peoples of The Grand Duchy of Lithuania*. Translated by Axel Holvoet. Vilnius, Lithuania: Aidai, 2002.

Power, Samantha. *"A Problem from Hell": America and the Age of Genocide*. New York: Perennial, 2002.

Rawicz, Slavomir. *The Long Walk: The True Story of a Trek to Freedom*. Guilford, CT: Lyons Press, 1997.

Reck, Friedrich. *Diary of a Man in Despair*. Translated by Paul Rubens. New York: New York Review of Books, 2000. Kindle edition.

Redel, Victoria. *The Border of Truth*. New York: Counterpoint, 2007.

Reese, Willy Peter. *A Stranger to Myself: The Inhumanity of War, Russia, 1941–44*. New York: Farrar, Straus and Giroux, 2005. Kindle edition.

Remarque, Erich Maria. *All Quiet on the Western Front*. Translated by A. W. Wheen. New York: Ballantine, 1958.

Rhodes, Richard. *Masters of Death: The SS-Einsatzgruppen and the Invention of the Holocaust*. New York: Vintage, 2002.

Riding, Alan. *And the Show Went On: Cultural Life in Nazi-Occupied Paris*. New York: Alfred A. Knopf, 2010.

Roberts, Andrew. *The Storm of War: A New History of the Second World War*. New York: HarperCollins, 2011.

Rose, Jonathan, ed. *The Holocaust and the Book: Destruction and Preservation*. Amherst: University of Massachusetts Press, 2001.

Rosen, Alan. *The Wonder of Their Voices: The 1946 Holocaust Interviews of David Boder*. New York: Oxford University Press, 2010. Kindle edition.

Rosenberg, Tina. *The Haunted Land: Facing Europe's Ghosts After Communism*. New York: Vintage, 1995. Kindle edition.

Ross, Henryk. *Łódź Ghetto Album*. Edited by Thomas Weber. London: Chris Boot, 2009.

Rubenstein, Joshua, and Vladimir P. Naumov, eds. *Stalin's Secret Pogroms: The Postwar Inquisition of the Jewish Anti-Fascist Committee*. Translated by Laura Esther Wolfson. New Haven, CT: Yale University Press, 2001. Kindle edition.

Sakowicz, Kazimierz. *Ponary Diary, 1941–1943: A Bystander's Account of a Mass Murder*. Edited by Yitzhak Arad. New Haven, CT: Yale University Press, 2005.

Schilde, Kurt, and Johannes Tuchel. *Columbia-Haus Berliner Konzentrationslager, 1933–1936*. Germany: Bezirksamt Tempelhof von Berlin, 1990.

Sepetys, Ruta. *Between Shades of Gray*. New York: Philomel, 2011.

Sereny, Gitta. *Into That Darkness: An Examination of Conscience*. New York: Vintage, 1983.

Shavit, Ari. *My Promised Land: The Triumph and Tragedy of Israel*. New York: Spiegel & Grau, 2013.

Shirer, William L. *The Rise and Fall of the Third Reich*. New York: Rosetta, 2011. Kindle edition.

Shore, Marci. *The Taste of Ashes: The Afterlife of Totalitarianism in Eastern Europe*. New York: Crown, 2013. Kindle edition.

Sirutavičius, Vladas, and Darius Staliūnas, ed. *A Pragmatic Alliance: Jewish-Lithuanian Political Cooperation at the Beginning of the 20th Century*. New York: Central European University Press, 2011.

Snyder, Timothy. *Bloodlands: Europe Between Hitler and Stalin*. New York: Basic Books, 2010.

——. *The Reconstruction of Nations: Poland, Ukraine, Lithuania, Belarus, 1569–1999*. New Haven, CT: Yale University Press, 2003.

Snyder, Timothy, and Ray Brandon, eds. *Stalin and Europe: Imitation and Domination, 1928–1953*. New York: Oxford University Press, 2014.

Sołtys, Maria, and Krzysztof Jaszczyński, eds. *1947: The Colors of Ruin; The Reconstruction of Warsaw and Poland in the Photographs of Henry N. Cobb*. Warsaw: Dom Spotkań z Historią, 2012.

Stang, Knut. *Kollaboration und Massenmord: Die litauische Hilfspolizei, das Rollkommando Hamann und die Ermordung der litauischen Juden*. Bern, Switzerland: Peter Lang, 1996.

Stille, Alexander. *The Force of Things: A Marriage in War and Peace*. New York: Farrar, Straus and Giroux, 2013.

Strassler, Robert B., ed. *The Landmark Herodotus*. New York: Anchor, 2007.

Šukys, Julija. *Epistolophilia: Writing the Life of Ona Šimaitė*. Lincoln: University of Nebraska Press, 2012. Kindle edition.

Shalamov, Varlam. *Kolyma Tales*. Translated by John Glad. New York: Penguin, 1994.

Tolstoy, Leo. *War and Peace*. Translated by Louise and Aylmer Maude. New York: Simon and Schuster, 1942.

Tuchman, Barbara W. *The Guns of August: The Outbreak of World War I*. New York: Random House, 2014. Kindle edition.

Turski, Marian. *Polish Witnesses to the Shoah*. London: Valentine Mitchell, 2010.

Von Kellenbach, Katharina. *The Mark of Cain: Guilt and Denial in the Post-War Lives of Nazi Perpetrators*. New York: Oxford University Press, 2013.

Von Manstein, Erich. *Lost Victories: The War Memoirs of Hitler's Most Brilliant General*. St. Paul, MN: Zenith, 2014.

Walton, Richard H., ed., *Cold Case Homicides: Practical Investigative Techniques*. Boca Raton, FL: Taylor & Francis, 2006.

The Wannsee Conference and the Genocide of the European Jews: Catalogue of the Permanent Exhibition. Berlin: House of the Wannsee Conference, Memorial and Education Site, 2009.

War After War: Armed Anti-Soviet Resistance in Lithuania in 1944–1953, Catalogue of the Exhibition. Vilnius: Museum of Genocide Victims of the Genocide and Resistance Research Center of Lithuania, 2008.

Wasserstein, Bernard. *On the Eve: The Jews of Europe Before the Second World War*. London: Profile, 2013.

Wiesel, Elie. *Open Heart*. Translated by Marion Wiesel. New York: Alfred A. Knopf, 2012.

FILMS

Elusive Justice: The Search for Nazi War Criminals. Directed by Johnathan Silvers. New York: Saybrook, 2011. DVD.

Partisans of Vilna: The Untold Story of Jewish Resistance During World War II. Directed by Josh Waletzky. Los Angeles: New Video Group, 2005. DVD.

ARTICLES AND WEBSITES

Cohen, Roger. "For a Priest and for Poland, a Tangled Identity." *New York Times*, October 10, 1999. http://www.nytimes.com/1999/10/10/world/for-a-priest-and-for-poland-a-tangled-identity.html.

International Commission for the Evaluation of the Crimes of the Nazi and Soviet Occupation Regimes in Lithuania website. http://www.komisija.lt/en. All material on this website was consulted; these articles were of particular significance:

Bubnys, Arūnas. "Lithuanian Police Battalions and the Holocaust." http://www.komisija.lt/en/body.php?&m=1194864300.

Dieckmann, Christoph. "Murders of the Prisoners of War." http://www.komisija.lt/en/body.php?&m=1194864157.

Dieckmann, Chistoph, and Saulius Sužiedėlis. "The Persecution and Mass Murder of Lithuanian Jews During Summer and Fall of 1941: Sources and Analysis." http://www.komisija.lt/en/body.php?&m=1194863926.

Jakubčionis, Algidas. "Occupation/Annexation and Sovietization of Lithuania." http://www.komisija.lt/en/body.php?&m=1194863351.

Streikus, Arūnas. "Destroying Religious Life in 1940–1941." http://www.komisija .lt/en/body.php?&m=1194863561.

The International Jewish Cemetery Project. http://www.iajgsjewishcemeteryproject.org.

JewishGen: The Home of Jewish Genealogy. http://www.jewishgen.org.

Kanc, Shimon, ed., "Svizian Region; Memorial Book of 23 Jewish Communities (Lithuania)." *JewishGen.* http://www.jewishgen.org/yizkor/svencionys/svencionys .html.

LitvakSIG: Lithuanian-Jewish Special Interest Group. http://www.litvaksig.org.

MacQueen, Michael. "The Context of Mass Destruction: Agents and Prerequisites of the Holocaust in Lithuania." *Holocaust Genocide Studies* 12, no. 1 (1998): 27–48. doi: 10.1093/hgs/12.1.27.

MacQueen, Michael, Jürgen Matthäus, and David G. Roskies. "Lithuania and the Jew: The Holocaust Chapter." Paper presented at the Center for Advanced Holocaust Studies, Holocaust Memorial Museum, Washington, DC, 2004. http://www .ushmm.org/m/pdfs/Publication_OP_2005-07-03.pdf.

U.S. Central Intelligence Agency. *Study, Review, and Analysis of All Capstan Agents' Personal Histories, Contacts and Associations.* March 23, 1953. http://www.foia.cia .gov/sites/default/files/document_conversions/1705143/AECHAMP%20%20%20 VOL.%201_0022.pdf.

U.S. Department of Justice. "Immigration Judge Orders Removal of Chicago-Area Man Accused of Participation of Nazi Massacre of Jews" (#99-118). April 5, 1999. http://www.justice.gov/opa/pr/1999/April/118crm.htm.

U.S. State Department. "Lithuanian Prosecutor Trying to Show Some Movement in Investigating War Criminals" (Docno: Vilnius 000148). January 2000. Freedom of Information Act Electronic Reading Room, 2005. http://www.foia.cia.gov/sites/ default/files/document_conversions/1705143/LILEIKIS,%20ALEKSANDRAS_0043 .pdf.

ARCHIVES (WITH ABBREVIATIONS USED IN NOTES)

AMC   Archive of Modern Conflict, London

BA   Bundesarchiv (Federal Archive), Berlin

BA-MA   Bundesarchiv-Militärarchiv (Federal Military Archive), Freiburg

BA-KO   Bundesarchiv Koblenz (Federal Archive), Koblenz

GARF   Gosudarstvennyj Archiv Russkoj Federaciji (State Archives of the Russian Federation), Moscow

ITS   International Tracing Service, Bad Arolsen

IPN   Instytut Pamięci Narodowej (Institute of National Remembrance), Warsaw

LCVA   Lietuvos Centrinis Valstybinis Archyvas (Central State Archive of Lithuania), Vilnius

LYA   Lietuvos Ypatingasis Archyvas (Lithuanian Special Archives), Vilnius

NARA   National Archives Record Administration, Washington, D.C.

USHMM United States Holocaust Memorial Museum, Washington, D.C.

YIVO   Institute for Jewish Research, New York

YVA   Yad Vashem Archives, Jerusalem

ZStL   Zentrale Stelle der Landesjustizverwaltungen zur Aufklärung nationalsozialistischer Verbrechen (Central Office of the State Justice Administrations for the Investigation of National Socialist Crimes), Ludwigsburg, Germany

A NOTE ON THE AUTHOR

RITA GABIS is an award-winning poet and prose writer. Her grants and fellowships include a New York Foundation for the Arts Award for creative nonfiction and residencies at Yaddo and the Fine Arts Work Center in Provincetown, Massachusetts. She is the author of the poetry collection *The Wild Field* (Alice James Books). Her work has appeared in *Harvard Review*, *Poetry*, and elsewhere. She lives and teaches in New York City.